Developmental Dysgraphia

AF716153

The ability to communicate with written language is critical for success in school and in the workplace. Unfortunately, many children suffer from developmental dysgraphia—impairment in acquiring spelling or handwriting skills—and this form of impairment has received relatively little attention from researchers and educators. This volume brings together, for the first time, theoretically grounded and methodologically rigorous research on developmental dysgraphia, presented alongside reviews of the typical development of spelling and writing skills. Leading experts on writing and dysgraphia shed light on different types of impairments that can affect the learning of spelling and writing skills, and provide insights into the typical development of these skills. The volume, which contributes both to the basic science of literacy and to the applied science of diagnosing and treating developmental dysgraphia, should interest researchers, educators, and clinicians.

The chapters in this book were originally published as a special issue of *Cognitive Neuropsychology.*

Brenda Rapp is Professor of Cognitive Science at Johns Hopkins University, USA, and editor-in-chief of the journal *Cognitive Neuropsychology*.

Michael McCloskey is Professor of Cognitive Science at Johns Hopkins University, USA.

Developmental Dysgraphia

Edited by
Brenda Rapp and Michael McCloskey

Routledge
Taylor & Francis Group
LONDON AND NEW YORK

First published 2018 by Routledge

2 Park Square, Milton Park, Abingdon, Oxfordshire OX14 4RN
52 Vanderbilt Avenue, New York, NY 10017

Routledge is an imprint of the Taylor & Francis Group, an informa business

First issued in paperback 2020

British Library Cataloguing in Publication Data
A catalogue record for this book is available from the British Library

ISBN 13: 978-1-138-49695-8 (hbk)
ISBN 13: 978-0-367-53574-2 (pbk)

Typeset in Myriad Pro
by RefineCatch Limited, Bungay, Suffolk

Publisher's Note
The publisher accepts responsibility for any inconsistencies that may have arisen during the conversion of this book from journal articles to book chapters, namely the possible inclusion of journal terminology.

Contents

Citation Information

The chapters in this book were originally published in *Cognitive Neuropsychology*, volume 34, issues 3–4 (May–June 2017). When citing this material, please use the original page numbering for each article, as follows:

Chapter 1
Developmental dysgraphia: An overview and framework for research
Michael McCloskey and Brenda Rapp
Cognitive Neuropsychology, volume 34, issues 3–4 (May–June 2017), pp. 65–82

Chapter 2
Learning to spell: Phonology and beyond
Rebecca Treiman
Cognitive Neuropsychology, volume 34, issues 3–4 (May–June 2017), pp. 83–93

Chapter 3
Developmental graphemic buffer dysgraphia in English: A single case study
Kristina Barisic, Saskia Kohnen and Lyndsey Nickels
Cognitive Neuropsychology, volume 34, issues 3–4 (May–June 2017), pp. 94–118

Chapter 4
Do reading and spelling share orthographic representations? Evidence from developmental dysgraphia
Christopher Hepner, Michael McCloskey and Brenda Rapp
Cognitive Neuropsychology, volume 34, issues 3–4 (May–June 2017), pp. 119–143

Chapter 5
Lexical decision performance in developmental surface dysgraphia: Evidence for a unitary orthographic system that is used in both reading and spelling
Andreas Sotiropoulos and J. Richard Hanley
Cognitive Neuropsychology, volume 34, issues 3–4 (May–June 2017), pp. 144–162

Chapter 6
Lexical processing and distributional knowledge in sound–spelling mapping in a consistent orthography: A longitudinal study of reading and spelling in dyslexic and typically developing children
Chiara Valeria Marinelli, Pamela Cellini, Pierluigi Zoccolotti and Paola Angelelli
Cognitive Neuropsychology, volume 34, issues 3–4 (May–June 2017), pp. 163–186

Chapter 7
Motor control of handwriting in the developing brain: A review
Sarah Palmis, Jeremy Danna, Jean-Luc Velay and Marieke Longcamp
Cognitive Neuropsychology, volume 34, issues 3–4 (May–June 2017), pp. 187–204

Chapter 8

Understanding handwriting difficulties: A comparison of children with and without motor impairment
Mellissa Prunty and Anna L. Barnett
Cognitive Neuropsychology, volume 34, issues 3–4 (May–June 2017), pp. 205–218

Chapter 9

The impact of developmental dyslexia and dysgraphia on movement production during word writing
Sonia Kandel, Delphine Lassus-Sangosse, Géraldine Grosjacques and Cyril Perret
Cognitive Neuropsychology, volume 34, issues 3–4 (May–June 2017), pp. 219–251

Notes on Contributors

Paolo Angelelli is Associate Professor in the Department of History, Society and Human Studies at the University of Salento, Lecce, Italy.

Kristina Barisic is a Senior Research Assistant in Cognitive Science at Macquarie University, Sydney, Australia.

Anna L. Barnett is Professor of Psychology at Oxford Brookes University, UK.

Pamela Cellini is based in the Department of Psychology at the Sapienza University of Rome, Italy.

Jeremy Danna is a Researcher in the Laboratoire de Neurosciences Cognitives, CNRS and Aix-Marseille Université, France.

Géraldine Grosjacques is based in the Centre de Référence des Troubles du Langage et des Apprentissages at the Centre Hospitalier Universitaire Grenoble Alpes, France.

J. Richard Hanley is Professor of Neuropsychology in the Department of Psychology at the University of Essex, UK.

Christopher Hepner is a Research Assistant in the Division of Cognitive Neurology/Neuropsychology at Johns Hopkins University, USA.

Sonia Kandel is Professor of Cognitive Science at the University of Grenoble Alps and Researcher in the GIPSA-lab (CNRS), France.

Saskia Kohnen is Clinical Director of the Macquarie University Reading Clinic and Senior Researcher in the Department of Cognitive Science at Macquarie University, Sydney, Australia.

Delphine Lassus-Sangosse is a Neuropsychologist based in the Centre de Référence des Troubles du Langage et des Apprentissages at the Centre Hospitalier Universitaire Grenoble Alpes, France.

Marieke Longcamp is Associate Professor in the Laboratoire de Neurosciences Cognitives, CNRS and Aix-Marseille Université, France.

Chiara Valeria Marinelli is a Researcher in the Department of History, Society and Human Studies at the University of Salento, Lecce, Italy.

Michael McCloskey is Professor of Cognitive Science at Johns Hopkins University, USA.

Lyndsey Nickels is Professor in the Department of Cognitive Science at Macquarie University, Sydney, Australia.

Sarah Palmis is a PhD candidate in the Laboratoire de Neurosciences Cognitives, CNRS and Aix-Marseille Université, France.

Cyril Perret is Maître de conferences based in the Centre de recherches sur la cognition et l'apprentissage (CERCA) at the Université de Poitiers, France.

Mellissa Prunty is a Lecturer in Occupational Therapy at Brunel University London, UK.

Brenda Rapp is Professor of Cognitive Science at Johns Hopkins University, USA, and editor-in-chief of the journal *Cognitive Neuropsychology*.

Andreas Sotiropoulos is a Data Scientist at Thomas Murray Data Services.

Rebecca Treiman is Professor in the Department of Psychology and Brain Sciences at Washington University in St. Louis, USA.

Jean-Luc Velay is a Researcher in the Laboratoire de Neurosciences Cognitives, CNRS and Aix-Marseille Université, France.

Pierluigi Zoccolotti is Professor of General Psychology at the Sapienza University, Rome, Italy and an Associate Researcher at the Institute of Cognitive Sciences and Technologies, Rome, Italy.

Developmental dysgraphia: An overview and framework for research

Michael McCloskey and Brenda Rapp

ABSTRACT
Developmental deficits in the acquisition of writing skills (developmental dysgraphias) are common and have significant consequences, yet these deficits have received relatively little attention from researchers. We offer a framework for studying developmental dysgraphias (including both spelling and handwriting deficits), arguing that research should be grounded in theories describing normal cognitive writing mechanisms and the acquisition of these mechanisms. We survey the current state of knowledge concerning developmental dysgraphia, discussing potential proximal and distal causes. One conclusion emerging from this discussion is that developmental writing deficits are diverse in their manifestations and causes. We suggest an agenda for research on developmental dysgraphia, and suggest that pursuing this agenda may contribute not only to a better understanding of developmental writing impairment, but also to a better understanding of normal writing mechanisms and their acquisition. Finally, we provide a brief introduction to the subsequent articles in this special issue on developmental dysgraphia.

The ability to write is a fundamental component of literacy, and is crucial for success not only in school but also in most workplace environments. Unfortunately, a significant proportion of children suffer from developmental dysgraphia—that is, impairment in acquisition of writing skills. Döhla and Heim (2016) recently estimated that 7–15% of school-age children exhibit some form of development writing deficit.[1]

In addition to disrupting the acquisition of writing skills, developmental dysgraphia often has broader detrimental effects. For many dysgraphic children any writing assignment is an ordeal; the struggle to spell words correctly or produce legible handwriting is immensely frustrating, and also diverts attention from the more substantive aspects of the assignment (e.g., Berninger, 1999; S. Graham, Berninger, Abbott, Abbott, & Whitaker, 1997). A child struggling with spelling while writing a paragraph about frogs will probably learn less about paragraph composition, and about frogs, than a child with typical spelling skills; and a child who struggles to write digits legibly and align them neatly will probably work longer and harder at maths homework, while learning less, than a child with typical handwriting skill. Nor are the detrimental effects of developmental dysgraphia limited to children. Adults with significant developmental writing deficits may face limitations in career choice or advancement, as well as experiencing difficulty with everyday tasks that draw upon writing skills.

Despite the prevalence and significant impact of developmental dysgraphia, the topic has received relatively little attention from researchers. A major purpose of this special issue is to highlight the need for a strong, sustained programme of research. An intensified research effort is crucial not only for advancing our knowledge of the underlying deficits in children and adults with developmental dysgraphia, but also for improving diagnosis and treatment. Furthermore, studies of developmental dysgraphia may enhance our understanding of normal cognitive writing skills and how these skills are acquired.

Writing and dysgraphia: Defining the scope

Writing and dysgraphia are both broad concepts, and the corresponding terms have been used in various ways. Hence, it is important at the outset to define the scope of our discussion and clarify our use of terminology. In discussing writing we focus on production of characters and individual words. Higher level writing skills, such as those involved in composing sentences and combining them into coherent texts, are beyond the scope of our discussion.

In other respects, however, we define the writing domain broadly. We include within our purview not only writing in print or script with a writing implement, but also other forms of written language production, such as typing on a laptop or texting on a smartphone. We also include both the ability to spell and the ability to plan and execute the motor processes required to generate an overt output. In the case of handwritten output we refer to the motor planning and production processes as handwriting processes, and include under this rubric both printing and cursive writing.

Turning now to writing impairments, the term *dysgraphia* has two different senses in the literature. Some researchers use the term to refer to impaired spelling, whereas others apply the label to deficits affecting the motor planning or production processes required for handwriting. We include both senses within the scope of our discussion. Finally, by *developmental dysgraphia* we mean impairment in acquisition of writing (spelling, handwriting, or both), despite adequate opportunity to learn, and absence of obvious neuropathology or gross sensory–motor dysfunction.

A theory-based approach

We advocate a strongly theory-based, as opposed to descriptive, approach to the study of cognitive deficits, including developmental dysgraphia. We argue that deficits affecting a cognitive function can be understood only by reference to a theory that specifies the normal cognitive representations and processes underlying the function (e.g., Caramazza, 1984; Caramazza & McCloskey, 1988; Castles & Coltheart, 1993; Hillis & Caramazza, 1992; McCloskey, 2001; McCloskey, Aliminosa, & Macaruso, 1991; McCloskey & Caramazza, 1988). Given such a theory, deficits can be characterized in terms of disruption to particular component (s) of the normal cognitive system.

Efforts to understand developmental deficits also require a theoretical framework specifying how the affected cognitive system is learned (Castles, Kohnen, Nickels, & Brock, 2014). Developmental deficits arise from disruption of normal learning processes. Consequently, a theory characterizing the learning processes is crucial for understanding the failures of learning that underlie developmental cognitive impairments. In the domain of writing, theories of learning are currently less well developed than theories of the normal adult system. Hence, we first describe a theoretical framework specifying the structure and functioning of the normal adult writing system, and illustrate the role of this framework in the study of acquired dysgraphia (writing deficits resulting from brain damage in adulthood). We then consider the processes involved in learning to write, and the potential roles of these processes in the genesis of developmental dysgraphias.

The normal adult writing system

Figures 1 and 2 illustrate a theory of the cognitive mechanisms making up the normal adult writing system. Figure 1 focuses primarily on spelling mechanisms and Figure 2 on the mechanisms for the production of handwriting. The theory illustrated in the figures reflects a consensus (although not universal agreement) among scientists who study writing (e.g., Margolin, 1984; Miceli & Capasso, 2006; Tainturier & Rapp, 2001; see N. L. Graham, 2014, for a different framework). We offer the theory as a set of working assumptions that, while subject to revision in light of new evidence, can serve as a foundation for the study of developmental writing deficits. Note also that the theory assumes an alphabetic writing system. Although some aspects are applicable to non-alphabetic systems, other aspects would require extensive modification to address non-alphabetic writing.

Cognitive spelling mechanisms

Figure 1 illustrates cognitive spelling mechanisms in the context of a spelling-to-dictation task in which a word is dictated, and then is written or spelled aloud. The theory assumes that if the dictated stimulus is a familiar word (e.g., CAT), the sequence of phonemes computed by speech recognition processes (e.g., /k æ t/) activates a representation in phonological long-term memory (often referred to as the phonological lexicon), leading in turn to activation of a lexical–semantic representation. (Note that these auditory comprehension processes are not specific to spelling tasks.) The semantic representation in turn activates a stored spelling representation in orthographic long-term memory (also referred to as the orthographic lexicon). Some theorists have proposed that representations in orthographic long-

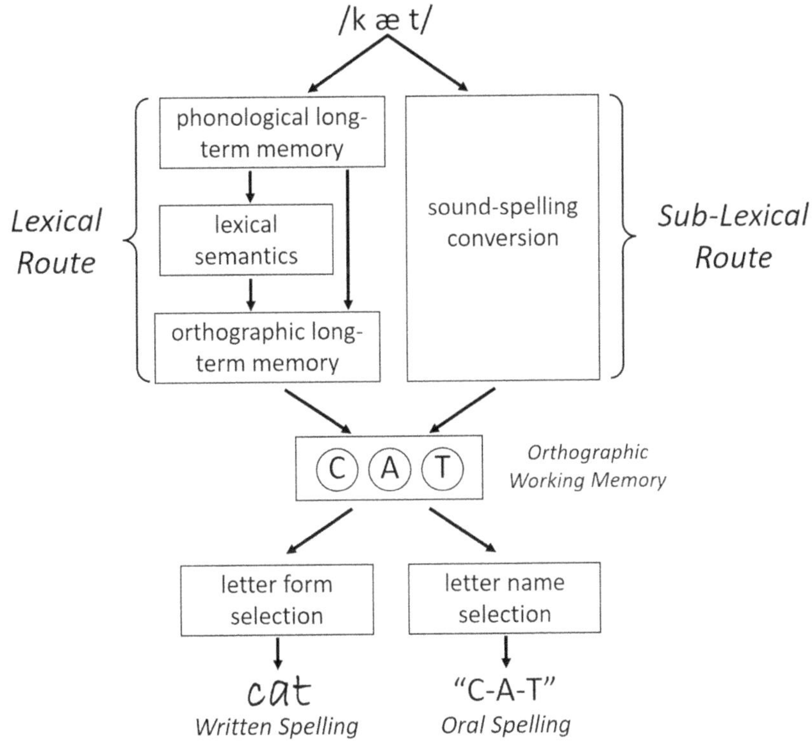

Figure 1. Schematic depiction of the cognitive mechanisms making up the normal adult writing system.

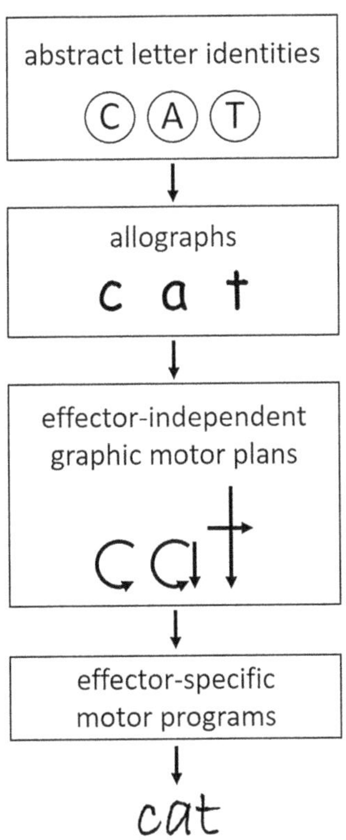

Figure 2. Schematic depiction of the cognitive handwriting mechanisms, which map abstract letter identities onto motor programmes for production of written responses.

term memory can also be activated directly from the phonological long-term memory (e.g., Margolin, 1984), or by a combination of inputs from phonological long-term memory and lexical semantics (e.g., Hillis & Caramazza, 1991).

The activated orthographic representation specifies the identity and ordering of letters making up the spelling of the word. The letter representations are assumed to be abstract (Rapp & Caramazza, 1997), in the sense that they specify only letter identity and not any aspects of letter form (e.g., the visual shape of a letter, or the strokes for writing it). The abstract orthographic representations provide the basis for producing various forms of output, including writing, oral spelling, and typing. Once activated, the sequence of abstract letter representations is held temporarily in an orthographic working memory (often referred to as the graphemic buffer) while the motor planning and production processes required for generating an overt response are carried out.

Spelling of unfamiliar words or pseudowords (e.g., GRAT) also implicates abstract orthographic representations. However, in this case no lexical–phonological, semantic, or lexical–orthographic representations are available in the lexical system. Instead a plausible spelling is assembled from the input sequence of phonemes (e.g., /g r æ t/), through a sub-lexical spelling process that applies sound–spelling correspondence knowledge. As Treiman (2017) argues, the sublexical process may apply not only simple phoneme–grapheme conversion rules (e.g., /g/ → G), but also more sophisticated context-sensitive rules (e.g., /s/ → C when followed by E, I, or Y). For this reason we refer to the sublexical process as sound-to-spelling conversion process rather than using the more common label of phoneme–grapheme conversion.[2]

Outputs of the sublexical process have the same form as representations of familiar words retrieved from orthographic long-term memory: sequences of abstract letter representations. Like the retrieved representations, spellings generated by the sublexical process are held in orthographic working memory, and production of the overt response proceeds just as for familiar words.

The lexical route, which involves retrieval of a learned spelling for a word, is necessary because (at least for most languages) the correct spelling of a word is not fully predictable from its phonological form. Accordingly, correct spellings cannot reliably be generated through sound–spelling conversion. For example, there is no way to predict from the sounds of the words KEEP and LEAP that the vowel is realized by the letters EE in the former and EA in the latter. Rather the spellings must be memorized (i.e., stored in orthographic long-term memory). Interestingly, studies show that even for languages with highly predictable spellings (e.g., Spanish and Italian) word spellings are learned and stored in orthographic long-term memory (e.g., Cuetos & Labos, 2001; Miceli, Benvegnù, Capasso, & Caramazza, 1997).

The sublexical sound-to-spelling conversion process is needed to generate plausible spellings for words whose spellings have not been learned, including words that have been encountered only in spoken form, and entirely unfamiliar words. For these words, the lexical route cannot supply the correct spelling, forcing reliance on the sublexical route.

A point we have not yet addressed concerns the interaction between the lexical and sublexical routes. One possibility is that the lexical route is first activated, and the sublexical route comes into play only if no stored spelling representation is activated. Perhaps more likely is that the two routes operate in parallel, such that both routes produce an output for familiar words (e.g., Houghton & Zorzi, 2003; Jones, Folk, & Rapp, 2009; Rapp, Epstein, & Tainturier, 2002; Tainturier, Bosse, Roberts, Valdois, & Rapp, 2013). Under this account any difference between lexical- and sublexical-route outputs would be resolved in favour of the lexical route. For example, if for the word LEAP the lexical route generated the spelling LEAP, and the sublexical route produced the output LEEP, the lexical spelling LEAP would be chosen for production.

Although we have introduced the writing theory in the context of a writing-to-dictation task, the theory also applies to the more common situation of spontaneous writing. We assume that in spontaneous writing the writer begins with a message to be conveyed, leading eventually to activation of semantic representations for the to-be-produced words. Activation of spelling representations in orthographic long-term memory, and subsequent processes, are then carried out as for writing to dictation.

For words whose spellings have not been learned, the spontaneous writing process is slightly more complex. Consider, for example, a writer who has encountered the word PLATYPUS only in spoken form, but now wants to write it. After activating the semantic representation, the writer cannot retrieve the spelling from orthographic long-term memory, because the spelling has not been learned. Instead the writer must retrieve the word's phonological representation from the phonological long-term memory, and then apply sublexical sound–spelling conversion processes to generate a potential spelling (e.g., PLATAPUSS).

Handwriting processes

Once an orthographic representation has been retrieved from long-term memory or assembled through sound–spelling conversion, additional processing is required to produce an overt response (e.g., Ellis, 1982, 1988; Hollerbach, 1981; Margolin, 1984; Van Galen, 1991). First, the abstract letter representations must be converted to a form appropriate for the chosen output format or modality. For handwritten output, letter-form representations (e.g., a representation of lower-case print f) must be activated, whereas for oral spelling letter name representations (e.g., /ɛf/) are required. For other forms of output (e.g., typing) different representations (e.g., keystroke representations) would need to be computed. Here we focus on the processes required for handwritten output.

As illustrated in Figure 2, some theorists (e.g., Ellis, 1982, 1988; Margolin, 1984) assume that in generating a handwritten response, abstract letter representations are first converted to allograph (letter shape) representations corresponding to the chosen form of written output (e.g., lower-case print). The allograph representations in turn activate effector-independent graphic motor plans, which are learned representations specifying the movements (i.e., the sequence of writing strokes) required to write the letter in the chosen form. The graphic motor plans are effector independent in the sense that they are not tied to particular effectors (e.g., the right hand), and do not specify movements with respect to specific muscles or joints. Hence, the graphic motor plan for upper-case print B could mediate writing of that letter with the right hand, left hand, left foot, or so forth.

Although the assumption of a progression from abstract letter identities to allographs to graphic motor plans is common, some theorists have proposed instead that abstract letter representations are mapped directly to graphic motor plans (e.g., Menichelli, Rapp, & Semenza, 2008; Miozzo & De Bastiani, 2002; Rapp & Caramazza, 1997; Van Galen, 1991).[3] Regardless of how graphic motor plans are activated, the final steps in the writing process involve the conversion of the graphic motor plans to effector-specific motor programmes, and the use of these plans by the motor system to execute the appropriate writing movements with the chosen effector. During the writing process visual feedback plays a significant role, not only in ensuring appropriate orientation and spacing of letters and words across the page, but also in monitoring and controlling the shapes of individual letters (e.g., Danna & Velay, 2015; Smyth & Silvers, 1987).

Theory of normal adult mechanisms and the study of deficits

An explicit theory specifying the representations and processes underlying a cognitive function provides a foundation for interpreting deficits affecting that function. In particular, deficits are interpreted as resulting from dysfunction of one or more components of the normal cognitive system. Ideally, the interpretation specifies which component(s) of the normal system are malfunctioning, how and to what extent they are malfunctioning, and how the malfunction(s) give rise to the specific pattern of impaired performance observed in an individual with a deficit. We first illustrate this point through an example from the literature on acquired dysgraphia in adults, and then consider the role of the normal adult theory in the study of developmental dysgraphia.

Theory-based interpretation of deficits

Goodman and Caramazza (1986a, 1986b) reported the case of J.G., a young woman with a spelling deficit resulting from a head injury. J.G.'s comprehension of dictated stimuli was intact, and she showed normal performance in spelling pseudowords (e.g., FEEN).[4] However, she was impaired in spelling words (e.g., CURTAIN), with errors taking the form of phonologically plausible misspellings (e.g., KERTIN). Her spelling performance also showed a regularity effect—better performance for words with spellings that are highly predictable from their sounds (e.g., CRIME) than for words with less predictable spellings (e.g., KNOCK). Finally, J.G.'s performance pattern was virtually identical in written and oral spelling tasks.

Goodman and Caramazza (1986a, 1986b) argued that J.G. suffered from a selective deficit affecting orthographic long-term memory, such that she was frequently unable to activate a learned spelling representation when attempting to spell a word. When retrieval of the orthographic representation failed, they argued, J.G. relied upon her intact sound-to-spelling conversion process to generate a spelling. These assumptions permit a clear and explicit interpretation for the various features of J.G.'s spelling performance. Her spelling is impaired for words but not for pseudowords because orthographic long-term memory is required for accurate spelling of words but not pseudowords (which are spelled sublexically). Her errors for words take the form of phonologically plausible misspellings because she often uses the sublexical sound–spelling conversion process to spell words, and this process generates spellings that, while plausible (e.g., KERTIN), are not always correct. The role of the sublexical route in J.G.'s spelling of words also explains the regularity effect: When she is forced to rely on sublexical spelling processes, she is more likely to produce the correct spelling for highly regular words than for less regular words, precisely because the more regular words have spellings that are more likely to be generated by application of sound–spelling correspondence rules. Finally, J.G.'s extremely similar performance in written and oral spelling tasks follows from basic assumptions about the functional architecture of the cognitive spelling mechanisms: Written and oral spelling recruit the same lexical and sublexical spelling processes.

In addition to illustrating that a theory of normal cognitive representations and processes provides a basis for interpreting deficits, this example makes another, closely related, point: A theory of normal mechanisms is crucial for developing systematic diagnostic methods. In choosing which tasks to present (e.g., word and pseudoword spelling, written and oral spelling), which variables to manipulate (e.g., regularity), and which analyses to carry out (e.g., analyses of error types) Goodman and Caramazza (1986a, 1986b) were guided by the theory of normal cognitive spelling mechanisms. Taken together, the tasks, manipulations, and analyses they chose in studying J.G. systematically assessed each of the processing components specified in the theory. For example, the functioning of J.G.'s sublexical sound-to-spelling process was assessed by examining her pseudoword spelling accuracy and her error types in spelling words. In the absence of a theory specifying the normal cognitive spelling mechanisms, Goodman and Caramazza would have had no solid basis for choosing diagnostic methods, or for interpreting results obtained with these methods.

Deficits as evidence about normal mechanisms

Thus far, we have emphasized that a theory of normal cognitive mechanisms plays an essential role in efforts to understand cognitive deficits. At the same time, however, deficits provide evidence bearing on the theory of normal cognitive mechanisms, supporting, disconfirming, or prompting further elaboration of assumptions about normal cognitive representations and processes. For instance, the results from J.G. supported fundamental assumptions about the cognitive architecture of the normal spelling system, such as the assumption of separate lexical and sublexical spelling routes (supported by the findings pointing to selective impairment of the former while the latter remained intact). In addition, systematic analyses of J.G.'s phonologically plausible misspellings led Goodman and Caramazza (1986a, 1986b) to formulate claims about the functioning of the sublexical spelling process. For example, Goodman and Caramazza presented evidence that in selecting letters to represent sounds the sublexical process is context sensitive, taking into account both syllable position (e.g., mapping /k/ to CK in syllable-final but not syllable-initial position) and the sound–letter mapping options chosen for adjacent positions in the word (e.g., mapping /s/ to C only when the letter selected for the immediately following position was E, I, or Y, as in CENTER or J.G.'s misspelling of SENATE as CENIT).

Developmental dysgraphia and the theory of normal adult writing mechanisms

The preceding discussion of cognitive theory and research on acquired dysgraphia has implications for the study of developmental dysgraphia. We assume that like acquired dysgraphias, developmental writing deficits can be interpreted by specifying which component(s) of the normal adult writing system (e.g., orthographic long-term memory, graphic motor plans) are deficient (which, in the case of developmental deficits, means that a component is less fully developed than expected).[5] Further, we assume that the study of developmental dysgraphia can shed light on normal cognitive writing mechanisms and their development. These assumptions may be incorrect, and indeed have been questioned in the context of other developmental deficits (e.g., Bishop, 1997; Karmiloff-Smith, 1997; but see Castles et al., 2014, for counter-arguments). Conceivably, atypical development could give rise to cognitive mechanisms that are both non-optimal and radically different in structure and functioning from the mechanisms acquired by typically developing children. If this were the case, we could not interpret deficits in terms of disruption to normal writing mechanisms, and we could not readily make inferences about the normal mechanisms from developmental writing deficits.

This possibility that individuals with developmental dysgraphia have grossly atypical cognitive writing mechanisms cannot be ruled out a priori. However, we suggest that neither should this possibility be assumed a priori. In our view it is more likely that in developmental dysgraphia some aspect(s) of an otherwise-typical system fail to develop fully, than that a completely different system is acquired. Regardless of relative likelihoods, however, we suggest that the appropriate research strategy is to adopt as a working hypothesis the normal-system-with-some-deficiency assumption, and ask whether the evidence comports with the assumption.[6] If the assumption is incorrect—that is, if individuals with developmental dysgraphia develop writing systems qualitatively different from those of typically developing writers—we should soon discover the error. Efforts to interpret developmental writing deficits by specifying disruption to the normal cognitive writing system should prove unsuccessful, and conclusions we draw about normal writing mechanisms through studies of developmental dysgraphia should fail to converge with conclusions from studies of normal writing and studies of acquired dysgraphia. On the other hand, if research founded on the normal-system-with-some-deficiency assumption proves fruitful in explaining deficits and advancing our understanding of normal writing processes, then we can have more confidence in the assumption. As we discuss in a later section, the available research on developmental dysgraphia, although still somewhat limited, provides grounds for optimism that developmental writing deficits will prove to be interpretable by reference to the normal adult system.

The developmental dimension

The developmental aspect of developmental dysgraphia raises another set of issues we have not yet considered. In acquired deficits (at least those with onset in adulthood) a cognitive system has developed normally, and then suffers disruption as a consequence of brain damage. In developmental deficits, however, the deficiency within the cognitive system occurs due to some malfunction in processes that support acquisition of the system. In the case of writing ability, the relevant knowledge and cognitive processes must be learned, and impairment affecting the ability to learn the knowledge and processes leads to deficiencies in the writing system.

Consider, for example, a deficit affecting orthographic long-term memory, in which an individual often cannot access representations of whole-word spellings. If this were an acquired deficit, we would assume that brain damage disrupted previously learned spelling representations, and/or the ability to retrieve these representations from orthographic long-term memory. However, if the deficit were developmental, we would probably assume that the individual was impaired in learning the spelling representations (or perhaps the procedures for retrieving the representations from memory). In this case—and indeed for any developmental deficit—interpreting the deficit involves not only specifying what component(s) of the writing system is/are deficient, but also characterizing the deficit(s) that led to impaired acquisition of the representations or processes making up the component.

This point brings up an important distinction, articulated by Coltheart (2015), between proximal and distal causes (see also Castles et al., 2014). Proximal causes are the deficiencies within a cognitive system that directly result in impaired performance, whereas distal causes are the causal factors that produced the deficiencies. In a case of developmental dysgraphia the proximal cause is the deficiency within the cognitive writing system that produces impaired writing performance (e.g., underdeveloped orthographic long-term memory, deficient knowledge of sound–spelling correspondence rules). The distal cause, in contrast, is the deficit that caused the failure in acquisition of cognitive spelling or handwriting mechanisms. For example, a deficit in encoding or retaining information about ordering of elements (such as the letters in a word) could impair the learning of word spellings, resulting in deficient orthographic long-term memory representations. In this instance, the distal cause is the deficit in sequence representation, and the proximal cause is the deficient orthographic long-term memory system.

Claims about proximal and distal causes address different questions, and should be carefully distinguished in theorizing about developmental dysgraphia. Claims about proximal causes speak to the question, "What aspect(s) of the cognitive writing system are deficient?", whereas for distal causes the question is, "What caused the failure of development for the deficient writing-system components?". Hence, proximal-cause interpretations (e.g., orthographic long-term memory deficit) are not alternatives to distal-cause accounts (e.g., impaired visual attention span). Rather, proximal- and distal-cause claims together provide a fuller interpretation for an impairment than either alone.

Of course, an adequate distal-plus-proximal-cause account should make clear how the proposed distal cause led to the posited proximal deficit. For example, if the proximal cause is claimed to be a deficient orthographic long-term memory, the distal cause should plausibly lead specifically to difficulty in learning word spellings.

Two points about distal causes merit brief discussion. First, although distal causes are typically assumed to involve rather general cognitive processes (e.g., learning, visual attention, or other processes implicated in a broad range of cognitive functions), distal causes could conceivably also include highly specific processes. For example, in an individual with a deficient orthographic long-term memory, the distal cause could conceivably be a highly selective deficit in learning word spellings, occurring in the presence of otherwise normal learning abilities, or the individual might have a learning deficit that, while not entirely specific to spelling, nevertheless affects learning only in a limited range of circumstances (e.g., a deficit in learning information in which the ordering of elements is critical).

Second, the distal cause for a deficit is probably best thought of not as a single causal state or event, but rather as a complex causal nexus that may include causes at several levels of explanation (e.g., cognitive, neural, genetic). For example, a genetic defect might (via several intervening causes) lead to an impairment in sequence encoding, which in turn causes a proximal deficit in orthographic long-term memory (see Coltheart, 2015, for further discussion). However, we limit our discussion of distal causes to the cognitive factors that most directly give rise to the proximal writing-system deficit.

Acquisition of writing ability

Our ability to understand the proximal and distal causes of developmental dysgraphias will depend importantly on our understanding of the processes involved in the normal acquisition of writing skills. Although some research has examined acquisition of spelling and handwriting (e.g., Apel, 2009; Berninger et al., 2006; Kandel & Perret, 2015; Kandel & Valdois, 2006; Kersey & James, 2013; Masterson & Crede, 1999; Treiman, 1993; Treiman & Kessler, 2014), we do not yet have a comprehensive theory of the processes implicated in development of writing skill, or the cognitive capacities required by these processes. Here we provide a very brief overview of this complex topic.

The end state of learning to write is the adult writing system schematized in Figures 1 and 2. How, though, is this system acquired? The acquisition process draws upon a broad range of abilities that are available to children when they begin learning to write, including spoken language, vision, attention, memory, and motor skills. More specific cognitive capacities that may be important for acquisition of writing include, but are not limited to, phonological awareness and phonological memory (Campbell & Butterworth, 1985; Snowling, Stackhouse, & Rack, 1986), visual attention span (Valdois et al., 2003), visual memory (Goulandris & Snowling, 1991), and processes for representing the order of elements in a sequence (e.g., Romani, Ward, & Olson, 1999).

With regard to the trajectory of writing acquisition, the process of learning to spell has most often been described in terms of stage theories (e.g., Ehri, 1986; Frith, 1980; Gentry, 1982). The various proposals differ in their specific assumptions, but most posit some type of preliterate stage in which children realize that written marks (other than drawings) can be used to represent meanings, followed by a phonological stage during which letters are used to represent sounds, and then one or more orthographic stages in which letters, letter groups, orthographic regularities, and eventually morphological information are incorporated into the spelling process. Importantly, however, Treiman and colleagues have shown that children begin to use various types of knowledge earlier than stage theories would predict. For example, children who would be classified as phonetic spellers nevertheless show evidence of familiarity with orthographic conventions concerning such matters as letter doubling (Treiman, 2003) and morphological boundaries (for more detailed discussion see Pollo, Kessler, & Treiman, 2009; Treiman, 1993; Treiman & Bourassa, 2000; Treiman & Kessler, 2014). Treiman and colleagues conclude that spelling development is not characterized by strict stages in which children draw solely upon only a particular type of knowledge (e.g., phonological as opposed to orthographic). Rather, they argue, multiple knowledge types are brought into play throughout the acquisition process, and stages can be more appropriately thought of as developmental time-periods marked by the predominant (but not exclusive) use of certain knowledge types (see also Temple, 1990; Varnhagen, McCallum, & Burstow, 1997).

Turning now to development of handwriting, the required motor control is quite demanding, and children's writing of letters is initially slow and variable. Only with extensive practice, around age 10–11 years, does letter production become automatized, fast, and less variable (e.g., Halsband & Lange, 2006; Van Galen, Portier, Smits-Engelsman, & Schomaker, 1993; see also Palmis, Danna, Velay, & Longcamp, 2017, in this special issue). Once handwriting is automatized, children can devote resources to other aspects of writing, such as sentence construction and text elaboration (Maggio, Lété, Chenu, Jisa, & Fayol, 2012; Pontart et al., 2013). Kandel and Perret (2015) argue that other consequences of growing automaticity include increasing interaction between central orthographic processing levels and more peripheral motor processes.

These proposals regarding normal spelling and handwriting acquisition represent valuable contributions to our understanding of writing development and developmental dysgraphia. Even taken together, however, they do not constitute a systematic theory of the knowledge and processes underlying the development of writing ability, and do not provide a firm foundation for systematically enumerating the possible distal causes for a developmental writing deficit. Therefore, a critical goal for research on developmental dysgraphia is the articulation of a more complete theory of writing acquisition.

Developmental dysgraphia: Current state of knowledge

The preceding discussion of normal adult writing mechanisms and their development provides a basis for considering the current state of knowledge regarding developmental dysgraphia. Here we provide a brief review of research regarding the proximal and distal causes.

Proximal causes

A growing literature describes individuals with developmental spelling deficits that closely resemble acquired forms of dysgraphia and can be understood as failures in developing particular components of the normal adult spelling system: orthographic long-term memory, the sublexical sound-to-spelling conversion process, or orthographic working memory (see Castles & Coltheart, 1993, for similar claims regarding developmental dyslexia).

Multiple reports have described individuals with developmental writing deficits attributable to a deficient orthographic long-term memory (as in the acquired case of J.G. studied by Goodman & Caramazza, 1986a, 1986b). Briefly, these individuals are impaired in spelling words (especially irregular words), and produce phonologically plausible errors, but have little or no difficulty spelling pseudowords. This pattern, sometimes referred to as developmental surface dysgraphia, has been reported in several languages (English: Brunsdon, Coltheart, & Nickels, 2005; Coltheart, Masterson, Byng, Prior, & Riddoch, 1983; Goulandris & Snowling, 1991; Hanley & Gard, 1995; Hanley, Hastie, & Kay, 1992; Romani et al., 1999; Seymour, 1986; Seymour & Evans, 1993; Temple, 1985, 1986; Italian: Angelelli, Judica, Spinelli, Zoccolotti, & Luzzatti, 2004; Angelelli, Notarnicola, Judica, Zoccolotti, & Luzzatti, 2010; Spanish: Afonso, Suárez-Coalla, & Cuetos, 2015; German: Cholewa, Mantey, Heber, & Hollweg, 2010; Stadie & van de Vijver, 2003; see also, in this special issue, Marinelli, Cellini, Zoccolotti, & Angelelli, 2017; Sotiropolous & Hanley, 2017; Hepner, McCloskey, & Rapp, 2017).

The complementary pattern—better spelling performance for words than pseudowords—has also been reported (Campbell & Butterworth, 1985; Cholewa et al., 2010; Funnell & Davison, 1989; Snowling et al., 1986; Temple, 1986; Temple & Marshall, 1983). This pattern, often labelled developmental phonological dysgraphia, can be understood as a selective deficit affecting the sound-to-spelling conversion process. In addition a few cases of developmental impairment in orthographic working memory have been reported (Roncoli & Masterson, 2016; Yachini & Friedmann, 2010). For example, Roncoli and Masterson (2016) described a 10-year-old boy who showed a pattern of spelling performance resembling that observed in acquired cases of orthographic working memory impairment: poor spelling of both regular and irregular words; errors in the form of letter omissions, insertions, substitutions, and transpositions; and effects of word length but not word frequency on spelling accuracy (see also Barisic, Kohnen, & Nickels, 2017, in this special issue).

Distal causes

Notwithstanding the limitations in our current knowledge concerning acquisition of writing ability, some progress has been made in exploring distal causes of developmental dysgraphia. The most commonly proposed distal cause is a deficit in phonological processing and/or phonological awareness, suggested by reports of phonological deficits in some individuals with developmental dysgraphia (e.g., Campbell & Butterworth, 1985; Snowling et al., 1986; but see Castles & Coltheart, 2004). According to this proposal, learning to spell (like learning to read) requires an explicit understanding that spoken words are composed from smaller phonological units (i.e., phonemes), as well as an ability to parse words into their constituent phonemes at a level of processing accessible to awareness. Individuals with deficiencies in these phonological skills might therefore have difficulty appreciating the relationships between the sounds and spellings of words, leading to difficulty in learning sound–spelling correspondences, and in memorizing whole-word spellings. Despite the apparent plausibility of this argument, we are not aware of any clear evidence for a causal link between phonological deficits and developmental dysgraphia (see, e.g., Castles & Coltheart, 2004). Also, numerous cases of developmental dysgraphia have been reported in which phonological processing skills were intact (Angelelli et al., 2004; Frith, 1978, 1980; Hanley et al., 1992; Hepner et al., 2017; Holmes & Quinn, 2009; Masterson, Laxon, Lovejoy, & Morris, 2007; Romani et al., 1999; Roncoli & Masterson, 2016). These cases demonstrate at the least that phonological impairment is not the sole distal cause of developmental dysgraphia.

Goulandris and Snowling (1991) suggested that deficits in the visual domain could lead to developmental dysgraphia. These researchers presented evidence of a visual memory impairment in an individual with developmental dysgraphia, and reasoned that the visual deficit would make it difficult to retain the information needed for building orthographic long-term memory representations. Also, Romani et al. (1999) described an individual with a deficit in encoding and learning the ordering of elements in a sequence of symbols (e.g., the ordering of letters in a written word), and argued that this sequence encoding deficit was the distal cause for the individual's developmental dysgraphia. (Romani et al., 1999, also presented evidence that the individual was intact in phonological processing and visual memory.)

With respect to developmental handwriting deficits, some form of motor-control deficit has most commonly been proposed as the distal cause (e.g., Smits-Engelsman, Niemeijer, & van Galen, 2001; Smits-Engelsman & Van Galen, 1997; Van Galen et al., 1993). For example, Van Galen et al. (1993) argued that poor writers are deficient at inhibiting noise in their neuromotor systems. Developmental handwriting deficits could also conceivably result from distal deficits that impair the learning of effector-independent or effector-specific motor programmes for characters.

These various results suggest that multiple forms of underlying impairment may lead to developmental dysgraphia. As our understanding of normal writing acquisition advances, we will have a stronger foundation for systematically exploring possible distal causes and relating these to particular types of proximal impairment within the writing system.

An agenda for research on developmental dysgraphia

The preceding discussion and overview of the literature provide a basis for defining an agenda for the study of developmental dysgraphia. The agenda has two closely interrelated goals: (a) advancing our understanding of the proximal and distal deficits underlying developmental writing impairments; and (b) advancing the development of theories concerning normal cognitive writing mechanisms and the development of these mechanisms. Many aspects of the agenda are already being pursued, and we hope that this special issue will contribute to moving the agenda forward.

With respect to characterizing the underlying deficits in developmental dysgraphia, we suggest that a fruitful research agenda can be defined by the following fundamental questions:

- What aspects of the cognitive writing system show impairment in cases of developmental dysgraphia (proximal causes)?
- What distal causes are implicated in the genesis of these deficits?

- How are distal and proximal causes linked? That is, how does each proximal deficit in cognitive writing mechanisms arise from the associated distal cause(s)?

These questions cannot, however, be addressed in isolation. As we have emphasized, answers must be built on a solid foundation of theory concerning normal cognitive writing mechanisms, and the development of these mechanisms. Hence, the second part of our proposed agenda concerns advancement of theory in these areas. The basic questions are as follows:

- What cognitive representations and processes underlie normal spelling and writing?
- How do these cognitive mechanisms develop as a child learns to write?

As we have discussed, considerable progress has been made regarding the first question: We have a reasonably well-specified theory of normal adult writing mechanisms. As with any cognitive theory, many aspects of the writing theory are in need of further development (and even the most basic assumptions of the theory could ultimately turn out to be wrong).[7] Nevertheless, the theory is sufficiently well developed and well supported that we can (at least to a first approximation) enumerate the possible proximal causes of developmental writing deficits and investigate these systematically.

In contrast, our knowledge concerning the acquisition of writing is not as far advanced, and consequently our foundation for elucidating distal causes of developmental dysgraphia is less complete. We hope that research on developmental dysgraphia will both contribute to, and benefit from, progress in our understanding of the normal development of writing ability.

Throughout this article we have focused on cognitive as opposed to neural representations and processes, because at present we have only limited knowledge about neural mechanisms in spelling and handwriting, and especially about neural dysfunctions in developmental dysgraphia. Accordingly, yet another important goal for future research is to advance our understanding of neural mechanisms and dysfunctions in writing and dysgraphia. (For discussions of neural substrates of writing see, e.g., Beeson et al., 2003; Palmis et al., 2017; Planton, Jucla, Roux, & Démonet, 2013; Purcell, Turkeltaub, Eden, & Rapp, 2011; Rapp & Dufor, 2011.)

In pursuing the research agenda we have sketched, it is important to recognize that developmental dysgraphias are heterogeneous, with respect to both proximal and distal causes. The writing system is complex, encompassing a broad range of cognitive and neural representations and processes. Disruption to any of these could potentially result in a writing deficit, with the nature of the deficit depending on the nature and extent of the disruption. Consequently, we should not expect disruption to the writing system (the proximal cause) to be the same in everyone suffering from developmental dysgraphia. To the contrary, we should recognize that deficits grouped under the heading developmental dysgraphia are diverse. Research on acquired dysgraphia in adults makes clear that there are multiple distinct forms of writing-system impairment, including but not limited to selective deficits affecting orthographic long-term memory (e.g., Beauvois & Dérouesné, 1981; Goodman & Caramazza, 1986a, 1986b), sublexical sound-to-spelling conversion (e.g., Shallice, 1981), orthographic working memory (e.g., Caramazza & Miceli, 1990; Caramazza, Miceli, Villa, & Romani, 1987; McCloskey, Badecker, Goodman-Schulman, & Aliminosa, 1994; Posteraro, Zinelli, & Mazzucchi, 1988), and graphic motor plans (e.g., Baxter & Warrington, 1986; Miozzo & De Bastiani, 2002). Furthermore, these diverse cognitive dysfunctions are associated with diverse loci of neural dysfunction (e.g., Rapp, Purcell, Hillis, Capasso, & Miceli, 2016). The evidence we have surveyed on developmental dysgraphia indicates that this category is comparably heterogeneous.

Similarly, with respect to distal causes, diverse proximal deficits are likely to stem from diverse distal impairments (e.g., impairments in phonological processing, visual memory, or sequence encoding). In addition, similar proximal deficits could potentially arise from quite different distal causes. For example, a deficient orthographic long-term memory could potentially result from several different distal causes, all of which cause difficulty in learning of word spellings.

This point has two crucial consequences. First, we should not take the goal of research to be that of determining *the* (proximal or distal) cause of, or *the* underlying (proximal or distal) deficit in, developmental dysgraphia. Almost certainly there are multiple proximal and distal causes that can lead to developmental writing deficits, and our goal should be to characterize the full constellation of these proximal and distal causes. The second consequence concerns research strategy: We cannot conduct research by selecting a group of developmental dysgraphics according to some diagnostic criteria, and then studying them as a group (e.g., averaging results across participants, looking for significant group effects). This research method assumes the group to be homogeneous in relevant respects, and in particular assumes that all have the same form of impairment. Rather, we must study participants individually, allowing commonalities and differences across individuals to emerge from the conclusions of detailed single-case investigations, rather than being assumed a priori.[8]

Overview of the special issue

The articles in this special issue explore many of the research topics we have discussed and contribute to advancing the agenda we have outlined. The first five articles focus primarily on spelling, whereas the final three address issues concerning handwriting.

Treiman (2017) reviews typical spelling development, with particular emphasis on sublexical spelling processes. Treiman argues that spelling patterns (regularities in sound–spelling mappings) are complex and multi-faceted, and hence that acquisition of sublexical knowledge is not a simple matter of learning context-free phoneme–grapheme mappings. She describes an integration of multiple patterns (IMP) framework, according to which children learn not only whole-word spellings, but also context-sensitive phonological, graphotactic, and morphological patterns that apply (although not without exceptions) to many words. For example, Treiman notes that /ɛ/ is typically (though not always) spelled EA when followed by D (e.g., HEAD), but as E when followed by other consonants (e.g., GET). She proposes that statistical learning processes play an important role in learning of spelling patterns and also suggests that learning a whole-word spelling is easier when multiple patterns converge on the correct spelling than when patterns conflict. Treiman's arguments and proposals have important implications for theory and research concerning normal spelling processes, the acquisition of spelling, and the nature of the deficiencies in developmental spelling deficits.

Barisic et al. (2017) report a single-case study of a 10-year-old boy, L.S. Examining L.S.'s performance across a variety of tasks chosen to probe the various components of the normal adult spelling system, Barisic and colleagues conclude that he suffers from a developmental deficiency at the level of the graphemic buffer (orthographic working memory). For example, like reported acquired cases of graphemic buffer impairment, L.S. predominantly makes letter errors in spelling (i.e., letter substitutions, transpositions, additions, and omissions). The Barisic et al. study adds to our understanding of the forms of developmental spelling impairment, as well as supporting the view that cognitive neuropsychological methods can fruitfully be applied to developmental deficits. In particular, the study highlights the value of theory-based assessment and interpretation of developmental dysgraphias.

Hepner et al. (2017) also apply theoretically grounded cognitive neuropsychological methods in their study of two children, P.J.T. and A.K.R., who present with poor spelling in the context of otherwise strong cognitive abilities. Hepner et al. argue that both children are impaired in learning lexical orthographic representations for use in spelling (with P.J.T. also showing deficiency in sublexical spelling processes) and examine potential distal causes for the spelling deficits. They also report a striking dissociation for P.J.T. between reading and spelling. Whereas P.J.T.'s spelling is severely deficient, a thorough assessment of his reading revealed normal (and in fact exceptionally strong) performance, with no evidence of weakness in either lexical or sublexical reading processes. This result has implications for issues concerning normal reading and spelling processes (e.g., shared vs. separate orthographic lexicons for reading and spelling) and suggests that at least some aspects of lexical orthographic representation and processing develop with considerable independence in reading and spelling.

Sotiropolous and Hanley (2017) also address issues concerning shared versus separate cognitive mechanisms for reading and spelling. These authors report intriguing results from six university students with developmental spelling and reading deficits. All six participants showed the same basic pattern of performance on reading and spelling assessment tasks (e.g., impaired reading and spelling of irregular words, but intact reading and spelling of pseudowords). This pattern is typically labelled surface dyslexia and dysgraphia, and is usually interpreted to reflect impaired lexical and intact sublexical reading and spelling processes. However, despite the similarity across participants in basic reading and spelling performance, testing with additional tasks (e.g., lexical decision, semantic decision, written picture naming) revealed clear differences among participants, indicating differences in the underlying impairments. In interpreting the observed performance patterns, Sotiropolous and Hanley argue that a single orthographic system mediates both reading and spelling. In addition to the specific empirical and theoretical contributions of the study, the Sotiropolous and Hanley findings highlight two points that we have emphasized in the present article: First, developmental dysgraphias (and dyslexias) are diverse, with multiple causes and manifestations; and second, detailed, theory-guided testing of individuals is necessary to identify the nature of the impairments.

Marinelli, Cellini, Zoccolotti, and Angelelli (2017) examined lexical and sub-lexical reading and spelling processes in Italian, a language with a largely transparent orthography. Marinelli and colleagues tested typically developing and dyslexic third- and fifth-grade children on spelling to dictation and orthographic judgment (i.e., lexical decision) tasks. Stimuli included not only words with regular spellings (which make up most of the Italian lexicon) but also words for which the spelling is not entirely predictable from the phonology (e.g., CUOCO, which is not fully predictable because /kw/ may be realized in Italian as either CU or, less commonly, as QU). In both spelling and orthographic judgment tasks, and for both typically developing and dyslexic children, results indicated that children were relying in part on lexical orthographic knowledge in performing the tasks (e.g., frequency and regularity effects were observed). However, the lexical knowledge was weaker in the dyslexic children (as evidenced, for example, by larger regularity effects for dyslexic than for typically developing children). Also, both dyslexic and typically developing children were sensitive to the frequencies of grapheme–phoneme mappings in Italian. For example, in spelling low-frequency words children were more accurate for those with high-frequency mappings (e.g., /kw/ → CU) than for those with low-frequency mappings (e.g., /kw/ → QU). Marinelli et al. suggest that sublexical knowledge, including knowledge about frequencies of sound–spelling mappings, contributes to lexical learning and, in dyslexic children, can compensate in part for deficient lexical–orthographic knowledge.

The final three articles in the special issue concern handwriting development and developmental handwriting deficits. Palmis et al. (2017) provide an overview of the cognitive and neural mechanisms in adult handwriting and typical handwriting development. Emphasizing the complex motor control processes required for handwriting, these authors characterize skilled handwriting in adults and then describe how writing is acquired over a number of years in childhood. According to Palmis and colleagues, acquisition of handwriting involves a variety of developmental changes, including a transition from production of characters as a series of discrete strokes (often separated by pauses or pen lifts) to a smoother, less variable, and more automatic production under the control of learned whole-character motor representations. Palmis et al. also offer insights into the brain networks that contribute to handwriting performance and the neural changes that occur in the course of handwriting development. This article provides a foundation for considering the nature of the proximal and distal deficits in children with developmental handwriting deficits.

Prunty and Barnett (2017) contrast children who have handwriting difficulties as a consequence of a general motor coordination deficit (developmental coordination deficit, or DCD) with children who struggle with handwriting in the absence of general motor impairment (referred to as dysgraphic children). DCD and dysgraphic groups were compared with typically developing control children on a variety of handwriting measures, including writing speed, pauses during writing, and quality of letter formation. Although the DCD and dysgraphic children performed more poorly than the typically developing children on most measures, few differences were found between the DCD and dysgraphic groups. However, considerable variation was observed within groups. These results highlight the importance—for diagnosis, remediation, and research—of considering children as individuals, and not just as members of a category such as DCD.

Finally, in a fitting conclusion to the special issue, Kandel, Lassus-Sangosse, Grosjacques, and Perret (2017) bring together the study of spelling and the study of handwriting. Although spelling and handwriting are usually treated separately in theory and research, Kandel and colleagues have argued previously that cognitive spelling processes (e.g., retrieval of lexical orthographic representations) are not completed prior to initiation of writing (e.g., Roux, McKeeff, Grosjacques, Afonso, & Kandel, 2013). Rather, the spelling processes are ongoing during the production of written output and may affect the motor processes in handwriting. Applying this perspective to the study of children diagnosed with developmental dysgraphia, Kandel and colleagues argue that in children who have difficulty spelling, the greater than normal cognitive load imposed by spelling processes may lead to handwriting deficiencies, including slow and dysfluent writing. In fact these authors suggest that the frequently observed poor handwriting in children with spelling deficits may often stem from the effects of spelling processes on handwriting, and not from deficiencies in handwriting per se.

We hope that this special issue will prove useful to researchers, educators, and clinicians interested in normal or impaired reading or writing. We especially hope that the special issue will stimulate further discussion and research on the important but understudied topic of developmental dysgraphia.

Notes

1. Dysgraphia (in the sense of impaired spelling) is often included in definitions of developmental dyslexia (see, e.g., the International Dyslexia Association's definition: "Dyslexia . . . is characterized by difficulties with accurate and/or fluent word recognition and by poor spelling and decoding abilities", "Definition of Dyslexia", 2017). The extent to which developmental spelling deficits associate with and dissociate from developmental reading deficits is an important issue for research, and we include within the scope of our discussion developmental dysgraphias occurring in either the presence or absence of reading impairments.
2. Sublexical spelling processes may also draw upon knowledge of morphology (e.g., Treiman, 2017). For example, in English the phoneme sequence /ʌs/ is likely to be spelled OUS when it corresponds to a suffix (as in FAMOUS) but not otherwise (e.g., STATUS, FUNGUS).
3. Note that the terms *allograph* and *allographic* are used somewhat inconsistently in the literature. Whereas some authors use these terms to refer to letter shape representations with no motoric content, others use the terms in referring to what we have called graphic motor plans.
4. A pseudoword spelling is scored correct if the spelling is plausible given the sound. Hence, for the dictated pseudoword /fi:n/, the spellings FEEN, FENE, and FEAN would all be counted as correct.
5. The normal system that provides a basis for characterizing deficits in developmental dysgraphia is not the fully developed adult system, but rather the partially developed form of that system we would expect to find in a typically developing child (e.g., the writing system of a typically developing 8-year-old if we are considering a developmentally dysgraphic 8-year-old). Consequently, interpretation of developmental dysgraphias requires not only a theory of the adult system, but also assumptions about how this system typically develops over time. Although some researchers (e.g., Bishop, 1997) have argued that developing cognitive systems may be so different from adult systems that theories of adult systems are not useful in interpreting developmental disorders, Castles et al. (2014) make a strong case for the value of adult-system theories in the study of developmental deficits.
6. This assumption is analogous to the assumption in adult cognitive neuropsychology that brain damage does not lead to creation of a cognitive system qualitatively different from the normal system (the "transparency" assumption; see Caramazza, 1986).
7. One important set of unresolved questions concerns relationships between writing and reading mechanisms (e.g., Coltheart & Funnell, 1987; Jones & Rawson, 2016; Tainturier & Rapp, 2001). For example, does a single orthographic long-term memory underlie both reading and spelling, or are there instead separate input (reading) and output (spelling) orthographic long-term memory systems, each specialized to perform different computations (mapping letter to word representations in reading, and word to letter representations in writing)? Research on developmental dysgraphia may shed light on these issues (see, e.g., Hepner et al., 2017; Sotiropoulos & Hanley, 2017, in this special issue).
8. This same point has been discussed extensively in the context of acquired deficits (see Caramazza & McCloskey, 1988; McCloskey & Caramazza, 1988).

Disclosure statement

No potential conflict of interest was reported by the authors.

Funding

Preparation of this article was supported by a Johns Hopkins Science of Learning Institute grant to Michael McCloskey; by National Institutes of Health [grant number DC006740] to Brenda Rapp; and by a generous gift from a donor to the Johns Hopkins University.

References

Afonso, O., Suárez-Coalla, P., & Cuetos, F. (2015). Spelling impairments in Spanish dyslexic adults. *Frontiers in Psychology*, *6*, 3. doi:10.3389/fpsyg.2015.00466

Angelelli, P., Judica, A., Spinelli, D., Zoccolotti, P., & Luzzatti, C. (2004). Characteristics of writing disorders in Italian dyslexic children. *Cognitive and Behavioral Neurology*, *17*, 18–31. doi:10.1097/00146965-200403000-00003

Angelelli, P., Notarnicola, A., Judica, A., Zoccolotti, P., & Luzzatti, C. (2010). Spelling impairments in Italian dyslexic children: Phenomenological changes in primary school. *Cortex*, *46*, 1299–1311. doi:10.1016/j.cortex.2010.06.015

Apel, K. (2009). The acquisition of mental orthographic representations for reading and spelling development. *Communication Disorders Quarterly*, *31*(*1*), 42–52. doi:10.1177/1525740108325553

Barisic, K., Kohnen, S., & Nickels, L. (2017). Developmental graphemic buffer dysgraphia in English: A single case study. *Cognitive Neuropsychology*.

Baxter, D. M., & Warrington, E. K. (1986). Ideational agraphia: A single case study. *Journal of Neurology, Neurosurgery & Psychiatry*, *49*, 369–374. doi:10.1136/jnnp.49.4.369

Beauvois, M. F., & Dérouesné, J. (1981). Lexical or orthographic agraphia. *Brain*, *104*, 21–49. doi:10.1093/brain/104.1.21

Beeson, P., Rapcsak, S., Plante, E., Chargualaf, J., Chung, A., Johnson, S., & Trouard, T. (2003). The neural substrates of writing: A functional magnetic resonance imaging study. *Aphasiology*, *17*, 647–665. doi:10.1080/02687030344000067

Berninger, V. W., Abbott, R. D., Jones, J., Wolf, B. J., Gould, L., Anderson-Youngstrom, M., … Apel, K. (2006). Early development of language by hand: Composing, reading, listening, and speaking connections; three letter-writing modes; and fast mapping in spelling. *Developmental Neuropsychology*, *29*, 61–92. doi:10.1207/s15326942dn2901_5

Berninger, V. W. (1999). Coordinating transcription and text generation in working memory during composing: Automatic and constructive processes. *Learning Disability Quarterly*, *22*, 99–112. doi:10.2307/1511269

Bishop, D. V. (1997). Cognitive neuropsychology and developmental disorders: Uncomfortable bedfellows. *The Quarterly Journal of Experimental Psychology Section A*, *50*, 899–923. doi:10.1080/713755740

Brunsdon, R., Coltheart, M., & Nickels, L. (2005). Treatment of irregular word spelling in developmental surface dysgraphia. *Cognitive Neuropsychology*, *22*, 213–251. doi:10.1080/02643290442000077

Campbell, R., & Butterworth, B. (1985). Phonological dyslexia and dysgraphia in a highly literate subject: A developmental case with associated deficits of phonemic processing and awareness. *The Quarterly Journal of Experimental Psychology Section A*, *37*, 435–475. doi:10.1080/14640748508400944

Caramazza, A. (1984). The logic of neuropsychological research and the problem of patient classification in aphasia. *Brain and Language*, *21*, 9–20. doi:10.1016/0093-934X(84)90032-4

Caramazza, A. (1986). On drawing inferences about the structure of normal cognitive systems from the analysis of patterns of impaired performance: The case for single-patient studies. *Brain and Cognition*, *5*, 41–66. doi:10.1016/0278-2626(86)90061-8

Caramazza, A., & McCloskey, M. (1988). The case for single-patient studies. *Cognitive Neuropsychology*, *5*, 517–527. doi:10.1080/02643298808253271

Caramazza, A., & Miceli, G. (1990). The structure of graphemic representations. *Cognition*, *37*, 243–297. doi:10.1016/0010-0277(90)90047-N

Caramazza, A., Miceli, G., Villa, G., & Romani, C. (1987). The role of the graphemic buffer in spelling: Evidence from a case of acquired dysgraphia. *Cognition*, *26*, 59–85. doi:10.1016/0010-0277(87)90014-X

Castles, A., & Coltheart, M. (1993). Varieties of developmental dyslexia. *Cognition*, *47*, 149–180. doi:10.1016/0010-0277(93)90003-E

Castles, A., & Coltheart, M. (2004). Is there a causal link from phonological awareness to success in learning to read? *Cognition*, *91*, 77–111. doi:10.1016/S0010-0277(03)00164-1

Castles, A., Kohnen, S., Nickels, L., & Brock, J. (2014). Developmental disorders: What can be learned from cognitive neuropsychology? *Philosophical Transactions of the Royal Society B: Biological Sciences*, *369*, 20130407. doi:10.1098/rstb.2013.0407

Cholewa, J., Mantey, S., Heber, S., & Hollweg, W. (2010). Developmental surface and phonological dysgraphia in German 3rd graders. *Reading and Writing*, *23*, 97–127. doi:10.1007/s11145-008-9153-7

Coltheart, M., & Funnell, E. (1987). Reading and writing: One lexicon or two? In D. A. Allport, D. G. Mackay, W. Prinz, & E. Scheerer (Eds.), *Language and production: Relationships between listening, speaking, reading, and writing* (pp. 313–339). London: Academic Press.

Coltheart, M. (2015). What kinds of things cause children's reading difficulties? *Australian Journal of Learning Difficulties*, *20*, 103–112. doi:10.1080/19404158.2015.1114000

Coltheart, M., Masterson, J., Byng, S., Prior, M., & Riddoch, J. (1983). Surface dyslexia. *The Quarterly Journal of Experimental Psychology Section A*, *35*, 469–495. doi:10.1080/14640748308402483

Cuetos, F., & Labos, E. (2001). The autonomy of the orthographic pathway in a shallow language: Data from an aphasic patient. *Aphasiology*, *15*, 333–342. doi:10.1080/02687040042000313

Danna, J., & Velay, J. L. (2015). Basic and supplementary sensory feedback in handwriting. *Frontiers in Psychology*, *6*, 57. doi:10.3389/fpsyg.2015.00169

Definition of Dyslexia. (2017). Retrieved from https://dyslexiaida.org/definition-of-dyslexia

Döhla, D., & Heim, S. (2016). Developmental dyslexia and dysgraphia: What can we learn from the one about the other? *Frontiers in psychology*, *6*, 700. doi:10.3389/fpsyg.2015.02045

Ehri, L. C. (1986). Sources of difficulty in learning to spell and read words. In M. Wolraich & D. Routh (Eds.), *Advances in developmental and behavioral pediatrics* (Vol. *7*, pp. 121–195). Greenwich, CT: JAI Press.

Ellis, A. W. (1982). Spelling and writing (and reading and speaking). In A. W. Ellis (Ed.), *Normality and pathology in cognitive functions* (pp. 113–146). London: Academic Press.

Ellis, A. W. (1988). Normal writing processes and peripheral acquired dysgraphias. *Language and Cognitive Processes, 3*, 99–127. doi:10.1080/01690968808402084

Frith, U. (1978). From print to meaning and from print to sound, or how to read without knowing how to spell. *Visible Language, 12*, 43–54.

Frith, U. (1980). Unexpected spelling problems. In U. Frith (Ed.), *Cognitive processes in spelling* (pp. 495–515). London: Academic Press.

Funnell, E., & Davison, M. (1989). Lexical capture: A developmental disorder of reading and spelling. *The Quarterly Journal of Experimental Psychology Section A, 41*, 471–487. doi:10.1080/14640748908402377

Gentry, J. R. (1982). An analysis of developmental spelling in "GNYS AT WRK". *The Reading Teacher, 36*, 192–200.

Goodman, R. A., & Caramazza, A. (1986a). Aspects of the spelling process: Evidence from a case of acquired dysgraphia. *Language and Cognitive Processes, 1*, 263–296. doi:10.1080/01690968608404678

Goodman, R. A., & Caramazza, A. (1986b). Phonologically plausible errors: Implications for a model of the phoneme-grapheme conversion mechanism in the spelling process. In G. Augst (Ed.), *New trends in graphemics and orthography* (pp. 300–325). Berlin: Walter de Gruyter.

Goulandris, N. K., & Snowling, M. (1991). Visual memory deficits: A plausible cause of developmental dyslexia? Evidence from a single case study. *Cognitive Neuropsychology, 8*, 127–154. doi:10.1080/02643299108253369

Graham, S., Berninger, V. W., Abbott, R. D., Abbott, S. P., & Whitaker, D. (1997). Role of mechanics in composing of elementary school students: A new methodological approach. *Journal of Educational Psychology, 89*, 170–182. doi:10.1037/0022-0663.89.1.170

Graham, N. L. (2014). Dysgraphia in primary progressive aphasia: Characterisation of impairments and therapy options. *Aphasiology, 28*, 1092–1111. doi:10.1080/02687038.2013.869308

Halsband, U., & Lange, R. K. (2006). Motor learning in man: A review of functional and clinical studies. *Journal of Physiology-Paris, 99*, 414–424. doi:10.1016/j.jphysparis.2006.03.007

Hanley, J. R, & Gard, F. (1995). A dissociation between developmental surface and phonological dyslexia in twoundergraduate students. *Neuropsychologia, 33*, 909–914.

Hanley, J. R., Hastie, K., & Kay, J. (1992). Developmental surface dyslexia and dysgraphia: An orthographic processing impairment. *The Quarterly Journal of Experimental Psychology Section A, 44*, 285–319. doi:10.1080/02724989243000046

Hepner, C., McCloskey, M., & Rapp, B. (2017). Do reading and spelling share orthographic representations? Evidence from developmental dysgraphia. *Cognitive Neuropsychology.*

Hillis, A. E., & Caramazza, A. (1991). Mechanisms for accessing lexical representations for output: Evidence from a category-specific semantic deficit. *Brain and Language, 40*, 106–144. doi:10.1016/0093-934X(91)90119-L

Hillis, A. E., & Caramazza, A. (1992). The reading process and its disorders. In D. I. Margolin (Ed.), *Cognitive Neuropsychology in Clinical Practice* (pp. 229–261). Oxford: Oxford University Press.

Hollerbach, J. M. (1981). An oscillation theory of handwriting. *Biological Cybernetics, 39*, 139–156. doi:10.1007/BF00336740

Holmes, V. M., & Quinn, L. (2009). Unexpectedly poor spelling and phonological-processing skill. *Scientific Studies of Reading, 13*, 295–317. doi:10.1080/10888430903001225

Houghton, G., & Zorzi, M. (2003). Normal and impaired spelling in a connectionist dual-route architecture. *Cognitive Neuropsychology, 20*, 115–162. doi:10.1080/02643290242000871

Jones, A. C., Folk, J. R., & Rapp, B. (2009). All letters are not equal: Subgraphemic texture in orthographic working memory. *Journal of Experimental Psychology: Learning, Memory, and Cognition, 35*, 1389–1402. doi:10.1037/a0017042

Jones, A. C., & Rawson, K. A. (2016). Do reading and spelling share a lexicon? *Cognitive Psychology, 86*, 152–184. doi:10.1016/j.cogpsych.2016.02.003

Kandel, S., Lassus-Sangosse, D., Grosjacques, G., & Perret, C. (2017). The impact of developmental dyslexia and dysgraphia on movement production during word writing. *Cognitive Neuropsychology.*

Kandel, S., & Perret, C. (2015). How does the interaction between spelling and motor processes build up during writing acquisition? *Cognition, 136*, 325–336. doi:10.1016/j.cognition.2014.11.014

Kandel, S., & Valdois, S. (2006). Syllables as functional units in a copying task. *Language and Cognitive Processes, 21*, 432–452. doi:10.1080/01690960400018378

Karmiloff-Smith, A. (1997). Crucial differences between developmental cognitive neuroscience and adult neuropsychology. *Developmental Neuropsychology, 13*, 513–524. doi:10.1080/87565649709540693

Kersey, A. J., & James, K. H. (2013). Brain activation patterns resulting from learning letter forms through active self-production and passive observation in young children. *Frontiers in Psychology, 4*, 567. doi:10.3389/fpsyg.2013.00567

Maggio, S., Lété, B., Chenu, F., Jisa, H., & Fayol, M. (2012). Tracking the mind during writing: Immediacy, delayed, and anticipatory effects on pauses and writing rate. *Reading and Writing, 25*, 2131–2151. doi:10.1007/s11145-011-9348-1

Margolin, D. I. (1984). The neuropsychology of writing and spelling: Semantic, phonological, motor, and perceptual processes. *The Quarterly Journal of Experimental Psychology Section A, 36*, 459–489. doi:10.1080/14640748408402172

Marinelli, C. V., Cellini, P., Zoccolotti, & Angelelli, P. (2017) Whole word processing and sensitivity to written regularity in a consistent orthography: A reading and spelling longitudinal study on dyslexic and typically developing children. *Cognitive Neuropsychology.*

Masterson, J. J., & Crede, L. A. (1999). Learning to Spell: Implications for Assessment and Intervention. *Language*

Speech and Hearing Services in Schools, *30*, 243–254. doi:10.1044/0161-1461.3003.243

Masterson, J., Laxon, V., Lovejoy, S., & Morris, V. (2007). Phonological skill, lexical decision and letter report performance in good and poor adult spellers. *Journal of Research in Reading*, *30*, 429–442. doi:10.1111/j.1467-9817.2007.00347.x

McCloskey, M., Aliminosa, D., & Macaruso, P. (1991). Theory-based assessment of acquired dyscalculia. *Brain and Cognition*, *17*, 285–308. doi:10.1016/0278-2626(91)90078-M

McCloskey, M., Badecker, W., Goodman-Schulman, R. A., & Aliminosa, D. (1994). The structure of graphemic representations in spelling: Evidence from a case of acquired dysgraphia. *Cognitive Neuropsychology*, *11*, 341–392. doi:10.1080/02643299408251979

McCloskey, M., & Caramazza, A. (1988). Theory and methodology in cognitive neuropsychology: A response to our critics. *Cognitive Neuropsychology*, *5*, 583–623. doi:10.1080/02643298808253276

McCloskey, M. (2001). The future of cognitive neuropsychology. In B. Rapp (Ed.), *What deficits reveal about the human mind/brain: A handbook of cognitive neuropsychology* (pp. 593–610). Philadelphia: Psychology Press.

Menichelli, A., Rapp, B., & Semenza, C. (2008). Allographic agraphia: A case study. *Cortex*, *44*(7), 861–868. doi:10.1016/j.cortex.2007.06.002

Miceli, G., Benvegnù, B., Capasso, R., & Caramazza, A. (1997). The independence of phonological and orthographic lexical forms: Evidence from aphasia. *Cognitive Neuropsychology*, *14*, 35–69. doi:10.1080/026432997381619

Miceli, G., & Capasso, R. (2006). Spelling and dysgraphia. *Cognitive Neuropsychology*, *23*, 110–134. doi:10.1080/02643290500202730

Miozzo, M., & De Bastiani, P. (2002). The organization of letter-form representations in written spelling: Evidence from acquired dysgraphia. *Brain and Language*, *80*, 366–392. doi:10.1006/brln.2001.2598

Palmis, S., Danna, J., Velay, J.-L., & Longcamp, M. (2017). Motor control of handwriting in the developing brain: A review. *Cognitive Neuropsychology*.

Planton, S., Jucla, M., Roux, F. E., & Démonet, J. F. (2013). The "handwriting brain": A meta-analysis of neuroimaging studies of motor versus orthographic processes. *Cortex*, *49*, 2772–2787. doi:10.1016/j.cortex.2013.05.011

Pollo, T. C., Kessler, B., & Treiman, R. (2009). Statistical patterns in children's early writing. *Journal of Experimental Child Psychology*, *104*, 410–426. doi:10.1016/j.jecp.2009.07.003

Pontart, V., Bidet-Ildei, C., Lambert, E., Morisset, P., Flouret, L., & Alamargot, D. (2013). Influence of handwriting skills during spelling in primary and lower secondary grades. *Frontiers in Psychology*, *4*, 818. doi:10.3389/fpsyg.2013.00818

Posteraro, L., Zinelli, P., & Mazzucchi, A. (1988). Selective impairment of the graphemic buffer in acquired dysgraphia: A case study. *Brain and Language*, *35*, 274–286. doi:10.1016/0093-934X(88)90112-5

Prunty, M., & Barnett, A. L. (2017). Understanding handwriting difficulties: A comparison of children with and without motor impairment. *Cognitive Neuropsychology*.

Purcell, J. J., Turkeltaub, P. E., Eden, G. F., & Rapp, B. (2011). Examining the central and peripheral processes of written word production through meta-analysis. *Frontiers in Psychology*, *2*, doi: 10.3389/fpsyg.2011.00239. doi:10.3389/fpsyg.2011.00239

Rapp, B., & Caramazza, A. (1997). From graphemes to abstract letter shapes: Levels of representation in written spelling.. *Journal of Experimental Psychology: Human Perception and Performance*, *23*, 1130–1152. doi:10.1037/0096-1523.23.4.1130

Rapp, B., & Dufor, O. (2011). The neurotopography of written word production: An fMRI investigation of the distribution of sensitivity to length and frequency. *Journal of Cognitive Neuroscience*, *23*, 4067–4081. doi:10.1162/jocn_a_00109

Rapp, B., Epstein, C., & Tainturier, M. J. (2002). The integration of information across lexical and sublexical processes in spelling. *Cognitive Neuropsychology*, *19*, 1–29. doi:10.1080/0264329014300060

Rapp, B., Purcell, J., Hillis, A. E., Capasso, R., & Miceli, G. (2016). Neural bases of orthographic long-term memory and working memory in dysgraphia. *Brain*, *139*, 588–604. doi:10.1093/brain/awv348

Romani, C., Ward, J., & Olson, A. (1999). Developmental surface dysgraphia: What is the underlying cognitive impairment? *The Quarterly Journal of Experimental Psychology Section A*, *52*, 97–128. doi:10.1080/713755804

Roncoli, S., & Masterson, J. (2016). 'Unexpected' spelling difficulty in a 10-year-old child with good reading skills: An intervention case study. *Writing Systems Research*, *8*, 143–166. doi:10.1080/17586801.2016.1159539

Roux, S., McKeeff, T. J., Grosjacques, G., Afonso, O., & Kandel, S. (2013). The interaction between central and peripheral processes in handwriting production. *Cognition*, *127*, 235–241. doi:10.1016/j.cognition.2012.12.009

Seymour, P. H. K, & Evans, H. M. (1993). The visual (orthographic) processor and developmental dyslexia. In D. M. Willows, R. S. Kruk, & E. Corcos (Eds.), *Visual processes in reading and reading disabilities* (pp. 347–376). Hillsdale, NJ: Lawrence Erlbaum Associates.

Seymour, P. H. K. (1986). *Cognitive analysis of dyslexia*. London, England: Routledge & Kegan Paul.

Shallice, T. (1981). Phonological agraphia and the lexical route in writing. *Brain: A Journal of Neurology*, *104*, 413–429. doi:10.1093/brain/104.3.413

Smits-Engelsman, B. C., Niemeijer, A. S., & van Galen, G. P. (2001). Fine motor deficiencies in children diagnosed as DCD based on poor grapho-motor ability. *Human Movement Science*, *20*, 161–182. doi:10.1016/S0167-9457(01)00033-1

Smits-Engelsman, B. C., & Van Galen, G. P. (1997). Dysgraphia in children: Lasting psychomotor deficiency or transient developmental delay? *Journal of Experimental Child Psychology*, *67*(2), 164–184. doi:10.1006/jecp.1997.2400

Smyth, M. M., & Silvers, G. (1987). Functions of vision in the control of handwriting. *Acta Psychologica*, *65*, 47–64. doi:10.1016/0001-6918(87)90046-1

Snowling, M., Stackhouse, J., & Rack, J. (1986). Phonological dyslexia and dysgraphia—a developmental analysis. *Cognitive Neuropsychology, 3*, 309–339. doi:10.1080/02643298608253362

Sotiropolous, A., & Hanley, J. R. (2017). The relationship between lexical decision and spelling in developmental surface dysgraphia: Evidence for a unitary orthographic system. *Cognitive Neuropsychology.*

Stadie, N., & van de Vijver, R. (2003). A linguistic and neuropsychological approach to remediation in a German case of developmental dysgraphia. *Annals of Dyslexia, 53*, 280–299. doi:10.1007/s11881-003-0013-5

Tainturier, M.-J., Bosse, M.-L., Roberts, D. J., Valdois, S., & Rapp, B. (2013). Lexical neighborhood effects in pseudoword spelling. *Frontiers in Psychology, 4*, 862.

Tainturier, M.-J., & Rapp, B. (2001). The spelling process. In B. Rapp (Ed.), *The handbook of cognitive neuropsychology: What deficits reveal about the human mind* (pp. 263–289). Philadelphia, PA: Psychology Press.

Temple, C. M. (1985). Developmental surface dysgraphia: A case report. *Applied Psycholinguistics, 6*, 391–405. doi:10.1017/S0142716400006329

Temple, C. M. (1986). Developmental dysgraphias. *The Quarterly Journal of Experimental Psychology Section A, 38*, 77–110. doi:10.1080/14640748608401586

Temple, C. M. (1990). Foop is still floop: A six year follow-up of phonological dyslexia and dysgraphia. *Reading and Writing, 2*(3), 209–221. doi:10.1007/BF00257972

Temple, C. M, & Marshall, J. C. (1983). A case study of developmental phonological dyslexia. *British Journal of Psychology, 74*(4), 517–533.

Treiman, R., & Bourassa, D. C. (2000). The development of spelling skill. *Topics in Language Disorders, 20*, 1–18. doi:10.1097/00011363-200020030-00004

Treiman, R., & Kessler, B. (2014). *How children learn to write words*. New York: Oxford University Press.

Treiman, R. (1993). *Beginning to spell*. New York: Oxford University Press.

Treiman, R. (2003). Phonology and spelling. In T. Nunes, & P. Bryant (Eds.), *Handbook of children's literacy* (pp. 31–42). Dordrecht: Kluver.

Treiman, R. (2017). Learning to spell: Phonology and beyond. *Cognitive Neuropsychology.*

Valdois, S., Bosse, M. L., Ans, B., Carbonnel, S., Zorman, M., David, D., & Pellat, J. (2003). Phonological and visual processing deficits can dissociate in developmental dyslexia: Evidence from two case studies. *Reading and Writing, 16*, 541–572. doi:10.1023/A:1025501406971

Van Galen, G. P. (1991). Handwriting: Issues for a psychomotor theory. *Human Movement Science, 10*, 165–191. doi:10.1016/0167-9457(91)90003-G

Van Galen, G. P., Portier, S. J., Smits-Engelsman, B. C., & Schomaker, L. R. (1993). Neuromotor noise and poor handwriting in children. *Acta Psychologica, 82*, 161–178. doi:10.1016/0001-6918(93)90010-O

Varnhagen, C. K., McCallum, M., & Burstow, M. (1997). Is children's spelling naturally stage-like? *Reading and Writing, 9*, 451–481. doi:10.1023/A:1007903330463

Yachini, M., & Friedmann, N. (2010). Developmental graphemic buffer dysgraphia. *Procedia - Social and Behavioral Sciences, 6*, 148–149. doi:10.1016/j.sbspro.2010.08.073

Learning to spell: Phonology and beyond

Rebecca Treiman

ABSTRACT
An understanding of the nature of writing systems and of the typical course of spelling development is an essential foundation for understanding the problems of children who have serious difficulties in learning to spell. The present article seeks to provide that foundation. It argues that the dual-route models of spelling that underlie much existing research and practice are based on overly simple assumptions about how writing systems work and about how spelling skills develop. Many writing systems include not only context-free links from phonemes to letters but also context-sensitive phonological patterns, morphological influences, and graphotactic patterns. According to an alternative framework, IMP (integration of multiple patterns), spellers acquire multiple sources of information through use of their statistical-learning skills and through direct instruction. Children learn the spelling of a word most easily when different patterns converge on the spelling, and they have difficulty when patterns conflict. Implications of these ideas for assessment and instruction are considered.

People in modern societies rely heavily on reading and writing to learn about the world and to communicate with others. To participate effectively in such societies, people must be good readers and good writers. Those who are poor at these skills will be disadvantaged. This article focuses on one skill that is important for writing and reading: the ability to spell individual words. Many skills are involved in writing, including developing and organizing one's ideas and choosing appropriate words. Knowing how to spell the words may seem minor in comparison, but it is an important part of the writing process. Dictionaries and spell-checkers can help, but writers cannot completely offload the task of spelling to outside tools. Use of these tools takes time, and it diverts attention from the goal of producing a well-reasoned and polished piece. Moreover, the productions of poor spellers may be so far off the mark that spell-checkers are of little help. Storing the conventional spelling of words in our heads rather than relying on outside tools benefits reading as well as writing. As Snow, Griffin, and Burns (2005, p. 86) state, "spelling and reading build and rely on the same mental representation of a word. Knowing the spelling of a word makes the representation of it sturdy and accessible for fluent reading".

Learning to spell is not a trivial task. Across languages, learning to spell words is harder than learning to read them (Bosman & Van Orden, 1997). Given the value of spelling for writing and for reading, the present article discusses how children learn to spell and the processes used by skilled spellers. I begin by considering the nature of writing systems. Two different theoretical frameworks for viewing the spelling process are then presented. The sections that follow discuss the sources of information that people use when deciding how to spell words and how children develop the ability to use each one. The focus, in these sections, is on typically developing spellers. Some implications for understanding and remediating the difficulties of poor spellers are considered at the end of the article.

Writing systems

Spoken language is a powerful method of communication, and it has allowed human societies to develop to a great degree. A limitation of spoken language, however, is that it is naturally evanescent. To overcome this limitation, people have developed methods of communication that are designed to last and that permit communication among those who are separated in time and space. Writing, the most prominent such communication system, achieves its power by piggybacking off language. Rather than trying to represent meaning directly, writing uses visual elements that represent units of a language. Many writing systems are *phonographic*, in that their visual elements represent phonological (sound) units of a language. *Alphabets*, a major type of phonographic writing system and the type on which I focus here, have letters that represent speech sounds, *phonemes*. For example, the letter form ‹р› stands for the phoneme /r/ in Russian and for /p/ in English. (This article uses angled brackets around letters when the letter forms themselves are the focus of discussion. Slashes signify phonemes, and italics are used to indicate words in general and to define terms.)

The English writing system, which has featured in much of the research on the learning and use of alphabetic writing systems, has been called "chaotic and unprincipled" (Dewey, 1971, p. 4), "the world's most awesome mess" (Pei, 1967, p. 337). These characterizations reflect the fact that the links between sounds and letters are not one-to-one. For example, /k/ may be spelled in a variety of ways, including ‹c› as in *sonic*, ‹ck› as in *haddock*, and ‹k› as in *kangaroo*. As another example, /æ/ is typically spelled as ‹a›, as in *hat* and *ham*. But *have* has ‹e› at the end as well as ‹a› in the middle, a spelling pattern that is more typical of words with /e/ (e.g., *hate*). As I will show, however, English spelling includes more regularities than often thought. The same is true for other writing systems that lack simple one-to-one relations from sounds to letters, such as French and Greek.

When a phoneme has more than one possible spelling, it is sometimes the case that one spelling tends to occur in certain phonological contexts and other spellings in other contexts. In English, for example, children are typically taught a simple *context-free* rule about how to spell /ɑ/: that it is spelled as ‹o›. This holds true for words like *pond* and *cod* but not for words like *wad*, *wand*, and *squash*. But these latter words are not isolated exceptions. They are examples of a *context-sensitive* pattern: /ɑ/ is usually spelled ‹a› after /w/. As another example of the effect of phonological context on English spelling, ‹ea› is a common alternative to ‹e› as a spelling of /ɛ/ when this vowel precedes /d/. *Head* is one of a number of words with ‹ea› in this context, joining *bread*, *dead*, *meadow*, and others. When /ɛ/ occurs before most consonants other than /d/, it is less likely to be spelled as ‹ea›. Additional examples of context-sensitive patterns in English may be found in Kessler and Treiman (2001). Many cases of context conditioning in modern English spelling reflect changes in the pronunciations of sounds that have occurred over time. For example, the vowel of *wad* and *wand* used to be pronounced the same as the vowel of *pad* and *hand*, but the pronunciation changed in the former words under the influence of the preceding /w/. The spellings, however, were not updated.

In some writing systems, the spelling of a phoneme may differ depending on whether it is part of a certain *morphological* unit (unit of meaning). For example, /o/ has a number of possible spellings in French, including ‹eau›, ‹o›, and ‹ot›. It is not the case, however, that a random subset of words with /o/ has each spelling. When /o/ is a diminutive suffix, as in *renardeau* "fox cub", which is based on the stem *renard* "fox", the spelling is almost always ‹eau›. When /o/ is not a diminutive suffix, as in *piano* and *escargot* "snail", other spellings are more common.

Still other patterns in writing are *graphotactic* in nature. These patterns concern the ordering and arrangement of letters. One example from English is that double consonants are uncommon before final ‹ic›. Thus, English has a number of words like *panic* and *magic* but few words like *tannic*. Before ‹ock› and ‹ick›, in contrast, double consonants (as in *haddock* and *derrick*) are common. The endings ‹ic›, ‹ick›, and ‹ock› are pronounced alike; it is the spelling of the ending rather than its phonological form that is associated with the presence of a single or double consonant in these cases. (See Berg, 2016, for further discussion of the influences on consonant doubling in English.) Another graphotactic pattern of English is that the choice between a double-letter and a single-letter spelling of /f/ and certain other phonemes in word-final position is influenced by the number of letters in the spelling of the preceding vowel. The double-letter spelling is used if the vowel is spelled with one letter (e.g., *Jeff*) but a single consonant is used if the vowel is spelled with more than one letter (e.g., *deaf*).

Having discussed some basic properties of writing systems, I turn to theories about how people spell and how they learn to do so.

Dual-route theories

The dominant theoretical framework for thinking about the mental processes involved in spelling is the *dual-route* framework (Barry, 1994; Tainturier & Rapp, 2001). Dual-route theorists propose that there are two ways to spell a word. The first method, the *lexical route*, is to look up the spelling of the word in one's mental dictionary. This route relies on spellings that have been previously encountered during the course of reading or other activities and that have been memorized as wholes and stored in long-term memory. The second method of spelling an item, the *nonlexical route*, is to generate a spelling based on rules that map individual phonemes to letters or groups of letters. The nonlexical route must be used for words that have not previously been seen and for nonwords that have been invented for purposes of an experiment. Spellers may use both routes for some types of items, and researchers have considered different ways in which the routes may interact (e.g., Tainturier, Bosse, Roberts, Valdois, & Rapp, 2013).

Researchers who adopt a dual-route framework have not usually provided much detail about the workings of the nonlexical route. For example, they have not laid out complete lists of the rules that are postulated for specific languages. Some instantiations of dual-route theory, as discussed by Barry and Seymour (1988), assume that the rules are context-free. That is, each phoneme is associated with the letter or letter group that is most often used to represent it in the words of the language. The nonlexical route of English thus includes rules that link /æ/ to ‹a›, /h/ to ‹h›, /v/ to ‹v›, and /ʃ/ (as in *shin*) to ‹sh›, these being the most common spellings of these phonemes in the language. Other instantiations of dual-route theory, including those favoured by Barry and Seymour and by Kreiner (1992), see each phoneme as having several spelling options, each with an associated strength. For example, the link between /u/ and ‹oo› is strong in English because /u/ has a fairly high probability of being spelled with ‹oo›, as in *moon* and *tooth*. The link between /u/ and ‹ew› (as in *screw*) is weaker, as are the links between /u/ and ‹eu› (as in *sleuth*) and between /u/ and ‹oe› (as in *shoe*). According to these instantiations of dual-route theory, the weights on the spelling options for a given phoneme do not vary depending on the surrounding context. Some other instantiations of dual-route theory allow for such variation, including variation as a function of whether a phoneme is in the initial, medial, or final position of a syllable (Goodman & Caramazza, 1986; Sanders & Caramazza, 1990). The version of dual-route theory proposed by Houghton and Zorzi (2003) can account for influences based on the identity of neighbouring phonemes. However, Treiman and Kessler (2016) showed that this computational model did not account for influences based on the spellings of those phonemes. In particular, the model failed to account for the above-described tendency for the doubling of certain final consonants to be more common after a vowel phoneme that is spelled with a single letter than after the same vowel phoneme that is spelled with more than one letter.

Whichever version of dual-route theory one adopts, words such as *hat*, *hash*, and *vat* are seen as *regular* words or, to use a term preferred by Barry and Seymour (1988), words with *high-contingency* sound-to-spelling correspondences. For these words, use of only the nonlexical route is guaranteed or almost guaranteed to produce the correct spelling. *Have* is an *irregular* word, one that contains a *low-contingency* spelling of the vowel. This is because the nonlexical rules generate an incorrect spelling, *hav*, with a probability of 1 or close to 1, depending on the version of dual-route theory that one adopts. *Shoe* is another example of an irregular word. Involvement of the lexical route is thought to be required in order to produce the correct spellings of irregular words.

The dual-route framework has guided not only studies of skilled spellers but also studies of developing spellers. A number of investigators who have applied dual-route theory to spelling development have suggested that beginning spellers rely largely on the nonlexical route (e.g., Sprenger-Charolles, Siegel, & Bonnet, 1998). Knowledge of basic letter-to-sound correspondences and ability to analyse spoken words into phonemes are essential for using this route. Over time, children build up a store of memorized spellings and become able to use the lexical route.

Although research within the dual-route framework has made many useful contributions, existing instantiations of this framework are based on an overly simple view of how writing systems work and of the patterns they afford. For example, *wand* is seen as an irregular word in most instantiations of the dual-route framework because it does not include the spelling of /ɑ/ that is most common in English as a whole, ‹o›. However, ‹a› is a common spelling of /ɑ/ when this vowel occurs after /w/, meaning that *wand* follows a context-sensitive phonological pattern. As another example, *have* is classified as irregular because of its final ‹e›;‹hav› would be the expected spelling according to the dual-route view. However, ‹hav› is highly unusual because English words hardly ever end with ‹v›; *live* and *love* are other examples of words that include an ‹e› that is phonologically unexpected in order to protect against a final ‹v›. To my knowledge, no existing version of dual-route theory can handle graphotactic patterns of this sort. As these examples show, some spellings that are considered irregular in the dual-route framework can be rationalized by considering graphotactics, morphology, and context-conditioned links from sounds to spellings. The next section discusses an alternative framework for thinking about the processes involved in spelling that takes these influences into account.

Integration of multiple patterns (IMP)

Integration of multiple patterns (IMP), a framework proposed by Treiman and Kessler (2014), is based on the idea that writing systems include a variety of patterns. Experienced spellers store information about the spellings of specific words and about patterns that apply across words—not only context-free links between phonemes and letters but also context-sensitive phonological patterns, graphotactic patterns, and morphological patterns. Because people use a variety of patterns, using multiple patterns even on the same word, they tend to learn a spelling most easily when several patterns converge upon it. Learning is slower when different sources of information conflict.

In using the term "patterns" rather than "rules", IMP acknowledges that the useful regularities within writing systems are not necessarily all or none. In English, for example, it is not the case that /ɛ/ is always spelled as ‹ea› before /d/ and always spelled as ‹e› before other consonants. However, ‹ea› is more common in the former context than in the latter. People use their knowledge of this probabilistic pattern when they entertain *stead* as a possible spelling of /stɛd/ but not *steab* as a possible spelling of /stɛb/. Learning of probabilistic patterns is enabled by *statistical-learning* skills: the ability to learn that certain objects and events tend to occur more often than others and that certain objects and events tend to occur together while others are less likely to do so. Statistical learning is often implicit, in that people pick up patterns from exposure even when the patterns are not explicitly pointed out to them and in that people may not be consciously aware of the patterns that they follow. This type of knowledge plays an important role in spelling, according to IMP.

People have the opportunity to use patterns that they know not only when generating spellings for novel words but also when remembering spellings that are commonly characterized as irregular. For example, even though ‹choir› is an unusual spelling for the phonological form /kwaɪr/, ‹ch› is a common spelling sequence in English, more common than ‹hc›, and it occurs at the beginning of a number of words. Learning and remembering a spelling like *choir* requires some information that is specific to this word, but it also draws on general information about English spelling that applies across words. That is, memory for even unusual spellings like *choir* is not based purely on rote memorization of letter sequences.

IMP's view of how children learn to spell differs in important ways from most dual-route views. Recall that most researchers who have applied the dual-route framework to development have seen phonology as paramount in the spelling of young children. The first step in learning to spell is said to be the acquisition of a set of rules that map phonemes to spellings, a nonlexical route. Only later do children begin to store in memory the spellings of specific words (Sprenger-Charolles et al., 1998). IMP, on the other hand, proposes that learning about the visual form of writing comes first. Young children use their statistical-learning skills to acquire some basic knowledge about what writing looks like and about how letters combine, and they begin to do this even before they learn how the spellings of words reflect the phonemes in their spoken forms. Somewhat older children apply their statistical-learning skills to the associations between sounds and spellings, learning not only about context-free associations from sounds to spellings but also about the role of phonological context in selecting among possible spellings of a sound. With experience, children also learn about how morphology can influence the choice among alternative spellings and about the more complex graphotactic patterns of their writing system. The following sections discuss these types of patterns in turn, beginning with graphotactics.

Graphotactics

Writing has two sides. It is an object in itself—marks on a surface—and it is a representation of something outside itself—a linguistic form. Research shows that children use their statistical-learning skills to begin learning about the outer form of writing before they learn how letters represent phonemes. As early as 3 or 4 years of age, for example, U.S. children have begun to learn that writing tends to be arranged along horizontal lines and that the same letter does not repeat multiple times. For example, children judge the repeated-letter string ‹TTTTT› as a poorer example of writing than the string ‹TOODLE› even though they cannot read either one (Ganapole, 1987; Lavine, 1977). Preschool children's beginning knowledge about letter arrangement also shows itself when they are asked to write words themselves. A number of children of around 4 and 5 years of age produce strings of letters that bear no phonological relation to the sounds of the words they are asked to write; they are *prephonological spellers*. Even though these children do not use phonologically plausible letters more often than expected by chance, they may arrange the letters along a line. They may use a variety of letters rather than repeating the same letter multiple times, and they may use letters and letter groups that are common in the language to which they have been exposed (Kessler, Pollo, Treiman, & Cardoso-Martins, 2013; Pollo, Kessler, & Treiman, 2009; Treiman, Kessler, Boland, Clocksin, & Chen, in press). These findings suggest that even prephonological spellers have some knowledge about what written words look like in their language—that is, some basic graphotactic knowledge. This knowledge increases over the period during which children spell in a prephonological manner (Treiman et al., in press), and the strength of such knowledge can help to predict a child's later success in learning to spell conventionally (Kessler et al., 2013).

Children do not learn about all of the graphotactic patterns of their writing system before they learn how letters represent units of language. Some graphotactic patterns are acquired later. In French, for example, double consonants are permitted after vowels but not after other consonants. Thus, *issoge* could be a word but *genssor* could not. Knowledge of this subtle pattern appears to develop around 8 years of age, several years after formal reading and spelling instruction have begun (Pacton & Fayol, 2000).

Graphotactic knowledge plays a role in the spelling of older children and adults as well as young children. Consider a fact about English spelling that was discussed earlier: the likelihood that a consonant is doubled may depend on the following letter sequence. For example, doubling is more common before final unstressed /ɪk/ that is spelled as ‹ick› or ‹ock› than before final /ɪk/ that is spelled as ‹ic›. Treiman and Boland (2017) found that adults' spellings reflect these patterns in that the tendency to double the middle consonant of a disyllabic nonword is influenced by the letters that spellers choose to represent the final part of the nonword. Teachers typically see the choice between single and double consonants as a purely phonological matter: Double consonants should be used after short vowels (e.g., *rabbit*), and single consonants should be used after long vowels (e.g., *rabies*; Carreker, 2005). Indeed, primary-school students are sometimes taught this pattern as the "rabbit rule". Adults' choices between single and double consonants are influenced by the phonological properties of the preceding vowel in the way suggested by the rabbit rule (Cassar & Treiman, 1997), but the results of Treiman and Boland show that graphotactic considerations are also influential. If a speller knows that a word ends with ‹ic›, for example, he could infer that the preceding consonant is unlikely to be doubled even if he has not previously seen the word's spelling. This means that spellings such as *panic* and *magic* do not need to be individually memorized as exceptions to a rule. These results are difficult to incorporate into dual-route theories of the spelling process, with their focus on phonology and on rote memorization of spellings that do not fit phonologically based patterns. However, the results fit well with the IMP framework.

Phonology

Although graphotactic knowledge plays an early and lasting role in spelling, phonology is undeniably important. A critical aspect of learning to use an alphabetic writing system is learning that letters symbolize sounds and how they do so. In the United States, this typically begins around the age of 5 or 6 as children move from prephonological spellings such as ‹dega› for *cut* and ‹bparo› for *fit* to spellings such as ‹k› or ‹cmo› for *cut* and ‹ft› for *fit*. Spellings that represent all of the phonemes in a word with letters that are used to symbolize them in some words of the language—spellings that researchers in the dual-route framework often call *phonetic*—do not emerge all at once. They are preceded by a period during which children fail to represent some phonemes within words and include some unexpected letters. As I show below, these errors arise for a variety of reasons.

Some spelling errors reflect a difficulty in conceptualizing spoken words as sequences of phonemes. Consonant clusters cause particular problems for phonemic analysis and for spelling. Children may write ‹sid› for *slide* and ‹pa› for *play*, for example, symbolizing the first consonant of the initial consonant cluster with the correct letter but not including a letter to represent the second consonant (Treiman, 1993). These errors, which occur even in children who pronounce the clusters correctly, reflect a difficulty in conceptualizing an initial cluster such as /pl/ as a sequence of two elements, both of which deserve representation in spelling. Words with consonant clusters at the ends also cause difficulties for phonemic analysis and spelling in learners of English and other languages (Treiman, Zukowski, & Richmond-Welty, 1995, for English; van Bon & Uit de Haag, 1997, for Dutch).

In other cases, children misspell words because their analyses of the spoken words do not agree with how the words are conventionally analysed for purposes of spelling. For example, U.S. children who can spell both phonemes of two-consonant initial clusters sometimes produce spellings such as ‹chruk› for *truck* and ‹chrap› for *trap* (Read, 1975; Treiman, 1993). A rule linking /t/ to ‹ch› is not part of the nonlexical route of dual-route theories for English, so these errors would be classified as nonphonetic. However, spellings like ‹chruk› for *truck* reflect pronunciation in that speakers tend to position the tongue farther back than usual when pronouncing the /t/ in order to reduce the distance that the tongue must move between /t/ and /r/. This results in a sound that approaches or reaches the /t͡ʃ/ that is heard in *chuck*. These facts explain why children sometimes spell the sound with ‹ch› or with the first letter of this sequence, ‹c›. As another example of an analysis that does not match that assumed by the conventional system, consider children's use of ‹d› in ‹sweder› for *sweater* and ‹prede› for *pretty* (Read, 1975; Treiman, Cassar, & Zukowski, 1994). In American English, the middle consonant of such words is pronounced as a quick tap of the tongue just behind the upper teeth. This *tap* is *voiced*, meaning that the vocal cords vibrate during its production. In this respect, the tap is more similar to /d/ than /t/. This explains why children sometimes spell it with ‹d›.

A third cause of errors in children whose spelling has begun to be influenced by phonology, in addition to difficulties in analysing spoken words into phonemes and analyses that disagree with conventional spelling, is use of letter names as guides to spelling. North American children are usually familiar with the names of many letters by the time they start to incorporate phonology into their spelling, and they sometimes spell a phoneme or a sequence of phonemes that is the name of a letter with the corresponding letter. The resulting spelling is often incorrect. Examples include ‹hom› for *home*, ‹tim› for *time*, and ‹hlp› for *help* (Treiman, 1993; Varnhagen, McCallum, & Burstow, 1997). A similar phenomenon occurs when young speakers of Portuguese use ‹q›, which is named /ke/, to spell the entire /ke/ sequence (Pollo, Treiman, & Kessler, 2008). Also, children sometimes spell a phoneme or a sequence of phonemes with a letter that is the name of a similar-sounding phoneme or sequence. For example, learners of Portuguese may use ‹q› for /ge/. They do this because /ge/ is phonologically similar to /ke/, the name of ‹q›, in all respects but the voicing of the consonant (Pollo et al., 2008).

The errors discussed so far in this section occur on a variety of words, including words such as *trap, brand*, and *help* that are regular from the standpoint of dual-route theory. Thus, learning to spell is not a trivial task even for words that have simple links between phonemes and spellings. When the mappings between phonemes and letters depend on context, as they sometimes do in English and other languages, learning to spell becomes more difficult. As discussed earlier, the choice among alternative spellings of a phoneme sometimes depends on the phonemes that come before or after it—that is, the phonological context. In one study, the vowel spellings of U.S. children began to be influenced by the following consonant around the age of 8 (Treiman & Kessler, 2006). Around this age, for example, children began to produce more ‹ea› spellings and fewer ‹e› spellings of /ɛ/ when this vowel occurred before /d/ than when it occurred before /b/. The ability to use phonological context improved gradually with age. Children do not usually receive explicit teaching about patterns of the sort investigated in the above mentioned study. It is likely that children acquire the patterns implicitly, through statistical learning. This learning takes time, in part, because many contextual patterns apply to small sets of words.

Morphology

In English, French, and some other languages, consideration of the morphological structure of a word can help people to spell it correctly. To take an example discussed earlier, a speller of French must determine whether a final /o/ is a diminutive suffix, in which case she should write ‹eau›, or whether it is not a suffix, in which case she has a variety of spelling options to consider. Learners of French begin to show an influence of morphology in the case of final /o/ around the age of 9 years (Pacton, Fayol, & Perruchet, 2005). As another example, a speller of English must consider whether the /pæst/ that he wishes to write is composed of a stem and a past-tense suffix, in which case he should write ‹passed›, or whether it is a single morpheme, in which case he should write ‹past›. In one study, correct ‹ed› spellings of past-tense /t/ became the majority around the age of 7 years (Varnhagen et al., 1997). Prior to this point, ‹t› spellings were most common. A final example of how children learn to use morphology to help choose among potential spellings of sounds involves taps. As mentioned earlier, children sometimes spell the taps of one-morpheme words like *water* with ‹d› rather than ‹t›. Children are less likely to produce such spellings for two-morpheme words like *waited* and *dirty* whose stems end with a /t/ that is not realized as a tap (Treiman et al., 1994). This effect, which has been found in U.S. children as young as 6 years old, suggests that children use their knowledge about a stem when spelling a word that contains that stem. Learning about these and other morphological influences occurs not all at once but over a period of years.

Supporting the idea that learning about morphological influences on spelling can take a long time, even adults sometimes fail to adhere to certain morphologically based patterns. For example, adults without a university education may pick the written word *trudze* as opposed to *truds* to fill in the blank in the sentence "He has three ___," not following the pattern that /z/ as a plural marker should be spelled with ‹s› (Mitchell, Kemp, & Dawson, 2011).

Spelling development in typical children: Summary

The results I have reviewed show that learning to spell words is a long process. Children begin by learning some basic facts about the visual appearance of writing. They then learn about how the spellings of words reflect their linguistic forms, including their phonological forms and their morphology. Children also learn that spelling is not simply a transcription of speech; it includes patterns that can only be described in terms of letters. Over time, therefore, children become more able to rationalize spellings in terms of patterns that hold across words, and less likely to memorize them as arbitrary sequences.

Existing theories within the dual-route theory have difficulty explaining a number of the findings reviewed here. The results are more compatible with IMP's view that many writing systems include context-conditioned links from sounds to letters, morphological influences, and graphotactic patterns and that learning to spell involves learning about all of these patterns. In fact, learning typically begins with the graphic aspect of spelling rather than the phonological aspect. Some patterns are explicitly taught to children, for example during the course of phonics instruction. Other patterns are not explicitly taught and are picked up implicitly, using statistical learning.

As IMP suggests, it is easier for children to learn the spelling of a word when several patterns converge on the correct spelling and harder when patterns conflict. Support for this idea comes from some of the findings reported in the study by Pacton et al. (2005) that was mentioned earlier. In that study, French primary-school students were most likely to spell /o/ as ‹eau› when two conditions were true: that /o/ was presented as a diminutive suffix and that the preceding letter and ‹eau› formed a sequence that was common in French, such as ‹teau›. In this case, both morphology and graphotactics support use of ‹eau›. The rate of ‹eau› spellings was lower when /o/ was presented as a diminutive suffix and when the spelling sequence consisting of the preceding consonant followed by ‹eau› did not occur in French, as with ‹feau›. In this case, morphology and graphotactics pull in different directions. The rate of ‹eau› spellings was lowest when neither morphology nor graphotactics promoted this spelling—that is, when /o/ was not a diminutive suffix and when use of ‹eau› would yield an uncommon or nonexistent spelling sequence. Bree, van der Ven, and van der Maas (2017), who examined Dutch children's spelling of past-tense forms, also found that the number of cues converging on the correct spelling was an indicator of the spelling difficulty of a word. Such findings do not support the idea that words fall into two discrete categories, regular and irregular, and that there is a sharp difference in difficulty between the two types of words.

Children with difficulties in learning to spell

Some children experience great difficulty as compared to their peers in learning to spell; these children usually have difficulty learning to read as well. The dual-route view has been the most common framework for thinking about the nature of these children's problems. According to the dual-route framework, children who have serious difficulties in learning to spell fall into different categories. Children with *surface dysgraphia* have a poorly developed lexical route. These children are good at spelling nonwords, in that they represent each phoneme with a letter or letter group that is sometimes used to represent it in words of the language. These children are also good at spelling words that dual-route theories classify as regular. However, children with surface dysgraphia are very poor at spelling irregular words. Their errors on these words are usually phonetic, in that the letters are plausible spellings of the phonemes. Other children are said to have *phonological dysgraphia*. Lacking a well-functioning nonlexical route, these children have great difficulty spelling novel items. They fail to spell some phonemes and spell others with letters that do not represent them in any word of the language, leading to a high proportion of nonphonetic errors. Still other children have difficulties with both the lexical and nonlexical routes or difficulties maintaining spelling sequences in short-term memory while preparing to produce them. Assessment, in the dual-route framework, involves examining children's performance on nonwords, regular words, and irregular words and classifying their misspellings as phonetic or nonphonetic (Angelelli, Notarnicola, Judica, Zoccolotti, & Luzzatti, 2010; Kohnen, Colenbrander, Krajendrink, & Nickels, 2015). If a child is found to have difficulty primarily with one route or process, instruction can concentrate on remediating that specific problem. If a child has trouble using both the lexical and nonlexical routes, then broader instruction is called for.

IMP offers some different ideas about the assessment and treatment of spelling difficulties. According to this framework, words cannot be neatly divided into regular and irregular categories. Words that do not follow simple context-free links between spellings and sounds may follow graphotactic, morphological, or context-sensitive phonological patterns. The existence of these multiple patterns needs to be acknowledged when assessing children with spelling difficulties. Some studies of children with serious spelling problems have begun to do this, as when Angelelli et al. (2010) included a category of words requiring context-sensitive sound-to-spelling rules and when Cassar, Treiman, Moats, Pollo, and Kessler (2005) tested knowledge about graphotactic patterns. IMP further suggests that it is important to go beyond scoring of whole spellings as correct or incorrect and as phonetically plausible or implausible. This is especially true for children with low levels of spelling skill, who perform at or close to floor levels on whole-word correctness and plausibility measures. For example, ‹ct›, ‹dega›, and ‹mmmm› are all incorrect spellings of *cut*, and none of them represents all of the phonemes in the word with plausible letters. However, ‹ct› shows more knowledge about the spelling of the word than does ‹dega›, and ‹dega› shows more knowledge about the general properties of English spelling than does ‹mmmm›. Researchers are beginning to develop methods of scoring children's productions that are sensitive to such differences and that may be helpful in identifying, at any early age, children who may go on to develop serious spelling (and reading) problems (Clemens, Oslund, Simmons, & Simmons, 2014; Kessler et al., 2013; Treiman et al., in press; Treiman, Kessler, Pollo, Byrne, & Olson, 2016).

Whereas dual-route theories see children with dysgraphia as differing from one another along two dimensions—knowledge of sound-to-spelling rules and memory for whole-word spellings—IMP sees multiple dimensions. For example, a child may be poor at using morphological cues to guide spelling but may show relatively good knowledge of graphotactic patterns. It will be important to include tests of these abilities in the assessment of children with spelling difficulties.

Research suggests that the difficulties faced by children with dysgraphia involve the same aspects of a writing system that are problematic for the general population of children (Cassar et al., 2005, for learners of English; Protopapas, Fakou, Drakopoulou, Skaloumbakas, & Mouzaki, 2013, for learners of Greek). Consonant clusters, for example, cause difficulty for spelling across the range of spelling ability. However, a typically developing child may have learned to represent all of the consonants in a cluster by the end of the first year of formal literacy instruction whereas a child with dysgraphia may not learn to do so until several years later. Thus, much of what we have learned about spelling development when studying the general population of children should apply, as well, to children with serious spelling problems.

IMP's idea that many sources of information contribute to spelling has implications not only for the assessment of children with spelling problems but also for the type of instruction that they need. Phonemic awareness and simple sound-to-spelling correspondences are important targets for teaching, as advocates of the dual-route view also suggest, but they are not the only targets. Children must also learn about context-conditioned phonological patterns, graphotactics, and morphology. This can be done through explicit instruction and by giving children systematic opportunities to observe and induce the patterns. For example, children can be presented with words that contain ‹c›, ‹k›, and ‹ck› spellings of /k/ or can generate such words themselves. The teacher can help children to discover that ‹c› and ‹k› appear in a variety of positions within words while ‹ck› does not occur at the beginnings. Spelling instruction is important because, although children gain some information about words' spellings as a result of encountering them in reading, they do not necessarily encode and remember all of the letters in words (Graham, 2000). Indeed, many of us have read the word *necessarily* a very large number of times, including in the preceding sentence, but still have difficulty remembering which consonant letters are doubled and which are not. The studies cited earlier suggest that spelling instruction should target the same skills across the range of ability. However, instruction should be more intensive for some children than for others, with more opportunities for practice and review.

Conclusions

Writing systems are complex, and some writing systems are especially complex. It is important to have a good understanding of these complexities in order to understand how children learn to spell and why some children have serious difficulties in this process. Dual-route theories of spelling describe the simpler links between sounds and letters that occur in alphabetic writing systems. However, writing systems include other types of patterns as well, including context-conditioned phonological patterns, morphological patterns, and graphotactic patterns. Theories about how children learn to spell need to account for the full range of patterns, as do theories about why some children have difficulty learning to spell and how we can help them.

Disclosure statement

No potential conflict of interest was reported by the author.

Funding

Preparation of this manuscript was supported in part by a grant from the National Science Foundation [grant number BCS-1421279].

References

Angelelli, P., Notarnicola, A., Judica, A., Zoccolotti, P., & Luzzatti, C. (2010). Spelling impairments in Italian dyslexic children: Phenomenological changes in primary school. *Cortex*, *46*, 1299–1311. doi:10.1016/j.cortex.2010.06.015

Barry, C. (1994). Spelling routes (or roots or rutes). In G. D. A. Brown & N. C. Ellis (Eds.), *Handbook of spelling: Theory, process and intervention* (pp. 27–49). Chichester: John Wiley & Sons.

Barry, C., & Seymour, P. H. K. (1988). Lexical priming and sound-to-spelling contingency effects in nonword spelling. *The Quarterly Journal of Experimental Psychology Section A*, *40*, 5–40. doi:10.1080/14640748808402280

Berg, K. (2016). Double consonants in English: Graphemic, morphological, prosodic and etymological determinants. *Reading and Writing*, *29*, 453–474. doi:10.1007/s11145-015-9610-z

Bosman, A. M. T., & Van Orden, G. C. (1997). Why spelling is more difficult than reading. In C. A. Perfetti, L. Rieben, & M. Fayol (Eds.), *Learning to spell: Research, theory, and practice across languages* (pp. 173–194). Mahwah, NJ: Lawrence Erlbaum Associates.

Bree, E., van der Ven, S., & van der Maas, H. (2017). The voice of Holland: Allograph production in written Dutch past tense inflection. *Language Learning and Development*, doi:10.1080/15475441.2016.1217777

Carreker, S. (2005). Teaching spelling. In J. R. Birsh (Ed.), *Multisensory teaching of basic language skills* (2nd ed., pp. 257–295). Baltimore, MD: Paul H. Brookes Publishing Company.

Cassar, M., & Treiman, R. (1997). The beginnings of orthographic knowledge: Children's knowledge of double letters in words. *Journal of Educational Psychology*, *89*, 631–644. doi:10.1037//0022-0663.89.4.631

Cassar, M., Treiman, R., Moats, L. C., Pollo, T. C., & Kessler, B. (2005). How do the spellings of children with dyslexia compare with those of nondyslexic children? *Reading and Writing: An Interdisciplinary Journal*, 27–49. doi:10.1007/s11145-004-2345-x

Clemens, N. H., Oslund, E. L., Simmons, L. E., & Simmons, D. (2014). Assessing spelling in kindergarten: Further comparison of scoring metrics and their relation to reading skills. *Journal of School Psychology*, *52*, 49–61. doi:10.1016/j.jsp.2013.12.005

Dewey, G. (1971). *English spelling: Roadblock to reading*. New York, NY: Teachers College Press.

Ganapole, S. J. (1987). The development of word consciousness prior to first grade. *Journal of Reading Behavior*, *19*, 415–436. doi:10.1080/10862968709547614

Goodman, R. A., & Caramazza, A. (1986). Aspects of the spelling process: Evidence from a case of acquired dysgraphia. *Language and Cognitive Processes*, *1*, 263–296. doi:10.1080/01690968608404678

Graham, S. (2000). Should the natural learning approach replace spelling instruction? *Journal of Educational Psychology*, *92*, 235–247. doi:10.1037//0022-0663.92.2.235

Houghton, G., & Zorzi, M. (2003). Normal and impaired spelling in a connectionist dual-route architecture. *Cognitive Neuropsychology*, *20*, 115–162. doi:10.1080/02643290242000871

Kessler, B., Pollo, T. C., Treiman, R., & Cardoso-Martins, C. (2013). Frequency analyses of prephonological spellings as predictors of success in conventional spelling. *Journal of Learning Disabilities*, *46*, 252–259. doi:10.1177/0022219412449440

Kessler, B., & Treiman, R. (2001). Relationships between sounds and letters in English monosyllables. *Journal of Memory and Language*, *44*, 592–617. doi:10.1006/jmla.2000.2745

Kohnen, S., Colenbrander, D., Krajendrink, T., & Nickels, L. (2015). Assessment of lexical and non-lexical spelling in students in Grades 1-7. *Australian Journal of Learning Difficulties*, *20*, 15–38. doi:10.1300/J108v05n03

Kreiner, D. S. (1992). Reaction time measures of spelling: Testing a two-strategy model of skilled spelling. *Journal of Experimental Psychology: Learning, Memory, and Cognition*, *18*, 765–776. doi:10.1037//0278-7393.18.4.765

Lavine, L. O. (1977). Differentiation of letterlike forms in prereading children. *Developmental Psychology*, *13*, 89–94. doi:10.1037/0012-1649.13.2.89

Mitchell, P., Kemp, N., & Dawson, J. (2011). Variations among adults in their use of morphemic spelling rules and word-specific knowledge when spelling. *Reading Research Quarterly*, *46*, 119–133. doi:10.1598/RRQ.46.2.2

Pacton, S., & Fayol, M. (2000). The impact of phonological cues on children's judgements of nonwords: The case of double letters. *Current Psychology Letters*, *1*, 39–54.

Pacton, S., Fayol, M., & Perruchet, P. (2005). Children's implicit learning of graphotactic and morphological regularities. *Child Development*, *76*, 324–339. doi:10.1111/j.1467-8624.2005.00848.x

Pei, M. (1967). *The story of the English language*. Philadelphia, PA: J. B. Lippincott.

Pollo, T. C., Kessler, B., & Treiman, R. (2009). Statistical patterns in children's early writing. *Journal of Experimental Child Psychology*, *104*, 410–426. doi:10.1016/j.jecp.2009.07.003

Pollo, T. C., Treiman, R., & Kessler, B. (2008). Preschoolers use partial letter names to select spellings: Evidence from Portuguese. *Applied Psycholinguistics*, *29*, 105–212. doi:10.1017/S0142716407080095

Protopapas, A., Fakou, A., Drakopoulou, S., Skaloumbakas, C., & Mouzaki, A. (2013). What do spelling errors tell us? Classification and analysis of errors made by Greek schoolchildren with and without dyslexia. *Reading and Writing*, *26*, 615–646. doi:10.1007/s11145-012-9378-3

Read, C. (1975). *Children's categorization of speech sounds in English*. Urbana, IL: National Council of Teachers of English.

Sanders, R., & Caramazza, A. (1990). Operation of the phoneme-to-grapheme conversion mechanism in a brain injured patient. *Reading and Writing*, *2*, 61–82. doi:10.1007/bf00383374

Snow, C. E., Griffin, P., & Burns, M. S. (2005). *Knowledge to support the teaching of reading: Preparing teachers for a changing world*. San Francisco, CA: John Wiley & Sons.

Sprenger-Charolles, L., Siegel, L. S., & Bonnet, P. (1998). Reading and spelling acquisition in French: The role of phonological mediation and orthographic factors. *Journal of Experimental Child Psychology*, *68*, 134–65. doi:10.1006/jecp.1997.2422

Tainturier, M.-J., Bosse, M.-L., Roberts, D. J., Valdois, S., & Rapp, B. (2013). Lexical neighborhood effects in pseudoword spelling. *Frontiers in Psychology*, *4*, 862. doi:10.3389/fpsyg.2013.00862

Tainturier, M.-J., & Rapp, B. (2001). The spelling process. In B. Rapp (Ed.), *Handbook of cognitive neuropsychology: What deficits reveal about the human mind* (pp. 263–289). Philadelphia, PA: Psychology Press.

Treiman, R. (1993). *Beginning to spell: A study of first-grade children*. New York, NY: Oxford University Press.

Treiman, R., & Boland, K. (2017). Graphotactics and spelling: Evidence from consonant doubling. *Journal of Memory and Language*, *92*, 254–264. doi:10.1016/j.jml.2016.07.001

Treiman, R., Cassar, M., & Zukowski, A. (1994). What types of linguistic information do children use in spelling? The case of flaps. *Child Development*, *65*, 1318–1337. doi:10.2307/1131501

Treiman, R., & Kessler, B. (2006). Spelling as statistical learning: Using consonantal context to spell vowels. *Journal of Educational Psychology*, *98*, 642–652. doi:10.1037/0022-0663.98.3.642

Treiman, R., & Kessler, B. (2014). *How children learn to write words*. New York, NY: Oxford University Press.

Treiman, R., & Kessler, B. (2016). Choosing between alternative spellings of sounds: The role of context. *Journal of Experimental Psychology: Learning, Memory, and Cognition*, *42*, 1154–1159. doi:10.1037/xlm0000225

Treiman, R., Kessler, B., Boland, K., Clocksin, H., & Chen, Z. (in press). Statistical learning and spelling: Older prephonological spellers produce more wordlike spellings than younger prephonological spellers. *Chlid Development*.

Treiman, R., Kessler, B., Pollo, T. C., Byrne, B., & Olson, R. K. (2016). Measures of kindergarten spelling and their relations to later spelling performance. *Scientific Studies of Reading*, *20*, 349–362. doi:10.1080/10888438.2016.1186168

Treiman, R., Zukowski, A., & Richmond-Welty, E. D. (1995). What happened to the "n" of sink? Children's spellings of final consonant clusters. *Cognition*, *55*, 1–38. doi:10.1016/0010-0277(94)00638-2

van Bon, W. H. J., & Uit de Haag, I. J. C. A. F. (1997). Difficulties with consonants in the spelling and segmentation of CCVCC pseudowords: Differences among Dutch first graders. *Reading and Writing*, *9*, 363–386. doi:10.1007/978-94-017-3054-9_4

Varnhagen, C. K., McCallum, M., & Burstow, M. (1997). Is children's spelling naturally stage-like? *Reading and Writing*, *9*, 451–481. doi:10.1023/A:1007903330463

Developmental graphemic buffer dysgraphia in English: A single case study

Kristina Barisic, Saskia Kohnen and Lyndsey Nickels

ABSTRACT

A single case study is reported of a 10-year-old, English-speaking boy, L.S., who presented with spelling errors similar to those described in acquired graphemic buffer dysgraphia (GBD). We used this case to evaluate the appropriateness of applying adult cognitive models to the investigation of developmental cognitive disorders. The dual-route model of spelling guided this investigation. L.S. primarily made "letter errors" (deletions, additions, substitutions, transpositions, or a combination of these errors) on words and nonwords and in all input (aural and visual) and output modalities (writing, typing, oral spelling); there was also some evidence of a length effect and U-shaped serial position curve. An effect of lexical variables on spelling performance was also found. We conclude that the most parsimonious account is an impairment at the level of the graphemic buffer and without systematic cognitive neuropsychological investigation, the nature of L.S.'s spelling difficulty would likely have been missed.

Introduction

Cognitive neuropsychologists use data from individuals with cognitive impairments to elucidate normal cognition. They also use theories of normal cognition to investigate cognitive impairments. However, most of this work has been conducted with adults who have acquired disorders after a brain injury. Since Marshall (1984) first advocated for the application of the cognitive neuropsychological framework to developmental abnormalities of cognition, it has been extensively applied to the study of developmental dyslexia with evidence of developmental descriptions of all acquired "subtypes" (see, for example, Coltheart & Kohnen, 2012; Friedmann & Coltheart, 2016; Temple, 2006). Dual-route models have also been used to study the typical acquisition of reading (e.g., Pritchard, Coltheart, Marinus, & Castles, 2016). Much less attention, however, has been paid to the application of cognitive neuropsychological models in typical and atypical acquisition of spelling.

Investigations into spelling difficulties in children to date have primarily focused on difficulties in learning and applying sound–letter rules (i.e., phonological dysgraphia, see Campbell & Butterworth, 1985; Snowling, Stackhouse, & Rack, 1986), difficulties acquiring orthographic representations (surface dysgraphia, see Brunsdon, Coltheart, & Nickels, 2005; Temple, 1985), and difficulties in learning and applying morphological spelling rules (e.g., Egan & Tainturier, 2011; Westwood, 2005). However, these difficulties would also be predicted based on other types of spelling models—most notably, developmental stage theories, where learning progresses through sound–letter, orthographic, and morphological stages (e.g., Ehri, 2000; Frith, 1985; Gentry, 1982). Importantly, there are some types of spelling difficulties that have been reported in cognitive neuropsychological case studies that would not be predicted to occur in the context of stage models of spelling acquisition. For example, it is not clear how graphemic buffer dysgraphia (see Miceli & Capasso, 2006, for a review of the acquired literature), neglect dysgraphia (e.g., Baxter & Warrington, 1983), deep dysgraphia (Bub & Kertesz, 1982), dyscravia (Gvion & Friedmann, 2010a), and letter position dysgraphia (Gvion & Friedmann, 2010b) fit into stage theories of spelling acquisition. This may be because developmental stage models of spelling, as currently developed, do not focus on the development of all relevant process (e.g., stages in the development of an orthographic working memory store). This paper focuses on one of these dysgraphias, graphemic buffer dysgraphia, thus testing the applicability of a "static" cognitive model of spelling of the graphemic buffer to a developmental case and investigating the acquisition of an orthographic working memory store.

There is an ongoing debate, however, regarding whether the "static" adult cognitive system is an appropriate framework for the investigation of development and developmental disorders (see, for example, Bishop, 1997; Castles, Kohnen, Nickels, & Brock, 2014; Temple, 2006). In particular, it has been brought into question whether "static" theories of adult cognitive systems, such as the dual-route cognitive model of spelling, can be used to understand difficulties that occur in a cognitive system in acquisition as the model is based on adult data and does not account for how learning occurs (Bishop, 1997). Castles et al. (2014), however, argued that these cognitive models can be meaningful as they represent the endpoint of development and provide a description of the key processes that are involved in performing a cognitive task at any point in development. Our case will therefore provide another test of Marshall's (1984) idea that models of cognitive processes, such as the dual-route cognitive model of spelling, can and should be applied to developmental cognitive difficulties.

Graphemic buffer dysgraphia (GBD) is a type of spelling difficulty that is attributed to an impairment in the orthographic working memory store (the graphemic buffer). GBD has been extensively documented in the adult acquired dysgraphia literature (e.g., *Italian*: seminal case L.B.: Caramazza & Miceli, 1990; Caramazza, Miceli, Villa, & Romani, 1987; cases G.S.I. and C.R.I.: Costa, Fischer-Baum, Capasso, Miceli, & Rapp, 2011; case F.M.: Tainturier & Caramazza, 1996. *English*: case A.S.: Jónsdóttir, Shallice, & Wise, 1996; case B.H.: Sage & Ellis, 2004; cases B.W.N., R.S.B.: Buchwald & Rapp, 2009). However, unlike other types of acquired dysgraphias, until recently there was only one brief report of the developmental equivalent of GBD (10 Hebrew-speaking children in Yachini & Friedmann, 2010) and one intervention study of a possible developmental case of GBD by Roncoli and Masterson (2016). We present the first study to systematically investigate a case of developmental GBD in English. Within the tradition of the cognitive neuropsychological approach, we draw on a dual-route cognitive model of spelling (e.g., Barry, 1994; Ellis, 1982) to determine whether our case's spelling performance was indicative of impairment at the level of the graphemic buffer. We first outline the theoretical framework within which we situate our discussion before describing the features of GBD.

Within dual-route models of spelling (see Figure 1), spelling occurs via two cognitive routes—the "lexical" route, which can be used to spell words (e.g., YACHT, DOG) that have a stored orthographic representation in an orthographic lexicon, and the "nonlexical" route, which can be used to spell novel words (e.g., LONT) and regularly spelled words (e.g., DOG) relying on phoneme–grapheme rules. The lexical and nonlexical routes converge at the graphemic buffer where the letters of the word or nonword are activated. Spelling is inherently a serial process—an individual cannot write or say more than one letter at a time. Therefore the graphemic buffer is an orthographic working memory store, which keeps letters active for as long as required to produce the spelling response. Production requires a number of "peripheral" processes (subsequent to the graphemic buffer), which differ according to the output modality (i.e., retrieving stroke sequences for writing, finding the correct letter on the keyboard for typing, or saying the letter name for oral spelling; Caramazza et al., 1987, Caramazza & Miceli, 1990). The graphemic buffer is uniquely located as the last central relay point for both lexical and nonlexical processes before peripheral processes begin (see Figure 1). Given these features, specific predictions can be made regarding the characteristics of spelling performance with an impaired graphemic buffer.

The symptoms of an impaired graphemic buffer were first described in adults with acquired spelling impairments (e.g., Caramazza & Miceli, 1990; Caramazza et al., 1987). One of the key features of GBD is spelling errors that are predominantly characterized by letter deletions (e.g., YACHT–<*yact*>), substitutions (<*yicht*>), transpositions (<*ycaht*>), or additions (<*yarcht*>). These types of errors ("letter errors") are attributed to the graphemic buffer's characteristic as an orthographic working memory store, responsible for keeping the correct letters active (role of "activation") in the correct sequence (role of "selection"; Rapp & Kong, 2002). Therefore, buffer dysfunction can result in incorrect letters being activated or errors in the sequence in which they are selected (Rapp & Kong, 2002).

Since the buffer is the last stage of central processing within the spelling system and is common to all spelling routes, all spelling modalities will be affected

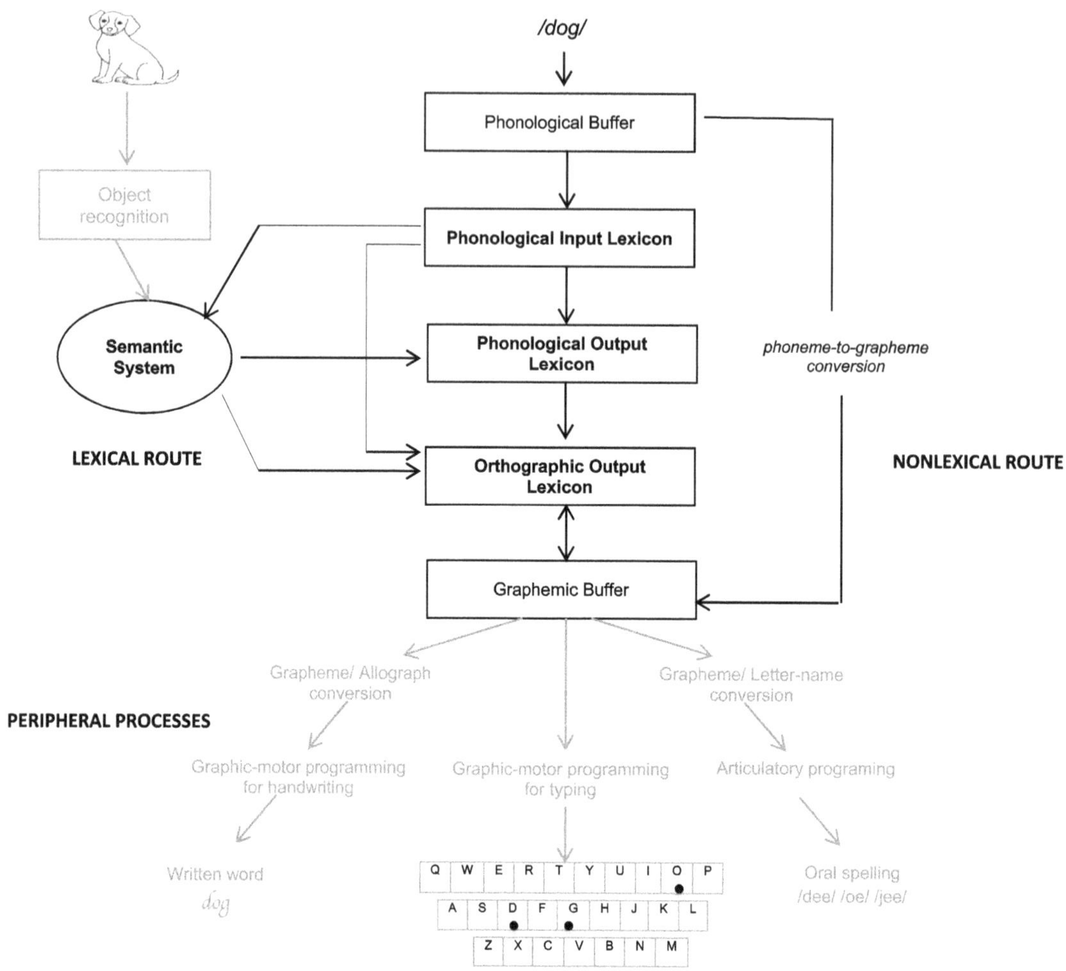

Figure 1. An example of a dual-route model of spelling with separate lexical and nonlexical routes that converge at the graphemic buffer.

by buffer dysfunction (Caramazza et al., 1987). Hence, these letter errors are reported to occur when spelling both words and nonwords and when spelling via different input modalities (spelling to dictation or written picture naming) and different response modalities (typing, handwriting, or oral spelling; de Partz, 1995; Miceli & Capasso, 2006).

A length effect is another defining feature of GBD whereby longer words are spelled less accurately than shorter words (Caramazza et al., 1987, 1990). This is hypothesized to be due to the reduced capacity of the impaired buffer—fewer letters than typical can be maintained active, or the correct number of letters can be held active but for a shorter period of time (Katz, 1991). In addition, it is proposed that the longer an item needs to be held active in a dysfunctioning buffer, the higher the likelihood of an error (Katz, 1991). Traditionally, the length effect has been investigated by analysing whole-word spelling accuracy over different word lengths. However, Buchwald and Rapp (2009) proposed that this analysis method could be misleading, as longer words simply provide greater opportunity for a letter error to emerge—regardless of whether or not the graphemic buffer is impaired. They suggested that analysing the proportion of letters correctly spelled, relative to the number of letters in the word, would mitigate this confound.

Investigators have also been interested in the distribution of letter errors within the word. Classically, cases of GBD demonstrate a U-shaped serial letter position curve whereby medial letters are spelled less accurately than initial and final letters (e.g., Caramazza et al., 1987; Jónsdóttir et al., 1996; McCloskey, Badecker, Goodman-Schulman, & Aliminosa, 1994). This is thought to be due to increased competition that occurs for medial letters in a string of letters within which neighbouring letters are competing for production (Costa et al., 2011; Glasspool, Shallice, & Cipolotti, 2006). While this error distribution is also observed in unimpaired spellers (Wing & Baddeley, 1980), it is enhanced in cases of GBD. However, a second letter error distribution has also been reported in GBD cases: a monotonic decrease in accuracy from initial to final positions of the word (e.g., Costa et al., 2011; Katz, 1991; Miceli, Capasso, Benvegnù, & Caramazza, 2004; Ward & Romani, 1998). This pattern is accounted for by a reduced capacity of the graphemic buffer and thus a faster decay of orthographic information, leaving the final positions more vulnerable to error.

In addition to the agreed features of GBD, there are some elements that are subject to ongoing debate. This includes whether GBD can result in effects of lexical variables, such as written frequency and imageability, on spelling. Classically, lexical variables have been claimed to have little impact on spelling performance in cases of selective buffer impairment (Caramazza et al., 1987). Under this view, it has been argued that any effect of lexical variables on spelling performance likely indicates an (additional) impairment at the level of the orthographic output lexicon (Aliminosa, McCloskey, Goodman-Schulman, & Sokol, 1993). Thus, "pure" cases of GBD (without additional impairments) should not show an effect of lexical variables. However, other authors argue that there can be mild effects of lexical variables on spelling performance even in "pure" cases of GBD (Buchwald & Rapp, 2009; Sage & Ellis, 2004). Buchwald and Rapp (2009), for example, propose that frequency effects may arise due to previous frequent, strong activation from the orthographic lexicon for letters in frequently occurring words. The authors suggest that these letters can be kept active for longer in a dysfunctioning buffer, leading to fewer errors for these words and a frequency effect in spelling performance of individuals with GBD. These mild effects of lexical variables are in contrast to the stronger effects evident when there is damage to lexical components.

In summary, GBD is typically characterized by letter errors (that occur in both words and nonwords and in different tasks and response modalities), a length effect, and a relative preservation of accuracy of initial letters in a spelled response. Lastly, lexical variables, if present, have been argued to have minimal effects on spelling performance.

In addition to the many acquired cases of GBD, as noted above, two studies have reported similar difficulties in developmental cases. Yachini and Friedmann (2010) described 10 Hebrew-speaking individuals with developmental spelling impairments whose spelling errors resembled those of acquired GBD: Their spelling was dominated by letter errors in all input (spelling-to-dictation, written naming, and spontaneous writing) and output (handwriting, typing, oral spelling, and pointing to letters) modalities. The participants also made a greater number of letter errors on longer words. More recently, Roncoli and Masterson (2016) described an intervention study with a 10-year-old boy, Alan. Alan is described as a case of developmental GBD as he demonstrated letter errors and an effect of word length on spelling accuracy similar to that reported in acquired adult cases of GBD. However, it is unclear whether Alan made significantly more letter errors than his peers. This is critical as all children in their study made these types of errors. In addition, the majority of Alan's errors were phonologically plausible spellings: an error type that is thought to indicate poor lexical spelling. Finally, there are no data on Alan's spelling performance in different modalities, nor his spelling of nonwords. It is therefore difficult to be confident that Alan's spelling difficulties are truly due to impairment at the level of the graphemic buffer.

In sum, to date, there is clear description of developmental GBD in Hebrew, while similarly thorough investigations with English cases are missing. If dual-route models can be applied to developmental populations, it would be predicted that a frequently described acquired spelling disorder such as GBD would also be found in children writing in English. This paper describes such a case: We present a description of an English-speaking child with some of the classic symptoms of GBD. We analyse this case within the framework of cognitive neuropsychology and apply the dual-route model of spelling (e.g., Barry, 1994; Ellis, 1982) to investigate whether he demonstrated the "classic" features of acquired GBD; specifically we address the following questions:

1. Are spelling errors primarily characterized by "letter errors"—deletions, substitutions, transpositions, or additions?

2. Do letter errors occur to an equal extent across:
    A. task modalities [spelling-to-dictation (aural input), written-picture-naming (visual input)], and
    B. response modalities (typing, handwriting, oral spelling)?
3. Do letter errors occur more often in longer words?
4. Is there a serial position effect?
5. Is there an effect of lexical variables on the occurrence of letter spelling errors?

Case report

L.S. was a 10-year-old boy in Grade 5 (6 years of formal schooling and literacy instruction as there is a Kindergarten year prior to Grade 1) who attended a school in suburban Sydney at the time of testing. L.S.'s mother originally contacted us regarding a spelling remediation study being run at the university at the time. She was concerned about L.S.'s spelling and reported that he frequently missed letters or mixed them up when writing. L.S.'s mother reported that he had normal hearing and vision and no spoken language impairment or history of developmental delay. L.S. was bilingual with no reported difficulties in speaking his other language. His mother spoke Spanish with him at home but he had almost no exposure to written Spanish and no formal or informal reading instruction in Spanish. No other family members were reported to have spelling or reading difficulties.

Background assessment

We conducted a detailed assessment of L.S.'s literacy and language in four testing sessions over six months at Macquarie University. Each session lasted between one and a half and two and a half hours. Several breaks were offered throughout testing sessions, and L.S. was able to appropriately attend to all tasks during testing. A summary of L.S.'s assessment results are presented in Table 1, and detailed descriptions of tests are available in Appendix A. Performance on these standardized measures was considered to be within normal limits if scores fell within one standard deviation of the normative sample mean (that is, between the 16th and 84th percentiles, corresponding to standard scores of 85–115). Below we summarize the results.

Spoken language assessment

Standardized assessment revealed no specific spoken language difficulties in receptive and expressive vocabulary (see Table 1). L.S. was able to repeat nonwords within normal limits (75%ile). These results were in line with parental report of no spoken language difficulties. However, on one spoken language task relevant to spelling (oral segmentation), L.S. performed below average (9%ile). Oral segmentation is a skill that may be used by spellers to separate out the individual sounds (phonemes) within a heard word. This skill may be important when children are learning new words as correctly identifying the separate phonemes within a word may be required in order to map each of these phonemes onto their appropriate letters (using the nonlexical process) to come to a spelling response that represents the sounds accurately. L.S. made two types of errors on this task: (a) adding a phoneme [e.g., nonword *SHAP* (3 phonemes) segmented into phonemes *sh-ə-a-p* (4 phonemes)] or (b) segmenting nonwords into units that were greater than single phonemes (e.g., nonword *DRAY* segmented into phonemes *dr-ay*, *TROAST* segmented into *t-r-oast*). Critically, these two error types cannot explain the errors that L.S. makes in spelling: Neither additions nor cluster reductions and multiple deletions were a main feature of L.S.'s spelling. As will become apparent below, none of the above features occur in L.S.'s spelling, thus making segmentation as the source of his spelling deficit an unlikely interpretation.

Reading assessment

L.S.'s irregular word reading skills fell within the normal range (34%ile). In contrast, his nonword reading fell below the normal range (13%ile, see Table 1 for more details). He also made many more transposition errors when reading anagram words (e.g., reading *slime* as "smile") than children in the same grade and reading level (2%ile). Text reading accuracy and comprehension were both within normal limits compared to children in the same grade at school (33%ile and 50%ile, respectively). Within a dual-route model of reading (e.g., Friedmann & Rahamim, 2007), L.S.'s pattern of results suggests that he has a deficit at the orthographic analysis stage[1] and in the nonlexical grapheme–phoneme procedure, while the orthographic input lexicon (and access to this lexicon) was developing age appropriately. An alternative explanation for L.S.'s performance

Table 1. Results of L.S.'s background assessment.

Measure	Task description	Skill assessed	Percentile	Evaluation	Implication
Spoken language					
Peabody Picture Vocabulary Test, 4th edition (PPVT–IV)	Spoken word–picture matching (e.g., "point to the picture that shows crying")	Receptive vocabulary (auditory comprehension)	95	Average	Age-appropriate receptive vocabulary. Object recognition, lexical access, and retrieval intact. Semantic system intact.
Woodcock–Johnson III Tests of Achievement (WJ–III ACH): Picture Vocabulary subtest	Spoken picture naming	Expressive vocabulary	75	Average	Age-appropriate expressive vocabulary. Object recognition, lexical access, and retrieval intact. Semantic system intact.
Developmental NEuroPSYchological Assessment, 2nd edition (NEPSY–II): Repetition of Nonsense Words subtest	Nonword repetition (e.g., *crumsee*)	Phonological encoding and decoding	75	Average	Age-appropriate phonological buffer.
Comprehensive Test of Phonological Processing, 2nd edition (CTOPP–2): Segmenting Nonwords subtest	Nonword segmentation (e.g., target: "mab", response "m-a-b")	Oral segmentation	9	Below average	Ability to segment nonwords into phonemes below age expectation.
Reading					
Castles and Coltheart Reading Test 2nd edition (CC2)	Irregular word list: Read irregular words (e.g., yacht) aloud	Lexical reading	34	Average	Age-appropriate lexical reading system.
	Nonword list: Read nonwords (e.g., gurve) aloud	Nonlexical reading	13	Below average	Impairment of nonlexical reading system.
Neale Analysis of Reading Ability, 3rd edition (NARA–3)	Read aloud paragraphs of text	Text reading accuracy	33	Average	Grade-appropriate text reading skills.
	Answer open-ended oral questions about the paragraph of text	Text comprehension	50	Average	Grade-appropriate text reading comprehension skills.
Letter Position Test (LetPos)	Read anagram words (e.g., slime) and their partners (i.e., smile) aloud	Letter-position coding	2	Below average	L.S. made many more transposition errors than children in the same grade and of the same reading level.
Spelling					
Cross-case letter copy	Transcribe 7 upper- and 7 lower-case letters into their opposite form (e.g., upper case <*T*> to lower case <*t*>)	Allographic/letter knowledge	No percentile available Raw: 14/14	No errors	Intact allograph/letter knowledge.
Test of Written Spelling, 3rd edition (TWS–3): Unpredictable Spelling subtest	Spell irregular words to dictation (e.g., two, people, fountain)	Lexical spelling	39	Average	Age-appropriate lexical spelling system.
Queensland University Inventory of Literacy (QUIL): Nonword Spelling subtest	Spell nonwords to dictation (e.g., dorf, strecker, churtlesneedee)	Nonlexical spelling	25	Average	Grade-appropriate nonlexical spelling system.

Note: All standardized measures administered following directions outlined in manual (see Appendix A for further details).

is that the proposed impairment of the graphemic buffer also impacts on his reading performance (Caramazza, Capasso, & Miceli, 1996; Tainturier & Rapp, 2003). We return to this account in the General Discussion.

Spelling assessment

L.S. made no errors in a cross-case letter copy task, suggesting that L.S. had access to both upper and lower case letter representations for writing and that any spelling errors were unlikely to be due to poor letter knowledge. His lexical and nonlexical spelling skills were both within the average range (39%ile and 25%ile, respectively).[2] This suggests that the orthographic output lexicon (and access to this lexicon) and nonlexical phoneme–grapheme (P–G) procedure were at an age-appropriate level.[3] Closer inspection of L.S.'s errors on the tests revealed an unusually high number of errors that are typical of that documented in acquired cases of GBD, including transpositions (e.g., WHISTLE as <*whitsle*>), deletions (PRINCIPAL as <*prinipal*>), substitutions (LEAGUE as <*leggue*>) and additions (OUGHT as <*oughtht*>). It was the frequency of these letter errors on standardized measures and an experimental word list (described below) and the fact that we had rarely observed them in other children that prompted a more thorough investigation of his spelling.

General procedure

Grade-matched controls

To determine whether L.S.'s spelling errors were unusual, we compared his spelling to that of seven typically developing children (five females), who were recruited from suburban Sydney primary schools. Control children were grade-matched, which meant they fell within one semester (two school terms) of L.S.'s initial testing session. All children completed tests of lexical (as measured by the Unpredictable Spelling subtest: the Test of Written Spelling, TWS–3; Larsen & Hammill, 1994) and nonlexical spelling (as measured by Nonword Spelling subtest: Queensland University Inventory of Literacy, QUIL; Dodd, Holm, Oerlemanns, & McCormick, 1996).[4] Control participants were selected to score within normal limits (within standard scores of 85 and 115, scaled scores between 7 and 13, which equates to 16th and 84th percentiles) on these tests, and the difference between their scores on two measures was within one standard deviation. The seven children's mean standard score for lexical spelling was 96.9 ($SD_{\text{standardscore}} = 7.3$), and mean scaled score nonlexical spelling was 8.6 ($SD_{\text{scaledscore}} = 1.0$), which equates to 42nd percentile and 32nd percentile, respectively.

In order to compare L.S.'s spelling performance to that of the control sample, Crawford's *t* tests (Crawford & Garthwaite, 2005; Crawford, Garthwaite, & Porter, 2010) were used. These statistics are designed to compare single cases to small control samples, controlling for Type 1 error rates (see Crawford et al., 2010).

Spelling error scoring procedure

The first author (K.B.) classified all spelling errors for L.S. and controls. A total of 28% (403 errors) were independently classified by the second author (S.K.). There was 87% agreement between the classifications. Any disagreements that emerged following independent coding were resolved by discussion.

Spelling errors were coded as one of six letter error types: (1) transposition (all target letters were present in the spelling response, but not in the correct order, e.g., QUESTION <*qeustion*>[5]); (2) deletion (all but one of the target letters were present in the spelling response with letters in the correct order, e.g., FIERCE <*firce*>); (3) addition (all target letters were present in the correct order with an additional letter, e.g., TOUGH <*tougth*>); (4) substitution (all target letters except for one were present in the correct order, and the missing letter was replaced by another letter, e.g., STAMP <*sramp*>); (5) multiple letter errors (two letter errors of the same type, e.g., ANOTHER <*anthore*> where two letters were transposed); (6) mixed letter errors (a combination of up to three buffer errors in words with five letters or more, e.g., NEITHER <*netir*>, which could be described as an adjacent transposition and two deletions). Furthermore, although not coded as an extra error category, spelling errors were noted that could be due to perseverative responding (letter/s added to the response that occurred within the target string, e.g., TOOTH <*toothooth*> and when letter/s were added from a previous response, e.g., Item 1–LEOPARD, Item 2–GUITAR <*gitard*>). Three additional categories were classified as "lexical" errors as these typically indicate difficulties in the lexical spelling process (e.g., Brunsdon et al., 2005; Temple, 1985). These included: (7) phonologically plausible spellings (e.g., CROCHET <*crowshay*>, where letters in the spelling response represented the sounds in the target word following phoneme–grapheme conversion (PGCs[6]); (8) homophone substitutions[7] (spelling response formed the correct spelling of homophone pair, e.g., SLEIGH <*slay*>); and (9) whole-word substitution (spelling response formed the correct spelling of another word, e.g., BOUGH <*bowl*>). L.S. made no semantically related spelling errors. Finally, two additional error types were coded: (10) ambiguous (responses that could be classified both as phonologically plausible errors and as a letter error, e.g., JEWEL <*jewl*>); (11) other (errors that were not clearly classifiable as any other error type, e.g., GIRAFFE <*griffarf*>). Importantly, as the origin of ambiguous errors (10) was unclear (may have arisen from an absence of a lexical representation in orthographic output lexicon and thus a reliance on nonlexical spelling route, or from a dysfunctioning buffer), these errors were not considered in any analysis.

Experimental studies

Are spelling errors primarily characterized by "letter" errors?

In this section we present data that aimed to investigate whether the main spelling errors that L.S. produced were letter errors.

Word spelling

List 1. L.S. (and controls) spelled a list of 182 irregular words to dictation. The words were 3–10 letters long and were sourced from the Oxford Wordlist (Bianco, Scull, & Ives, 2008), a database of words used by Australian primary school children in free writing and thus words that L.S. (and the control participants) should know. Each word was read aloud by the tester with a short three-to-four-word definition (e.g., "GUY, man or boy, GUY") before each child was asked to write their response.[8]

List 2. L.S. spelled an additional 218 words, 2–10 letters long, to dictation over the four sessions to gain a larger sample of spelling performance that extended to regular words. Control children did not spell these words. Words were once again sourced from the Oxford Wordlist (Bianco et al., 2008). These additional words, along with the 182 words already administered, created a total corpus of 400 words for analysis. Overall, these 400 words varied in item characteristics including length ($M_{\text{LEN}} = 5.30$, $SD_{\text{LEN}} = 1.61$, range = 2–10), log written frequency ($M_{\text{freq}} = 1.67$, $SD_{\text{freq}} = 0.83$, range = 0–4.48), imageability ($M_{\text{Img}} = 484.16$, $SD_{\text{Img}} = 125.52$, range = 202–661), orthographic neighbourhood size ($M_N = 3.58$, $SD_N = 4.46$, range = 0–23), age of acquisition ($M_{\text{AoA}} = 6.02$, $SD_{\text{AoA}} = 1.99$, range = 2.50–13.29), and regularity[9] ($M_{\text{pgc}} = .10$, $SD_{\text{pgc}} = .29$). Data on length, written frequency, imageability, and orthographic neighbourhood size were taken from *N*-Watch (Davis, 2005). Age of acquisition data were from the Kuperman, Stadthagen-Gonzalez, and Brysbaert (2012) database. Data for imageability and age of acquisition were only available for part of the corpus ($n = 323$ and $n = 394$ words, respectively).

Word spelling results List 1. L.S. performed as accurately as the controls on List 1 (see Table 2), Crawford's $t = 0.47$, $p = .33$, one-tailed, and did not differ significantly from controls in the number of lexical spelling errors, Crawford's $t = -0.78$, $p = .23$, one-tailed. However, L.S. made significantly more letter errors (Error Categories 1–6) than controls, Crawford's $t = 2.77$, $p = .02$, one-tailed, and this was his most common error type (48%).

A total of 28% of L.S.'s total errors were "single" letter errors (only one letter error in the string, i.e., Error Categories 1–4). These results confirmed our initial impression that L.S. made more than the usual number of letter errors. L.S. made fewer lexical spelling errors than letter errors—only 7% of his errors were phonologically plausible, with another 2% of errors being homophone substitutions. There were only two whole-word substitutions (1%). A total of 36% of L.S.'s errors were considered either "ambiguous" or "other" and were not considered for analysis.

Word spelling results Lists 1 and 2 combined. As can be seen in Table 2, L.S.'s most common spelling error on this combined list was letter errors (48%). Of the total errors, 31% were "single" letter errors (Error Categories 1–4). Only 12% of L.S.'s errors were clearly lexical errors (phonologically plausible, homophone

Table 2. Example responses and frequency of errors made on spelling to dictation on a list of words compared to controls (List 1) and an extra list of words that only L.S. spelled (List 2).

			List 1: 182 irregular words		List 2: All 400 words
	Stimulus	L.S. example response	L.S. total raw [total %]	Controls ($n = 7$) Mean raw (*SD*) [*M* %]	L.S. total raw [total %]
Total errors (1–11)	—	—	92 [50.5]	85.1 (*13.8*)[a] [46.8]	131 [32.8]
Letter errors (1–6)	—	—	44 [47.8]	27.4 (*5.6*)[b] [32.2]*	63 [48.1]
(1) transposition	GUITAR	<*gutiar*>	9	6.3 (*3.9*)	12
(2) deletion	CHILDREN	<*chidren*>	12	7.3 (*2.6*)	17
(3) addition	CHEF	<*cheif*>	5	2.7 (*2.5*)	10
(4) substitution	AREA	<*erea*>	0	2.9 (*1.7*)	2
(5) multiple letter errors	OUGHT	<*oughtht*>	2	1.9 (*1.2*)	3
(6) mixed letter errors	MOVIE	<*moivei*>	16	6.4 (*2.0*)	19
Lexical errors (7–9)	—	—	15 [16.3]	20.6 (*6.7*)[c] [24.2]	16 [12.2]
(7) phonologically plausible	CROCHET	<*crowshay*>	7	15.7 (*7.1*)	7
(8) homophone substitution	WEIGHT	<*wait*>	6	3.7 (*1.6*)	7
(9) whole-word substitution	BOUGH	<*bowl*>	2	1.1 (*0.7*)	2
Additional errors (10–11)	—	—	33 [35.9]	37.1 (*10.6*)[d] [43.6]	52 [39.7]
(10) ambiguous	CHEESE	<*chese*>	24	28.7 (*10.7*)	40
(11) other	NEIGHBOUR	<*nabiour*>	9	8.4 (*2.8*)	12

Note: Crawford's *t*-test (one-tailed) compared L.S. to controls. List 2 was administered to investigate L.S.'s spelling performance on both irregular and regular words. Control data were not available for List 2. Standard deviations in parentheses. Percentages in brackets.
[a]Control range for total errors: $min = 66$, $max = 106$; $p = .33$. [b]Control range for letter errors: $min = 19$, $max = 35$; $p = .02$*. [c]Control range for lexical errors: $min = 12$, $max = 29$; $p = .23$. [d]Control range for additional errors: $min = 23$, $max = 53$; $p = .36$.
*Indicates that L.S. produces statistically significantly more errors than controls.

substitutions, or whole-word substitution). A total of 40% of L.S.'s errors were unclear in terms of their origin and largely consisted of phonologically plausible responses that could also have resulted from a buffer dysfunction, for example, spelling CHEESE as <*chese*>.

Given the small number of items, the results should be interpreted with caution. Nonetheless, L.S.'s spelling pattern is consistent with the type of spelling errors he was making on the word lists, with investigations of individuals with acquired GBD and with the hypothesized impairment in the graphemic output buffer.

Nonword spelling

We investigated the nature of spelling errors in nonword spelling using the data from 24 nonwords from the QUIL (Dodd et al., 1996; see Table 1). All seven grade-matched control children completed this task.

All responses that were phonologically plausible[10] were accepted as correct (e.g., CRAID, <*crade*>, <*craid*>, <*krade*>, <*kraid*>). We considered the following error types in this analysis: letter errors (Category 1–6), whole-word substitutions (Category 9, e.g., KLEPERING, <*cleaning*>), or other errors (Category 11, e.g., TRUCKOW, <*tokour*>).

Nonword spelling results. L.S. performed as accurately as the controls (see Table 3) Crawford's $t = 1.47$, $p = .095$, one-tailed; however, he made significantly more letter errors (Error Category 1–6: L.S. 50%, controls mean 32%, $SD = 6.2\%$), Crawford's $t = 2.68$, $p = .018$, one-tailed. That is, L.S. was more likely to make a letter error on nonwords than his peers.

Table 3. Frequency of errors made on spelling to dictation on 24 nonwords from QUIL Nonword subtest.

	L.S. Total raw [total %]	Control ($n = 7$) Mean raw (*SD*) [*M* %]
Total errors (1–6; 9; 11)	12 [50.0]	9.4 (*1.6*)[a] [39.2]
Letter errors (1–6)	12 [100]	7.7 (*1.5*)[b] [81.9]*
(1) transposition	0	0.3 (*0.5*)
(2) deletion	0	1.9 (*0.7*)
(3) addition	2	0.9 (*0.7*)
(4) substitution	6	2.1 (*0.9*)
(5) multiple letter errors	2	1.6 (*1.3*)
(6) mixed letter errors	2	1.0 (*1.8*)
Lexical errors (9)	0 [0.0]	0.0 (*0.0*) [0.0]
(9) whole-word substitution	0	0.0 (*0.0*)
Additional errors (11)	0 [0.0]	1.6 (*1.8*)[c] [17.0]
(11) other	0	1.6 (*1.8*)

Note: Error Categories 7 (phonologically plausible) and 10 (ambiguous) were not coded as these responses are correct for this task. Error Category 8 (homophone) was not coded as the stimuli are nonwords. Crawford's *t*-test (one-tailed) compared L.S. to controls. Standard deviations in parentheses. Percentages in brackets.
[a]Control range for total errors: $min = 7$, $max = 11$; $p = .095$. [b]Control range for letter errors: $min = 6$, $max = 10$; $p = .018$*. [c]Control range for additional errors: $min = 0$, $max = 4$; $p = .219$.
*Indicates that L.S. produces statistically significantly more errors than controls.

Discussion: Are spelling errors primarily characterized by "letter" errors?

The graphemic buffer is argued to hold letters active until more peripheral output mechanisms finalize their operations. A dysfunctional buffer will struggle to maintain and select the letters it holds (Rapp & Kong, 2002), resulting in "letter errors". Given the location of the graphemic buffer within the spelling model, both lexical and nonlexical spelling should reveal letter errors (Caramazza et al., 1987, 1990). The analyses above confirm these predictions for L.S.: The majority of his spelling errors on words and nonwords were letter errors. L.S. made significantly more of these types of errors than grade-matched controls while he made similar number of other errors that may reflect the, as yet, imperfect acquisition of lexical knowledge in children of this age (e.g., spelling CROCHET as <*crowshay*>). This is in line with spelling performance reported in cases of acquired (e.g., Caramazza et al., 1987; Miceli & Capasso, 2006) and developmental GBD (Yachini & Friedmann, 2010). In contrast, Roncoli and Masterson's (2016) case, Alan, made predominantly phonologically plausible errors (56%), and it remains unclear whether he made more letter errors than age- and spelling-matched controls.

Do letter errors occur to an equal extent across different input and output modalities?

In GBD letter errors are expected regardless of input or output modality. The next set of tasks was designed to examine whether L.S. showed this pattern.

Input modalities (aural or visual)

L.S. was asked to perform written picture naming (visual input task) and spelling to dictation (aural input task) of the same set of 80 highly imageable words (e.g., ghost, cheese) (Krajenbrink, Nickels, & Kohnen, 2015). Words were selected to have a minimum imageability rating of 500 ($M_{IMG} = 594.08$, $SD_{IMG} = 29.98$) based on the MRC Psycholinguistic Database (Coltheart, 1981). In written picture naming, L.S. was given explicit instruction not to say his response out loud before writing the name of the picture. If he wrote a semantically related word (e.g., <*CHAIR*> for BENCH), he was prompted to think of another name for the picture.[11] Two hours later (in the same session) these same words were presented to spell to dictation (e.g., "Write BENCH").

Table 4. Frequency of errors on written naming and spelling to dictation tasks for a list of 80 highly imageable words.

	Written naming Raw total [%]	Spelling to dictation Raw total [%]
Total errors (1–11)	19 [23.8]	21 [26.3]
Letter errors (1–6)	13 [68.4]	11 [52.4]
(1) transposition	4	4
(2) deletion	2	2
(3) addition	1	0
(4) substitution	1	1
(5) multiple letter errors	0	1
(6) mixed letter errors	5	3
Lexical errors (7–9)	0 [0.0]	0 [0.0]
(7) phonologically plausible	0	0
(8) homophone substitution	0	0
(9) whole-word substitution	0	0
Additional errors (10–11)	6 [31.6]	10 [47.6]
(10) ambiguous	6	9
(11) other	0	1

Note: Krajenbrink et al. (2015). Percentages in brackets.

The frequencies of L.S.'s errors for each task are presented in Table 4. Analysis revealed that L.S. was equally accurate in both tasks, McNemar's exact test $p = .815$, two-tailed. Again, L.S.'s spelling errors were mainly letter errors in both modalities (68% visual input; 52% aural input) with no significant differences between the modalities, McNemar's exact test $p = .791$, two-tailed. L.S. made no errors that could be clearly attributed to lexical impairment (Categories 7–9). Importantly, the written naming task attracts as many letter errors as spelling to dictation, suggesting that the letter errors that L.S. produces are unlikely to be due to the oral segmentation difficulty reported above.

Output modalities (handwriting, typing, oral spelling)

L.S. and controls[12] were asked to handwrite, type, and orally spell 66 words to dictation across three testing blocks. Words were selected from the Oxford Wordlist (Bianco et al., 2008) and varied in all lexical variables but were matched across subsets for average written frequency, length, imageability, regularity, and orthographic neighbourhood size (see Appendix B and above section for explanation of variables). In each session a third of the list was spelled in each modality; hence, by the completion of the three blocks, every word had been spelled in each modality. L.S. spelled each block in a different session, whereas the control children spelled all blocks in a single session.

Once again, in all modalities L.S. produced more letter errors (Error Categories 1–6) than lexical spelling

Table 5. Frequency of L.S.'s errors on spelling to dictation tasks written, typed, and spelled orally for a list of 66 words.

	Handwriting Raw total [%]	Typing Raw total [%]	Oral spelling Raw total [%]
Total errors (1–11)	16 [24.2]	15 [22.7]	22 [33.3]
Letter errors (1–6)	8 [50.0]	8 [53.3]	15 [68.2]
(1) transposition	1	1	1
(2) deletion	3	2	4
(3) addition	0	1	2
(4) substitution	3	0	0
(5) multiple letter errors	0	0	4
(6) mixed letter errors	1	4	4
Lexical errors (7–9)	2 [12.5]	2 [13.3]	1 [4.5]
(7) phonologically plausible	0	1	0
(8) homophone substitution	1	0	1
(9) whole-word substitution	1	1	0
Additional errors (10–11)	6 [37.5]	5 [33.3]	6 [27.3]
(10) ambiguous	6	5	6
(11) other	0	0	0

Note: Percentages in brackets.

errors (Error Categories 7–9; see Table 5). The difference in the number of letter errors between modalities approached significance, Cochran's *Q* test $Q(2) = 5.76$ $p = .056$. Follow-up analyses revealed no significant differences in the number of letter errors produced by L.S. between any of the output modalities: specifically, no significant differences between handwriting or typing, McNemar's exact test $p = 1.000$, two-tailed; handwriting or oral spelling, McNemar's exact test $p = .118$, two-tailed; or typing or oral spelling, McNemar's exact test $p = .092$, two-tailed. Therefore L.S. produced similar numbers of letter errors when spelling in all modalities.

Although producing fewer letter errors overall, controls showed a similar pattern across tasks to L.S.: They produced on average 4.8 letter errors when typing ($SD = 0.84$), 5.0 letter errors when handwriting ($SD = 2.65$), and 8.2 when orally spelling ($SD = 1.79$). That is, the control children also made more letter errors when in oral spelling than in the other modalities, suggesting that this is the harder task for these children. To evaluate this statistically, we compared the differences in relative frequency of letter errors across pairs of modalities produced by L.S. with that of the control sample (Crawford, Howell, & Garthwaite, 1998; Crawford & Garthwaite, 2002): There were no significant differences between L.S. and controls for handwritten spelling or typing $t = -2.243$, $p = .088$, two-tailed; between handwritten spelling or oral spelling $t = -2.169$, $p = .096$, two-tailed; or between typing or oral spelling, $t = -0.014$, $p = .989$, two-tailed.

Discussion: Do letter errors occur to an equal extent across different input and output modalities?

The graphemic buffer is argued to be a central relay point in the dual-route model of spelling (see Figure 1, earlier). Therefore, to ensure that L.S.'s spelling pattern was not the result of impairment to one of the input processes (e.g., auditory processing) nor due to a deficit in a peripheral process (e.g., letter formation) we investigated his spelling given different task and response modalities. We found no significant differences in the number of letter errors that L.S. made across different input modalities (visual compared with aural) or output modalities (handwriting, typing, and oral spelling). This is in line with many cases of GBD (e.g., Costa et al., 2011; Katz, 1991; Tainturier & Rapp, 2003; Yachini & Friedmann, 2010) and can be explained by the position of the buffer within the spelling process (e.g., Caramazza et al., 1987, 1990).

Do letter errors occur more often on longer words?

Cases with acquired GBD make more spelling errors on long words than on short words (Miceli & Capasso, 2006), and this length effect is considered one of the primary features of GBD (Caramazza et al., 1987). However, Sage and Ellis (2004) and Buchwald and Rapp (2009) have shown that this effect may have been confounded by certain stimulus characteristics that have been poorly controlled (e.g., longer words tend to have smaller orthographic neighbourhoods). Indeed, in the corpus of words that L.S. spelled to dictation ($n = 400$), as expected, many variables intercorrelated.[13] Thus, clear delineation of a length effect requires careful matching of items and/or choice of statistics.

We investigated the impact of word length (number of letters in a word) on L.S.'s spelling in three analyses, first using matched lists; second using regression to examine whether word length predicts the occurrence of a letter error occurring using the entire corpus of words spelled to dictation; third, as suggested by Buchwald and Rapp (2009), using regression to determine whether word length predicts individual letter accuracy within words spelled to dictation.

In developmental cases, spelling knowledge is still being acquired. Therefore, there is a greater possibility that participants may be unfamiliar with the correct spelling and hence produce a phonologically plausible error. While phonologically plausible errors are often considered a sign of lexical impairment in adults, children with age-appropriate lexical skills may produce phonologically plausible spellings for words they have not yet learned. For this reason, spelling accuracy was not the main dependent variable in our analyses; rather we predicted the likelihood that L.S. would make a letter error compared with any other response.

Letter errors on words in matched word lists

Four matched word lists of words of four letters ($n = 14$), five letters ($n = 20$), six letters ($n = 20$), and seven letters ($n = 20$) were created from the corpus of 400 words that L.S. spelled. These lists were matched on written log frequency, $M_{freq} = 1.70$, $SD_{freq} = 0.05$; orthographic neighbourhood size, $M_N = 1.32$, $SD_N = 0.20$; age of acquisition, $M_{AoA} = 6.49$, $SD_{AoA} = 0.17$; and regularity, $M_{PGC} = .07$, $SD_{PGC} = .06$ (see Appendix C). L.S. made letter errors on 4, 4, 5, and 10 words in each list, respectively; there was a trend for L.S. to make more letter errors as the number of letters in a word (word length) increased, Jonckheere trend exact test $p = .052$, one-tailed. When considering all error types, L.S. made a total of 5, 8, 9, and 13 errors in each list respectively—that is, L.S. made significantly more letter errors as word length increased.

Regression analyses

We conducted regression analyses to determine whether the number of letters in a word (word length) would predict the occurrence of letter errors (i.e., the error types that are thought to be due to buffer dysfunction) across the entire corpus that L.S. spelled ($n = 400$, see earlier). Hence each response was coded as containing either a letter error or another type of response (correct or other error type). First, we looked at the correlations: The occurrence of letter errors was significantly correlated with word length, $r = .256$, $p < .0001$, orthographic neighbourhood size, $r = .241$, $p < .0001$, written frequency, $r = -.111$, $p = .027$ and regularity, $r = -.117$, $p = .020$ (see Table D1 in Appendix D). As these variables were significantly intercorrelated in this corpus, to determine which of these four variables uniquely contributed to L.S.'s letter errors, logistic regression was undertaken with a model reduction strategy of backward (Wald) elimination: A test of the full model against a constant only model was statistically significant, indicating that all of the predictors as a set reliably added predictive value, $\chi^2(4) = 42.311$, $p < .001$. Following reduction, the final model was also statistically significant from a constant only model, $\chi^2(2) = 39.159$, $p < .001$ and provided a good fit of the data, Hosmer–Lemeshow test, $\chi^2(8) = 5.255$, $p = .730$. In both the full and reduced model, only orthographic neighbourhood size significantly predicted whether a letter error would occur (see Table 6), while written frequency approached significance: A letter error was more likely to occur on words that have a smaller neighbourhood size, and words with smaller written frequencies were associated with a greater likelihood that L.S. would make a letter error.

Given concerns about the high intercorrelations between lexical variables (Table D1, Appendix D), we also conducted this same analysis without orthographic neighbourhood size. Results revealed that only word length significantly predicted whether a letter error occurred, Wald criterion = 24.334, $p < .001$ (see Table D2, Appendix D), whereby longer words were more likely to be associated with a letter error occurring.

Individual letter accuracy[14]

As longer words provide a greater opportunity for a letter error to emerge, Buchwald and Rapp (2009) suggested analysing individual letter accuracy instead of whole-word spelling accuracy. This is because when using whole-word spelling accuracy scoring method (as conducted above) a word with multiple errors would count as a single error, whereas according to an individual letter scoring method, each letter error would be counted separately. The following analysis therefore investigated whether the proportion of letters that L.S. spelled correctly was related to word length (number of letters in a word).

Individual letter accuracy scoring procedure. To determine the number of letters correct in each word, the scoring procedure based on Caramazza and Miceli (1990) and adapted by Buchwald and Rapp (2009) was applied. In this procedure, the target spelling and response are maximally aligned such that any letter in the correct relative position receives a score of 1. We use the spelling error <*chidren*> for CHILDREN to explain the procedure. The letters C, H, I, all receive a score of 1, *D* results in

Table 6. Summary of logistic regression predicting the occurrence of "letter errors" for entire corpus L.S. spelled to dictation.

							95% CI for odds ratio	
	B	*SE*	Wald	*df*	*p*	Odds ratio	Lower	Upper
Initial model								
Word length	0.151	0.112	1.830	1	.176	1.164	0.934	1.449
Written frequency	−0.322	0.194	2.768	1	.096	0.724	0.495	1.059
Orthographic *N*-size	−0.251	0.087	8.325	1	.004*	0.778	0.656	0.923
Regularity	−0.962	1.058	0.827	1	.363	0.382	0.048	3.038
Constant	−1.476	0.847	3.048	1	.810	0.228		
Reduced model								
Written frequency	−0.344	0.189	3.317	1	.069	0.709	0.489	1.027
Orthographic *N*-size	−0.333	0.077	18.772	1	<.001***	0.717	0.616	0.833
Constant	−0.455	0.336	1.834	1	.176	0.634		

Note: *N* = 400 items. Method: Backward stepwise (Wald). Initial model −2 log likelihood was 302.72. Reduced model −2 log likelihood was 305.87. *N*-size = neighbourhood size; CI = confidence interval.
$^{*}p < .05$. $^{**}p < .01$. $^{***}p < .001$.

the score of 1 as it appears in the correct relative position to adjacent letters (despite not being present in the correct absolute position), and the following letters all receive a score of 1. Therefore, the total score for this is 7/8 = .875. If a letter is present in the wrong position of the string (transposed) it is given a score of .5. Adjacent transpositions are scored .75 for both letters. For example, WHISTLE written as <*whitsle*> receives a score of 1 + 1+1 + .75 + .75 + 1 + 1, therefore total individual letter accuracy is calculated as 3.5 out of 5 letters, and thus proportion correct is 3.5/5 = .7. This scoring procedure was applied to a subset of 335 words L.S. spelled to dictation. We only included correctly spelled words and letter errors (Error Categories 1–6). Other errors were not included, as they could not be consistently coded with the above scoring procedure.

Analyses. First we correlated lexical variables with proportion of letters spelled correctly. Word length, $r = -.306$, $p < .0001$, written frequency, $r = .156$, $p = .004$, age of acquisition, $r = -.132$, $p = .016$, orthographic neighbourhood size, $r = .283$, $p < .0001$, and regularity, $r = .131$, $p = .016$, were all significantly correlated with proportion of individual letters correct (see Table D3 in Appendix D). These variables were therefore included in a regression model to determine which uniquely predicted individual letter accuracy. Two items were excluded as age of acquisition ratings were missing, leaving a total of 333 items in the following multiple regression analysis. Backward elimination was again used to define a model that explained the most variance with the least number of variables.

The initial regression model and the final model were both statistically significant [adjusted $R^2 = .109$, $F(5, 327) = 9.132$, $p < .001$; adjusted $R^2 = .113$, $F(3, 329) = 15.120$, $p < .001$. respectively]. The final model explained slightly more of the variance (11.3%). In the final model, the three predictors letter length, written frequency, and orthographic neighbourhood size all made significant independent contributions (see Table 7). Words with fewer letters, higher in written frequency, and with a higher orthographic neighbourhood size were associated with increased individual letter accuracy.

Discussion: Do letter errors occur more often on longer words?

When the buffer is impaired, fewer letters than normal can be maintained active or the correct number of letters can only be held active for a shorter period of time (Katz, 1991). Since longer words are required to be maintained in the buffer for longer, they are more error-prone in people with GBD (Katz, 1991). Hence the length effect (longer words are spelled less accurately than shorter words) is one of the defining features of GBD (e.g., Buchwald & Rapp, 2009; Caramazza et al., 1987; Hillis & Caramazza, 1989; Katz, 1991; Sage & Ellis, 2004).

For L.S., length also impacted on spelling performance. First, L.S. tended to make more letter errors on longer words in matched word lists. Although a regression analysis revealed that only lexical variables (orthographic neighbourhood size and a trend for an effect of written frequency) predicted the likelihood that L.S. would produce a response with a letter error, both length and lexical variables predicted individual letter accuracy.

An impact of lexical variables on spelling performance is not an uncommon finding in cases of GBD in the literature (e.g., Buchwald & Rapp, 2009; Kay & Hanley, 1994). As Sage and Ellis (2004) argued, the

Table 7. Summary of multiple regression analysis predicting individual letter accuracy.

						95% CI for β	
	B	SE_B	β	*t*	*p*	Lower	Upper
Initial model							
Intercept	0.993	0.032		30.961	<.001***	0.930	1.056
Word length	−0.011	0.004	−0.188	−2.840	.005**	−0.018	−0.003
Written frequency	0.011	0.006	0.107	1.926	.055	0.000	0.023
Age of acquisition	−0.001	0.003	−0.029	−0.512	.609	−0.007	0.004
Orthographic *N*-size	0.003	0.001	0.146	2.181	.030*	0.000	0.005
Regularity	0.007	0.016	0.023	0.420	.675	−0.025	0.038
Reduced model							
Intercept	0.985	0.026		37.699	<.001***	0.934	1.036
Word length	−0.011	0.004	−0.193	−2.938	.004**	−0.018	−0.004
Written frequency	0.012	0.006	0.115	2.198	.029*	0.001	0.023
Orthographic *N*-size	0.003	0.001	0.156	2.399	.017*	0.001	0.006

Note: $N = 333$ items. Method: backward. Initial model adjusted $R^2 = .109$. Reduced model adjusted $R^2 = .113$. *N*-size = neighbourhood size; CI = confidence interval.
*$p < .05$. **$p < .01$. ***$p < .001$.

relationship between length and lexical variables such as frequency and orthographic neighbourhood size is strong (e.g., short words have many more orthographic neighbours than longer words). The analysis using matched word lists tried to control for these naturally occurring confounds; however, we were left with few items per conditions. The regression analysis attempted to control for these factors statistically, but there remain debates in the statistical literature regarding the extent to which multicollinearity is a problem in these cases. We return to the issue of lexical effects on spelling below.

Is there a serial position effect?

In addition to length, the serial position of a letter within a word has been shown to impact on error patterns in acquired cases of GBD. Traditionally, acquired GBD cases have demonstrated a U-shaped accuracy function whereby letters at the beginning and end are spelled more accurately than medial letters (e.g., Caramazza et al., 1987).

We investigated the serial-position effect by first scoring individual letter accuracy as described above (see individual letter accuracy scoring procedure). Then we divided the total individual letter accuracy by the total number of target letters in that position to provide percentage correct per position.

Letter errors

For this analysis, we only included word lengths that were present in the corpus more than five times. Hence, this included 326 words from 3 to 9 letters long that L.S. spelled to dictation, of which 62 had resulted in letter errors. Again, only letter errors (both single letter errors and unambiguous multiple letter errors) and correct responses were considered for this analysis as other errors, such as phonologically plausible errors, could not be consistently coded with the above individual letter accuracy scoring procedure. These different lengths were normalized to five positions using the method described by Wing and Baddeley (1980). Figure 2 shows a shallow U-shaped distribution where Medial Positions B, C, and D were spelled less accurately than Positions A and E.

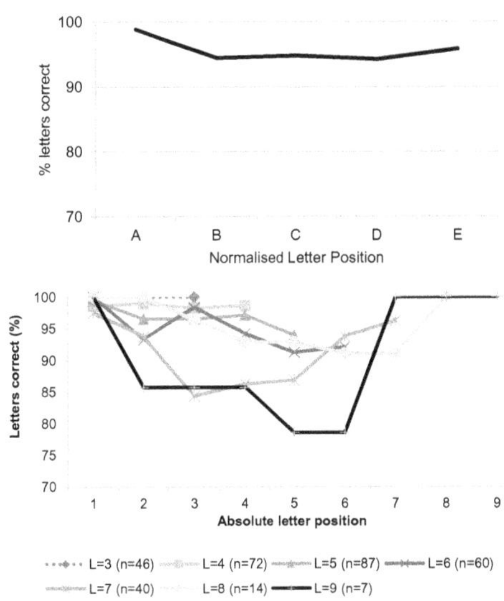

Figure 2. L.S.'s spelling accuracy as a function of serial position within a word normalized across five letter positions (top panel) and L.S.'s spelling accuracy as a function of word length across absolute positions (bottom panel) for letter errors and correctly spelled words ($n = 326$ items). [To view this figure in colour, please see the online version of this Journal.]

There has been some criticism of the Wing and Baddeley (1980) normalization approach. Machtynger and Shallice (2009) and Olson, Romani, and Caramazza (2010) argue that combining words of different lengths into normalized positions could obscure important information about serial behaviour (see also, Goldberg & Rapp, 2008, for a discussion on the effect of length on accuracy at specific positions). Therefore we analysed the same data again using absolute positions, as presented in Figure 2. Here a similar serial position pattern is evident: Medial positions are spelled less accurately across letter lengths.

Furthermore, visual inspection of Figure 2 indicates that longer words are vertically displaced below shorter words. This means that L.S. makes more letter errors in each position as words increase in length (statistical comparison of Position 4 across different lengths, Jonckheere trend test $z = 2.26$, $p = .012$, one-tailed). Thus, the probability that a letter will be written correctly in each position is also influenced by the total number of letters to be produced (Olson et al., 2010).

Discussion: Is there a serial position effect?

The length effects typically found in GBD can be caused by different types of impairments. A linear decrease in accuracy across letter strings is thought to be caused by rapid decay of information in the buffer (e.g., case G.S.I.: Costa et al., 2011). The U-shaped position function has been attributed to the role of the buffer in selecting letters for production (see Costa et al., 2011). It has been proposed that medial letters in a dysfunctioning buffer are subject to greater natural competition of neighbouring letters, whereas initial and final letters are not, making them more resistant to error (Glasspool et al., 2006).

L.S. spelled medial letters less accurately than initial and final letters, resulting in a shallow U-shaped individual letter accuracy function on both normalized and raw data. This pattern of performance is in line with some of the classic cases of GBD (e.g., Caramazza et al., 1987; Jónsdóttir et al., 1996; McCloskey et al., 1994) and most of the developmental cases reported in Yachini and Friedmann's (2010) short report. Hence, L.S.'s graphemic buffer impairment might be in selecting letters for production (Costa et al., 2011) or increased vulnerability to lateral competition (Glasspool et al., 2006).

Is there an impact of lexical variables on the occurrence of letter errors?

There is a debate in the acquired literature regarding the role of lexical variables in GBD. Traditionally, they were thought not to play a role (e.g. Caramazza & Miceli, 1990), whereas others have argued that GBD is compatible with lexical influences (e.g., Sage & Ellis, 2004). In our analysis of the effects of length (above) we found some evidence that lexical variables may influence L.S.'s production of letter errors using logistic regression. Here we further explore this in experimentally matched word lists (treating variables as categorical).

Matched word lists

Matched word lists were created from the corpus of words that L.S. spelled to dictation to investigate the influence of different lexical variables: imageability, orthographic neighbourhood (Coltheart's N), (log) written word frequency (from *N*-Watch, Davis, 2005), and age of acquisition (Kuperman et al., 2012). Each list manipulated one variable and controlled for (matched) the others as well as length (number of letters). For example, for imageability, we had one list of words that were high in imageability, one list of words with a mid-range rating of imageability, and one with low imageability ratings. These three lists were matched for orthographic neighbourhood size, (log) written word frequency, age of acquisition, and word length (number of letters in a word). The frequencies of L.S.'s letter errors on each list are presented in Table 8. Tables E1–E4 in Appendix E outline means and standard deviations of lexical variables for each matched list.

Imageability. The likelihood that L.S. made a letter error significantly increased as imageability decreased, Jonckheere trend test $z = 1.72$, $p = .043$, one-tailed.

Orthographic neighbourhood size. The likelihood that L.S. made a letter error significantly decreased with larger orthographic neighbourhood size, Fisher exact $z = 3.07$, $p = .002$, two-tailed.

Written logarithmic frequency. The likelihood that L.S. would make a letter error was not related to written frequency, Jonckheere trend test, $z = 0.63$, $p = .264$, one-tailed.

Table 8. Frequencies of L.S.'s letter errors on each matched list when spelling to dictation.

Lexical variable	Low	Medium	High
Imageability	10/31 [32]	11/33 [33]	4/33 [12]
Orthographic *N*-size	28/71 [39]		12/77 [16]
Written frequency	14/38 [37]	9/43 [21]	12/42 [29]
Age of acquisition	8/37 [22]	16/52 [31]	11/38 [29]

Note: *N*-size = neighbourhood size; percentages in brackets.

Age of acquisition. The likelihood that L.S. would make a letter error was not related to age of acquisition, Jonckheere trend test, $z = -0.57$, $p = .284$, one-tailed.

In summary, on matched word lists, the likelihood that L.S. made a letter error significantly increased as imageability and orthographic neighbourhood size decreased. Written frequency and age of acquisition were not related to the likelihood that L.S. would make a letter error.

Discussion: Is there an effect of lexical variables on the occurrence of letter errors?

An ongoing debate in the literature concerns the question of whether or not lexical variables can influence spelling performance in people with selective impairment of the graphemic buffer. Across analyses (matched sets, Table 8, and regressions, Tables 6 and 7, earlier) we found that the likelihood that L.S. made a letter error was related to lexical variables, including neighbourhood size (more letter errors on low *N*-size items; regression and matched sets), imageability (more letter errors on low imageability items; matched sets only), frequency (more letter errors on low frequency items; matched sets and regression), while age of acquisition did not predict letter errors.

These results were in contrast to findings in cases of Hebrew-speaking developmental GBD cases (Yachini & Friedmann, 2010) where lexical variables did not affect performance. However, many acquired GBD cases demonstrate effects of lexicality (e.g., Buchwald & Rapp, 2009; Kay & Hanley, 1994; McCloskey et al., 1994; Sage & Ellis, 2004). We return to this issue in the General Discussion.

General discussion

We have presented evidence that L.S. demonstrates most of the characteristics expected in cases of GBD: a higher rate of letter errors than compared to his peers; letter errors that predominate his spelling performances for both words and nonwords; letter errors when spelling given various input and response modalities; and evidence for an effect of length and an effect of serial position. L.S. also demonstrated an effect of lexical variables on the buffer, which has been reported in many acquired cases in the literature. These results provide strong evidence for a graphemic buffer-level impairment underlying L.S.'s spelling performance.

We now turn to alternative interpretations of L.S.'s impairment and discuss features of performance that are relevant for current theoretical debates.

Lexical effects and the graphemic buffer

Aliminosa et al. (1993) argue that effects of lexical variables on spelling in GBD, along with phonologically plausible spelling errors, suggest there is an additional impairment at the orthographic output lexicon. One clear difference between acquired and developmental cases of GBD is that developmental cases are still acquiring their orthographic lexicon. Hence, the occurrence of phonologically plausible errors is not necessarily an indicator of a lexical weakness—it may instead reflect the natural strategy used (by adults and children) when encountering an unfamiliar word. Particular care needs to be taken when choosing words for studies with developmental cases to ensure that they are appropriate for children of that age. Indeed, we chose words from a database based on spellings of primary school children to increase the chance that L.S. would be familiar with these words. L.S. both spelled these words as accurately as his peers and demonstrated within normal range performance on a normed lexical spelling test. This would seem to argue against a lexical spelling impairment.

Furthermore, our detailed error analyses across the different tasks showed consistently that errors that are taken to indicate lexical impairment (i.e., phonologically plausible errors, whole-word and homophone substitutions) were less common than letter errors, and L.S. did not make more of these errors than his peers. Finally, lexical variables may be especially influential in development, children are still acquiring their lexical knowledge, and these variables indeed do influence the ease at which word spellings are learnt. Taken together, this suggests that his orthographic lexicon, and access to this lexicon, were developing at an age-appropriate rate, and a lexical impairment is an unlikely account for L.S.'s spelling performance.

There is still considerable contention in the acquired literature regarding the role of lexical variables within the graphemic buffer (see Aliminosa et al., 1993; Sage & Ellis, 2004). Buchwald and Rapp (2009) offer two possible accounts for mild lexical effects in cases of GBD. Firstly, the authors argue that words, such as those with a large orthographic neighbourhood size, have more robust representations in the lexicon and therefore have stronger "activation-histories" with the buffer. It is this feature that makes these letters, and by extension these words, more resistant to error (Buchwald & Rapp, 2009; Sage & Ellis, 2004). Secondly, the authors also argue that given these more robust representations, there is stronger feedback between the working memory store (buffer) and long-term store (lexicon) which may play a role in improved performance (Buchwald & Rapp, 2009; McCloskey, Macaruso, & Rapp, 2006). Thus, lexical factors, like orthographic neighbourhood size, may have an impact on performance, even in cases of pure buffer impairments, due to the interactive nature of the spelling system. We would argue that the evidence from L.S. together with many recent accounts of lexical factors in acquired cases of GBD (see Miceli & Capasso, 2006, for a review), support the position that effects of lexicality do not provide evidence against (pure) buffer impairment. Rather, we suggest that L.S. provides further support for a theoretical account where activation in a buffer is supported by interaction within the spelling system.

Relationship between letter-position coding and the graphemic buffer

An interesting association appeared between L.S.'s errors in reading and spelling: L.S. demonstrated a high rate of transposed letters both when reading and when spelling. There are two possible hypotheses. The first is that L.S.'s reading and spelling errors are both caused by the same underlying graphemic buffer deficit. Alternatively, L.S.'s reading and spelling errors have different underlying causes, with the reading errors caused by an orthographic analyser deficit and spelling errors caused by a graphemic buffer deficit. We suggest that the latter is most likely. First, while transposition errors dominated L.S.'s reading performance, this was not the case for his spelling where other letter errors were as frequent or even more frequent (see Table 2). Second, other than transposition errors, few other types of letter error appeared in L.S.'s reading. If the same component were responsible for both reading and spelling errors, it is unclear why transpositions would be more frequent in L.S.'s reading than his spelling.

For L.S. we conclude that his transposition errors in reading stem from an impairment at the level of the orthographic analyser, while transpositions in spelling arose at the level of the graphemic buffer. Nevertheless, an association between poor letter position coding and spelling has also been reported in previous cases. Of the five English-speaking cases of developmental letter position dyslexia (a selective impairment of the letter position function, which results in anagram errors, e.g., reading *slime* as "smile"), four had spelling impairments (Kezilas, Kohnen, McKague, & Castles, 2014; Kohnen, Nickels, Castles, Friedmann, & McArthur, 2012). However, like L.S., none of these children's spelling was dominated by transposition errors. It seems most likely then that the association between transposition errors in reading and poor spelling is not the result of a shared underlying deficit.

Nonetheless, the alternative interpretation of a single impairment accounting for the association between reading and spelling errors cannot be ruled out by our data. Specifically, some authors argue that the graphemic buffer is shared for reading and spelling (e.g., Caramazza et al., 1996; Tainturier & Rapp, 2003). Moreover, these accounts predict that nonword reading is compromised (more than word reading), which was the case for L.S. While our data do not allow us clearly determine which of the two proposed accounts best explain his performance (two impairments as outlined in the previous paragraph or a single impairment to a shared graphemic buffer), L.S.'s poor nonword reading and letter position mistakes in reading are generally consistent with the idea that the graphemic buffer is shared for reading and spelling.

Developmental stage models and dual-route models of spelling

The use of cognitive neuropsychological approaches to studying the typical and atypical development of spelling is contentious (see Bishop, 1997; Castles et al., 2014). So-called stage models have been more often used to guide research and clinical practice of spelling development (e.g., Ehri, 2000; Frith, 1885; Gentry, 1982). However, we would argue that these models, in their current inceptions, struggle to explain the occurrence of letter errors both in L.S. and in the typical controls. Within stage models, phonologically implausible errors are taken to indicate difficulties with acquiring the skill of associating sounds with letters (often called alphabetic stage). This stage has to be completed before the next stage (the orthographic stage) is entered. Phonologically plausible errors are said to occur because alphabetic skills have been acquired but the orthographic stage has not been reached yet. If we take an age-appropriate level performance on a nonword spelling task to indicate that the alphabetic stage has been acquired sufficiently, and an age-appropriate performance on a word spelling task to indicate that the orthographic stage has been acquired sufficiently (both of which is the case for L.S. and his controls), it is unclear how the occurrence of phonologically implausible letter errors can be interpreted within stage theories (also see Varnhagen, McCallum, & Burstow, 1997). In contrast, with a theory in which the skilled spelling system includes lexical and nonlexical procedures as well as a graphemic buffer, the interpretation is straightforward: L.S. has acquired the lexical and nonlexical procedures whereas the buffer function in L.S.'s spelling system is suboptimal leading to a higher frequency of letter errors.

In addition to assisting the description of the atypical acquisition of the spelling process, cognitive neuropsychological models also describe typical spelling. Spelling errors that occur due to dysfunction (e.g., of the graphemic buffer) can often also be observed in typical spellers. The idea is that spelling errors occur in the same processing component in the spelling model in all spellers; however, in impaired spellers these errors occur at a much higher frequency. Wing and Baddeley (1980) described letter errors in adult spellers. Our work, together with that of Roncoli and Masterson (2016), revealed that letter errors also occur in the spelling performance of typically developing primary-school aged children. Given the difficulties that stage-models have in explaining letter errors in any but the earliest stages of spelling acquisition, we would argue that models that include an orthographic working memory component are better placed to describe not only the atypical but also the typical development of spelling.

Another relevant feature of L.S.'s performance when discussing models of spelling used in developmental research is the selectiveness of L.S.'s spelling impairment. If we are correct in interpreting his lexical and sublexical routes as being acquired at a normal rate, then the only subskill of spelling that is being suboptimally acquired is that of the graphemic buffer. That is, lexical and sublexical processes can be acquired even if graphemic buffer function is impaired. These selective impairments are taken to indicate that the acquisition process is modular (Castles, Bates, & Coltheart, 2006; Marshall, 1984) and that "static" models of skilled cognition are well placed to explain this process.

What is the functional impact of developmental GBD?

While more severe cases of developmental GBD may score in the impaired range on standardized tests of lexical and nonlexical spelling, L.S. did not. From a clinical or educational point of view, one may wonder what is the functional impact of L.S.'s spelling impairment, given his average performance on standardized spelling tests. Does L.S. actually have a spelling deficit? The answer is multifaceted. Of course, as "dysgraphia" is defined as an impairment to a component within the spelling system necessary to complete the task of accurate spelling, the answer could be "Yes" as our research demonstrated that L.S.'s overall rates of letter errors were different to those of a matched control group and were similar to those reported in the (albeit restricted) developmental GBD literature (Yachini & Friedmann, 2010), indicating an impairment. In addition, L.S.'s mother and teachers reported difficulties with his spelling (and hence enrolled him in our spelling treatment study), which suggests a possible functional impact at home and school. While not always accurate, parent and teacher concerns warrant careful consideration. Nevertheless, typically used, standardized spelling assessments did not validate these concerns from L.S.'s mother and teacher. It may be the case that only in mild cases of developmental GBD, perhaps like L.S., is overall spelling accuracy not severely affected. Alternatively, this may be because these standardized spelling tests were not sensitive enough to detect L.S.'s graphemic impairment, and a more sensitive and specific test of functional spelling is required. Indeed, many of the items in the lexical list that we used (TWS–3: Unpredictable Spelling; Larsen & Hammill, 1994) are quite short (only 8 out of the 21 words that L.S. got correct were longer than 5 letters, and 3 of these 8 were morphologically complex). Further to this, while the number of letters per item increases across the nonlexical list used (QUIL: Nonword Spelling; Dodd et al., 1996), the items are pseudo-morphologically complex (e.g., "strimperdiction", "strecker", "clondly"), which may hide graphemic buffer deficits. Certainly, a specific standardized and normed test of graphemic buffer functioning may have detected L.S.'s problems. However, no such test currently exists, but this is an important avenue for future research.

Summary and conclusions

This single case study had two aims: first, to utilize the cognitive neuropsychological framework to investigate whether L.S., following an initial presentation of high rates of the types of spelling errors typical of dysfunction at the orthographic working memory, demonstrated the characteristics of GBD; and, second, to provide a demonstration of the role that cognitive theories can play in defining and describing developmental disorders and, in turn, show the potential for such disorders to inform theory of spelling and spelling acquisition.

Our investigation revealed that L.S. demonstrated most of the characteristics of GBD as reported in the acquired and developmental literature (Caramazza et al., 1987; Yachini & Friedmann, 2010). In addition, he demonstrated effects of lexicality on his spelling performance, which have been previously reported in the literature on acquired deficits (e.g., Sage & Ellis, 2004). Alternative explanations for his spelling performance, such as an additional impairment at the orthographic lexicon, were excluded, and we conclude that the most parsimonious locus of impairment for L.S. is the graphemic buffer. We also suggest that L.S. provides further support for theories where effects of lexicality on spelling, and particularly in GBD, are to be expected due to interactivity between lexical and post-lexical spelling components.

At present, we do not know the prevalence of GBD in developmental cases. While L.S. is, to the best of our knowledge, the most thoroughly tested developmental GBD case in English, we predict that many children's GBD has been missed. Some of the reasons for this may be a lack of knowledge about the relevant features of this type of spelling difficulty because developmental spelling models do not include an orthographic working memory store. But even within the developmental cognitive neuropsychological literature, reports of GBD are rare. It may be missed, or misdiagnosed as mixed dysgraphia, especially in the absence of widely available normative control data on the frequency of occurrence of letter errors in typically developing spellers. Our own and other careful reports may help alert researchers and clinicians to the possibility of working with a case of developmental GBD. Future research into the role of the buffer in developmental cases is warranted to contribute further to our understanding of the heterogeneous presentation of dysgraphias in children and by extension the developmental trajectory of the spelling system.

Notes

1. Significantly higher proportions of letter position errors in reading have been suggested to indicate a deficit in the orthographic analyser (e.g., Friedmann & Rahamim, 2007; Kezilas et al., 2014; Kohnen et al., 2012). Some of L.S.'s reading mistakes on the nonwords were letter position errors (e.g., reading *salpy* as "slappy"), possibly indicating that the suggested impairment of the orthographic analyser impacted on word and nonword reading.
2. In all spelling tasks for this investigation, self-corrections were accepted if they occurred before the examiner administered the next item.
3. Given that L.S.'s performance on standardized spelling tests were within normal limits, the reader may wonder whether L.S. has a "deficit" at all. We will demonstrate that indeed L.S.'s performance on a number of tasks was qualitatively different from that of his peers, indicating a dysfunctioning graphemic buffer. We will return to the puzzle of his "deficit" in the General Discussion.
4. The QUIL (Dodd et al., 1996) was chosen as a selection measure as it is one of the purest measures of nonlexical spelling knowledge with Australian normative data (Kohnen, Nickels & Castles, 2009). The TWS–3 was used to assess lexical spelling skills as it was reviewed as the most appropriate measure available (Kohnen et al., 2009).
5. All examples presented are from L.S.'s written samples.
6. Spelling responses were considered phonologically plausible if each phoneme in the target corresponded to a grapheme in the response as reported by PGC rules used by Perry, Ziegler, and Coltheart (2002). Any ambiguities were resolved through discussion between authors.

7. Substitutions of irregular homophones could also be classified as phonologically plausible or whole-word substitution errors. We always classified these as homophone substitutions.
8. We also asked L.S. to read these 182 words aloud. He read 91% correctly, suggesting that L.S. was familiar with the written form for most of the words presented in this spelling task.
9. Regularity was coded based on the predictability of PGCs within each word. Predictability was defined in reference to the work by Perry et al. (2002). A rating of 1 indicates that all phonemes in a word are spelled using the most frequent spelling for a phoneme on the Perry list (e.g., RING). A rating of 0 indicates that one or more phonemes in a word are spelled not using the most frequent spelling on the Perry list (e.g., SIGN).
10. Criteria for phonologically plausible spelling as outlined above in spelling error scoring procedure.
11. While naming agreement was high for these pictures, some ambiguity remained even in adults for whom this task was designed originally.
12. Five of the seven control children were available for this follow-up experimental testing.
13. Specifically, orthographic neighbourhood size was significantly and strongly negatively correlated with number of letters (word length), $r = -.619$, $p < .0001$, two-tailed. Number of letters was also significantly correlated with age of acquisition $r = .204$, $p < .0001$, two-tailed; regularity $r = -.256$, $p < .0001$, two-tailed; and with written frequency $r = -.188$, $p < .0001$, two-tailed; however, it was not correlated with imageability, $r = .025$, $p = .656$, two-tailed (see Table D1, Appendix D for more details).
14. Readers are reminded that the term "letter errors" refers to when a word was coded as containing an error that is typical in cases of GBD. "Individual letter accuracy" refers to the accuracy of an individual letter within a word.

Acknowledgements

We are very grateful to L.S. and his mother, and to the control participants and their families, for their participation in this study. We are also grateful to Trudy Krajenbrink, Yvette Kezilas, Nathan Caruana, Naama Friedmann, Teresa Schubert, Greg Savage, and reviewers for valuable discussions and feedback. Many thanks to Nicholas Badcock and Kathryn Preece for their assistance in recruitment.

Disclosure statement

No potential conflict of interest was reported by the authors.

Funding

This research is part of a larger project on spelling disorders funded by an Australian Research Council (ARC) Project grant [grant number DP110103822]. Lyndsey Nickels was funded by an Australian Research Council - Future Fellowship [grant number FT120100102] and Saskia Kohnen by a Macquarie University Research Fellowship; Centre of Excellence in Cognition and its Disorders, Australian Research Council

ORCID

Lyndsey Nickels http://orcid.org/0000-0002-0311-3524

References

Aliminosa, D., McCloskey, M., Goodman-Schulman, R., & Sokol, S. M. (1993). Remediation of acquired dysgraphia as a technique for testing interpretations of deficits. *Aphasiology, 7*(1), 55–69.

Barry, C. (1994). Spelling routes (or routes or rutes). In G. G. A. Brown & N. C. Ellis (Eds.), *Handbook of spelling: Theory, process and intervention* (pp. 27–50). Chichester, UK: John Wiley & Sons Ltd.

Baxter, D. M., & Warrington, E. K. (1983). Neglect dysgraphia. *Journal of Neurology, Neurosurgery & Psychiatry, 46*(12), 1073–1078.

Bianco, J. L., Scull, J., & Ives, D. (2008). *The words children write: Research summary of the Oxford wordlist research study: An investigation of high frequency words in young children's writing and reading development*. Oxford: Oxford University Press.

Bishop, D. V. (1997). Cognitive neuropsychology and developmental disorders: Uncomfortable bedfellows. *The Quarterly Journal of Experimental Psychology Section A, 50*(4), 899–923.

Brunsdon, R., Coltheart, M., & Nickels, L. (2005). Treatment of irregular word spelling in developmental surface dysgraphia. *Cognitive Neuropsychology, 22*(2), 213–251.

Bub, D., & Kertesz, A. (1982). Deep agraphia. *Brain and Language, 17*, 146–165.

Buchwald, A., & Rapp, B. (2009). Distinctions between orthographic long-term memory and working memory. *Cognitive Neuropsychology, 26*(8), 724–751.

Campbell, R., & Butterworth, B. (1985). Phonological dyslexia and dysgraphia in a highly literate subject: A developmental case with associated deficits of phonemic processing and awareness. *The Quarterly Journal of Experimental Psychology Section A, 37*(3), 435–475.

Caramazza, A., Capasso, R., & Miceli, G. (1996). The role of the graphemic buffer in reading. *Cognitive Neuropsychology, 13*, 673–698.

Caramazza, A., & Miceli, G. (1990). The structure of graphemic representations. *Cognition, 37*(3), 243–297.

Caramazza, A., Miceli, G., Villa, G., & Romani, C. (1987). The role of the graphemic buffer in spelling: Evidence from a case of acquired dysgraphia. *Cognition, 26*, 59–85.

Castles, A., Bates, T., & Coltheart, M. (2006). John Marshall and the developmental dyslexias. *Aphasiology, 20*(9), 871–892.

Castles, A., Coltheart, M., Larsen, L., Jones, P., Saunders, S., & McArthur, G. (2009). Assessing the basic components of reading: A revision of the castles and coltheart test with new norms. *Australian Journal of Learning Difficulties*, *14*, 67–88.

Castles, A, Kohnen, S, Nickels, L, & Brock, J. (2014). Developmental disorders: what can be learned from cognitive neuropsychology. *Philosophical Transactions of the Royal Society of London B: Biological Sciences*, *369*(1634).

Coltheart, M., & Kohnen, S. (2012). Acquired and developmental disorders of reading and spelling. In M. Faust (Ed.), *The handbook of the neuropsychology of language* (pp. 892–920). New York, NY: Wiley.

Coltheart, M. (1981). The MRC psycholinguistic database. *The Quarterly Journal of Experimental Psychology Section A*, *33* (4), 497–505.

Costa, V., Fischer-Baum, S., Capasso, R., Miceli, G., & Rapp, B. (2011). Temporal stability and representational distinctiveness: Key functions of orthographic working memory. *Cognitive Neuropsychology*, *28*(5), 338–362.

Crawford, J. R, & Garthwaite, P. H. (2002). Investigation of the single case in neuropsychology: Confidence limits on the abnormality of test scores and test score differences. *Neuropsychologia*, *40*(8), 1196–1208.

Crawford, J. R., & Garthwaite, P. H. (2005). Testing for suspected impairments and dissociations in single-case studies in neuropsychology: Evaluation of alternatives using Monte Carlo simulations and revised tests for dissociations. *Neuropsychology*, *19*(3), 318–331.

Crawford, J. R., Garthwaite, P. H., & Porter, S. (2010). Point and interval estimates of effect sizes for the case-controls design in neuropsychology: Rationale, methods, implementations, and proposed reporting standards. *Cognitive Neuropsychology*, *27*(3), 245–260.

Crawford, J. R., Howell, D. C., & Garthwaite, P. H. (1998). Payne and Jones revisited: Estimating the abnormality of test score differences using a modified paired samples *t*-test. *Journal of Clinical and Experimental Neuropsychology*, *20*, 898–905.

Davis, C. (2005). N-Watch: A program for deriving neighbourhood size and other psycholinguistic statistics. *Behavior Research Methods*, *37*(1), 65–70.

de Partz, M. P. (1995). Deficit of the graphemic buffer: Effects of a written lexical segmentation strategy. *Neuropsychological Rehabilitation*, *5*(1-2), 129–147.

Dodd, B., Holm, A., Oerlemanns, M., & McCormick, M. (1996). *QUIL: Queensland university inventory of literacy*. St. Lucia, Queensland: University of Queensland, Department of Speech Pathology & Audiology.

Dunn, L. M., & Dunn, D. M. (2007). *Peabody picture vocabulary test – Fourth Edition (PPVT-4)*. melbourne: Pearson Australia Group Pty Ltd.

Egan, J., & Tainturier, M. J. (2011). Inflectional spelling deficits in developmental dyslexia. *Cortex*, *47*(10), 1179–1196.

Ehri, L. C. (2000). Learning to read and learning to spell: Two sides of a coin. *Topics in Language Disorders*, *20*, 19–36.

Ellis, A. W. (1982). Spelling and writing (and reading and Speakindg). In A. W. Ellis (Ed.), *Normality and pathology in cognitive functions* (pp. 113–146). London: Academic Press.

Friedmann, N., & Coltheart, M. (2016). Types of developmental dyslexia. In A. Bar-on, & D. Ravid (Eds.), *Handbook of communication disorders: Theoretical, empirical, and applied linguistics perspectives* (pp. 1–37). Berlin: De Gruyter Mouton.

Friedmann, N., & Rahamim, E. (2007). Developmental letter position dyslexia. *Journal of Neuropsychology*, *1*(2), 201–236.

Frith, U. (1985). Beneath the surface of developmental dyslexia. In K Patterson, J. C Marshall, & M Coltheart (Eds.), *Surface dyslexia: Neuropsychological and cognitive studies of phonological reading* (pp. 301–330). London, England: Erlbaum.

Gentry, J. R. (1982). An analysis of developmental spelling in "GNYS AT WRK". *The Reading Teacher*, *36*, 192–200.

Glasspool, D. W., Shallice, T., & Cipolotti, L. (2006). Towards a unified process model for graphemic buffer disorder and deep dysgraphia. *Cognitive Neuropsychology*, *23*(3), 479–512.

Goldberg, A., & Rapp, B. (2008). Is compound chaining the serial-order mechanism of spelling? A simple recurrent network investigation. *Cognitive Neuropsychology*, *25*(2), 218–255.

Gvion, A, & Friedmann, N. (2010). Dyscravia: Voicing substitution dysgraphia. *Neuropsychologia*, *48*(7), 1935–1947.

Gvion, A., & Friedmann, N. (2010). Letter position dysgraphia. *Cortex*, *46*(9), 1100–1113.

Hillis, A. E., & Caramazza, A. (1989). The graphemic buffer and attentional mechanisms. *Brain and Language*, *36*(2), 208–235.

Jónsdóttir, M. K., Shallice, T., & Wise, R. (1996). Phonological mediation and the graphemic buffer disorder in spelling: Cross-language differences? *Cognition*, *59*(2), 169–197.

Katz, R. B. (1991). Limited retention of information in the graphemic buffer. *Cortex*, *27*(1), 111–119.

Kay, J., & Hanley, J. (1994). Peripheral disorder of spelling: The role of the graphemic buffer. In G. D. A.Brown, & N. C. Ellis (Eds.), *Handbook of spelling: Theory, process and intervention* (pp. 295–315). New York, NY: John Wiley.

Kezilas, Y., Kohnen, S., McKague, M., & Castles, A. (2014). The locus of impairment in developmental letter position dyslexia. *Frontiers in Human Neuroscience*, *8*(356), 1–14.

Kohnen, S., Marinus, E., Friedmann, E., Anandakumar, T., Nickels, L., McArthur, G., & Castles, A. (2012). Letter position test. Retrieved from www.motif.org.au

Kohnen, S., Nickels, L., Castles, A., Friedmann, N., & McArthur, G. (2012). When "slime" becomes "smile": developmental letter position dyslexia in English. *Neuropsychologia*, *50*(14), 3681–3692.

Kohnen, S., Nickels, L., & Castles, A. (2009). Assessing spelling skills and strategies: A critique of available resources. *Australian Journal of Learning Difficulties*, *14*(1), 113–150.

Korkman, M., Kemp, S., & Kirk, U. (2007). *Developmental neuropsychological assessment* (2nd ed.). Melbourne: Pearson Australia Group Pty.

Krajenbrink, T., Nickels, L., & Kohnen, S. (2015). *Graphemic buffer impairment with fragment errors: A case of reduced activation from the buffer*. Manuscript submitted for publication.

Kuperman, V., Stadthagen-Gonzalez, H., & Brysbaert, M. (2012). Age-of-acquisition ratings for 30,000 English words. *Behavior Research Methods*, *44*(4), 978–990.

Larsen, S. C., & Hammill, D. D. (1994). *The test of written spelling* (3rd ed.). Austin, Texas: Pro-ed.

Machtynger, J., & Shallice, T. (2009). Normalizing serial position analyses: The proportional accountability algorithm. *Cognitive Neuropsychology*, *26*(2), 217–222.

Marshall, J. C. (1984). Toward a rational taxonomy of the developmental dyslexias. In R. N. Malatesha, & H. A. Whitaker (Eds.), *Dyslexia: A global issue* (pp. 45–58). The Hague: Nijhoff.

McCloskey, M., Badecker, W., Goodman-Schulman, R. A., & Aliminosa, D. (1994). The structure of graphemic representations in spelling: Evidence from a case of acquired dysgraphia. *Cognitive Neuropsychology*, *11*(3), 341–392.

McCloskey, M, Macaruso, P, & Rapp, B. (2006). Grapheme-to-lexeme feedback in the spelling system: Evidence from a dysgraphic patient. *Cognitive Neuropsychology*, *23*(2), 278–307.

Miceli, G., Capasso, R., Benvegnù, B., & Caramazza, A. (2004). The categorical distinction of vowel and consonant representations: Evidence from dysgraphia. *Neurocase*, *10*(2), 109–121.

Miceli, G., & Capasso, R. (2006). Spelling and dysgraphia. *Cognitive Neuropsychology*, *23*(1), 110–134.

Neale, M. D. (1999). *Neale analysis of reading ability* (3rd ed.). Melbourne: ACER Press.

Olson, A., Romani, C., & Caramazza, A. (2010). Analysis and interpretation of serial position data. *Cognitive Neuropsychology*, *27*(2), 134–151.

Perry, C., Ziegler, J. C., & Coltheart, M. (2002). How predictable is spelling? Developing and testing metrics of phoneme-grapheme contingency. *The Quarterly Journal of Experimental Psychology Section A*, *55*(3), 897–915.

Pritchard, S. C., Coltheart, M., Marinus, E., & Castles, A. (2016). Modelling the acquisition of grapheme–phoneme correspondences within the dual-route cascaded model of reading aloud. *Scientific Studies of Reading*, *20*(1), 49–63.

Rapp, B., & Kong, D. L. (2002, October). Revealing the component functions of the graphemic buffer. *Brain and Language*, *83*(1), 112–114.

Roncoli, S., & Masterson, J. (2016). "Unexpected" spelling difficulty in a 10-year-old child with good reading skills: An intervention case study. *Writing Systems Research*, *8*(2), 143–166.

Sage, K., & Ellis, A. W. (2004). Lexical influences in graphemic buffer disorder. *Cognitive Neuropsychology*, *21*(2-4), 381–400.

Snowling, M., Stackhouse, J., & Rack, J. (1986). Phonological dyslexia and dysgraphia—A developmental analysis. *Cognitive Neuropsychology*, *3*(3), 309–339.

Tainturier, M. J., & Caramazza, A. (1996). The status of double letters in graphemic representations. *Journal of Memory and Language*, *35*(1), 53–73.

Tainturier, M. J., & Rapp, B. (2003). Is a single graphemic buffer used in reading and spelling? *Aphasiology*, *17*(6-7), 537–562.

Temple, C. M. (1985). Developmental surface dysgraphia: A case report. *Applied Psycholinguistics*, *6*, 391–405.

Temple, C. M. (2006). Developmental and acquired dyslexias. *Cortex*, *42*(6), 898–910.

Varnhagen, C. K, McCallum, M, & Burstow, M. (1997). Is children's spelling naturally stage-like. *Reading and Writing*, *9*, 451–481

Wagner, R. K, Torgesen, J. K, & Rashotte, C. A. (2013). *Comprehensive Test of Phonological Processing - SecondEdition: CTOPP-2*. Pearson, Melbourne.

Ward, J., & Romani, C. (1998). Serial position effects and lexical activation in spelling: Evidence from a single case study. *Neurocase*, *4*(3), 189–206.

Westwood, P. (2005). *Spelling: Approaches to teaching and assessment*. Melbourne, Australia: ACER.

Wing, A. M., & Baddeley, A. D. (1980). Spelling errors in handwriting: A corpus and a distributional analysis. In *U. Frith (Ed.), Cognitive Processes in Spelling*. London: Academic Press.

Woodcock, R. W., McGrew, K. S., & Mather, N. (2008). *Woodcock-Johnson III Tests of Achievement - Australian Adaptation*. Jannali, NSW: Psychological Assessments Australia.

Yachini, M., & Friedmann, N. (2010). Developmental graphemic buffer dysgraphia. *Procedia-Social and Behavioral Sciences*, *6*, 148–149.

Appendices

Appendix A

Below are detailed descriptions of norm-referenced assessments administered to gain more information regarding L.S.'s and/or controls' literacy profiles.

Spoken language assessment

Receptive vocabulary. Receptive vocabulary was assessed using the Peabody Picture Vocabulary Test (PPVT–4; Dunn & Dunn, 2007). L.S. was asked to identify the correct pictorial representation of the concept conveyed by a single, orally presented word from an array of four options (e.g., "point to the picture that shows crying"). The test consists of 228 items with different, age-appropriate, starting points. Words increased in difficulty, and a discontinue rule of 8 errors in a set of 12 words was applied. Scores are expressed as standard scores, with a mean of 100 and standard deviation of 15.

Expressive vocabulary. The Picture Naming subtest of the Woodcock–Johnson III Tests of Achievement battery (WJ–ACH–III; Woodcock, McGrew, & Mather, 2008) was used to assess expressive vocabulary. L.S. was asked to provide the name for the object in the picture. The test consists of 44 pictures, which increase in difficulty. Grade-based starting points, basal continuation rules (6 lowest items must be correct to progress), and a discontinue rule of 6 consecutive incorrect responses were applied. Scores are expressed as standard scores, with a mean of 100 and standard deviation of 15.

Oral segmentation. An important skill for spelling is oral segmentation. The Segmenting Nonwords subtest from Comprehensive Test of Phonological Processing (Wagner, Torgesen, Rashotte & Pearson, 2013) was used to assess this skill. L.S. was asked to verbally segment auditorily presented nonwords into their phonemic parts (e.g., target: "mab", correct response "m-a-b"). This test consists of 20 items, and the standard discontinue rule of 3 consecutive errors was applied. Scores are expressed as scaled scores with a mean of 10 and standard deviation of 3.

Phonological encoding and decoding. The Repetition of Nonsense Words subtest from the Developmental NEuroPSYchological Assessment battery (NEPSY–II; Korkman, Kemp, & Kirk, 2007) was administered to assess phonological processing. L.S. was asked to repeat single nonwords played on an iPod (e.g., *crumsee*). A discontinue rule of 4 consecutive incorrect responses was applied. Scores are expressed as scaled scores with a mean of 10 and standard deviation of 3.

Reading assessment

Lexical reading. Single word reading accuracy was assessed using the irregular word stimuli of the Castles and Coltheart Reading Test (CC2; Castles et al., 2009). Participants were asked to read aloud 40 irregular (e.g., *good, ceiling*) words presented on flashcards. As is standard in CC2 administration, words from this subtest were presented intermixed with the other stimuli (regular words and nonwords) from the CC2 (Castles et al., 2009). Words increased in difficulty, and a stopping rule of 5 incorrect responses to irregular words was applied. Scores are expressed as *z*-scores with a mean of 0 and a standard deviation of 1.

Nonlexical reading. Nonlexical reading skills (the ability to successfully convert graphemes to phonemes for novel words) were assessed using the nonword reading stimuli of the CC2 (Castles et al., 2009). The nonword stimuli were administered in the same manner as described above for irregular word reading. The 40 nonwords increased in length and complexity (e.g., *norf, gwextoint*), and a stopping rule of 5 incorrect was applied. Scores are expressed as *z*-scores with a mean of 0 and a standard deviation of 1.

Letter position coding. To test letter-position coding in reading, the Letter Position Test (LetPos; Kohnen, Marinus, Friedmann, Anandakumar, Nickels, McArthur, & Castles, 2012 Kohnen, Marinus, Friedman, Anandakumar, Nickels, McArthur, & Castles, 2012) was administered. This test consists of 30 anagram word pairs (e.g., *slime, smile*). Words are presented on 2 pages. Each page had a single word from a pair (pairs never occurred on the same page). Children were asked to read each word aloud. There are no discontinue rules for this test. The primary measure used was the total number of transposition errors (reading *slime* as "smile"). Australian normative data are based on grade and reading level (derived from CC2 performance). Scores are expressed as *z*-scores with a mean of 0 and a standard deviation of 1.

Text reading accuracy and comprehension. Text reading and comprehension were assessed with the Neale Analysis of Reading Ability (NARA–3; Neale, 1999). This test required L.S. to read aloud up to six passages of text that increased in length and word difficulty. L.S.'s accuracy errors were corrected during reading. Once he finished reading a passage, he was asked a series of questions about the text. A stopping rule was applied after 16–20 reading errors on a single passage. The number of questions answered correctly provided the reading comprehension raw score. Scores are expressed as standard scores, with a mean of 100 and SD of 15.

Spelling assessment

Letter knowledge. We assessed L.S.'s letter knowledge with a cross-case copying task. L.S. was asked to transcribe seven upper- and seven lower-case letters that differ in upper- and lower-case shape into its opposite form (e.g., upper case <*T*> to lower case <*t*>). There are no norms for this test; however, children L.S.'s age are expected to perform this task without difficulty.

Lexical spelling. Lexical spelling was assessed using the Unpredictable Spelling subtest of the Test of Written Spelling (TWS–3; Larsen & Hammill, 1994). This test assesses participants' ability to spell 50 words with unpredictable phoneme-to-grapheme conversions (e.g., *two, people, fountain*). Words were presented with brief sentence contexts (e.g., "two, there are two birds in the tree, two") following which participants were asked to write a response. Words increased in difficulty, and a stopping rule of 5 consecutive errors was applied. Scores are expressed as standard scores, with a mean of 100 and standard deviation of 15.

Nonlexical spelling. The Nonword Spelling subtest from the Queensland University Inventory of Literacy battery (QUIL, Dodd et al., 1996) was administered to measure nonlexical spelling skills. Participants listened to 24 nonwords that increased in length and difficulty (e.g., *dorf, churtlesneedee*) presented on an iPod. Children were asked to write how they thought each nonword would be spelled. Spellings received a score of 1 if the response was a phonologically plausible spelling of the nonword target (i.e., had acceptable phoneme-to-grapheme correspondences). Scores are expressed as grade scaled scores with a mean of 10 and standard deviation of 3.

Appendix B

Table B1. Means of item characteristics of matched word-lists for output analysis.

	n	Written frequency	Word length	Regularity	Orthographic *N*-size
List 1	22	2.12 (0.77)	5.73 (2.19)	.55 (.51)	3.64 (4.50)
List 2	22	2.12 (0.69)	5.64 (2.01)	.59 (.50)	4.23 (5.01)
List 3	22	2.14 (0.70)	5.77 (2.50)	.55 (.48)	4.50 (5.25)

Note: *N*-size = neighbourhood size. Standard deviations in parentheses.

Appendix C

Table C1. Means of item characteristics of word-lists matched for word length.

	n	Written frequency	Orthographic *N*-size	AoA	Imageability	Regularity
4-letter words	14	1.78 (0.87)	1.50 (0.85)	6.42 (1.80)	393.71 (130.86)	.14 (.36)
5-letter words	20	1.65 (0.88)	1.40 (0.99)	6.46 (1.04)	338.05 (112.02)	.05 (.22)
6-letter words	20	1.59 (0.62)	1.35 (1.27)	6.48 (1.95)	335.55 (87.53)	.05 (.22)
7-letter words	20	1.62 (0.83)	1.35 (1.09)	6.52 (1.79)	342.85 (132.37)	.00 (.00)

Note: *N*-size = neighbourhood size; AoA = age of acquisition. Standard deviations in parentheses.

Appendix D

Table D1. Correlations for 400 words spelled to dictation: Letter errors and item characteristics.

	Written freq	Word length	Orthographic *N*-size	AoA[a]	IMG[b]	Regularity
Letter errors	−.105*	.259***	−.237***	.097	−.072	−.115*
Written freq		−.188***	.092	−.374***	−.425***	−.001
Word length			−.619***	.204***	.025	−.256***
Orthographic *N*-size				−.181***	.002	.331***
Age of acquisition (AoA)					−.126**	−.178***
Imageability (IMG)						.092

Note: *N*-size = neighbourhood size; freq = frequency.
[a]AoA ratings only available for $n = 394$ items. [b]IMG ratings only available for $n = 323$ items.
$^{*}p < .05$. $^{**}p < .01$. $^{***}p < .001$.

Table D2. Summary of logistic regression predicting letter errors for entire corpus that L.S. spelled to dictation without orthographic neighbourhood size

							95% CI for odds ratio	
	B	*SE*	Wald	*df*	*p*	Odds ratio	Lower	Upper
Initial model								
Word length	0.381	0.090	17.868	1	<.001**	1.464	1.227	1.747
Written frequency	−0.287	0.192	2.225	1	.136	0.751	0.515	1.094
Regularity	−1.421	1.039	1.873	1	.171	0.241	0.032	1.849
Constant	−3.343	0.656	25.971	1	<.001**	0.035		
Reduced model								
Word length	0.431	0.189	24.334	1	<.001**	1.539	1.296	1.826
Constant	−4.141	0.336	57.828	1	<.001**	0.016		

Note: Method: Backward stepwise (Wald). Initial model −2 log likelihood was 345.03. Reduced model −2 log likelihood was 319.16. Entire corpus: $n = 400$ items. CI = confidence interval.
$^{*}p < .05$. $^{**}p < .01$. $^{***}p < .001$.

Table D3. Correlations for 335 words spelling-to-dictation: Letter accuracy and item characteristics.

	Written freq	Word length	Orthographic *N*-size	AoA[a]	IMG[b]	Regularity
Proportion letters correct	.156**	−.306***	.283***	−.132*	.046	.131*
Written frequency		−.172**	.074	−.338***	−.469***	−.026
Word length			−.604***	.201***	.035	−.257***
Orthographic *N*-size				−.170**	.003	.338***
Age of acquisition (AoA)					−.181**	−.173**
Imageability (IMG)						.089

Note: *N*-size = neighbourhood size; freq = frequency.
[a]AoA ratings only available for $n = 333$ items. [b]IMG ratings only available for $n = 277$ items.
$^{*}p < .05$. $^{**}p < .01$. $^{***}p < .001$.

Appendix E

Table E1. Means of item characteristics of matched word-lists for imageability.

	n	*M*	Written frequency	Word length	Orthographic *N*-size	AoA
Low imageability	31	304.61 (52.49)	1.60 (0.94)	5.55 (0.99)	1.65 (1.80)	6.38 (1.95)
Medium imageability	33	464.24 (47.79)	1.61 (0.79)	5.52 (1.33)	1.61 (1.94)	6.40 (2.20)
High imageability	33	603.82 (28.83)	1.56 (0.57)	5.45 (1.06)	1.58 (1.62)	6.38 (1.62)

Note: *N*-size = neighbourhood size; AoA = age of acquisition. Standard deviations in parentheses.

Table E2. Means of item characteristics of matched word-lists for orthographic neighbourhood size.

	n	*M*	Written frequency	Word length	AoA	Imageability
Low *N*-size	71	0.18 (0.39)	1.53 (0.79)	5.72 (1.02)	6.48 (2.20)	474.02 (141.65)
High *N*-size	77	3.74 (2.91)	1.61 (0.74)	5.32 (1.08)	6.40 (2.18)	443.54 (130.40)

Note: *N*-size = orthographic neighbourhood size; AoA = age of acquisition. Standard deviations in parentheses.

Table E3. Means of item characteristics of matched word-lists for (log) written frequency.

	n	*M*	Word length	Orthographic *N*-size	AoA	Imageability
Low written frequency	38	0.74 (0.28)	5.61 (1.37)	1.92 (2.91)	6.12 (1.71)	352.05 (112.14)
Medium written frequency	43	1.53 (0.24)	5.53 (1.01)	2.02 (2.71)	6.02 (1.83)	340.74 (130.74)
High written frequency	42	2.48 (0.51)	5.55 (1.13)	1.95 (2.14)	6.03 (1.57)	332.00 (128.63)

Note: *N*-size = neighbourhood size; AoA = age of acquisition. Standard deviations in parentheses.

Table E4. Means of item characteristics of matched word-lists for age of acquisition.

	n	*M*	Written frequency	Word Length	Orthographic *N*-size	Imageability
Low age of acquisition	37	4.36 (0.63)	1.74 (0.81)	5.38 (1.16)	1.57 (1.85)	375.70 (132.35)
Medium age of acquisition	52	6.13 (0.60)	1.42 (0.61)	5.63 (1.21)	1.69 (2.10)	405.83 (121.15)
High age of acquisition	38	8.95 (1.44)	1.43 (0.69)	5.74 (1.03)	1.61 (1.82)	329.08 (133.78)

Note: *N*-size = neighbourhood size. Standard deviations in parentheses.

Do reading and spelling share orthographic representations? Evidence from developmental dysgraphia

Christopher Hepner, Michael McCloskey and Brenda Rapp

ABSTRACT

Both spelling and reading depend on knowledge of the spellings of words. Despite this commonality, observed dissociations between spelling and reading in cases of acquired and developmental deficits suggest some degree of independence between the cognitive mechanisms involved in these skills. In this paper, we examine the relationship between spelling and reading in two children with developmental dysgraphia. For both children, we identified significant deficits in spelling that affected the processing of orthographic long-term memory representations of words. We then examined their reading skills for similar difficulties. Even with extensive testing, we found no evidence of a reading deficit for one of the children. We propose that there may be an underlying difficulty that specifically affects the learning of orthographic word representations for spelling. These results lead us to conclude that at least some components of lexical orthographic representation and processing develop with considerable independence in spelling and reading.

The relationship between perception and action has been investigated in a variety of domains (e.g., vision, spoken language processing). In the written language domain, the issues concern the relationship between reading (perception) and writing (action). Researchers have asked such questions as: Do we use the same knowledge about the spellings of words when we read and write? Does knowledge about how letters are written influence the ability to recognize letters or words? Do visual representations of letters play a role in writing? Questions of this sort have been asked not only with regard to adult expert users of written language, but also in the context of literacy acquisition. Improving our understanding of the relationship between learning to read and learning to write is important not only for enhancing theoretical knowledge concerning the structure and development of cognitive reading and writing mechanisms, but also for development of effective teaching methods and strategies for remediating deficits.

In the research reported here, we examine the relationship between reading and spelling in two children with developmental dysgraphia. As a foundation for discussion of these cases, we first provide an overview of the cognitive representations and processes making up the adult writing system. We then summarize evidence from adults regarding shared representations and processes in reading and spelling, as well as evidence from studies of developmental dyslexia and dysgraphia. It is important to note that the term *dysgraphia* has different senses in the literature, sometimes referring to impaired spelling and sometimes to deficits affecting the motor planning or production processes required for handwriting. In this article we focus on spelling, although we also consider and discuss handwriting. By *developmental dysgraphia* we mean difficulties in the acquisition of writing (spelling, handwriting, or both), despite adequate learning opportunities, and the absence of obvious neuropathology or gross sensory–motor dysfunction.

The adult reading and spelling systems

Figure 1a depicts the adult cognitive mechanisms for single-word reading. When a visual stimulus such as STEAK is presented, letter identification processes map the visual letter shapes onto abstract representations specifying the identity and ordering of letters

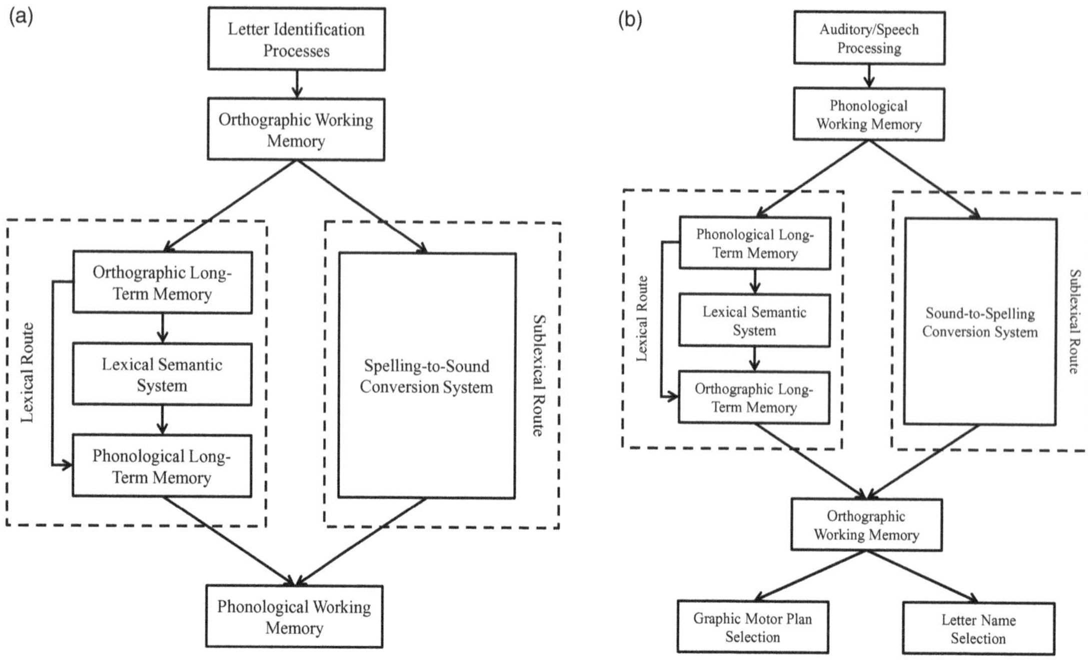

Figure 1. Depictions of the cognitive architectures for (a) reading and (b) spelling in adults.

(e.g., Caramazza & Hillis, 1990a, 1990b; McCloskey, Fischer-Baum, & Schubert, 2013; Rapp & Caramazza, 1989; Schubert & McCloskey, 2013). The letter identity/order representations are processed in *orthographic working memory* (O-WM; sometimes referred to as the graphemic buffer) pending subsequent operations.[1]

If the stimulus is a familiar word, the representation of letter identity and order will activate a stored lexical–orthographic representation in *orthographic long-term memory* (O-LTM; sometimes referred to as the orthographic input lexicon). The activated lexical representation in turn activates the meaning of the word in the *lexical semantic system*. If the word is to be read aloud, a lexical–phonological representation is activated in *phonological long-term memory* (P-LTM; also referred to as the phonological output lexicon). The phonological representation is activated from the lexical–semantic representation; according to many theorists, it can also be activated via direct links between O-LTM and P-LTM (e.g., Schwartz, Saffran, & Marin, 1980).

In addition to whole-word lexical representations, reading also draws upon knowledge about the relationships between sublexical orthographic units (letters and letter groups) and their corresponding sounds. These spelling–sound mappings (sometimes referred to as grapheme–phoneme mappings or correspondences) form the basis of the *spelling-to-sound conversion system* that takes as input the letter identity/order representation (e.g., P-L-O-F-E), and generates a plausible pronunciation (e.g., /ploʊf/). This sublexical reading process is critical for pronouncing unfamiliar letter strings (e.g., words not previously encountered or invented pseudowords). The sublexical process may also contribute to oral reading of familiar words, but is not adequate for consistently generating correct word-reading responses. Because most letters and letter groups have multiple alternative mappings to phonemes or phoneme sequences (e.g., EA may correspond to /iː/ or /ɛ/), the sublexical reading process generates pronunciations that, although plausible, may be incorrect (e.g., STEAK → /stiːk/). The likelihood of error is especially high for words that instantiate uncommon spelling-to-sound mappings (e.g., CHUTE, with the infrequent CH → /ʃ/ mapping).

As depicted in Figure 1b, the cognitive processes for spelling and writing are in many respects the converse of those implicated in reading. Orthographic production can be initiated by hearing words (e.g., taking notes in a lecture, spelling to dictation), from word meanings (e.g., generating a grocery list, writing a letter), or from seen objects (e.g., writing picture names). Consider the case of hearing a spoken word (e.g., /wʌns/). After auditory and phonological speech processing, the P-LTM store of familiar word sounds is addressed, followed by access to the lexical semantic system. Access to semantic representations forms the basis for the retrieval of the lexical orthographic representations in O-LTM that specify the letter identities and ordering constituting the word's spelling (e.g., O-N-C-E). In addition to the semantically mediated lexical route, a direct, non-semantic lexical route between P-LTM and O-LTM has been posited (Bub, Cancelliere, & Kertesz, 1985; Funnell, 1983; Sartori, Masterson, & Job, 1987; Schwartz et al., 1980). Parallel to reading, there is also a sublexical system, the *sound-to-spelling-conversion system*, which uses knowledge about the systematic relations between speech sounds and letters or letter groups. This sublexical spelling system generates phonologically plausible spellings for unfamiliar words. If a word has a (regular) spelling that consists of a few common sound–spelling correspondences, it will probably be spelled correctly via the sound-to-spelling conversion system, but if it contains uncommon correspondences or letters/letter groups with multiple possible spellings (e.g., /jɑt/), an incorrect spelling is likely to be generated (e.g., YOT instead of YACHT). (For more detailed reviews, see: Rapp & Fischer-Baum, 2015; Tainturier & Rapp, 2001).

Orthographic information generated by either the lexical or the sublexical system is then processed by O-WM. This information consists of symbolic letter representations and their order. O-WM maintains the activity of the representations and carries out the serial selection of the constituent letter identities for subsequent production. Orthographic knowledge can be expressed in a variety of formats (e.g., written spelling, oral spelling, typing, drawing with a toe in the sand). For written spelling, abstract, effector-independent motor plans of letter strokes are retrieved to direct the generation of effector-specific motor programmes that drive production of the written response. For oral spelling, the names of the letters must be selected and produced on the basis of the same abstract orthographic representations as those used for written spelling.

Shared representations and processes in reading and spelling? Evidence from adults

In the literature on adult orthographic processing, discussion of shared cognitive mechanisms for reading and spelling has focused largely on O-LTM representations, although a small amount of work has considered shared processes for O-WM (e.g., Caramazza, Capasso, & Miceli, 1996; Tainturier & Rapp, 2003; see Footnote 1), allograph selection (e.g., Rapp & Caramazza, 1997), and sound–spelling/spelling–sound conversion processes (e.g., Beauvois & Dérouesné, 1979, 1981). In this paper we also focus on the question of shared O-LTM representations and processes in reading and spelling.

It may seem intuitively plausible that when we encounter word spellings during reading, we form long-term memory representations that would be available for recognizing the word on subsequent encounters (reading) or for producing the spelling (writing). Empirical evidence bearing on this intuition of shared O-LTM representations comes from behavioural, cognitive neuropsychological, and neuroimaging studies. Several studies of neurotypical adults have reported evidence consistent with shared lexical orthographic representations. Monsell (1987) reported significant repetition priming in reading words that had been spelled earlier (without visual feedback). In addition, Holmes and Carruthers (1998) and Burt and Tate (2002) reported that words that individuals could not spell correctly also elicited slower or less accurate responses in reading tasks (see also Holmes & Davis, 2002; Holmes, Malone, & Redenbach, 2008). These findings are consistent with the proposal that reading and spelling share lexical orthographic representations in LTM. However, this interpretation has not gone unchallenged (e.g., Beauvois & Derouesne, 1979, 1981; Frith, 1978, 1980). For example, priming effects might arise not from shared representations for reading and spelling, but rather from episodic memories that are created in one task (e.g., spelling), which then influence performance on the other (e.g., reading). In terms of cross-task associations of performance speed or accuracy, one alternative account is that similarities across tasks are driven by some factor involved in both reading and spelling rather than by shared orthographic representations; another is that representations activated for reading trigger automatic "updates" of spelling representations, and vice versa.

In the cognitive neuropsychological literature, several cases have been reported of associated reading and spelling impairments that seem to originate in O-LTM (Behrmann & Bub, 1992; Coltheart &

Funnell, 1987; Philipose et al., 2007; Rapcsak & Beeson, 2004). However, the interpretation of these associations is uncertain because associated deficits could indicate either a shared process or, alternatively, damage that coincidentally affects neurally adjacent O-LTM components for reading and spelling. Furthermore, in addition to the associations, dissociations have been reported in which either reading or spelling is intact in the context of O-LTM impairment in the other modality (Hillis, Rapp, & Caramazza, 1999). Dissociations such as these are also subject to multiple interpretations as they could result from damage to distinct O-LTM memory components for reading and spelling, but could alternatively occur if lesions affect modality-specific access to a shared O-LTM system.

Possibly the strongest evidence of shared O-LTM processes and representations comes from neuroimaging studies probing whether reading and spelling recruit the same neural substrates for O-LTM. The small number of functional magnetic resonance imaging (fMRI) studies that have examined the neural substrates of both reading and spelling in the same individuals (Purcell, Napoliello, & Eden, 2011; Rapp & Dufor, 2011; Rapp & Lipka, 2011) have all found co-activation for the two tasks in the left mid-fusiform and inferior frontal gyri. Evidence that these areas are involved in O-LTM comes from Rapp and colleagues (Rapp & Dufor, 2011; Rapp & Lipka, 2011), who found both areas to be sensitive to the lexical frequency of the words that were read and spelled. Overlapping activation for reading and spelling is, nonetheless, consistent with the possibility of distinct O-LTM components for reading and spelling supported by different subpopulations of neurons within the region. Purcell, Jiang, and Eden (2017) challenged this interpretation using the neural adaptation approach, which is based on the assumption that repeated activation of a neural population leads to a decreasing neural response. Purcell et al. (2017) examined neural adaptation for words that were first spelled and then read, or first repeated and then read. They found neural adaptation in a left ventral fusiform area (visual word form area, VWFA) when words were spelled and then read, but not when they were repeated and then read.

In sum, while the preponderance of evidence from behavioural and neuroimaging studies of neurotypical adults favours the hypothesis of shared O-LTM for reading and spelling, the issue is certainly not resolved, as there is considerable room for alternative interpretations of the existing evidence. Furthermore, the findings from the adult system do not necessarily extend in a straightforward manner to the developing system. Conceivably, for example, O-LTM processes may initially develop independently for reading and spelling, becoming unified only later in the developmental trajectory.

Shared representations and processes in reading and spelling? Evidence from developmental dyslexia/dysgraphia

In research with typically developing children, a close relationship has been documented between reading and spelling skill levels, with Ehri (2000) reporting correlations of reading and spelling scores of .68–.86 across six studies involving first graders to adults. However, drawing conclusions about shared processes from these findings is problematic, given that there are many possible reasons for the strong correlations other than shared processes and representations. Similarly, in studies of developmental deficits, dysgraphia is very commonly found to co-occur with developmental dyslexia (Ehri, 2000; Greenberg, Ehri, & Perin, 1997). However, here too there could be many reasons for high co-occurrence rates, and, furthermore (as we discuss in more detail below), some cases of dissociations between developmental dyslexia and dysgraphia have also been reported.

In discussing specific patterns of developmental dysgraphia and dyslexia, it is useful to consider the distinction made by Coltheart (2015) between *proximal* and *distal* causes of developmental disorders. Proximal causes refer to abnormalities in the cognitive system mediating the skill of interest. In the case of developmental dysgraphia, for example, proximal causes are deficiencies in developing one or more components of the cognitive spelling/writing system (Figure 1b). Distal causes, often referred to as underlying causes, are the factors responsible for proximal deficits. Distal causes arise outside the cognitive system of interest and may include general cognitive dysfunctions (e.g., a phonological awareness deficit that impairs learning of sound–spelling correspondences) or external factors such as poor teaching (for further discussion, see McCloskey & Rapp, 2017).

Researchers studying proximal causes of developmental dysgraphia have reported several performance patterns that appear to reflect deficiencies in developing specific components of the spelling system (for a review of similar claims regarding developmental dyslexia, see Castles & Coltheart, 1993). In one such pattern, referred to as developmental surface dysgraphia, spelling of irregular words is impaired (with errors taking the form of phonologically plausible misspellings) but spelling of pseudowords/unfamiliar words is largely intact. This pattern, which is attributable to deficient development of O-LTM, has been reported in multiple languages, including English (Brunsdon, Coltheart, & Nickels, 2005; Coltheart, Masterson, Byng, Prior, & Riddoch, 1983; Goulandris & Snowling, 1991; Hanley & Gard, 1995; Hanley & Kay, 1992; Romani, Ward, & Olson, 1999; Seymour, 1986; Seymour & Evans, 1993; Temple, 1984, 1985), German (Bergmann & Wimmer, 2008; Cholewa, Mantey, Heber, & Hollweg, 2010), Italian (Angelelli, Judica, Spinelli, Zoccolotti, & Luzzatti, 2004; Angelelli, Marinelli, & Zoccolotti, 2010), and Greek (Douklias, Masterson, & Hanley, 2009). The complementary pattern, labelled developmental phonological dysgraphia, involves better spelling of words (including irregular words) than pseudowords, and is attributed to difficulty in developing the sound-to-spelling conversion system (Campbell & Butterworth, 1985; Funnell & Davison, 1989; Snowling, Goulandris, Bowlby, & Howell, 1986; Temple, 1986; Temple & Marshall, 1983). In addition, recent reports have described children with spelling difficulties suggesting selective impairment in the development of O-WM (Barisic, Kohnen, & Nickels, 2017; Gvion & Friedmann, 2010; Roncoli & Masterson, 2016; Yachini & Friedmann, 2010).

Cases such as these—of developmental deficits selectively affecting a specific processing component—provide precisely the type of opportunity needed to examine the relationship between spelling and reading during development. To our knowledge, however, only a very few studies have evaluated whether individuals show the same proximal deficit, affecting the same cognitive component, in both reading and spelling (e.g., Roncoli & Masterson, 2016; Sotiropoulos & Hanley, 2017), with these providing some evidence in support of shared O-WM and O-LTM systems in reading and spelling.

When considering *distal causes* of developmental dysgraphia (and dyslexia), it is key to keep in mind that, because written language is a recent human invention, there has not been enough evolutionary time to develop a genetic blueprint for neural networks that carry out written language processing. Developmental deficits in reading and spelling are, therefore, generally assumed to stem from underlying difficulties in evolutionarily older domains such as spoken language, vision, attention, and motor processes. A number of hypotheses have been proposed regarding the underlying causes of developmental dysgraphia, most of which have also been posited as underlying causes of developmental dyslexia. In this investigation, we examine phonological awareness and processing, motor processing, visual attention span, visual learning and memory, verbal learning and memory, letter order encoding and memory, and orthographic learning. A better understanding of the underlying deficits will allow us to evaluate the extent to which developmental reading and spelling deficits have common underlying causes. In turn, this will further our understanding of the complex trajectory involved in the acquisition of reading and spelling in normally developing individuals.

The current investigation

To make progress on the issue of whether developmental dysgraphia and dyslexia affect shared or separate cognitive representations and processes, we need detailed investigations that evaluate the integrity of specific components in both reading and spelling. In this article, we report on an investigation guided by the theoretical framework described above, involving two children with developmental dysgraphia. We first investigated proximal causes of the dysgraphias, identifying clear difficulties in the acquisition of O-LTM. Based on this understanding of the children's spelling deficits, we carried out a detailed examination of their reading skills to assess the possibility of shared O-LTM between reading and spelling. Finally, we considered a range of potential distal deficits to develop a more in-depth understanding of the genesis of the developmental dysgraphia in these cases.

Our results shed light on the proximal and distal causes of impaired spelling for both children. However, the most striking result from our study is the finding of a clear dissociation in one of the children between superior reading skills and impaired spelling. This finding leads us to conclude that at least some aspects of lexical orthographic representation and processing can develop independently in reading and spelling.

Case histories

P.J.T. is a right-handed Canadian boy who was enrolled in a French immersion programme for two years (kindergarten and first grade) and thereafter was enrolled in an English-language programme. He was 8 years 4 months old and had finished the second grade at the time of most of the testing carried out for this study (July 2015), although some additional testing was carried out until July 2017. When we began our testing with him, P.J.T. had attended an all-English programme for one full school year. We additionally report on testing administered by a clinical psychologist prior to our study, when P.J.T. was 6 years 11 months old. The clinical testing was initiated by the parents who had noticed that P.J.T. was having academic difficulties during his time in the French immersion programme. On the basis of that testing, a discrepancy between reading and spelling performance was reported, and P.J.T. was diagnosed with attention deficit hyperactivity disorder–combined type (ADHD–C).

A.K.R. is a right-handed American girl with a history of articulation delay related to motor planning difficulty that had resolved by the time of this investigation. She was 10 years 5 months old and enrolled in the fifth grade at the time most of the testing was carried out (November 2015), although some additional testing was carried out until March 2017. In addition, an evaluation was conducted by an occupational therapist in October 2015, and an assessment of general cognitive functions and academic achievement was carried out by her school in November 2015.

General cognitive function

General intelligence, spoken language, and academic achievement were evaluated with the following tests: Wechsler Intelligence Scale for Children (WISC; P.J.T.: Fourth Edition, WISC–IV; Wechsler, 2003; February 2014; A.K.R.: Fifth Edition, WISC–V; Wechsler, 2014; 25 September 2015); Peabody Picture Vocabulary Test (PPVT; P.J.T.: Fourth Edition, PPVT–4; Dunn & Dunn, 2007; February 2014; A.K.R.: Revised Edition, PPVT–R; Dunn & Dunn, 1981; 9 November 2015); Wechsler Individual Achievement Test–Third Edition (WIAT–III, Psychological Corporation, 2009; P.J.T.: February 2014; A.K.R.: 12 November 2015); and Expressive Vocabulary Test–Second Edition (EVT–2; Williams, 2007; P.J.T.: February 2014). Because some of these tests were administered in outside evaluations, there are some differences in the test versions and subtests administered to the two children.

WISC results (see Table 1) indicate very high cognitive ability levels for both children, with a General Ability Index of 160 (99th percentile) for P.J.T. and a Full Scale IQ of 123 (94th percentile) for A.K.R. Both P.J.T. and A.K.R. obtained high scores in Verbal Comprehension subtests (Similarities and Vocabulary), scoring below the 50th percentile only in Letter–Number Sequencing and Coding (P.J.T.) and Matrix Reasoning (A.K.R.).

Spoken language tests on the WISC and WIAT (Table 2) revealed high levels of functioning, consistent with school reports and our own observations. Also, on the PPVT, which evaluates comprehension of aurally presented words, both children scored at the 99th percentile with standard scores of 160. In addition, P.J.T. scored at the 95th percentile (standard score 125) on the EVT, a test of expressive word vocabulary.

The WIAT evaluates academic achievement, providing a useful overview of performance in basic skill areas. Scores for both P.J.T. and A.K.R. were well above average (and often very high) on most of the language, reading, and maths measures. Notably, the lowest scores were on the Spelling subtest, with both children scoring at the 23rd percentile. Reading subtest scores, in contrast, ranged from the 50th to the 99th percentile.

In summary, both children have very high intellectual capacity and excellent spoken language skills. Academic achievement ranged from average to far above

Table 1. Performance on the WISC subtests for P.J.T. and A.K.R.

		P.J.T.	A.K.R.
Verbal comprehension	Similarities	19 (99)	16 (98)
	Vocabulary	19 (99)	18 (99)
	Comprehension	15 (95)	—
Perceptual reasoning	Block Design	16 (98)	10 (50)
	Picture Concepts	19 (99)	—
	Matrix Reasoning	19 (99)	8 (25)
Working memory	Digit Span	13 (84)	15 (95)
	Letter–Number Sequencing	8 (25)	—
Processing speed	Coding	9 (37)	14 (91)
	Symbol Search	11 (63)	18 (99)
Other	Spatial Span Forward	14 (91)	—
	Spatial Span Backward	11 (63)	—
	Visual Puzzles	—	10 (50)
	Figure Weights	—	11 (63)

Note: Standard scores are reported with percentile ranks in parentheses. WISC = Wechsler Intelligence Scale for Children.

Table 2. Results from WIAT–III.

	P.J.T.	A.K.R.
Listening comprehension	—	132 (98)
Receptive vocabulary	—	122 (93)
Oral discourse comprehension	145 (99)	130 (98)
Reading comprehension	126 (96)	111 (77)
Math problem solving	125 (95)	127 (96)
Sentence composition	122 (93)	113 (81)
Sentence building	—	124 (95)
Sentence combining	—	100 (50)
Word reading	133 (99)	101 (53)
Pseudoword decoding	100 (50)	129 (97)
Spelling	89 (23)	89 (23)
Essay composition	—	159 (99)
Word count	—	147 (99)
Theme development and text organization	—	154 (99)
Grammar and mechanics	—	156 (99)
Numerical operations	111 (77)	122 (93)
Oral expression	—	155 (99)
Expressive vocabulary	—	135 (99)
Oral word fluency	—	139 (99)
Sentence repetition	—	157 (99)
Oral reading fluency	—	116 (86)
Oral reading accuracy	—	117 (87)
Oral reading rate	—	112 (79)
Math fluency: addition	—	101 (53)
Math fluency: subtraction	—	105 (63)
Math fluency: multiplication	—	94 (34)

Note: The table reports standard scores with percentiles in parentheses. WIAT–III: Wechsler Individual Achievement Test—3rd Edition.

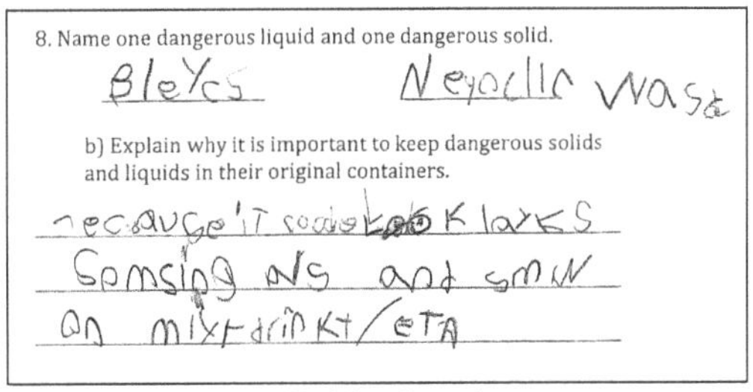

A. Writing Sample

Bleycs Neyoclir wasd

because it coode look layks
somsing als and smw
on miyt drinkt / eta

B. Transcription

Bleach Nuclear waste

because it could look like
something else and some
one might drink / eat

C. Intended Text

Figure 2. (a) P.J.T. writing sample. (b) Literal transcription. (c) Text P.J.T. intended to write.

average in all areas except spelling. These results confirm the impression of the parents, teachers, and the children themselves that spelling was an area of particular difficulty for both children, in striking contrast with their otherwise high levels of ability and achievement. More specifically, the results are consistent with the impression that the children's spelling difficulties are at odds with their reading abilities and interests, as exemplified by their extensive reading for pleasure. Figures 2 and 3 present writing samples from P.J.T. and A.K.R., respectively. The samples, produced shortly before our testing of each child (P.J.T.: age 8, A.K.R.: age 10), illustrate the difficulty in spelling experienced by these children despite their high level of intellectual ability and language skills.

Spelling: Proximal sources of impairment

For both children we carried out testing aimed at identifying the proximal cause(s) of their impaired spelling—that is, the specific components of the cognitive spelling system that had not developed adequately.

Written versus oral spelling

Deficits affecting central components of the spelling system—orthographic long-term memory, sound-to-spelling conversion, and orthographic working memory—should manifest in both written and oral spelling (see Figure 1b), whereas deficits at subsequent levels should affect output modalities selectively. For example, an impairment in handwriting processes should affect written but not oral spelling.

For both P.J.T. and A.K.R., performance was comparable on written and oral spelling tasks, pointing to a central locus (or loci) of impairment. Specifically, for P.J.T., 309 words from the Dolch (1948) word sets (words that children are expected to read by "sight" without sounding them out, at pre-primer through third-grade levels) were tested for written spelling and, in separate sessions, for oral spelling. He was 53% correct in written spelling (165/309) and 46% correct (141/309) in oral spelling, $\chi^2(1, N = 618) = 3.42$, $p > .05$. For A.K.R., both forms of the WRAT–3 (Wide Range Achievement Test, 3rd edition; Wilkinson, 1993) Spelling test were administered, one for written and one for oral spelling. She was 35% correct in written spelling (14/40) and 33% correct in oral spelling (13/40), $\chi^2 < 1$.

Direct copy transcoding

Given that comparable performance in written and oral spelling suggests that the children's spelling

A. Writing Sample

The local restrant with an unknow name got a very bad reivew today. Well trying to acomadate a custerms allergys the custormer was give a very bland plate. It was not clorful and delitful. In the custororms worts "(It) was more like a lage snak plate than a dinner." The cholclate coverd bannas at the end hardly made up for it. Plus the the custormor was tanted by the smelles of a s?in-ff of one of her favrote dishes wich she can not eat due to allergys.

B. Transcription

The local restaurant with an unknown name got a very bad review today. While trying to accommodate a customer's allergies the customer was given a very bland plate. It was not colorful and delightful. In the customer's words, "(It) was more like a large snack plate than a dinner." The chocolate covered bananas at the end hardly made up for it. Plus the customer was taunted by the smells of a sniff of one of her favorite dishes which she cannot eat due to allergies.

C. Intended Text

Figure 3. (a) A.K.R. writing sample. (b) Literal transcription (ignoring crossed-out letters and occasional use of upper-case in place of lower-case letter forms). (c) Text A.K.R. intended to write.

difficulties arise from central components of the spelling system, we would expect good performance in direct copy transcoding, a task in which words and pseudowords are presented in either upper or lower case, and the participant is asked to copy transcode them in the other case. This task can be performed without recruiting central spelling processes (although one cannot prevent participants from engaging these processes). Consistent with our expectation, P.J.T. was 100% correct in copy transcoding (20/20), and A.K.R. was 93% correct (25/27). A.K.R.'s two errors were letter transpositions: AFRAID → AFIARD and QUAINT → QUANIT.

Pseudoword spelling

For purposes of evaluating sublexical sound-to-spelling conversion processes, a pseudoword spelling-to-dictation task was administered to both P.J.T. and A.K.R. The Diagnostic Spelling Test–Nonwords (DiSTn; Kohnen, Colenbrander, Krajenbrink, & Nickels, 2013) consists of 74 pseudoword stimuli (e.g., YARSH) with a wide variety of phoneme–grapheme correspondences. Norms are available by grade level based on a sample of over 600 Australian children 6–14 years of age.

A.K.R. scored at the 46th percentile (raw score 46), suggesting adequate development of sublexical spelling processes. Examination of her pseudoword spelling responses supported this conclusion. According to the scoring criteria for the test, A.K.R. misspelled 28 of the 74 pseudowords; in other words, she failed to produce phonologically plausible spellings for these items. In assessing A.K.R.'s sublexical spelling ability it may be useful to consider that six of her responses, although not included among the correct spellings listed in the scoring criteria, are not grossly incorrect. In fact, they would be considered phonologically plausible if they were evaluated against possible English spellings for their component sounds (for a given syllable position) according to Hanna, Hanna, Hodges, and Rudorf (1966). This is a more lenient criterion that is sometimes used in scoring spelling (e.g., Bruck & Treiman, 1990; McCann & Besner, 1987; Rapp, Epstein, & Tainturier, 2002). Examples from A.K.R.'s responses include /zɛl/ → ZEL (cf. GEL), /kuːv/ → KOVE (cf. MOVE), and /ʃʌs/ → SHOUSS (cf. ROUGH). The remaining responses scored incorrect were rather subtle vowel errors (e.g., /lɛŋ/ → LANG), and four instances of /kw/ realized as QW rather than QU (e.g., /kwiːd/ → QWEED). The latter error suggests that A.K.R. has not learned the sound–spelling correspondence rule /kw/ → QU, but her sublexical spelling otherwise appears entirely adequate. This assessment is also supported by the observation that in spelling tasks with word stimuli A.K.R. typically produced plausible spellings even for long, polysyllabic words that were presumably unfamiliar to her (e.g., VICISSITUDE → VISISATTUDE, IRIDESCENCE → EARADESANCE).

P.J.T., in contrast to A.K.R., exhibited clear difficulties in pseudoword spelling, scoring at the 6th percentile on the DiSTn when tested with written responses (raw score 13), and at the 8th percentile (raw score 14) when the test was administered for oral spelling. Examination of his responses indicated deficient knowledge of sound-to-spelling correspondence rules. P.J.T. consistently produced incorrect mappings for /ʧ/, /ð/, /ʃ/, /θ/, and /kw/. For example, in 18 attempts to spell /θ/ and /ð/, he never produced TH, instead producing T 14 times, H twice, and S twice (e.g., /θɪf/ → TIF, /fleɪθ/ → FLAS). In addition, he consistently realized /ɝ/ as R (rather than ER, IR, or UR), yielding orthographically illegal spellings (e.g., /zɝn/ → ZRN). He had similar difficulties producing the highest probability mappings for /iː/ and /uː/, which were always realized by a single E or O, respectively, and never by EE, E_E, or OO. As these examples illustrate, P.J.T. had particular difficulty with sound–spelling correspondence rules in which phonemes are mapped to multiple letters (e.g., /θ/ → TH), although he also made occasional errors involving one-to-one phoneme–grapheme mappings.

Pseudoword spelling requires not only sound-to-spelling conversion processes, but also orthographic working memory: The spellings assembled by the sublexical process must be held in working memory while the processes required for generation of overt responses (e.g., handwriting processes) are carried out (see Figure 1). Accordingly, A.K.R.'s normal performance in pseudoword spelling suggests that her orthographic working memory is intact, whereas P.J.T.'s impaired pseudoword spelling raises the question of whether he may suffer from a deficient orthographic working memory in addition to underdeveloped sound-to-spelling conversion processes.

To obtain additional evidence concerning P.J.T.'s orthographic working memory we generated a new list of pseudowords. This list consisted of 40 one- and two-syllable pseudowords constructed to avoid as much as possible the sound–spelling mappings that proved problematic for P.J.T. in the DiSTn task (e.g., θ → TH). In this way, we hoped to evaluate P.J.T.'s orthographic working memory without complications introduced by his deficient knowledge of sound-to-spelling correspondences.

The list was administered twice, once for written and once for oral spelling. P.J.T. produced a phonologically plausible spelling for 73 of the 80 stimuli (91%). Two of his seven phonologically implausible responses (/ʤiːvɔk/ spelled GVOK twice) apparently stemmed from a sound–spelling conversion error often observed in children learning to spell, in which a letter name (in this case, /ʤiː/ for G) is used as the basis for mapping from sound to spelling (e.g., Treiman, 1993). Hence, P.J.T. made errors not readily attributable to deficient sound–spelling correspondence knowledge for only 5 of the 80 stimuli (e.g., /sæfzeɪm/ → SAFTAIZ, /tɔnɪd/ → TOND). This 6% error rate seems unexceptional for an 8-year-old spelling pseudowords. Consequently, we suggest that P.J.T.'s orthographic working memory is normal, and that his spelling errors do not reflect dysfunction in working memory processes.

Spelling irregular words

The Diagnostic Spelling Test–Irregular Words (DiSTi; Kohnen, Colenbrander, Krajenbrink, & Nickels, 2015) was administered to both P.J.T. and A.K.R. The DiSTi consists of 74 words with low-probability phoneme–grapheme mappings (e.g., BISCUIT). Accurate spelling of these words requires orthographic long-term memory (i.e., stored knowledge of whole-word spellings), because sublexical spelling processes will not reliably generate the correct spelling. A.K.R. was tested on the DiSTi for written spelling. For P.J.T., the test was split into even- and odd-numbered items, which were administered separately for written and oral spelling.

Both children performed well below average for their age and grade level (P.J.T.: raw score 6, 15th percentile; A.K.R.: raw score 23, 14th percentile). Their very high levels of performance on tests of auditory word comprehension (e.g., PPVT) rule out difficulties in phonological and semantic processing of the dictated stimulus words. Furthermore, we have presented evidence that their spelling difficulties do not arise from deficits in orthographic working memory or peripheral production processes (e.g., handwriting processes). Consequently, a deficiency in orthographic long-term memory is the most likely proximal cause of their difficulties in spelling irregular words. That is, both P.J.T. and A.K.R. show impairment in learning the spellings of words.

Evaluation of the children's spelling errors supports the conclusion of deficient lexical–orthographic knowledge. A.K.R.'s errors were examined on the 153 words she spelled from the DiSTi and the two forms of the WRAT-3 Spelling task. Her error rate on these words was 67% (103/153).[2] The vast majority of her errors (83/103, or 81%) were phonologically plausible misspellings (e.g., PURCHASE → PURCHES, BISCUIT → BISCKET). These errors may be interpreted by assuming that A.K.R. had not learned the spelling of the word and relied instead on her well-developed sublexical sound-to-spelling conversion processes. Most of the remaining errors involved letter omissions, transpositions, or insertions in long, low-frequency words (e.g., ENTHUSIASM → ENTHUSAM, OPPORTUNITY → OPPORTINY, CACOPHONY → CONCAFONY). These errors may reflect occasional (and unremarkable) difficulty in spelling long words sublexically, and/or partial knowledge of the word's spelling.

For P.J.T., we considered word stimuli from the WRAT-3, DiSTi, and Dolch Word tasks. Across these tasks, his error rate was 53% (354/672). Phonologically plausible misspellings (e.g., BOX → BOCS, RAIN → RANE) accounted for 60% of the errors (211/354). The phonologically plausible errors presumably represent instances in which P.J.T. had not learned the spelling of the word, but succeeded in spelling it sublexically using his sound-to-spelling correspondence knowledge. The remainder of his errors were implausible spellings. Most of these errors apparently reflected the deficient sublexical spelling processes evident in the pseudoword spelling tasks. For example, P.J.T. mapped /θ/ to T rather than TH in spelling TOGETHER as TEGETER and THINK as TINGK; he realized /ɝ/ as R in BIRD → BRD, UNDER → UNDR, and NEVER → NEVR; and he spelled /aʊ/ variously as O, U, AW, and AU in errors such as GROUND → GROND, ABOUT → ABUT, COW → CAW, and DOWN → DAUN.

P.J.T. also made errors that appeared to reflect partial learning of a word's spelling. Examples include ELEPHANT → ELAPINT, in which /f/ is mapped to P, and KNOW → KOW, in which /n/ is mapped to K. These mappings never occur in English words, and P.J.T. never produced the mappings in spelling pseudowords—for example, he always realized /f/ as F in pseudoword spelling tasks. Consequently, it is likely that the errors reflect partial knowledge of the spellings for ELEPHANT and KNOW. Partial lexical knowledge may also underlie a number of errors in which P.J.T. produced the correct letters but in the wrong order (e.g., MOTHER → MHTOER, THEY → THYE, BLUE → BULE). He almost never made letter transposition errors in pseudoword spelling, indicating that these errors in spelling words are unlikely to reflect deficient sublexical sound-to spelling conversion processes or orthographic working memory failures. Rather the ordering errors probably represent cases in which P.J.T. had learned the letters in a word's spelling, but had not entirely mastered the ordering.

Proximal sources of impairment: Conclusions

P.J.T. and A.K.R. are both significantly impaired in spelling. The results we have presented indicate that the spelling deficits do not originate in word comprehension, orthographic working memory, or peripheral production processes. For A.K.R., sublexical sound-to-spelling conversion processes are also normal, but for P.J.T. these processes are deficient. Finally, both children show clear impairment in orthographic long-term memory: With respect to stored knowledge of word spellings, P.J.T. and A.K.R. are well below the level expected given their ages and grade levels. Furthermore, the home-training results for P.J.T. (discussed in a later section) suggest continued difficulty in learning of word spellings. This deficiency in learning the spellings of words is especially striking in light of their very strong cognitive abilities and apparently excellent reading skills.

These conclusions raise two important sets of questions. The first concerns the relationship between spelling and reading in P.J.T. and A.K.R. If the same lexical–orthographic knowledge underlies both reading and spelling, we might expect the children to show orthographic long-term memory impairment in reading tasks; yet both P.J.T. and A.K.R. appear to be excellent readers. The second set of questions concerns distal causes of the children's spelling impairments: Why do P.J.T. and A.K.R. have difficulty learning the spellings of words, and why does P.J.T. also have difficulty acquiring knowledge of sound-to-spelling correspondences? We take up these questions in the following sections.

Reading

Sublexical reading processes were evaluated via pseudoword reading tasks, and lexical reading processes were assessed with several tasks involving word stimuli.

Reading pseudowords

Both P.J.T. and A.K.R. read aloud the 40 pseudowords on the Castles and Coltheart Reading Test 2 (CC2; Castles et al., 2009) and the 45 pseudowords making up the Word Attack subtest of the Woodcock Reading Mastery Test–Revised (WRMT–R; Woodcock, 1987). On both tasks A.K.R. scored slightly below the mean for her age and grade level, but within the average range (27th percentile on the CC2 pseudowords, and 37th percentile on the WRMT Word Attack subtest). Examination of her responses revealed that most of her errors were rather subtle (e.g., CEDGE → /kɛʤ/, in which she read C as /k/ despite the following E), and that she frequently read long, polysyllabic pseudowords correctly (e.g., SPOLTCHURB, HOPDALHUP). Note also that A.K.R. scored at the 97th percentile on the WIAT Pseudoword Decoding task. Hence, A.K.R.'s sublexical reading processes, like her sublexical spelling processes, appear to be adequate.

P.J.T.'s pseudoword reading performance was average to superior: He scored at the 47th percentile for the CC2 pseudowords, and at the 84th percentile on the WRMT Word Attack subtest. These results stand in clear contrast to his deficient performance (below the 10th percentile) on pseudoword spelling tasks. Examination of P.J.T.'s pseudoword reading performance revealed that he was usually able to perform accurate spelling-to-sound conversion even for the correspondences between single phonemes and multiple graphemes that proved so difficult for him in pseudoword spelling. For example, he successfully read the pseudowords ZOATH, BRINTH, MORSHAB, PHET, and PLEECH, despite his inability to produce TH, SH, PH, or CH correctly in spelling. P.J.T., then, evidenced strong sublexical reading skills despite his impairment in sublexical spelling processes.

Reading regular and irregular words

Both P.J.T. and A.K.R. read aloud the 40 regular and 40 irregular words on the CC2, and both children showed high levels of performance for both sets of words: P.J.T. scored at the 88th and 97th percentiles for regular and irregular words, respectively, and A.K.R. scored at the 98th and 87th percentiles. These results demonstrate very strong orthographic long-term memory representations and processes for reading in both children. That is, both P.J.T. and A.K.R. have strong stored knowledge of the orthographic forms of words, and can access this knowledge when reading. Their scores for irregular words are especially diagnostic, given that reliably accurate reading of irregular words can be accomplished only by accessing stored knowledge of the words in orthographic long-term memory.

Discriminating words from pseudohomophones

Additional evidence of strong lexical reading processes emerged from the Test of Orthographic Choice (Kohnen, Anandakumar, McArthur, & Castles, 2012). In this task, 30 word–pseudohomophone pairs (e.g., GLANCE–GLANSE) are presented, and the examinee is asked to select the real word in each pair. This task requires knowledge of the spellings of words, because the decisions cannot be made on the basis of the pronunciation of the word. Both P.J.T. and A.K.R. showed excellent performance, with percentile ranks of 91 and 85, respectively.

Defining homophones

In this task P.J.T. and A.K.R. were asked to provide definitions for homophones presented visually (e.g., MANE, PEACE). A.K.R. was tested with 46 homophones, and P.J.T. with 30. Both children showed excellent performance: 45/46 (98%) for A.K.R., and 26/30 (87%) for P.J.T. In a separate homophone discrimination task, P.J.T. was asked to define paired homophones (e.g., PLANE and PLAIN) and indicate which definition went with each spelling. He defined 29/30 (97%) of the homophones correctly and matched each of those definitions to the correct spelling. Like the word–pseudohomophone discrimination task, the homophone definition task requires knowledge of the spellings of words. For example, to give the correct definition for PEACE, one must be able to distinguish this word from PIECE, and this distinction can only be made via knowledge stored in orthographic long-term memory. The children's definitions demonstrated not only their strong lexical–orthographic knowledge, but also their exceptional intellectual ability. For instance, P.J.T. defined BEE as "the insect that most people are afraid of that stings but also makes honey", and A.K.R. defined WRITE as "using an agreed on set of symbols to create messages that others can understand".

Reading migratable words

The Letter Position Test (Kohnen, Marinus, et al., 2012) was administered to both P.J.T. and A.K.R. Stimuli are 30 word pairs in which the two words in each pair are anagrams (e.g., LOTS–LOST, BOLT–BLOT, THERE–THREE). The words are presented one at a time for reading aloud, with the first 30 trials consisting of one word from each pair, and the second 30 trials including the remaining word from each pair. High rates of letter migration errors (e.g., reading LOTS as LOST) are taken to suggest difficulty in perceiving or encoding letter order. Errors are categorized as migration errors, other word errors, or other errors.

Results are presented in Table 3. P.J.T. clearly had no difficulty with the migratable words, scoring at the 95th percentile for overall accuracy and making very few letter migration errors. A.K.R.'s performance was in the low-average range, with accuracy at the 27th percentile and migration errors at the 21st percentile. She made seven letter migration errors (e.g., WARP → WRAP), whereas P.J.T. (who is two years younger) produced only two. Although A.K.R.'s performance was not severely impaired, these results raise the possibility of a mild deficit in encoding or retaining the ordering of letters. This test was administered for a second time to A.K.R. in March 2017 to determine whether the difficulty with migratable words was reliable; these results are also reported in Table 3 and indicate a continued, consistent difficulty with migratable word reading.

Reading: Conclusions

Whereas P.J.T. demonstrated clear lexical (orthographic long-term memory) and sublexical deficits in spelling, we were not able to find any evidence of lexical or sublexical reading difficulties. His performance was well above average in reading regular words, irregular words, migratable words, and pseudowords (the only exception being an average score on one of the two pseudoword reading tasks). In addition, he showed excellent performance in defining homophones and distinguishing homophones from pseudohomophones. We conclude that P.J.T. shows a striking dissociation between significantly impaired spelling and very strong reading ability.

A.K.R. also performed very well on most of the reading tasks, including reading regular and irregular words, distinguishing homophones from pseudohomophones, and defining homophones. Her performance on pseudoword reading tasks was more variable, ranging from low average to superior, suggesting little if any deficiency in sublexical reading processes. However, a potential reading deficiency is indicated by her frequent letter migration errors (e.g., FILES → "flies") on the Letter Position Test. While her performance at the 21st percentile does not indicate a severe impairment, it is striking in the context of her otherwise high levels of word reading. This result raised the possibility of impairment in encoding or retaining letter order information. In discussing distal sources of impairment in the following section, we report some additional relevant evidence.

Spelling: Distal sources of impairment

We next explore possible distal (underlying) causes of the developmental spelling deficiencies evidenced by P.J.T. and A.K.R. Specifically, we consider potential deficits in phonological processing, motor skills, visual attention span, learning and memory (visual and

Table 3. Results from the Letter Position Test.

	P.J.T.			A.K.R.			A.K.R. retest		
Errors	Score	Percentile	*z*	Score	Percentile	*z*	Score	Percentile	*z*
Total errors	5	95	1.64	11	27	−0.60	7	30	−0.54
Migration errors	2	92	1.43	7	21	−0.80	6	21	−0.82
Word errors	1	86	1.08	3	27	−0.60	1	41	−0.23
Other errors	2	66	0.41	1	27	−0.60	0	44	−0.16

Note: Letter Position Test: Kohnen, Marinus, et al. (2012).

verbal), letter order representation, and orthographic learning.

Phonological processing

Deficits in phonological awareness and/or phonological processing are widely thought to be prominent underlying causes of developmental dyslexia (e.g., Bradley & Bryant, 1978, 1983; Bruck, 1993; Liberman, 1973; Stanovich, 1988; Wagner & Torgesen, 1987), and many theorists have suggested that phonological deficits are also implicated in developmental dysgraphia (e.g., Campbell & Butterworth, 1985; Snowling et al., 1986; but see Castles & Coltheart, 2004). For P.J.T. and A.K.R. the possibility of phonological impairment was assessed with the Comprehensive Test of Phonological Processing (CTOPP; P.J.T.: CTOPP; Wagner, Torgesen, & Rashotte, 1999; A.K.R.: Second Edition, CTOPP-2; Wagner, Torgesen, Rashotte, & Pearson, 2013). The CTOPP includes multiple tasks probing phonological awareness, phonological memory, and other aspects of phonological processing. The results, presented in Table 4, indicate normal levels of performance for both children. Therefore, despite the fact that impaired phonological processing/awareness is the most widely held and entrenched hypothesis regarding underlying causes of developmental dyslexia and dysgraphia, we find no evidence of phonological deficits in P.J.T. or A.K.R.

Handwriting and motor skills

Both families expressed concern about the children's poor and effortful handwriting. The writing samples in Figures 2 and 3 illustrate that both children's handwriting is often unclear. Our observations indicated that P.J.T. had especial difficulty and experienced considerable frustration with handwriting. However, both

Table 4. Performance of P.J.T. and A.K.R. on the Comprehensive Test of Phonological Processing.

	P.J.T.		A.K.R.	
Composite measure	Score	Percentile	Score	Percentile
Phonological awareness	105	63	112	79
Phonological memory	113	81	112	79
Rapid naming (symbolic)	104	61	106	65
Alternative phonological awareness	—	—	118	89
Alternative rapid naming (non-symbolic)	98	45	97	42

Note: Standard scores and percentiles are reported.

children showed normal performance on tests probing the general motor skills required for writing. On the Visual–Motor Integration (VMI) Motor Coordination Test (Beery & Beery, 2010), which assesses fine motor control in drawing geometric figures, P.J.T. achieved a standard score of 103, placing him in the 58th percentile. On the Fine Motor Precision, Fine Motor Integration, and Manual Dexterity subtests of the Bruininks–Oseretsky Test of Motor Proficiency (Bruininks & Bruininks, 2005), A.K.R.'s scaled scores were 22, 15, and 20 respectively, all in the average to above-average range. Also, on the Test of Handwriting Skills–Revised (Milone, 2007), all of her skill scores were average or better, and her overall standard score was 115.

Also relevant is that both P.J.T. and A.K.R. showed comparable spelling impairment in written and oral spelling tasks, suggesting that handwriting difficulties were not playing a significant role in their spelling performance. Conceivably, struggles with handwriting could have contributed to difficulty in learning the spellings of words, especially for P.J.T., who expended much more effort with handwriting, and experienced much more frustration, than A.K.R. The need to focus on mechanical aspects of writing could perhaps have reduced the amount of attention available for learning to spell. Nevertheless, it seems unlikely that handwriting difficulties can entirely account for the spelling deficiency in either P.J.T. or A.K.R.

Visual attention span

Valdois and colleagues (Ans, Carbonnel, & Valdois, 1998; Bosse, Tainturier, & Valdois, 2007; Bosse & Valdois, 2009; Valdois, 1996; Valdois et al., 2003) have proposed that reduced visual attention span is the underlying cause in some cases of developmental dyslexia. According to their argument, difficulty in processing multiple letters in parallel impairs the ability to learn the orthographic forms of words, as well as the ability to recognize words rapidly during reading. To the extent that reduced visual attention span impairs orthographic learning, one might expect visual attention span deficiencies to affect the development of spelling as well. Accordingly, we evaluated visual attention span in P.J.T. and A.K.R. via two tasks developed by Valdois et al. (2003; see also Bosse & Valdois, 2009). The task of principal interest was a global report task, in which strings of five consonants are presented briefly (200 ms), and the participant is asked to report as many of the letters as possible, in any order. This task requires distribution of visual attention across multiple letters. The second task was a letter identification control task designed to assess whether weak performance in global report could be due to deficient processing of individual letters. Single letters are presented at one of five exposure durations ranging from 33–101 ms, and the participant is asked to name each letter. Bosse and Valdois (2009) report control data from French children in Grades 1, 3, and 5.

Both P.J.T. and A.K.R. showed entirely normal performance on both the letter identification and global report tasks. In letter identification, their scores were 142 (P.J.T.) and 150 (A.K.R.), which are well above average relative to the Bosse and Valdois (2009) control children. On the global report task P.J.T. reported 76% of the letters correctly, and was entirely correct on 20% of the strings. On both measures his performance fell between the means for Grade 1 and Grade 3 (Bosse & Valdois, 2009), consistent with his second-grade placement. A.K.R. correctly reported 98% of the letters and 90% of the whole strings, well above average for her grade level. We conclude that reduced visual attention span is not a distal cause of the spelling deficiency for either P.J.T. or A.K.R.

Encoding and representing letter order

Romani et al. (1999) proposed that an impairment in processing letter order is the distal cause in some cases of developmental surface dysgraphia. As discussed above, P.J.T.'s spelling errors included some letter transpositions (e.g., BLUE → BULE), although he evidenced no difficulty with letter order in reading. A.K.R. did not make large numbers of letter transposition errors in spelling, but in reading migratable words she made letter migration errors at a higher than normal rate (e.g., reading WARP as WRAP).

Romani et al. (1999) specifically proposed a deficit in the learning and recall of letter order information. We were not able to examine these specific skills with P.J.T. and A.K.R., although we did briefly examine their perception of letter order in a letter string reading task. P.J.T. and A.K.R. were presented with 12 strings of 12 consonants each and were asked to name the consonants in order. A.K.R. read 99.3% of the letters correctly (143/144), and P.J.T. was correct on 98.6% (142/144). Neither child made any letter order errors. As an informal basis for comparison, a college student with a letter order encoding deficit tested in our lab read correctly only 83% of the letters in 12-letter strings, making frequent letter transpositions.

These results do not rule out some forms of letter order impairment (e.g., selective impairment in retaining information about letter order in orthographic long-term memory). However, the absence of letter order errors in reading aloud long consonant strings does suggest that neither child is significantly impaired in the perception of letter order.

Visual and verbal learning and memory

Deficits affecting O-LTM in spelling could result from an underlying deficit in learning and long-term retention of verbal and/or visual information. These possibilities were assessed with three tests.

WRMT–R Visual–Auditory Learning Task

The Visual-Auditory Learning Task (Woodcock, 1987) assesses short-term learning of associations between written symbols and spoken words. The participant is shown a small set of symbols and is told that each symbol corresponds to a particular word or morpheme (e.g., a triangle inside a circle = BOB, and a small circle on top of a big circle = ON). The participant is then shown strings made up of the symbols and is asked to "read" them as phrases or sentences. This process repeats, adding a few more symbols with each iteration until there are a total of 28 symbols to be remembered. Both P.J.T. and A.K.R. showed excellent performance, scoring at the 97th and 71st percentiles, respectively.

Children's Memory Scale

P.J.T.'s visual and verbal short-term learning and memory were also evaluated with the Children's Memory Scale (CMS; Cohen, 1997). Visual tests include dot locations and faces, and verbal tests include stories and word pairs. The delayed conditions evaluate retention after 30 minutes. P.J.T. performed above the 75th percentile on all subtests (see Table 5).

Visual learning task (Gascoigne et al., 2014)

Because the orthographic learning required for skilled reading and spelling involves memory over a longer time scale than that evaluated by either the WRMT

Table 5. P.J.T.'s performance on the CMS.

	Index score	Percentile rank
Visual immediate	112	79
Visual delayed	115	84
Verbal immediate	137	99
Verbal delayed	137	99
General memory index	136	99
Learning index	125	95
Delayed recognition	115	84

Note: CMS = Children's Memory Scale.

or the CMS, we administered a visual learning task from Gascoigne et al. (2014) that included assessment of learning following a one-week delay. The task was based on a spatial memory task from Hepworth and Smith (2002), and evaluated retention after 30 min (short delay) and 7 days (long delay).

The to-be-learned stimuli consist of 10 visual designs that occupy specific positions within a 6×4 grid. In the initial learning phase, the participant views the designs in the grid. Then an empty grid is presented with the 10 designs off to one side, and the participant is asked to drag and drop each design into the appropriate grid location. The study/test process is then repeated until perfect performance is achieved on two consecutive learning trials, up to a maximum of 12 trials. Recall is then tested (using the same procedure as that in the learning phase) at short (30-min) and long (7-day) delays; the 7-day assessment also includes a recognition test. Results are reported in Table 6. No data were recorded for P.J.T.'s learning and short-delay recall phases due to accidental premature closure of the online program (although his mother estimates that three or four learning trials were required to reach the learning criterion). Both P.J.T. and A.K.R. show normal performance on all measures (trials needed for initial learning and memory at all delays).

Orthographic learning

In P.J.T.'s case, given the lack of evidence for the distal deficits that were examined, we considered the possibility of a specific impairment of lexical orthographic learning (Hanley, Hastie, & Kay, 1992). To examine this possibility, we developed a home training programme for P.J.T. in which his mother worked with him to help him learn word spellings. The programme was principally aimed at remediation, but also allowed us to assess informally the extent to which P.J.T. continued to struggle in learning to spell words. Training stimuli were 76 words from the Dolch List (Dolch, 1948) that P.J.T. had spelled incorrectly in both written and oral spelling. It is important to point out that these are all words that P.J.T. can easily read. Training sessions were carried out several days per week. For the first session, 6 of the 76 training stimuli were selected as the initial training set. In each training session, training words were presented for writing to dictation. If P.J.T. spelled a word incorrectly, he copied it three times and then was asked to spell it to dictation again. A training word that was spelled correctly on the first attempt in three consecutive training sessions was moved to a "learned" set, and a new word was added to the training set. Three words from the learned set were retested in each training session. When a learned word was correct at retest, it remained in the learned set; however, if it was spelled incorrectly the word was returned to the training set and underwent the training process again. Three to five words were trained on each session.

Over a period of 15 months (82 training sessions) P.J.T. reached the learning criterion (correct spelling in three consecutive sessions) for 68 of the 76 training words. He took an average of 4.8 training sessions to learn the spelling of a word. However, some words required many more sessions. For example, BLUE,

Table 6. Performance of P.J.T. and A.K.R. on the Gascoigne et al. (2014) visual learning task.

	P.J.T.		Controls (*N* = 12)		A.K.R.		Controls (*N* = 8)	
	M	%	*M*	%	*M*	%	*M*	%
Age	9.8		10.1 (0.8)		11.4		10.5 (0.4)	
Learning trials	—		8.3 (2.6)		8		8.7 (2.8)	
Short-delay recall	—			95 (8)		100		96 (8)
Long-delay recall		60		50 (36)		50		35 (31)
Long-delay recognition (hits/false alarms)	3/1		2.9 (1.6)/2.0 (1.8)		4/1		2.6 (1.7)/2.4 (1.7)	

Note: The table shows means for controls; standard deviations in parentheses.

PLEASE, and BETTER each required more than 12 sessions to reach the learning criterion. Furthermore, 17 of the 68 words that reached criterion were subsequently misspelled during retesting.

The following examples illustrate the progression of training and retraining. The spellings shown are those P.J.T. produced when the training word was first tested in each session.

- "blue": BULE × 2 → BULY → BULE → BLUE × 3 → BULE × 2 → BLUE × 4
- "floor": FLORE → FLOR → FLUR → FLOUR → FOORE → FLOOR × 5 → FOOR → FLOOR × 4
- "brown": BROWN → BROMN → BRON → BRAWN → BROWN → BROUN → BRAWN → BROWN × 4
- "does": DUZE → DOSE × 6 → DOES × 4 → DOSE × 3 → DOES × 4 → DOSE → DOES × 2

To formally assess training effects, a spelling to dictation task was administered with 37 trained and 37 untrained control words matched for length, frequency, and phoneme–grapheme mapping probability. P.J.T.'s accuracy on the trained words increased from 64.9% on the first training attempt to 75.7% after training, a difference that was not statistically significant, $\chi^2(1, N = 74) = 1.03$, $p = .31$. Further, the accuracy on the trained words was not statistically different from the accuracy on the matched untrained words (62.2%), $\chi^2(1, N = 74) = 1.58$, $p = .21$. Similar results were observed when we scored P.J.T.'s spelling responses in terms of letter accuracy: Accuracy on trained words increased by an average of 4.3% from pre- to post-training (89.8% to 94.0%), $t(36) = 1.39$, $p = .17$, and post-training letter accuracy on trained words did not differ statistically from accuracy on untrained words (90.5%), $t(36) = 1.09$, $p = .28$.

The very limited improvement in P.J.T.'s spelling accuracy for trained words shows a very striking level of difficulty with orthographic learning. Although we do not have the necessary control data to establish that P.J.T.'s learning performance is impaired, the results seem at odds with his strong learning and memory abilities, and especially with his superior learning of the lexical orthographic knowledge required for reading. Hence, the results suggest that P.J.T. continues to experience significant difficulty in acquiring the lexical orthographic knowledge necessary for successful spelling of words.

Probing orthographic word knowledge

With the goal of developing a better understanding of the difficulties P.J.T. faces in learning lexical orthographic representations, we administered a spelling-probe task in which words were dictated, and P.J.T. was asked whether specific letters were present in the spellings of the words. This task tests knowledge about the letter identities in a word's spelling independent of knowledge about letter order. In studies of acquired dysgraphia, spelling-probe performance has been shown to generally mirror spelling performance (Rapp & Kong, 2002). Furthermore, the spelling-probe task has been shown to recruit the same neural network as that activated by writing (Rapp & Dufor, 2011). Given P.J.T.'s frustration with producing written or oral spelling, we hoped that this task would provide a less stressful means of collecting detailed and targeted spelling data.

We tested P.J.T. in two probe conditions, both of which involved asking, on each trial, about two letters. In the dual-letter condition a word was dictated, and P.J.T. was asked, for each of the two letters, whether the letter was present in the word—for example, the word TEN was dictated, followed by the questions, "Is there a T in TEN?", and "Is there an N?". In the repeated-letter condition the same letter was queried twice—for example, dictated stimulus DID with questions "Is there a D in DID?", and (contingent upon a "yes" response) "Is there another D?".

Stimuli were taken from the pool of words that P.J.T. had already spelled in prior testing. For the repeated-letter condition we constructed sets of four words: one with a repeated letter (e.g., DID), two controls with a single instance of the letter (DAY and HAD), and one foil that did not contain the letter (HIM). The words in each set were matched in length and lexical frequency. The first and second control words included the probed letter in the same positions as the first and second occurrences of that letter in the repeated letter word. For the dual-letter condition the four-word sets consisted of one word with both probed letters (e.g., TEN for probe letters T and N), two controls with one of the letters (TOP and RAN), and a foil with neither letter (BOX). We created 15 sets of 4 items for each condition, and randomized the ordering of items within conditions.

To allow for meaningful comparisons between letter-probe and spelling results, we scored P.J.T.'s prior spellings of the probed words as if the probe questions had been answered on the basis of those spellings. For example, in the repeated-letter condition the word AGAIN was presented with the probe letter A. P.J.T. had previously spelled AGAIN as AGGANE and AGEN. For the first probe question ("AGAIN, is there an A in AGAIN?") the corresponding scores for both prior spellings would be 1 (i.e., correct), because both AGGANE and AGEN include an A. For the second probe question ("Is there another A?"), AGGANE was scored 1 because it has two As, but AGEN, which includes only one A, was scored 0.

Collapsing across conditions and probe questions (first and second), P.J.T.'s accuracy in the letter probe task was almost identical to his spelling accuracy. Probe-task accuracy was 90.6% (203/224), compared to 89.3% (393/440) for prior spelling responses scored for comparability with probe responses, $\chi^2(1, N = 664) = 0.15$, $p = .70$.

In both repeated and dual-probe conditions, the control words showed lower accuracy for letters occurring later in the word: Probe-task accuracy decreased from 100% (30/30) for the earlier letter (or instance of a repeated letter) to 80% (24/30) for the later letter ($p = .024$, Fisher's exact test). For spelling, the accuracy difference between earlier (89.3%) and later (74.1%) letters was marginally significant, $\chi^2(1, N = 114) = 3.40$, $p = .065$.

In dual-letter words (i.e., words containing both of the probed letters), the decrease in accuracy from the earlier to the later letter was similar to that observed for the control words (100% to 80% in the letter-probe task, 93.5% to 83.9% for spelling). Probably as a result of the small sample sizes (15 observations per cell for the letter-probe task, 31 per cell for spelling), these differences did not reach significance [probe task, $p = .22$, Fisher's exact test; spelling, $\chi^2(1, N = 62) = 0.64$, $p = .42$].

For repeated-letter words (e.g., DID) the accuracy decrease between the questions probing the first and second occurrences of the letter was substantially larger and highly reliable. In the letter probe task, P.J.T.'s accuracy decreased from 100% (15/15) on the first probe to 53.3% (8/15) on the second; $p = .006$, Fisher's exact test. His spelling performance was nearly identical, dropping from 96.7% correct (29/30) on the first instance of the letter to 53.3% (16/30) on the second instance ($p < .001$, Fisher's exact test).

These results support several conclusions. First, the strong similarity between P.J.T.'s spelling-probe and written spelling performance suggests that spelling-probe task is a viable alternative to traditional spelling tasks, and one that may provide a less stressful means for evaluating spelling representations and processes. Second, P.J.T.'s poorer performance on later than earlier letters in a word suggests that his difficulty in learning the letter identities making up the spelling of a word is affected by their position in the word. This conclusion is confirmed by the results shown in Figure 4, which depicts accuracy by normalized position (as in Wing & Baddeley, 1980) for P.J.T.'s spelling data. The position effects raise a number of questions that could be investigated in future work. Finally, P.J.T.'s surprising difficulty with repeated letters suggests that he may have some specific difficulty in learning or processing representations involving multiple tokens of the same abstract letter identity. However, additional testing would be required to clarify the nature of the difficulty.

General discussion

We have reported on an investigation of two children with developmental dysgraphia, P.J.T. and A.K.R. The aims of the study were to identify causes of the children's spelling impairments and to examine the relationship between their spelling and reading. The design, selection of tasks, and interpretation of results were guided by a theoretical framework specifying the representations and processes involved in adult spelling and reading. We first evaluated a number of potential proximal causes of the spelling impairments—that is, potential deficiencies within the spelling system. This evaluation identified clear

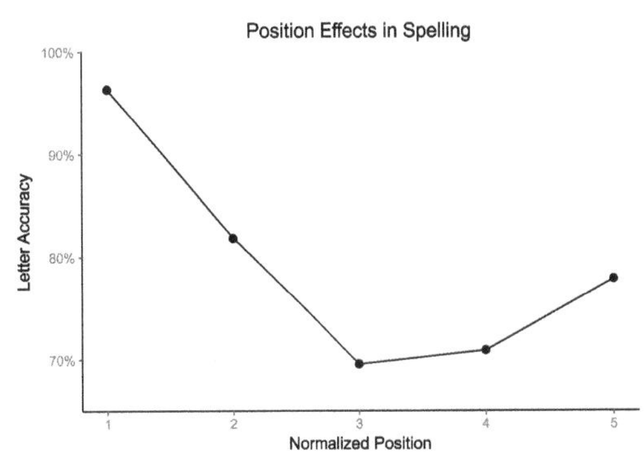

Figure 4. Accuracy by normalized position in P.J.T.'s spelling data.

and significant deficits in orthographic long-term memory in both children, as well as an additional impairment in the sound-to-spelling conversion system in P.J.T. Based on these findings, we then examined orthographic long-term memory and sub-lexical spelling-to-sound conversion processes in reading. We found no evidence of any reading impairment for P.J.T., indicating a striking dissociation between impaired spelling and superior reading. For A.K.R. we found evidence of mild difficulty with letter order in reading, revealed by errors in reading migratable words (e.g., reading TRIED as TIRED). Whether this letter order difficulty is related to A.K.R.'s spelling impairment is, however, uncertain, especially given that letter order errors were not prominent in her misspellings.

Finally, we explored potential distal deficits that could have led to the children's proximal deficits within the spelling system. We considered phonological processing and awareness, motor skills, visual attention span, encoding and representing letter order, and visual and verbal learning and memory. Neither child exhibited distal deficits that could clearly account for their difficulty in learning word spellings or (in the case of P.J.T.) sound-to-spelling conversion. A.K.R.'s difficulty with migratable words in reading may indicate an underlying difficulty with letter order that affects both reading and spelling. Conceivably, the letter order difficulty could reflect a more general underlying deficit in sequence processing. However, based on the limited testing results we are not able to reach firm conclusions regarding the distal cause of her difficulty in reading migratable words, nor about whether this distal cause would also explain some of her difficulties in spelling.

Distal causes for developmental dysgraphia

Although we evaluated P.J.T. and A.K.R. for the deficits most commonly proposed as distal causes of developmental dysgraphia (e.g., phonological processing deficit, impaired visual attention span), we failed to find distal deficits that would account for the spelling impairment in either child. This outcome allows several possible interpretations. First, and most obvious, our testing clearly did not examine every cognitive process that could conceivably contribute to acquisition of orthographic long-term memory representations (or, for P.J.T., sound–spelling correspondence knowledge). Hence, the distal deficits in P.J.T. and A.K.R. may affect cognitive processes that we did not examine.

A second possibility is that the distal deficits in P.J.T. and A.K.R. lay in processes that were deficient at an earlier period, but that have now "caught up" in their development and are functioning normally. On this account, the earlier distal deficiencies delayed the acquisition of spelling knowledge, with effects on spelling performance that were clearly detectable in our study. However, the distal deficiencies could not themselves be detected, because they had resolved by the time of our study. For example, for P.J.T. one might consider whether his early literacy experiences in the French immersion programme could have delayed his acquisition of English spelling. This possibility cannot be ruled out entirely, although we note that the French programme clearly did not prevent him from attaining a high degree of proficiency in English reading. More generally, we cannot exclude for either child the possibility of an earlier distal deficit that had resolved by the time of our testing, but at least for P.J.T. this account seems rather implausible, given his continuing struggle to learn spellings in the home training programme.

A final possibility, and perhaps the most interesting one, is that the underlying cause of the spelling impairment in P.J.T. and/or A.K.R. is not a deficiency in some general cognitive function (e.g., visual attention span), but rather a highly selective deficit that affects only the acquisition of orthographic knowledge and perhaps (at least for P.J.T.) only the orthographic knowledge required for spelling. Given such a deficit we would not expect to see difficulty in tasks probing more general cognitive processes. In support of the plausibility of a selective deficit in orthographic learning is the notion that although spelling and reading must rely on evolutionarily older underlying skills, they cannot be reduced to these skills. In other words, something new must be learned when literacy is acquired. This new learning may involve tuning evolutionarily older processes and representations in ways that are specifically appropriate for written language processing and creating connections that are needed to support orthographic knowledge and processing. It is conceivable that the specific type of learning that is required to tune and interconnect brain areas is disrupted in certain individuals while the underlying skills themselves are intact.

Further research and theory development will be important for advancing our understanding of distal causes in developmental dysgraphia (and dyslexia). For example, advances in theory concerning the cognitive processes implicated in acquiring lexical orthographic representations would be helpful for systematically defining the set of general cognitive deficits that could potentially act as distal causes of developmental dysgraphia, and for evaluating the plausibility of hypotheses positing highly specific orthographic learning deficits.

Implications of P.J.T.'s spelling–reading dissociation

The most striking result from the present study is the dramatic dissociation between P.J.T.'s impaired orthographic long-term memory processes in spelling, and superior orthographic long-term memory processes in reading. This dissociation reveals that at least certain aspects of the system for processing lexical orthographic representations are not shared between reading and spelling.

There are two general classes of interpretation for this dissociation. The first posits distinct sets of lexical orthographic representations for reading and spelling, whereas the second assumes distinct processes for activation/retrieval of information from a single orthographic long-term memory system shared between reading and spelling. We discuss each of these in turn and suggest a specific interpretation that builds on theoretical proposals in the domain of spoken word production.

In the adult neuropsychological literature, dissociations in orthographic long-term memory between reading and spelling are often described as surface dyslexia without surface dysgraphia, and vice versa (Behrmann & Bub, 1992; Coltheart & Funnell, 1987). To account for these findings, some researchers have posited different orthographic long-term memory stores for reading and spelling (often referred to as the orthographic input and output lexicons, respectively; see, e.g., Allport & Funnell, 1981; Caramazza, Miceli, Villa, & Romani, 1987; Hanley & McDonnell, 1997; Margolin, 1984; Patterson & Shewell, 1987). We refer to this account as the *modality-specific orthographic representations hypothesis* (here using *modality* to refer to reading vs. spelling). According to this hypothesis, P.J.T. has a well-developed reading O-LTM system while his spelling O-LTM system is deficient.

A modality-specific representations hypothesis could assume either that the orthographic representations for reading and spelling have identical, duplicated content, or that the two sets of representations differ in some way. A proposal of duplicated content appears somewhat unappealing on grounds of parsimony, and because independent motivation for positing such duplication is lacking. The possibility of different types of orthographic lexical representations for reading and spelling is more interesting, but until specific proposals are put forth regarding the nature of the differences, this potential version of the modality-specific representations hypothesis is little more than a promissory note.

Also worth noting is that neither version of the modality-specific hypothesis provides a straightforward account of the various reported associations between reading and spelling that we discussed in the introduction, and neither version straightforwardly allows for the generalization of orthographic lexical knowledge from reading to spelling.

A second approach to interpreting P.J.T.'s reading–spelling dissociation is to posit lexical orthographic representations that are shared between reading and spelling, with modality-specific processes for accessing and/or processing the stored orthographic knowledge. In reading, lexical orthographic information is accessed from representations of letter identities and order (see Figure 5), whereas in spelling the lexical orthographic knowledge is accessed from phonological or semantic representations. This *shared orthographic representations hypothesis* would interpret dissociations between reading and spelling by positing deficits to procedures that are specific to reading or spelling. For P.J.T. the interpretation would be as follows: The shared lexical orthographic representations were well learned, as were the processes for accessing these representations in reading; however, P.J.T. had difficulty developing the processes required for accessing the lexical orthographic representations from phonological LTM and/or the semantic system. As a consequence, when P.J.T. attempts to spell a word, the process of activating the lexical-orthographic representation may yield only weak, fragmentary activation, or may fail entirely, leading to a spelling error.

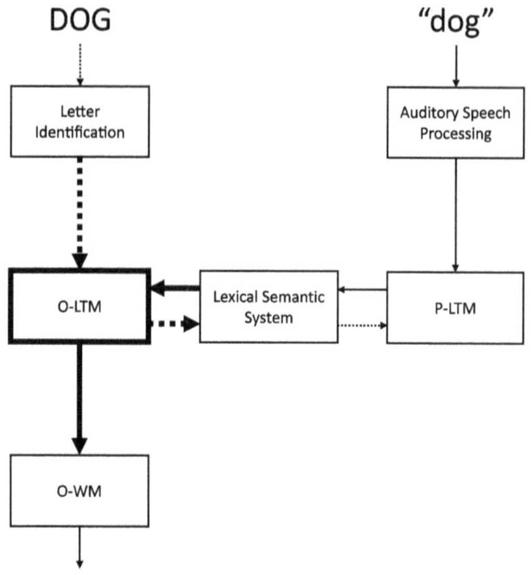

Figure 5. A model of a cognitive architecture for written language processing with modality-independent lexical orthographic representations. Sublexical processes are omitted. Solid lines are used for processes and representations involved in spelling and dashed lines for those involved in reading. Bold indicates processes and representations involved specifically in lexical orthographic processing in reading and spelling. O-LTM = orthographic long-term memory; P-LTM = phonological long-term memory; O-WM = orthographic working memory.

One challenge for this hypothesis concerns the difficulty of testing the critical assumption that lexical–orthographic representations are intact in cases of impairment attributed to access deficits (see Rapp & Caramazza, 1989). For example, how could we find evidence that the lexical–orthographic representations that mediate spelling are intact in P.J.T.?

Progress in evaluating these theoretical alternatives empirically, and even in assessing their plausibility, will depend on advances in our thinking about the nature of lexical orthographic representations and computations. For example, implicit in the preceding discussion is the notion that orthographic long-term memory in some sense contains information about the orthographic forms of words (e.g., the information that the word DOG corresponds to the letter sequence D-O-G). Given this implicit assumption, the hypothesis of separate lexical orthographic representations for reading and spelling runs the risk of positing duplicate representations of this information, as we have discussed. Consider, however, the somewhat different conceptualization illustrated in Figure 6. According to this view, orthographic lexical representations consist of word nodes that do not "contain" information about letter sequences; rather the word nodes are linked to letter nodes, and thereby provide a basis for activating (in the case of spelling) or being activated by (in the case of reading) the corresponding sequence of letter representations.

Within this general perspective, we could formulate both modality-specific and shared orthographic representations hypotheses. In fact, we could develop a broad range of hypotheses, depending upon whether we assume that the word nodes, the letter nodes, and the word–letter connections are shared or separate for reading and spelling. Figure 6 illustrates a version in which lexical nodes are shared between reading and spelling, but the letter nodes, and the links between letter and word nodes, are separate for reading and spelling. This nodes-and-links perspective is consistent with a widely adopted theoretical framework for spoken word production (Dell, 1986; Levelt, Roelofs, & Meyer, 1999), which posits that production involves two stages: activation of a word node (lexical selection), leading in turn to activation of the nodes for the constituent phonological segments (segmental encoding).

Applied to reading and spelling, the nodes-and-links perspective is not radically different from the conceptual framework in which we think of the orthographic LTM system as "containing" knowledge about letter sequences. Indeed, in Figure 6 we could draw a box encompassing the word nodes, the letter nodes for spelling, and the word–letter connections, and

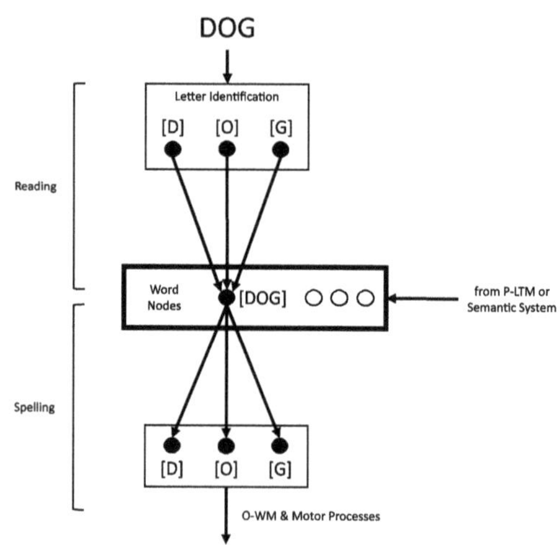

Figure 6. A model of a cognitive architecture for written language processing from a nodes-and-links perspective. Labels on nodes are only for clarification, and do not indicate content "inside" a node. O-LTM = orthographic long-term memory; P-LTM = phonological long-term memory.

we could then label this box *orthographic LTM system for spelling*. Nevertheless, the nodes-and-links perspective is potentially valuable, for a number of reasons. First, as we have just mentioned, this perspective is helpful in articulating potential versions of the modality-specific and shared orthographic representations hypotheses. Second, this perspective may encourage us to rethink the distinction between separate representations and separate procedures. For example, does Figure 6 illustrate a modality-specific orthographic representations hypothesis, or a modality-specific procedures hypothesis? If we consider the orthographic representations to consist solely of the word nodes, then the figure shows representations that are shared between reading and spelling, with modality-specific processes for accessing and using these representations. However, if we conceive of orthographic representations as encompassing the word nodes, the letter nodes, and the links between them, then Figure 6 shows largely (although not entirely) separate representations for reading and spelling.

The nodes-and-links perspective may also affect our views on the plausibility of various theoretical alternatives. If we conceive of orthographic LTM as a container holding knowledge of letter sequences, then positing two separate orthographic LTM systems may seem implausible. However, the hypothesis illustrated in Figure 6 may appear more plausible, despite positing largely separate orthographic knowledge (embodied in the word–letter links) for reading and spelling.

We do not intend to suggest that theorists should abandon the lexicon-as-knowledge-container perspective in favour of a nodes-and-links perspective. Rather, our principal point is that contrasting these conceptual frameworks reveals the extent to which our formulation of theoretical alternatives, our assessment of their plausibility, and perhaps even our arguments relating empirical evidence to theoretical claims rest upon implicit assumptions that have not been cashed out. Considerable theoretical development is needed if we are to make progress in understanding the relationship between reading and spelling in a way that accounts for the detailed patterns of data available in the literature. Our hope is that this theoretical work, in conjunction with the documentation of increasingly detailed and distinct performance patterns such as those reported here, will move us towards a position in which we will be able to develop proposals with predictions that would adjudicate between them.

Summary and conclusions

We have presented a strong case of a dissociation between reading and spelling that clearly reveals that at least certain representations and/or processes involved in reading and spelling develop independently from one another. These findings provide important additional constraints on theories of reading and spelling. We have suggested that the full set of available findings seem to be well accommodated in a system in which reading and spelling share at least some components of orthographic long-term memory with modality-specific access and segmental encoding processes. This provides a reasonably parsimonious framework for understanding both the associations and the dissociations between reading and spelling that have been reported to date.

Notes

1. The role of O-WM in reading is a rather under-researched topic. However, it has been argued (Caramazza et al., 1996; Tainturier & Rapp, 2003) that the degree to which O-WM is engaged is determined by task demands. While spelling always places demands on O-WM, "normal" horizontal word reading is typically carried out in parallel with few demands placed on O-WM. In contrast, vertical word reading, reading words with letters presented serially, or even pseudoword reading places greater demands on O-WM. In support of the hypothesis of shared O-WM processes in reading and spelling, Caramazza et al. (1996) and Tainturier and Rapp (2003) reported cases of individuals with acquired dysgraphia with deficits affecting O-WM in spelling who showed similar patterns of errors and length effects in spelling, pseudoword reading, and reading with alternative formats (e.g., mirror-reversed and orally presented letters).
2. Note that both the DiSTi and the WRAT include words that a child of A.K.R.'s age would not be expected to spell correctly (e.g., CACOPHONY, IRIDESCENCE). Accordingly, although her 67% error rate is higher than expected for a child of her age, it does not reflect catastrophic spelling impairment. Note also that the spelling corpus for P.J.T., described below, includes a larger proportion of words a child of his age would be expected to spell correctly, and hence his somewhat lower error rate (53%) does not imply a less severe spelling impairment.

Acknowledgements

We are grateful to P.J.T., A.K.R., and their families for their support for this project and their cheerful participation in long hours of testing. We are also grateful to Michael Gascoigne for his help with testing materials and normative data for the visual learning task.

Disclosure statement

No potential conflict of interest was reported by the authors.

Funding

Preparation of this article was supported by a Johns Hopkins Science of Learning Institute grant to Michael McCloskey; by the National Institutes of Health [grant number DC006740] to Brenda Rapp; and by a generous gift from a donor to the Johns Hopkins University.

ORCID

Christopher Hepner http://orcid.org/0000-0001-8999-1231

References

Allport, D. A., & Funnell, E. (1981). Components of the mental lexicon. *Philosophical Transactions of the Royal Society B: Biological Sciences, 295*(1077), 397–410. https://doi.org/10.1098/rstb.1981.0148

Angelelli, P., Judica, A., Spinelli, D., Zoccolotti, P., & Luzzatti, C. (2004). Characteristics of writing disorders in Italian dyslexic children. *Cognitive and Behavioral Neurology, 17*(1), 18–31. https://doi.org/10.1097/00146965-200403000-00003

Angelelli, P., Marinelli, C. V., & Zoccolotti, P. (2010). Single or dual orthographic representations for reading and spelling? A study of Italian dyslexic-dysgraphic and normal children. *Cognitive Neuropsychology, 27*(4), 305–333. https://doi.org/10.1080/02643294.2010.543539

Ans, B., Carbonnel, S., & Valdois, S. (1998). A connectionist multiple-trace memory model for polysyllabic word reading. *Psychological Review, 105*(4), 678–723. https://doi.org/10.1037/0033-295X.105.4.678-723

Barisic, K., Kohnen, S., & Nickels, L. (2017). Developmental graphemic buffer dysgraphia in English: A single case study. *Cognitive Neuropsychology*. https://doi.org/10.1080/02643294.2017.1359154

Beauvois, M.-F., & Dérouesné, J. (1979). Phonological alexia: Three dissociations. *Journal of Neurology, Neurosurgery & Psychiatry, 42*(12), 1115–1124. https://doi.org/10.1136/jnnp.42.12.1115

Beauvois, M.-F., & Dérouesné, J. (1981). Lexical or orthographic Agraphia. *Brain, 104*(1), 21–49. https://doi.org/10.1093/brain/104.1.21

Beery, K. E., & Beery, N. A. (2010). *The Beery-Buktenica developmental test of visual-motor integration (Beery VMI) with supplemental developmental tests of visual perception and motor coordination and stepping stones age norms, from birth to age six: Administration, scoring, and teaching manual* (6th ed.). Bloomington, MN: Pearson.

Behrmann, M., & Bub, D. (1992). Surface dyslexia and dysgraphia: Dual routes, single lexicon. *Cognitive Neuropsychology, 9*(3), 209–251. https://doi.org/10.1080/02643299208252059

Bergmann, J., & Wimmer, H. (2008). A dual-route perspective on poor reading in a regular orthography: Evidence from phonological and orthographic lexical decisions. *Cognitive Neuropsychology, 25*(5), 653–676. https://doi.org/10.1080/02643290802221404

Bosse, M.-L., Tainturier, M. J., & Valdois, S. (2007). Developmental dyslexia: The visual attention span deficit hypothesis. *Cognition, 104*(2), 198–230. https://doi.org/10.1016/j.cognition.2006.05.009

Bosse, M.-L., & Valdois, S. (2009). Influence of the visual attention span on child reading performance: A cross-sectional study. *Journal of Research in Reading, 32*(2), 230–253. https://doi.org/10.1111/j.1467-9817.2008.01387.x

Bradley, L., & Bryant, P. E. (1978). Difficulties in auditory organisation as a possible cause of reading backwardness. *Nature, 271*(5647), 746–747. https://doi.org/10.1038/271746a0

Bradley, L., & Bryant, P. E. (1983). Categorizing sounds and learning to read—A causal connection. *Nature, 301*(5899), 419–421. https://doi.org/10.1038/301419a0

Bruck, M. (1993). Word recognition and component phonological processing skills of adults with childhood diagnosis of dyslexia. *Developmental Review, 13*(3), 258–268. https://doi.org/10.1006/drev.1993.1012

Bruck, M., & Treiman, R. (1990). Phonological awareness and spelling in normal children and dyslexics: The case of initial consonant clusters. *Journal of Experimental Child Psychology, 50*(1), 156–178. https://doi.org/10.1016/0022-0965(90)90037-9

Bruininks, R. H., & Bruininks, B. D. (2005). *Bruininks-Oseretsky test of motor proficiency* (2nd ed.). Circle Pines, MN: AGS Publishing.

Brunsdon, R., Coltheart, M., & Nickels, L. (2005). Treatment of irregular word spelling in developmental surface dysgraphia. *Cognitive Neuropsychology, 22*(2), 213–251. https://doi.org/10.1080/02643290442000077

Bub, D., Cancelliere, A., & Kertesz, A. (1985). Whole-word and analytic translation of spelling-to-sound in a non-semantic reader. In K. Patterson, J. C. Marshall, & M. Coltheart (Eds.), *Surface dyslexia: Neuropsychological and cognitive studies of phonological reading* (pp. 15–34). London: Lawrence Erlbaum Associates.

Burt, J. S., & Tate, H. (2002). Does a reading lexicon provide orthographic representations for spelling? *Journal of Memory and Language, 46*(3), 518–543. https://doi.org/10.1006/jmla.2001.2818

Campbell, R., & Butterworth, B. (1985). Phonological dyslexia and dysgraphia in a highly literate subject: A developmental case with associated deficits of phonemic processing and awareness. *The Quarterly Journal of Experimental Psychology*

Section A, 37(3), 435–475. https://doi.org/10.1080/14640748508400944

Caramazza, A., Capasso, R., & Miceli, G. (1996). The role of the graphemic buffer in reading. *Cognitive Neuropsychology, 13* (5), 673–698. https://doi.org/10.1080/026432996381881

Caramazza, A., & Hillis, A. E. (1990a). Levels of representation, co-ordinate frames, and unilateral neglect. *Cognitive Neuropsychology, 7*(5–6), 391–445. https://doi.org/10.1080/02643299008253450

Caramazza, A., & Hillis, A. E. (1990b). Spatial representation of words in the brain implied by studies of a unilateral neglect patient. *Nature, 346*(6281), 267–269. https://doi.org/10.1038/346267a0

Caramazza, A., Miceli, G., Villa, G., & Romani, C. (1987). The role of the graphemic buffer in spelling: Evidence from a case of acquired dysgraphia. *Cognition, 26*(1), 59–85. https://doi.org/10.1016/0010-0277(87)90014-X

Castles, A., & Coltheart, M. (1993). Varieties of developmental dyslexia. *Cognition, 47*(2), 149–180. https://doi.org/10.1016/0010-0277(93)90003-E

Castles, A., & Coltheart, M. (2004). Is there a causal link from phonological awareness to success in learning to read? *Cognition, 91*(1), 77–111. https://doi.org/10.1016/S0010-0277(03)00164-1

Castles, A., Coltheart, M., Larsen, L., Jones, P., Saunders, S., & McArthur, G. (2009). Assessing the basic components of reading: A revision of the Castles and Coltheart test with new norms (CC2). Retrieved from http://www.motif.org.au/

Cholewa, J., Mantey, S., Heber, S., & Hollweg, W. (2010). Developmental surface and phonological dysgraphia in German 3rd graders. *Reading and Writing, 23*(1), 97–127. https://doi.org/10.1007/s11145-008-9153-7

Cohen, M. J. (1997). *Children's memory scale*. San Antonio, TX: The Psychological Corporation.

Coltheart, M. (2015). What kinds of things cause children's reading difficulties? *Australian Journal of Learning Difficulties, 20*(2), 103–112. https://doi.org/10.1080/19404158.2015.1114000

Coltheart, M., & Funnell, E. (1987). Reading and writing: One lexicon or two? In A. Allport, D. G. MacKay, & W. Prinz (Eds.), *Language perception and production: Relationships between listening, speaking, reading and writing* (pp. 313–339). San Diego, CA: Academic Press.

Coltheart, M., Masterson, J., Byng, S., Prior, M., & Riddoch, J. (1983). Surface dyslexia. *The Quarterly Journal of Experimental Psychology Section A, 35*(3), 469–495. https://doi.org/10.1080/14640748308402483

Dell, G. S. (1986). A spreading-activation theory of retrieval in sentence production. *Psychological Review, 93*(3), 283–321. https://doi.org/10.1037/0033-295X.93.3.283

Dolch, E. W. (1948). *Problems in reading*. Champaign, IL: Garrard Press.

Douklias, S. D., Masterson, J., & Hanley, J. R. (2009). Surface and phonological developmental dyslexia in Greek. *Cognitive Neuropsychology, 26*(8), 705–723. https://doi.org/10.1080/02643291003691106

Dunn, L. M., & Dunn, L. M. (1981). *Peabody picture vocabulary test, revised* (Rev. ed). Circle Pines, MN: American Guidance Service.

Dunn, L. M., & Dunn, D. M. (2007). *Peabody picture vocabulary test* (4th ed.). Minneapolis, MN: Pearson Assessments.

Ehri, L. C. (2000). Learning to read and learning to spell: Two sides of a coin. *Topics in Language Disorders, 20*(3), 19–36. https://doi.org/10.1097/00011363-200020030-00005

Frith, U. (1978). From print to meaning and from print to sound, or how to read without knowing how to spell. *Visible Language, 12*(1), 43–54.

Frith, U. (1980). Unexpected spelling problems. In U. Frith (Ed.), *Cognitive processes in spelling* (pp. 495–515). London: Academic Press.

Funnell, E. (1983). Phonological processes in reading: New evidence from acquired dyslexia. *British Journal of Psychology, 74*(2), 159–180. https://doi.org/10.1111/j.2044-8295.1983.tb01851.x

Funnell, E., & Davison, M. (1989). Lexical capture: A developmental disorder of reading and spelling. *The Quarterly Journal of Experimental Psychology Section A, 41*(3), 471–487. https://doi.org/10.1080/14640748908402377

Gascoigne, M. B., Smith, M. L., Barton, B., Webster, R., Gill, D., & Lah, S. (2014). Accelerated long-term forgetting in children with temporal lobe epilepsy. *Neuropsychologia, 59*, 93–102. https://doi.org/10.1016/j.neuropsychologia.2014.04.012

Goulandris, N. K., & Snowling, M. (1991). Visual memory deficits: A plausible cause of developmental dyslexia? Evidence from a single case study. *Cognitive Neuropsychology, 8*(2), 127–154. https://doi.org/10.1080/02643299108253369

Greenberg, D., Ehri, L. C., & Perin, D. (1997). Are word-reading processes the same or different in adult literacy students and third–fifth graders matched for reading level? *Journal of Educational Psychology, 89*(2), 262–275. https://doi.org/10.1037/0022-0663.89.2.262

Gvion, A., & Friedmann, N. (2010). Letter position dysgraphia. *Cortex, 46*(9), 1100–1113. https://doi.org/10.1016/j.cortex.2009.09.008

Hanley, J. R., & Gard, F. (1995). A dissociation between developmental surface and phonological dyslexia in two undergraduate students. *Neuropsychologia, 33*(7), 909–914. https://doi.org/10.1016/0028-3932(95)00038-5

Hanley, J. R., Hastie, K., & Kay, J. (1992). Developmental surface dyslexia and dysgraphia: An orthographic processing impairment. *The Quarterly Journal of Experimental Psychology Section A, 44*(2), 285–319. https://doi.org/10.1080/02724989243000046

Hanley, J. R., & Kay, J. (1992). Does letter-by-letter reading involve the spelling system? *Neuropsychologia, 30*(3), 237–256. https://doi.org/10.1016/0028-3932(92)90003-5

Hanley, J. R., & McDonnell, V. (1997). Are reading and spelling phonologically mediated? Evidence from a patient with a speech production impairment. *Cognitive Neuropsychology, 14*(1), 3–33. https://doi.org/10.1080/026432997381600

Hanna, P. R., Hanna, J. S., Hodges, R. E., & Rudorf, E. H., Jr. (1966). Phoneme-grapheme correspondences as cues to spelling improvement. Retrieved from http://eric.ed.gov/?id=ED128835

Hepworth, S., & Smith, M. L. (2002). Learning and recall of story content and spatial location after unilateral temporal-lobe excision in children and adolescents. *Child Neuropsychology (Neuropsychology, Development and Cognition: Section C)*, *8* (1), 16–26. https://doi.org/10.1076/chin.8.1.16.8718

Hillis, A. E., Rapp, B., & Caramazza, A. (1999). When a rose is a rose in speech but a tulip in writing. *Cortex*, *35*(3), 337–356. https://doi.org/10.1016/S0010-9452(08)70804-9

Holmes, V. M., & Carruthers, J. (1998). The relation between reading and spelling in skilled adult readers. *Journal of Memory and Language*, *39*(2), 264–289. https://doi.org/10.1006/jmla.1998.2583

Holmes, V. M., & Davis, C. W. (2002). Orthographic representation and spelling knowledge. *Language and Cognitive Processes*, *17*(4), 345–370. https://doi.org/10.1080/01690960143000263a

Holmes, V. M., Malone, A. M., & Redenbach, H. (2008). Orthographic processing and visual sequential memory in unexpectedly poor spellers. *Journal of Research in Reading*, *31*(1), 136–156. https://doi.org/10.1111/j.1467-9817.2007.00364.x

Kohnen, S., Anandakumar, T., McArthur, G., & Castles, A. (2012). The test of orthographic choice (TOC). Retrieved from http://www.motif.org.au/

Kohnen, S., Colenbrander, D., Krajenbrink, T., & Nickels, L. (2013). Diagnostic spelling test – Nonwords with normative data. Retrieved from http://www.motif.org.au/

Kohnen, S., Colenbrander, D., Krajenbrink, T., & Nickels, L. (2015). Assessment of lexical and non-lexical spelling in students in grades 1–7. *Australian Journal of Learning Difficulties*, *20*(1), 15–38. https://doi.org/10.1080/19404158.2015.1023209

Kohnen, S., Marinus, E., Friedmann, N., Anandakumar, T., Nickels, L., McArthur, G., & Castles, A. (2012). Letter position test. Retrieved from http://www.motif.org.au/

Levelt, W. J. M., Roelofs, A., & Meyer, A. S. (1999). A theory of lexical access in speech production. *Behavioral and Brain Sciences*, *22*(1), 1–38. https://doi.org/10.1017/s0140525x99001776

Liberman, I. Y. (1973). Segmentation of the spoken word and reading acquisition. *Bulletin of the Orton Society*, *23*(1), 64–77. https://doi.org/10.1007/BF02653842

Margolin, D. I. (1984). The neuropsychology of writing and spelling: Semantic, phonological, motor, and perceptual processes. *The Quarterly Journal of Experimental Psychology Section A*, *36*(3), 459–489. https://doi.org/10.1080/14640748408402172

McCann, R. S., & Besner, D. (1987). Reading pseudohomophones: Implications for models of pronunciation assembly and the locus of word-frequency effects in naming. *Journal of Experimental Psychology: Human Perception and Performance*, *13*(1), 14–24. https://doi.org/10.1037/0096-1523.13.1.14

McCloskey, M., Fischer-Baum, S., & Schubert, T. (2013). Representation of letter position in single-word reading: Evidence from acquired dyslexia. *Cognitive Neuropsychology*, *30*(6), 396–428. https://doi.org/10.1080/02643294.2014.880675

McCloskey, M., & Rapp, B. (2017). Developmental dysgraphia: An overview and framework for research. *Cognitive Neuropsychology*. https://doi.org/10.1080/02643294.2017.1369016

Milone, M. (2007). *Test of handwriting skills, revised* (Rev. ed). Novato, CA: Academic Therapy Publications.

Monsell, S. (1987). On the relation between lexical input and output pathways for speech. In A. Allport, D. G. MacKay, & W. Prinz (Eds.), *Language perception and production: Relationships between listening, speaking, reading and writing* (pp. 273–311). San Diego, CA: Academic Press.

Patterson, K., & Shewell, C. (1987). Speak and spell: Dissociations and word-class effects. In M. Coltheart, G. Sartori, & R. Job (Eds.), *The cognitive neuropsychology of language* (pp. 273–294). London: Lawrence Erlbaum Associates.

Philipose, L. E., Gottesman, R. F., Newhart, M., Kleinman, J. T., Herskovits, E. H., Pawlak, M. A., … Hillis, A. E. (2007). Neural regions essential for reading and spelling of words and pseudowords. *Annals of Neurology*, *62*(5), 481–492. https://doi.org/10.1002/ana.21182

Psychological Corporation. (2009). *Wechsler individual achievement test* (3rd ed.). San Antonio, TX: Author.

Purcell, J. J., Jiang, X., & Eden, G. F. (2017). Shared orthographic neuronal representations for spelling and reading. *NeuroImage*, *147*, 554–567. https://doi.org/10.1016/j.neuroimage.2016.12.054

Purcell, J. J., Napoliello, E. M., & Eden, G. F. (2011). A combined fMRI study of typed spelling and reading. *NeuroImage*, *55*(2), 750–762. https://doi.org/10.1016/j.neuroimage.2010.11.042

Rapcsak, S. Z., & Beeson, P. M. (2004). The role of left posterior inferior temporal cortex in spelling. *Neurology*, *62*(12), 2221–2229. https://doi.org/10.1212/01.WNL.0000130169.60752.C5

Rapp, B., & Caramazza, A. (1989). Letter processing in reading and spelling: Some dissociations. *Reading and Writing*, *1*(1), 3–23. https://doi.org/10.1007/BF00178834

Rapp, B., & Caramazza, A. (1997). From graphemes to abstract letter shapes: Levels of representation in written spelling. *Journal of Experimental Psychology: Human Perception and Performance*, *23*(4), 1130–1152. https://doi.org/10.1037/0096-1523.23.4.1130

Rapp, B., & Dufor, O. (2011). The neurotopography of written word production: An fMRI investigation of the distribution of sensitivity to length and frequency. *Journal of Cognitive Neuroscience*, *23*(12), 4067–4081. https://doi.org/10.1162/jocn_a_00109

Rapp, B., Epstein, C., & Tainturier, M.-J. (2002). The integration of information across lexical and sublexical processes in spelling. *Cognitive Neuropsychology*, *19*(1), 1–29. https://doi.org/10.1080/0264329014300060

Rapp, B., & Fischer-Baum, S. (2015). Uncovering the cognitive architecture of spelling. In A. E. Hillis (Ed.), *The handbook of adult language disorders* (pp. 47–69). New York, NY: Psychology Press.

Rapp, B., & Kong, D. L. (2002). Revealing the component functions of the graphemic buffer. *Brain and Language*, *83*(1), 112–114. https://doi.org/10.1016/S0093-934X(02)00059-7

Rapp, B., & Lipka, K. (2011). The literate brain: The relationship between spelling and reading. *Journal of Cognitive Neuroscience*, *23*(5), 1180–1197. https://doi.org/10.1162/jocn.2010.21507

Romani, C., Ward, J., & Olson, A. (1999). Developmental surface dysgraphia: What is the underlying cognitive impairment? *The Quarterly Journal of Experimental Psychology Section A*, *52*(1), 97–128. https://doi.org/10.1080/027249899391241

Roncoli, S., & Masterson, J. (2016). "Unexpected" spelling difficulty in a 10-year-old child with good reading skills: An intervention case study. *Writing Systems Research*, *8*(2), 143–166. https://doi.org/10.1080/17586801.2016.1159539

Sartori, G., Masterson, J., & Job, R. (1987). Direct route reading and the locus of lexical decision. In M. Coltheart, G. Sartori, & R. Job (Eds.), *The cognitive neuropsychology of language* (pp. 59–78). London: Lawrence Erlbaum Associates.

Schubert, T., & McCloskey, M. (2013). Prelexical representations and processes in reading: Evidence from acquired dyslexia. *Cognitive Neuropsychology*, *30*(6), 360–395. https://doi.org/10.1080/02643294.2014.880677

Schwartz, M. F., Saffran, E. M., & Marin, O. S. M. (1980). Fractionating the reading process in dementia: Evidence for word-specific print-to-sound associations. In M. Coltheart, J. C. Marshall, & K. Patterson (Eds.), *Deep dyslexia* (pp. 259–269). London: Routledge & Kegan Paul.

Seymour, P. H. K. (1986). *Cognitive analysis of dyslexia*. London: Routledge & Kegan Paul.

Seymour, P. H. K., & Evans, H. M. (1993). The visual (orthographic) processor and developmental dyslexia. In D. M. Willows, R. S. Kruk, & E. Corcos (Eds.), *Visual processes in reading and reading disabilities* (pp. 347–376). Hillsdale, NJ: Lawrence Erlbaum Associates.

Snowling, M., Goulandris, N., Bowlby, M., & Howell, P. (1986). Segmentation and speech perception in relation to reading skill: A developmental analysis. *Journal of Experimental Child Psychology*, *41*(3), 489–507. https://doi.org/10.1016/0022-0965(86)90006-8

Sotiropoulos, A., & Hanley, J. R. (2017). Developmental surface and phonological dyslexia in both Greek and English. *Cognition*, *168*, 205–216. https://doi.org/10.1016/j.cognition.2017.06.024

Stanovich, K. E. (1988). The right and wrong places to look for the cognitive locus of reading disability. *Annals of Dyslexia*, *38*(1), 154–177. https://doi.org/10.1007/BF02648254

Tainturier, M.-J., & Rapp, B. (2001). The spelling process. In B. Rapp (Ed.), *The handbook of cognitive neuropsychology: What deficits reveal about the human mind* (pp. 263–289). Philadelphia, PA: Psychology Press.

Tainturier, M.-J., & Rapp, B. (2003). Is a single graphemic buffer used in reading and spelling? *Aphasiology*, *17*(6/7), 537–562. https://doi.org/10.1080/02687030344000021

Temple, C. M. (1984). Surface dyslexia in a child with epilepsy. *Neuropsychologia*, *22*(5), 569–576. https://doi.org/10.1016/0028-3932(84)90021-6

Temple, C. M. (1985). Developmental surface dysgraphia: A case report. *Applied Psycholinguistics*, *6*(4), 391–405. https://doi.org/10.1017/S0142716400006329

Temple, C. M. (1986). Developmental dysgraphias. *The Quarterly Journal of Experimental Psychology Section A*, *38*(1), 77–110. https://doi.org/10.1080/14640748608401586

Temple, C. M., & Marshall, J. C. (1983). A case study of developmental phonological dyslexia. *British Journal of Psychology*, *74*(4), 517–533. https://doi.org/10.1111/j.2044-8295.1983.tb01883.x

Treiman, R. (1993). *Beginning to spell: A study of first-grade children*. New York,NY: Oxford University Press.

Valdois, S. (1996). A case study of developmental surface dyslexia and dysgraphia. *Brain and Cognition*, *32*(2), 229–231. https://doi.org/10.1006/brcg.1996.0065

Valdois, S., Bosse, M.-L., Ans, B., Carbonnel, S., Zorman, M., David, D., & Pellat, J. (2003). Phonological and visual processing deficits can dissociate in developmental dyslexia: Evidence from two case studies. *Reading and Writing*, *16*(6), 541–572. https://doi.org/10.1023/a:1025501406971

Wagner, R. K., Torgesen, J. K., & Rashotte, C. A. (1999). *Comprehensive test of phonological processing* (1st ed.). Austin, TX: Pro-Ed.

Wagner, R. K., & Torgesen, J. K. (1987). The nature of phonological processing and its causal role in the acquisition of reading skills. *Psychological Bulletin*, *101*(2), 192–212. https://doi.org/10.1037/0033-2909.101.2.192

Wagner, R. K., Torgesen, J. K., Rashotte, C. A., & Pearson, N. A. (2013). *Comprehensive test of phonological processing* (2nd ed.). Austin, TX: Pro-Ed.

Wechsler, D. (2003). *Wechsler intelligence scale for children* (4th ed.). San Antonio, TX: Psychological Corporation.

Wechsler, D. (2014). *Wechsler intelligence scale for children* (5th ed.). San Antonio, TX: Psychological Corporation.

Wilkinson, G. S. (1993). *Wide range achievement test*. Wilmington, DE: Wide Range, Inc.

Williams, K. T. (2007). *Expressive vocabulary test* (2nd ed.). Minneapolis, MN: Pearson Assessments.

Wing, A. M., & Baddeley, A. D. (1980). Spelling errors in handwriting: A corpus and a distributional analysis. In U. Frith (Ed.), *Cognitive processes in spelling* (pp. 251–285).

Woodcock, R. W. (1987). *Woodcock reading mastery tests, revised* (Rev. ed). Circle Pines, MN: American Guidance Service.

Yachini, M., & Friedmann, N. (2010). Developmental graphemic buffer dysgraphia. *Procedia – Social and Behavioral Sciences*, *6*, 148–149. https://doi.org/10.1016/j.sbspro.2010.08.073

Lexical decision performance in developmental surface dysgraphia: Evidence for a unitary orthographic system that is used in both reading and spelling

Andreas Sotiropoulos and J. Richard Hanley

ABSTRACT

The relationship between spelling, written word recognition, and picture naming is investigated in a study of seven bilingual adults who have developmental surface dysgraphia in both Greek (their first language) and English (their second language). Four of the cases also performed poorly at orthographic lexical decision in both languages. This finding is consistent with similar results in Italian that have been taken as evidence of a developmental impairment to a single orthographic system that is used for both reading and spelling. The remaining three participants performed well at orthographic lexical decision. At first sight, preserved lexical decision in surface dysgraphia is less easy to explain in terms of a shared orthographic system. However, the results of subsequent experiments showed clear parallels between the nature of the reading and spelling difficulties that these three individuals experienced, consistent with the existence of a single orthographic system. The different patterns that were observed were consistent with the claims of Friedmann and Lukov (2008. Developmental surface dyslexias. *Cortex*, *44*, 1146–1160) that several distinct sub-types of developmental surface dyslexia exist. We show that individual differences in spelling in surface dysgraphia are also consistent with these sub-types; there are different developmental deficits that can give rise, in an individual, to a combination of surface dyslexia and dysgraphia. Finally, we compare the theoretical framework used by Friedmann and her colleagues that is based upon the architecture of the DRC model with an account that relies instead upon the Triangle model of reading].

Introduction

Developmental surface dysgraphia in the English writing system is an impairment that allows individuals to spell nonwords and regular words accurately but disrupts their ability to learn the spellings of irregular words. Irregular words (e.g., *pint*) have atypical correspondences between one or more of the phonemes and the graphemes that they contain. In case studies of individuals with surface dysgraphia, disorders of reading and spelling tend to co-occur, with individuals having problems in learning to read as well as to spell irregular words (e.g., Castles & Coltheart, 1996; Goulandris & Snowling, 1991; Hanley & Gard, 1995; Hanley, Hastie, & Kay, 1992; Romani, Ward, & Olson, 1999; Temple, 1985).

A co-occurrence of reading and spelling impairments has also been observed in studies of developmental surface dyslexia and dysgraphia in more transparent alphabetic writing systems such as German, Greek, and Italian. Although these orthographies contain very few words that are irregular for the purposes of reading, they are less transparent for the purposes of writing and contain many words with atypical spelling to sound correspondences. Douklias, Masterson, and Hanley (2009) showed that Greek surface dysgraphics experience selective problems in spelling words of this kind and also tend to read familiar Greek words relatively slowly. Douklias et al. argued that slow reading and inaccurate spelling are both the consequence of the same developmental impairment. Bergmann and Wimmer (2008) found that German-speaking dyslexics had particular problems in spelling irregular German words. They showed that such individuals also found it difficult to distinguish correctly spelled words from pseudohomophones on a written lexical decision task even though they could successfully distinguish pseudohomophones from phonologically incorrect spellings. Angelelli, Marinelli, and Zoccolotti (2010) found that Italian surface dysgraphic children who were impaired at spelling irregular words were also impaired on written lexical decision tasks where they had to distinguish correct spellings from their own phonologically plausible misspellings. Normally developing Italian children in this study also found it difficult to distinguish a correct spelling from their own misspellings. In English, consistent findings have been obtained in developmental surface dyslexia/dysgraphia (e.g., Hanley et al., 1992), in acquired surface dyslexia/dysgraphia (e.g., Behrmann & Bub, 1992), and in skilled adult readers/spellers (e.g., Holmes & Carruthers, 1998). Such findings suggest that the same orthographic units (or lexicon) support spelling, reading aloud, and lexical decision. They are therefore consistent with the results of Rapp and Lipka's (2011) functional magnetic resonance imaging (fMRI) investigation in which the same area in the left mid-fusiform appeared to be involved in both recognizing and spelling written words.

In this paper, we describe the performance of three cases of developmental surface dysgraphia who perform well at lexical decision (Experiment 1). A key issue that we investigate is whether the performance of these three individuals is nonetheless consistent with the single lexicon account. We also examine the assumption that the fundamental impairment in developmental surface dyslexia/dysgraphia is to the development of the orthographic lexicon itself (rather than to its input or output pathways). We provide evidence that this assumption is only true in some cases of surface dyslexia/dysgraphia, and that there are important individual differences in the core deficit that lead to impaired reading and spelling of irregular words.

The claim that qualitatively different impairments can be observed in individuals with an irregular word reading deficit has been advanced on several occasions with regard to acquired surface dyslexia (e.g., Ellis, Lambon Ralph, Morris, & Hunter, 2000; Ellis & Young, 1988). More recently, Friedmann and Lukov (2008) and Gvion and Friedmann (2016) have suggested that different types of underlying impairment can also be observed in developmental surface dyslexia in Hebrew, a Semitic language with a relatively opaque alphabetic orthography. Some of the developmental surface dyslexics studied by Friedmann and Lukov performed badly at written lexical decision, consistent with an impairment to the development of the orthographic lexicon itself. Friedmann and Lukov referred to this condition as *input* surface dyslexia. However, other surface dyslexics performed well at lexical decision but showed poor performance on a test that required access from written words to the semantic system. Friedmann and Lukov argued that in these cases the orthographic lexicon had developed normally, and referred to this condition as *orthographic output* surface dyslexia.

Friedmann and Lukov (2008) attempted to explain these differences in terms of the architecture of the dual-route cascaded (DRC) model of reading aloud (Coltheart, Rastle, Perry, Langdon, & Zeigler, 2001). Advocates of the DRC model (e.g., Coltheart & Funnell, 1987) have long argued that the same lexicon is used for both reading and spelling. Figure 1 therefore presents Purcell, Shea, and Rapp's (2014) version of the DRC model in which there is just one orthographic lexicon (orthographic long-term memory, LTM). We refer to it as the DRC–single lexicon account (DRC–SLA). In this model, familiar words can be read aloud both by the semantic pathway (orthography > semantics > phonology) and by the direct lexical route from the orthographic lexicon to the phonological lexicon.

Friedmann and Lukov (2008) argued that although the orthographic lexicon itself is impaired in input surface dyslexia, the problems in reading familiar words in orthographic output surface dyslexia are instead caused by an impairment that impedes access from the orthographic lexicon to both the semantic system and the phonological lexicon. In other surface dyslexics, however, Friedmann and Lukov observed good lexical decision performance *and* preserved access to semantics. These individuals also performed well at picture naming. Friedmann and Lukov suggested there might be a third type of developmental surface dyslexia that they termed *interlexical* surface dyslexia. Individuals with interlexical surface dyslexia, they claimed, have an intact orthography–semantic reading route that allows good performance on lexical decision and semantic decision tasks. Their poor reading of irregular words is instead caused by impaired development of the direct connection from the orthographic lexicon to the phonological lexicon (although, if so, it is surprising that these individuals could not read irregular words aloud via the semantic system). Finally, Gvion and Friedmann (2016) also observed impaired reading aloud of irregular words in Hebrew in eight developmental cases with preserved access to the meaning of written words but poor picture naming. Consequently, Gvion and Friedmann claimed that a problem at the level of the phonological lexicon can also make it necessary

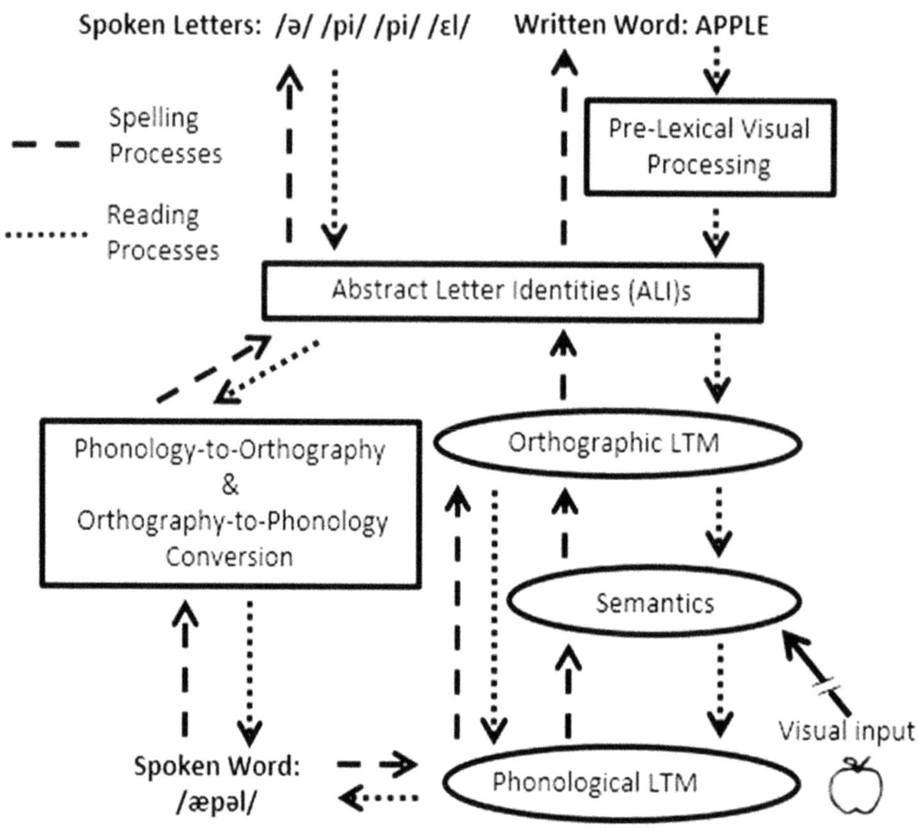

Figure 1. A dual-route model of reading, spelling, and picture naming that is taken from Purcell et al. (2014) in which the same lexicon (orthographic long-term memory, LTM) is used for reading and spelling. Ovals indicate lexical processing for orthography, phonology, or semantics. The short dotted lines and the dashed lines between the ovals indicate reading processes and spelling processes, respectively.

for individuals to read via the non-lexical route and show a pattern that is consistent with surface dyslexia.

The present study investigates individual differences in seven bilingual adults with surface dyslexia and dysgraphia. In a previous report (Sotiropoulos & Hanley, 2017), we have shown that all seven perform accurately when reading and spelling nonwords and regular words in both Greek (their first language) and English (their second language). However, consistent with developmental surface dysgraphia in both Greek and English, all seven made a disproportionately large number of spelling errors on English and Greek words with atypical spelling–sound correspondences. They were also inaccurate at reading irregular English words and slow at reading familiar Greek words consistent with impaired development of the orthographic lexicon in both Greek (Douklias et al., 2009; Niolaki, Terzopoulos, & Masterson, 2014) and English. The present study investigates their performance on tests of orthographic lexical decision (Experiment 1), on a test of semantic access from written words (Experiment 2), and on written (Experiment 3) and spoken picture-naming tests (Experiment 4). In so doing, we attempt to accommodate their reading and spelling performance in English and Greek within the theoretical framework that Friedmann and Lukov (2008) and Gvion and Friedmann (2016) devised in order to explain surface dyslexia in Hebrew. In particular, we examine whether, consistent with the DRC–SLA model that is presented in Figure 1, the performance of all seven can be explained without the need to postulate the existence of separate orthographic lexicons for reading and spelling.

Experiment 1: Orthographic lexical decision

Method

Participants

All of the participants were Greek nationals who were students at British universities at the time of testing. They were aged between 20 and 38 years. Their first language was Greek, and their second language was English. They were recruited as part of a doctoral study (Sotiropoulos, 2015) that examined the reading and spelling performance of 30 Greek students who had experienced developmental literacy difficulties in childhood. Approval for the study was obtained from the Ethics Committee of the University of Essex. Seven of the 30 dyslexics fitted the criteria for surface dyslexia/dysgraphia in Greek and English and were therefore included in the present study. All seven had been classified as dyslexic by educational psychologists in Greece during their school years. Eighteen participants who had normal reading and spelling ability (as reported to the first author) acted as controls. The time that the dyslexics and had spent in the UK, the age at which they learnt English, and the length of their exposure to English were all fairly similar to those of the controls (see Table 1).

The reading and spelling performance of these seven cases in Greek and English has previously been reported by Sotiropoulos and Hanley (2017). Their performance when reading and spelling in English is summarized in Table 2. Sotiropoulos and Hanley demonstrated that all seven were significantly less accurate than controls at spelling English and Greek words that contained atypical spelling–sound correspondences. Over 90% of the spelling errors that they made in both English and Greek were phonologically appropriate. They also performed slowly, though accurately, at reading familiar Greek and English words and made regularization errors when reading aloud irregular English words. They performed at normal levels of accuracy relative to controls when reading and spelling both Greek and English nonwords. All seven therefore suffered from surface dyslexia/dysgraphia in both languages.

Materials

Twenty-four English words along with their corresponding pseudohomophones (e.g., *feel* and *feal*) were used (48 letter strings in total; see Appendix A) for the English lexical decision test. Thirty-four Greek words (e.g., "παγκόσμιος" = global) along with their corresponding pseudohomophones (e.g., "παγγόσμειος") were used (68 letter strings in total; see Appendix B) for the Greek lexical decision test. The pseudohomophones were derived from the words by changing one or two vowels or consonants. Pseudohomophones and words were identical in pronunciation.

Procedure

In each language, the items were presented in one pseudorandomized list. This procedure allowed counterbalancing of the order with which the two items of a word–pseudohomophone pair was presented. The sequence was word before pseudohomophone for half of the pairs and the opposite for the other half. Moreover, close proximity of a word and its pseudohomophone was avoided. The Greek lexical decision test was administered approximately six months before the English version of the test.

The experimental materials were presented on the screen of an Apple Mac PowerBook G3 computer. Microsoft Office Powerpoint software was used for the presentation of the stimuli. Words were presented in font size 44 in lower case. The Audacity software program (available at http://audacityteam.org/) was used to extract reading latencies in milliseconds. Presentation of each word was accompanied by an auditory tone that was visible in Audacity. The latency reflected the time in milliseconds from the onset of the tone to the onset of the first soundwave that was detected on the audacity recording of the speech signal corresponding to the response.

The experimenter controlled the presentation. Participants were presented with one item at a time and had to decide whether the presented word was correctly written. They were required to give a "yes" or "no" response orally to each item. Only when participants gave a "yes" answer for the word and a "no" answer for its corresponding pseudohomophone was performance for the pair considered to be correct. Scores could potentially vary from 0 (reflecting zero correct decisions) to 24 (reflecting 24 correct decisions), and from 0–34 in Greek.

Results and discussion

Results are presented in Table 3. *T*-tests that were modified for use in single case studies (Crawford & Howell, 1998) were used to compare the performance of the dysgraphics with the mean score of the controls. The accuracy of four of the participants was significantly impaired on the English lexical decision task (T.T.: $t = -10.73$, $p < .001$; N.T.: $t = -4.42$, $p < .001$; M.B.: $t = -4.49, p < .001$; N.S.: $t = -3.20, p < .001$). These response times for these four individuals were also significantly slower than those for the controls for both words (T.T.:

Table 1. The amount of time spent in the UK and the amount of exposure to the English language of the 7 dysgraphics/dyslexics and 18 control participants.

	Controls	T.T.	N.T.	M.B.	M.R.	N.S.	A.H.	G.M.
Time spent in UK (years)	4.22 (1.8)	10	4	3	7	2	8	6
First exposure to English (years)	8.6 (2.1)	8	9	9	8	10	8	8
Total time of exposure (years)	15.8 (3.4)	21	15	14	19	12	20	17

Note: Standard deviations in parentheses.

$t = 4.57$, $p < .001$; N.T.: $t = 2.42$, $p < .05$; M.B.: $t = 2.757$, $p < .01$; N.S.: $t = 2.07$, $p < .05$) and pseudohomophones (T.T.: $t = 8.94$, $p < .001$; N.T.: $t = 3.03$, $p < .01$; M.B.: $t = 3.79$, $p < .01$; N.S.: $t = 2.32$, $p < .05$). However, the accuracy and speed of the other three cases (M.R., A.H., G.M.) was normal and did not differ significantly from those of the controls.

The four participants whose scores were impaired at English lexical decision in Experiment 1 also performed significantly less accurately than controls at lexical decision in Greek (T.T.: $t = -6.47$, $p < .001$; N.T.: $t = -4.84$, $p < .001$; M.B.: $t = -3.20$, $p < .001$; N.S.: $t = -3.20$, $p < .001$). Their responses were also significantly slower than those of controls on both words (T.T.: $t = 4.39$, $p < .001$; N.T.: $t = 2.34$, $p = .016$; M.B.: $t = 2.859$, $p = .005$; N.S.: $t = 2.19$, $p < .05$) and pseudohomophones (T.T.: $t = 6.83$, $p < .001$; N.T.: $t = 2.26$, $p < .05$; M.B.: $t = 3.18$, $p < .01$; N.S.: $t = 2.17$, $p < .05$). The speed and accuracy of the three participants who performed well at lexical decision in English (M.R., A.H., G.M.) did not differ significantly from those of the controls in Greek.

The results show a consistent pattern. Four of the cases were impaired at lexical decision in both languages, and three were unimpaired. As the participants who were impaired at English lexical decision were also impaired at Greek lexical decision, it seems unlikely that their poor English lexical decision performance is associated with any of the variables reported in Table 1. In addition, a comparison of the scores in Tables 2 and 3 provides no evidence that the four individuals with poor lexical decision were more impaired at reading and spelling irregular English words than the three individuals with good lexical decision performance. It does not appear, therefore, that the overall severity of the dyslexic impairment is responsible for the observed differences in lexical decision performance.

Instead, the results suggest that the literacy problems that these individuals experience have distinct causes. It appears that T.T., N.T., N.S., and M.B. are suffering from what Friedmann and Lukov (2008) have categorized as *input* surface dyslexia in which the impairment is considered to be at the level of the orthographic lexicon itself. Input surface dyslexia cannot, however, be reasonably attributed to M.R., A.H., and G.M. for whom preserved lexical decision performance in Experiment 1 suggests that the orthographic lexicon in both Greek and English is working relatively well.

One possible explanation for a dissociation between lexical decision and spelling performance is that there are separate orthographic systems for reading and spelling and that surface dyslexics with impaired lexical decision have impairments to both systems (e.g., T.T., N.T., and M.B.) while those with preserved lexical decision (e.g., M.R., A.H., and G.M.) have impairments to just the spelling system. But if M.R., A.H., and G.M. have no impairment to the orthographic units that are used for reading, why do they read familiar Greek words slowly and irregular English words inaccurately (Sotiropoulos & Hanley, 2017)? Instead we investigate the possibility that this dissociation can be explained in terms of a single orthographic lexicon for reading and spelling, as in Figure 1. It appears that T.T., N.T., and M.B. have an impairment to the orthographic lexicon itself (input surface dyslexia). In Experiment 2, we investigate whether the performance of M.R., A.H., and G.M. is consistent with an impairment to the development of connections from the orthographic lexicon to the semantic system (orthographic output surface dyslexia).

Experiment 2: English semantic decision task

Friedmann and Lukov (2008) showed that when there is good performance at lexical decision, surface dyslexia is sometimes associated with poor performance on a semantic decision test for written words. Experiment 2 investigated whether M.R., A.H., and G.M. would perform in an analogous manner. In Experiment 2, the task required that the appropriate meaning of a written word be accessed. If M.R., A.H., and G.M. have a problem that affects reading immediately after processing by an intact

Table 2. Performance at reading and spelling English words and nonwords by 7 surface dyslexics in comparison with 18 normal readers/spellers.

	Controls	M.R.	T.T.	G.M.	M.B.	A.H.	N.T.	N.S.
Regular word reading accuracy (out of 20)	19.3 (0.77)	20	20	19	19	20	20	20
Regular word reading latency (ms)	554 (66)	703*	769*	686*	718*	742*	741*	701*
Irregular word reading accuracy (out of 20)	17.1 (1.89)	13*	8*	11*	12*	11*	11*	13*
Nonword reading accuracy (out of 30)	24.6 (1.88)	22	25	23	24	24	24	23
Regular word spelling accuracy (out of 20)	19.3 (0.75)	18	20	20	19	20	20	19
Irregular word spelling accuracy (out of 20)	18.5 (1.10)	15*	4*	14*	11*	11*	11*	16*
Nonword spelling accuracy (out of 30)	24.7 (2.05)	23	27	23	23	26	24	23

Note: Data are taken from Sotiropoulos and Hanley (2017). Standard deviations in parentheses.
*$p < .05$ (significance test: Crawford & Howell, 1998).

orthographic lexicon, then these three individuals should perform poorly on a task that requires access to the semantic system for written words. The target words were irregular English words in an attempt to ensure that the task could not be accomplished by using a non-lexical reading route.

Method

Materials

Table 4 presents the materials that were used in Experiment 2. Following Friedmann and Lukov (2008), a target phrase or word that was always regular was presented on the screen. A pair of homophones (e.g., *sun/son*) or potentiophones (e.g., *now/know*) was presented to its immediate right (e.g., *family: sun/son; be informed: now/know*; see Appendix C). One member of each pair was semantically related to the target word or phrase; the other word was either a homophone or a potentiophone of the target word or phrase. Potentiophones are words that, when read via grapheme-to-phoneme conversion, could potentially be read as other words (e.g., "now", which can be sounded out as the word "know"). Participants had to choose whether the word on the right or the left of each pair was semantically associated with the target word. Eighteen pairs of homophones contained an irregular word and a regular one. The irregular word was always the word that was semantically related to the target word, and so participants should choose it as the correct response. In half of those pairs the correct word (irregular) appeared first (e.g., *fruit:* ***pear****/pair*), and in half of the pairs the incorrect word (regular) appeared second (e.g., *part of: sum/****some***). Fourteen pairs of potentiophones were presented. In half of those pairs the correct word appeared first (e.g., *miss:* ***lose*** *loose*), and in half of the pairs the incorrect word appeared second (e.g., *drink: bear/****beer***). Among the 14 word–potentiophone pairs that were used in the semantic decision task, there were two pairs of words in which both items were potentiophones of each other ("now" and "know", "whose" and "hose"). Scores could potentially vary from 0, reflecting zero correct pairs, to 32, reflecting 32 correct pairs.

Procedure

The task was presented on a computer screen in font size 44 in lower case. SuperLab for Mac software was used for the presentation of the decision tasks. Participants indicated an answer by pressing a key on the keyboard according to whether the correct answer was on the left or right of the pair of words. Measures of both accuracy and speed were taken.

Table 3. The English and Greek lexical decision accuracy and latency for real words and pseudohomophones of 7 dysgraphic individuals in comparison with those for 18 controls.

Lexical decision		Controls	T.T.	N.T.	M.B.	N.S.	M.R.	A.H.	G.M.
English	Accuracy (out of 24)	21.2 (1.6)	4*	14*	14*	15*	23	22	20
	Latency in ms (*Yes* responses)	907 (233)	2001*	1485*	1567*	1403*	1058	1130	859
	Latencyin ms (*No* responses)	1008 (255)	3349*	1803*	2000*	1615*	1332	1236	1074
Greek	Accuracy (out of 34)	27.8 (3.0)	8*	13*	18*	18*	24	25	28
	Latencyin ms (*Yes* responses)	1066 (321)	2515*	1836*	2009*	1788*	1104	1192	977
	in ms (*No* responses)	1202 (341)	3603*	1995*	2317*	1963*	1358	1381	1186

Note: Real words: "yes responses"; pseudohomophones: "no responses". RT = reaction time. Standard deviations in parentheses.
*$p < .05$ (significance test: Crawford & Howell, 1998).

Table 4. Pairs of potentiophones used in the English semantic task.

Triad (target meaning: pair of homophones)	
drink: bear / **beer**	*"bear"* could be read as *"beer"* if read like *"clear"*
which person owns: **whose** / hose	*"hose"* could be read as *"whose"* if read like *"lose"*
water pipe: **hose** / whose	*"whose"* could be read as *"hose"* if read like *"chose"*
be informed: now / **know**	*"now"* could be read as *"know"* if read like *"snow"*
at the moment: **now** / know	*" know"* could be read as *"now"* if read like *"how"*
miss: **lose** / loose	*"loose"* could be read as *"lose"* if read like *"choose"*
look carefully: pear/ **peer**	*"pear"* could be read as *"peer"* if read like *"dear"*
hair brush: **comb** / come	*"come"* could be read as *"comb"* if read like *"dome"*
TV: shoe / **show**	*"shoe"* could be read as "show" if read like *"toe"*
clothes: **stain** / stein	*"stein"* could be read as "stain" if read like *"vein"*
dog: bread / **breed**	*"bread"* could be read as *"breed"* if read like *"read"*
oxygen: **air** / ear	*"ear"* could be read as "air" if read like *"wear"*
dislike: height / **hate**	*"height"* could be read as *"hate"* if read like *"weight"*
all: **whole** / howl	*"howl"* could be read as "whole" if read like *"bowl"*

Note: Correct item in bold.

Results and discussion

Results are presented in Table 5. As would be expected if they had a problem at the level of the orthographic lexicon, all four of the individuals who performed badly at lexical decision in Experiment 1 also showed poor semantic decision accuracy relative to controls (T.T.: $t = -2.99$, $p < .01$; N.T.: $t = -2.43$, $p = .01$; M.B.: $t = -1.88$, $p < .05$; N.S.: $t = -2.99$, $p < .01$). Accuracy problems in the semantic decision task were accompanied by significantly slowed latencies (T.T.: $t = 6.14$, $p < .001$; N.T.: $t = 3.85$, $p < .01$; M.B.: $t = 3.77$, $p < .01$; N.S.: $t = 3.53$, $p < .01$).

Importantly, one of the remaining surface dysgraphic individuals (M.R.) also performed significantly less accurately ($t = -3.55$, $p < .01$) and more slowly than controls $t = 2.77$, $p < .01$) on the semantic task despite unimpaired lexical decision in Experiment 1. M.R.'s pattern of performance is therefore consistent with Friedmann and Lukov's (2008) definition of orthographic output surface dyslexia, a problem in accessing semantic representations from otherwise intact orthographic representations. The possibility that M.R. has an additional problem in accessing the phonological lexicon is investigated in Experiment 4, which examines spoken picture naming.

Table 5. Semantic decision performance in English of 7 dysgraphic individuals in comparison with that of controls.

	Accuracy (out of 34)	Latency (ms)
Controls (n = 18)	28.4 (1.8)	1934 (339)
T.T.	23*	4072*
N.T.	24*	3276*
M.B.	25*	3247*
N.S.	23*	3164*
M.R.	22*	2897*
A.H.	29	2303
G.M.	27	1896

Note: Standard deviations in parentheses.
*$p < .05$ (significance test: Crawford & Howell, 1998).

A.H. and G.M., however, were unimpaired at making semantic decisions in terms of either speed or accuracy. This outcome suggests that their orthographic system has developed normally and that there is good access from the orthographic lexicon to the semantic system. The cause of their impaired ability to read irregular words aloud is further investigated in Experiment 4. Experiment 3, however provides a comparison of spelling to dictation with written spelling of picture names.

Experiment 3: Spelling the names of pictures

In this experiment, we further investigate irregular word spelling. A.H. and G.M.'s good lexical decision performance (Experiment 1) suggested that their orthographic lexicon is intact. If the same lexicon is used for spelling as for reading, then it might be possible for A.H. and G.M. to access the orthographic lexicon from the semantic system despite their problems in spelling to dictation. According to the model outlined in Figure 1, such an outcome would also require that the link from the semantic system to the orthographic lexicon is preserved. This seems quite possible in light of A.H. and G.M.'s ability to access the meanings of irregular English words during reading (Experiment 2). Experiment 3, therefore, compares A.H. and G.M.'s spelling of picture names that are irregular English words with their spelling of the same words to dictation.

M.R. also performed well at lexical decision (Experiment 1) but could not access the semantic representations of irregular written words (Experiment 2), consistent with an impairment to the pathway from the orthographic lexicon to the semantic system. It seems quite possible that M.R. would have a corresponding impairment to the connections from the semantic system to the orthographic lexicon (see Figure 1). If so, despite his preserved orthographic lexicon, it would follow that he would not perform any better at spelling picture names than at spelling to dictation.

The results of Experiment 1 suggested that T.T., N.T., N.S., and M.B. have a problem at the level of the orthographic lexicon. Consequently they should also be as impaired at spelling picture names as they are at spelling to dictation.

Method

Materials and procedure

Twenty-two objects were selected from Snodgrass and Vanderwart's (1980) set of pictures. They all had one-syllable names in English: *axe, ball, bow, bowl, bread, coat, comb, book, door, eye, flute, fly, glove, key, knife, shirt, shoe, skirt, swan, thumb, tie, watch.* They comprised words with a phoneme that has a low-contingency spelling. Three had low-contingency spellings of their consonants (*comb*, *thumb*, and *knife*), and the remainder had low-contingency spellings of their vowels. Spelling contingency was determined on the basis of the analysis of phoneme-to-spelling correspondences provided by Barry and Seymour (1988). Low-contingency words contained neither the first nor the second most common spelling of phonemes. For example, the most common spelling of the long vowel /u:/ is OO, as in *moon*, which occurs in 47.9% of words with this vowel, and the second most common spelling is EW, as in *shrewd* and *brew*, which occurs in 10.1% of words; the low-contingency spelling in *flute* is the third most common and occurs in only 9.6% of words. Although these words have low-contingency spellings, they are not necessarily irregular for reading. For example, for both the high-contingency spelling *OO* (as in *moon* and *boot*) and the low-contingency spelling *U-E* (as in *flute* and *dune*), the major spelling-to-sound correspondence is /u:/. The word *flute* therefore has a low-contingency spelling of its vowel, but it is regular for reading.

Table 6. Naming performance of 71 pictures in English and in Greek by 7 dysgraphic individuals in comparison with that of 18 controls.

	Pictures			
	English		Greek	
	Accuracy	Naming latency (ms)	Accuracy	Naming latency (ms)
Controls	64.0 (2.8)	1112 (156)	67.4 (2.1)	1001 (131)
T.T.	69	912	70	850
N.T.	63	1123	67	1014
M.B.	66	1201	69	1112
M.R.	68	1053	70	1045
N.S.	64	1295	69	1234
A.H.	54*	1676*	57*	1603*
G.M.	53*	2111*	57*	1995*

Note: Standard deviations in parentheses.
*$p < .05$ (significance test: Crawford & Howell, 1998).

Each item was presented twice during separate testing sessions to each participant, once as a picture and once as a spoken word. Participants were asked to write down the word. There was a gap of at least one month between testing sessions. Half of the participants (T.T., N.S., G.M., A.H., and nine controls) received the written picture-naming test first, and half received the spelling to dictation test first (M.B., N.T., M.R., and nine controls). A percentage score was also calculated that comprised the number of items spelt correctly to dictation as a percentage of the items that were spelt correctly from pictures. For instance, if a participant spelt only five items correctly in the spelling to dictation task but was able to spell 10 of these items accurately from pictures, a score of 50% would be given.

Results and discussion

Consistent with the surface dysgraphic profile of the participants, over 97% of the errors that were made in the spelling to dictation test were phonologically appropriate responses. The corresponding figure for written picture naming errors was 77%. However, the remaining errors on written picture naming were not spelling errors; 17% were omissions, and 7% were superordinate errors.

Mean accuracy and latency scores are shown in Table 6. The most important finding is that, consistent with the single orthographic lexicon account, the performance of A.H. and G.M. showed no evidence of any impairment relative to controls when spelling picture names. Nevertheless, the spelling of both A.H. ($t = 3.89$, $p < .01$) and G.M. ($t = 4.38$, $p < .01$) remained severely impaired when they were asked to write the same items to dictation. By contrast all of the remaining participants were impaired on both versions of the test. T.T. was impaired at spelling to dictation ($t = -7.30$, $p < .01$) and written spelling ($t = -6.83$, $p < .01$). N.T. was impaired at spelling to dictation ($t = -3.89$, $p < .01$) and written spelling ($t = -3.81$, $p < .01$). M.B. was impaired at spelling to dictation ($t = -4.38$, $p < .01$) and written spelling ($t = -3.81$, $p < .01$). M.R. was impaired at spelling to dictation

($t = -2.43$, $p < .05$) and written spelling ($t = -2.81$, $p < .01$). N.S. was impaired at spelling to dictation ($t = -1.95$, $p < .05$) and written spelling ($t = -2.36$, $p < .05$).

The Revised Standardised Difference Test (RSDT; Crawford & Garthwaite, 2005) was used to investigate the dissociation between written spelling and spelling to dictation. A significant dissociation was found for both A.H. and G.M., who performed well at written picture naming but badly at spelling to dictation of the same items [A.H. RSDT: $t(17) = 5.89$, $p < .001$; G.M. RSDT: $t(17) = 8.85$, $p < .001$]. The remaining surface dysgraphics showed no significant dissociation between the two modalities, consistent with equal impairments on both tasks. The third row in Table 7 shows that, apart from A.H. and G.M., the participants did not spell correctly in written picture naming any items that they had been unable to spell to dictation. Performance in the two different output modalities was highly correlated in controls ($r = .92$, $p < .01$).

The results of Experiment 3 show that there are strong parallels between the way in which all seven of these surface dysgraphic individuals read and spell familiar English words. T.T., N.T., N.S., and M.B. appear to have a problem at the level of the orthographic lexicon that impairs irregular word reading and the spelling of irregular words from pictures and to dictation. The two participants (A.H. and G.M.) who could access the meanings of written words from print in Experiment 2 appeared able to access the representations of words in the orthographic lexicon from their semantic representations and so spell correctly the names of pictures that they could not spell to dictation. M.R., conversely, who was impaired at accessing the meaning of written words from print in Experiment 2, seemed unable to use the semantic pathway to spell words. These findings provide strong support for the view that the same orthographic lexicon is involved in reading and spelling.

The parallels between A.H. and G.M.'s ability to spell picture names and to access the meaning of written words and between M.R.'s inability to spell picture names and access the meaning of written words are also striking. They are consistent with the view that, contrary to the model presented in Figure 1, the same orthography > semantics pathway as the one that is used in the reading of irregular English words can be used in reverse to support the spelling of these words. We return to this issue in the General Discussion.

Experiment 4: Spoken picture naming

In Experiment 4, we investigate further the reason why A.H. and G.M. are poor at reading and spelling irregular words to dictation given their preserved ability to make lexical decisions and semantic decisions about written words (Experiments 1 and 2). One possibility is that these two individuals have an anomic impairment of the kind that was described by Gvion and Friedmann (2016). Although they appear to have an intact orthography–semantic reading route that allows good performance on lexical decision tasks and on semantic decision tasks, they may have a developmental impairment that prevents them from activating the representations of familiar words in the phonological output lexicon. Alternatively, A.H. and G.M. may have what Friedmann and Lukov (2008) refer to as interlexical surface dyslexia in which there is an impairment to the connection from the orthographic lexicon to the phonological lexicon.

The obvious way to test these alternatives is to examine spoken picture naming. Interlexical surface dyslexia is associated with preserved spoken picture naming (Friedmann & Lukov, 2008). Conversely, if A.H. and G.M. suffer from an impairment to the speech output system, their picture naming should be significantly worse than that of controls. The other five surface dyslexics should perform relatively well because their impairment is to the orthographic

Table 7. A comparison of spelling to dictation with the spelling of picture names together with the proportion correct on spelling to dictation conditionalized on correct written picture naming.

	Controls (n = 18)	T.T.	N.T.	M.B.	N.S.	M.R.	A.H.	G.M.
Spelling to dictation (out of 22)	20.0 (1.6)	5*	12*	11*	16*	15*	12*	11*
Spelling picture names (out of 22)	19.6 (1.9)	6*	12*	12*	15*	14*	17	19
Spelling to dictation/Picture name spelling	1.0 (.02)	1.0	1.0	1.0	1.0	1.0	.71	.58

Note: Standard deviations in parentheses.
*$p < .05$ (significance test: Crawford & Howell, 1998).

system (T.T., N.T., M.B., N.S.), or to the connections between the orthographic system and the semantic system (M.R.). Because the orthographic system is not involved in picture naming (visual input > semantics > phonology in Figure 1), the semantic representations and, subsequently, the names of the pictures should be readily available to these five individuals.

Method

Materials and procedure

The picture naming task comprised 71 pictures (see Appendix D) taken from Snodgrass and Vanderwart (1980). An Apple Mac PowerBook G3 computer using Microsoft Office Powerpoint software was used for the presentation of the stimuli. Responses were recorded using the Audacity software program, and measures of both accuracy and latency were taken. The experimenter controlled the presentation. Participants were asked to give the name of each picture orally in Greek, as quickly and accurately as possible. They were also able to correct their answers as only the final answers were taken into account for the accuracy measure. Between four and six months later, the same pictures were again presented, and the participants were asked to respond in English.

Results and discussion

The results are presented in Table 6. As was expected, none of T.T., N.T., N.S., M.B., and M.R. experienced any difficulties with spoken picture naming. There appears to be no impairment that is associated with the retrieval of words from the phonological lexicon in any of these five cases. This finding confirms that the overall performance of T.T., N.T., N.S., and M.B. is consistent with Friedmann and Lukov's (2008) definition of input surface dyslexia and that M.R.'s overall performance is consistent with their definition of output surface dyslexia.

The picture naming performance in English of A.H. and GH was significantly impaired on measures of both accuracy (A.H.: $t = -3.48$, $p < .01$; G.M.: $t = -3.82$, $p < .01$) and speed (A.H.: $t = -3.52$, $p < .01$; G.M.; $t = -6.23$, $p < .001$). Fourteen of the 17 English picture-naming errors made by A.H. were classified as semantic, and the remaining three were omissions (e.g., *bow*–"I don't know"). Semantic errors included superordinate categories and circumlocutions (e.g., *ant*–"bee", *pig*–"animal", *anchor*:–"this thing in the ships", I can't remember the name of it"). Twelve of the 18 errors made by G.M. were semantic errors (e.g., *pig*–"sheep", *goat*–"animal", *anchor*–"an instrument, I can't remember the name of it"), and four were omissions (e.g., rabbit–"I don't know"). There was one visual error (*flute*–"pen") and one phonological error (*thumb*–"/θʌmb/").

A similar pattern was observed when these participants were asked to respond in Greek. Both A.H. and G.M. made significantly more errors than controls (A.H.: $t = -4.91$, $p < .001$; G.M.: $t = -4.91$, $p < .001$). A.H. ($t = 4.47$, $p < .001$) and G.M. ($t = 7.39$, $p < .001$) also named the pictures significantly more slowly than controls. Once again, none of T.T., N.T., M.B., M.R. and N.S. experienced any speed or accuracy problems.

These results clearly show that A.H. and G.M. were impaired at spoken picture naming. Their impaired accuracy and speed and the type of errors that they made are similar to those for the developmental surface dyslexic participants reported by Gvion and Friedmann (2016). It therefore appears that A.H. and G.M. make regularization errors when reading aloud irregular words because the lexical route is disrupted by a problem that is associated with the phonological output lexicon. This impairment resembles that observed not only in Gvion and Friedmann's developmental surface dyslexics but also in Watt, Jokel, and Behrmann's (1997) case of acquired surface dyslexia.

In light of their impaired ability to access phonology from semantics, we also investigated whether A.H. and G.M. would have difficulties in accessing the meaning of spoken words. Importantly, their auditory comprehension ability revealed no evidence of any impairment. First, following their attempt to name the pictures aloud in English, A.H. and GH were shown the items that they had previously failed to name correctly. They were then asked to match each picture with one of two orally presented words: a false name and the correct name (e.g., *is this an ant or bee?*). In the case of an omission or a superordinate error, a semantically related word was given instead. A.H. corrected all his false answers (17/17), and G.M. gave 15 out of 18 correct responses in the picture identification task, correcting all the semantic errors that he previously made. Both individuals, therefore, appeared able to access the meaning of auditorily presented words that they had been unable to produce during spoken picture naming.

Second, A.H. (39/40) and G.M. (37/40) both performed within the normal range when given a test of spoken word–picture matching that was taken from the Psycholinguistic Assessments of Language Processing in Aphasia (PALPA) battery (Test 47; Kay, Lesser, & Coltheart, 1992). Controls, however, performed at ceiling on this task (38.6/40, *SD* = 1.20) so these data do not represent a robust examination of A.H. and G.M.'s ability to understand spoken words.

Third, we administered an auditory comprehension test that was based on the vocabulary sub-test of the Wechsler Abbreviated Scale of Intelligence (WASI; Wechsler, 1999). It was first given in Greek, and 6 months later it was given in English. Participants heard 34 words and were asked to provide a definition. A score of two was awarded on each trial where an accurate definition was given (e.g., *improvise > ad lib*). A score of one was awarded when a less precise definition was provided (e.g., *improvise > to adjust to new conditions and demands*). A score of zero was given for an incorrect answer (e.g., *improvise > compromise*). The 34 English words with their 34 Greek translations are presented in Appendix E. Mean scores are shown in Table 8. It can be seen that control performance was not at ceiling and that all of the dysgraphic participants, including A.H. and G.M., performed within the normal range on both English and Greek versions of the test.

There is therefore no evidence that either A.H. or G.M. has a problem in understanding spoken words. Such an outcome is consistent with the existence of separate pathways between semantics and phonology that support speech comprehension and production (see Figure 1). In A.H. and G.M., the link from phonology to semantics appears to be unimpaired even though the link from semantics to phonology has not developed normally.

Since A.H. and G.M. could spell accurately irregular English words from pictures (Experiment 3), it appeared that A.H. and G.M. could make use of the semantic system when spelling irregular words from pictures but not when spelling irregular words to dictation. Because they can access the meaning of spoken words (Experiment 4) and because the connections between semantics and orthography are intact (Experiments 2 and 3), it is surprising that A.H. and G.M. cannot use the semantic route to activate the orthographic representations of irregular words when spelling to dictation. It appears as if the nonlexical route in some way captures the spelling process when target words are spoken aloud, impeding the semantics > orthography pathway from generating the correct spelling of words with atypical sound–spelling correspondences.

General discussion

Previous research has shown that individuals with developmental surface dysgraphia in orthographies such as English (e.g., Hanley et al., 1992), German (Bergmann & Wimmer, 2008), and Italian (Angelelli et al., 2010) frequently perform badly on tests of lexical decision. Such a pattern of performance has been taken as support for the view that the same orthographic lexicon is used in reading and spelling and that a developmental impairment to this lexicon affects both spelling and lexical decision. In the present study, consistent with such findings, we have reported the performance of four individuals with surface dysgraphia (T.T., N.T., N.S., M.B.) who were impaired at orthographic lexical decision in both English and Greek. However, contrary to those earlier reports, the present study has provided evidence of three individuals (M.R., A.H., G.M.) with developmental surface dysgraphia who performed well at orthographic lexical decision tasks in both English and Greek. Preserved lexical decision performance raises the possibility that separate orthographic lexicons exist for reading and spelling. Any suggestion that these three individuals might have an impaired spelling lexicon but an unimpaired reading lexicon was discounted, however. This is because all three of these individuals read familiar words in Greek and English more slowly than controls, and their oral reading of irregular English words was inaccurate (Sotiropoulos & Hanley, 2017).

Table 8. Mean accuracy on the auditory comprehension test in both Greek and English.

	Controls *M (SD)*	*n*	T.T.	N.T.	M.B.	N.S.	M.R.	A.H.	G.M.
English	48.0 (6.1)	14	59	51	51	46	48	45	47
Greek	55.0 (7.5)	9	64	59	58	54	56	48	50

Note: Accuracy: out of 68. Standard deviations in parentheses.

Three types of developmental surface dyslexia and dysgraphia

Instead, we have claimed that this pattern of performance can be readily explained in terms of a single orthographic lexicon. In so doing, we have employed the framework used by Friedmann and Lukov (2008) and by Gvion and Friedmann (2016) to explain the existence of different types of developmental surface dyslexia in Hebrew. Friedmann and her colleagues observed these differences in a Semitic language (Hebrew) in which the cues to phonology from orthography are relatively limited. Our results suggest that these distinctions can be applied equally effectively to surface dyslexia in less opaque orthographies than Hebrew such as English. Most importantly, we have extended Friedmann's framework to also accommodate developmental spelling impairments in surface dysgraphia in terms of the DRC–SLA (see Figure 1).

The four cases (T.T., N.T., N.S., and M.B.) who were impaired at orthographic lexical decision appeared unable to read and spell irregular words because of a problem at the level of an orthographic lexicon that encodes the identity and the order of the graphemes that familiar written words contain (input surface dyslexia and dysgraphia). The three individuals (M.R., A.H., G.M.) who performed well at lexical decision had an intact orthographic lexicon but appeared to have suffered damage to other components of the reading and writing system. In the case of M.R., who performed poorly when making semantic decisions about written words, it appeared that his orthographic lexicon was intact but that there was a developmental impairment to the connections between the orthographic lexicon and the semantic system (orthographic output surface dyslexia and dysgraphia). As a consequence, he found it difficult to access the meaning of written words in Experiment 2 and to access the orthographic representations of words from semantics when spelling the names of pictures (Experiment 3).

The good lexical decision performance of A.H. and G.M. in Experiment 1 was again consistent with an intact orthographic lexicon. Their unimpaired ability to access the meaning of written words (Experiment 2) is consistent with a preserved pathway from orthography to semantics. As with the developmental surface dyslexics reported by Gvion and Friedmann (2016), it appears that A.H. and G.M.'s impaired ability to read irregular words aloud is the consequence of a difficulty in accessing the phonological system from the semantic system during spoken word production (Experiment 4). Experiment 3 revealed a striking dissociation between their impaired spelling to dictation and preserved spelling of picture names. It appears that A.H. and G.M. had preserved access to the orthographic lexicon from semantics when spelling the names of pictures despite their inability to spell the same words to dictation.

Our results have therefore shown that a single lexicon account can provide a plausible explanation of the finding that a developmental spelling impairment that is selective to irregular words (developmental surface dysgraphia) can co-occur with both impaired (T.T., N.T., N.S., and M.B.), and preserved (M.R., A.H., G.M.) lexical decision performance for words of this kind. The core impairment in those with impaired lexical decision appears to be to the development of the orthographic lexicon itself. The core developmental impairment in those with unimpaired lexical decision appears to be to the connections between the orthographic lexicon and the semantic system (M.R.) or to the connections from the semantic system to the phonological system (A.H. and G.M.). Therefore, there are at least three distinct developmental deficits that can give rise, in an individual, to a combination of surface dyslexia and dysgraphia. All three are consistent with the claim that the same orthographic lexicon is used for both reading and spelling. Such an outcome provides further evidence that the same neurophysiological substrate(s) supports learning to read and learning to spell familiar words (Rapp & Lipka, 2011).

It is also important to note that in Experiments 1 and 4, the nature of the processing impairment that these seven individuals experienced in English was identical to the processing impairment that they experienced in Greek. This outcome strengthens the claims of Sotiropoulos and Hanley (2017) that the foundation skills that are important for learning to read and spell in English are the same as those that are required for learning to read and spell in Greek. The results of these two experiments provide further evidence that the neurophysiological substrate that supports the connections between orthography and semantic that are involved in learning to read and spell is the same in both Greek and English.

Consequently, a developmental weakness in part of this underlying substrate will inevitably lead to an impairment that affects development of literacy in different orthographies in an analogous way.

The DRC versus the triangle model

To maintain consistency with the approach taken by Friedmann and her colleagues, we have so far explained the findings in terms of a version of the DRC model (Coltheart et al., 2001). In order to accommodate both reading and spelling, the expanded DRC–single lexicon account (DRC–SLA) that is represented in Figure 1 has been used. In this section, we further scrutinize the effectiveness of the DRC–SLA and contrast it with an account that relies instead upon the *triangle* model of reading (Harm & Seidenberg, 1999; Plaut, McClelland, Seidenberg, & Patterson, 1996; Woollams, 2014). We discuss whether the architecture of the triangle model (see Figure 2) can provide a more or less satisfactory account than the DRC–SLA model of the individual differences in reading and spelling that have been observed in Experiments 1–4.

According to the triangle model, there are separate pathways from orthography to semantics (the semantic route) and from orthography to phonology (the phonological route). The orthographic units do not contain information about the way in which individual words are spelled. Instead this information is instantiated in the connections between orthography and phonology and in the connections between orthography and semantics. Early versions of the model (Seidenberg & McClelland, 1989) demonstrated that both regular and irregular words could be read reasonably accurately by a single orthography > phonology pathway. When, however, an orthography > semantics pathway was incorporated into the model in subsequent simulations (Plaut et al., 1996), the semantic pathway assumed primary responsibility for reading all but the most frequent irregular words. Proponents of the triangle model therefore assume that, for the majority of readers, the correct pronunciations of both regular and irregular English words are generated by first activating their meaning from the orthographic units (see Figure 2). This claim has been criticized because a small number of acquired dyslexics with semantic impairments can read irregular words despite being unable to define them (e.g., Blazely, Coltheart, & Casey, 2005). In response, adherents of the triangle model claim that there exist a minority of readers of English who rely more heavily on the orthography > phonology than on the orthography > semantics pathway when reading words with atypical spelling–sound correspondences (Plaut, 1997; Woollams, Lambon Ralph, Madrid, & Patterson, 2016).

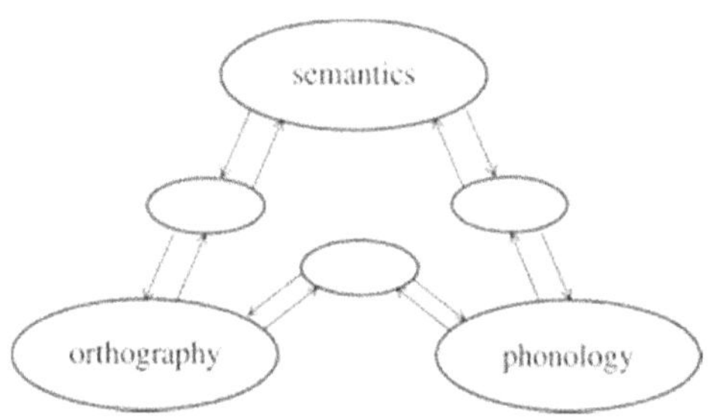

Figure 2. The basic architecture of the triangle model of reading in which the connections between orthography, phonology, and semantics are bidirectional.

Because the semantic pathway is so important for the accurate reading of irregular English words, its impaired development is assumed to cause surface dyslexia (Woollams, 2014). Nonwords, regular words, and irregular words of high familiarity can be read on the basis of direct mappings between orthographic units and phonological units (the phonological route). It is assumed that this pathway develops relatively normally in surface dyslexia. Poor nonword reading in phonological dyslexia is explained in terms of a developmental impairment to the phonological units themselves (Harm & Seidenberg, 1999).

Whether or not exactly the same units and connections are used in spelling and reading has not been made explicit by supporters of the triangle model. Nevertheless, such a proposal is certainly consistent with the *primary systems* approach that is frequently advocated by supporters of the triangle model (Patterson & Lambon Ralph, 1999; Woollams, 2014) in which the systems that subserve the acquisition of literacy rely upon connections with more basic underlying knowledge systems. Furthermore, although the triangle model has rarely been used to investigate spelling performance, Loosemore, Brown, and Watson (1991) reported a successful simulation of the phonological spelling route. They used a similar architecture to that which the triangle model employs during simulations of the phonological route in reading. In this model, the spellings of regular English words were more easily acquired than the spellings of irregular words, and some of the symptoms of surface dysgraphia were simulated.

The cases of T.T., N.T., N.S., and M.B.: Input surface dyslexia and dysgraphia

As we have seen, the DRC–SLA can parsimoniously explain the poor reading, spelling, and lexical decision performance of T.T., N.T., N.S., and M.B. in terms of a single impairment to the development of the orthographic lexicon. In the triangle model, the orthography > semantics pathway is involved in making lexical decisions (e.g., Plaut & Booth, 2006). T.T., N.T., N.S., and M.B.'s impaired lexical decision and poor reading performance would be the result of very weak connections between the orthographic units and the semantic system. If the same pathway between orthography and semantics is also involved in written word production then this impairment would explain T.T., N.T., N.S., and M.B.'s impaired spelling of irregular words. Otherwise an additional semantics > orthography impairment would be necessary to explain their spelling deficit.

The case of M.R.: Orthographic output surface dyslexia and dysgraphia

Can the triangle model explain M.R.'s inability to access meaning from print despite preserved lexical decision as the consequence of an impairment to the connections between the orthographic and semantic systems? If the orthography > semantics pathway is involved in making orthographic lexical decisions, then an orthography > semantics impairment might be expected to produce poor lexical decision performance. However, a simulation by Plaut and Booth (2006, p. 198) showed that it was possible to lesion the orthography > semantics pathway such that lexical decision was "relatively unaffected over a range of lesion severities that produced substantial semantic impairment". The dissociation between T.T., N.T., N.S., and M.B.'s impaired and M.R.'s preserved lexical decision performance could therefore be explained by the triangle model in terms of differences in the severity of the orthography > semantic impairment. M.R.'s poor spelling of picture names could be seen as reflecting the impaired development of the same pathway between orthography and semantics or the impaired development of a separate spelling route from semantics to orthography.

According to the DRC–SLA, M.R. has developmental impairments to the connections from the orthographic lexicon to the semantic system (poor access to the meaning of irregular English words when reading), and to the connections from the orthographic lexicon to the semantic system (poor spelling of picture names that are irregular English words). In the DRC–SLA, however, there is also a direct lexical reading route that can read familiar words aloud via a connection between the orthographic lexicon and the phonological lexicon without the need for semantic mediation. In order to explain M.R.'s poor reading of irregular words, it would therefore be necessary to assume that there is an additional phonology > orthography deficit that has inhibited the development of the direct lexical reading route (see Figure 1). Poor spelling of irregular words would indicate an additional impairment to the development of the orthography > phonology spelling route in Figure 1.

According to the triangle model, the direct connection from the orthographic system to the phonological system is primarily used to process regular words and nonwords. M.R. is relatively proficient at reading and spelling regular words and nonwords (Table 1). Unlike the DRC–SLA, therefore, it would *not* be necessary to assume that M.R. has any additional developmental impairment to the connections between orthography and phonology unless he is one of the small number of readers who rely on the phonological pathway to process irregular words (Woollams et al., 2016).

The cases of A.H. and G.M.: Phonological output surface dyslexia

The triangle model can explain A.H. and G.M.'s reading and picture naming problems as the consequence of a single developmental impairment to the pathway from the semantic system to the phonological system (Figure 2). A.H. and G.M.'s preserved ability to comprehend the meanings of spoken words despite their impaired spoken word output is consistent with the existence of separate pathways between semantics and phonology that are involved in speech production and comprehension (see Figures 1 and 2). As with M.R., there is no need to assume a developmental impairment to the pathway between orthography and phonology because, according to the triangle model, this route is not primarily responsible for the way in which most individuals read irregular words. A.H. and G.M. could not have a developmental impairment at the level of the phonological units themselves because, according to the triangle model, the outcome would be developmental phonological dyslexia (Harm & Seidenberg, 1999).

In terms of the DRC–SLA, A.H. and G.M.'s impaired picture naming and reading aloud of irregular words could be seen as the consequence of developmental impairments to the connections from the semantic system to the phonological lexicon. If so, as with the case of M.R., it would be necessary to assume a second developmental impairment to the pathway from the orthographic lexicon to the phonological lexicon in order to explain their poor irregular word reading. Alternatively, if as Gvion and Friedmann (2016) suggest, the impairment was at the level of the phonological output lexicon itself, then this would prevent both the lexical–semantic and direct lexical reading routes from producing the correct pronunciations of irregular words. Nonword reading ability would not be affected in this scenario (see Figure 1). If, however, A.H. and G.M. have a problem at the level of the phonological output lexicon itself, it becomes difficult to explain their unimpaired ability to comprehend the meaning of spoken words without the assumption that separate phonological lexicons are used in auditory comprehension and production. This assumption is not implausible but it requires a more elaborate model than that presented in Figure 1. In summary, in order to explain A.H. and G.M.'s impaired reading of irregular words, the DRC–SLA model requires separate impairments to the lexical–semantic and direct lexical routes or else it requires separate input and output phonological lexicons.

What about A.H. and G.M.'s spelling of words with atypical phoneme > grapheme correspondences? Both the DRC–SLA and the triangle model can explain A.H. and G.M.'s accurate spelling of the names of pictures that are irregular English words (Experiment 3) in terms of an unimpaired pathway from semantics to orthography. A.H. and G.M.'s poor spelling to dictation of words with atypical sound–spelling correspondences is less easy to explain, however. In the DRC–SLA, there must be a developmental impairment to the connection from the phonological lexicon to the orthographic lexicon. An orthography–phonology impairment is not required by the triangle model as this pathway would not be considered responsible for the way in which most people spell irregular words. But neither model can explain why A.H. and G.M.'s spelling to dictation of irregular words cannot proceed via the intact semantics > orthography pathway.

Conclusion

In summary, both the DRC–SLA (Figure 1) and the triangle model can accommodate most of the main findings reported in this study. However, both models have relative strengths and weaknesses, and neither model can readily accommodate all of them.

The DRC–SLA provides the most straightforward explanation of lexical decision impairments. T.T., N.T., N.S., and M.B.'s impaired lexical decision, reading, and spelling (Tables 2 and 3) can be explained in terms of a single lesion to the orthographic representations themselves. M.R.'s preserved lexical decision but impaired semantic access is consistent with a developmental impairment to the pathway from orthography to semantics. The triangle model assumes instead that a severe developmental impairment to the orthography > semantics pathway disrupts lexical decision (T.T., N.T., N.S., M.B.), and that a weaker impairment to this pathway can impair semantic access but not lexical decision (M.R.). Unless the same orthography–semantics pathway is used for both reading and spelling, the triangle model would also require an additional impairment in order to explain T.T., N.T., N.S., and M.B.'s irregular word spelling deficits. Both models would require an additional impairment to this pathway to explain M.R.'s spelling deficit. Nonetheless, the existence of a single pathway between orthography and semantics would explain the parallels between the way in which M.R., A.H., and G.M. access the meaning of written words and spell the names of pictures (Experiments 2 and 3). Figures 1 and 2 both contain two separate orthography–semantics pathways, but both models could be easily modified to include just one.

In the DRC–SLA, there must be developmental impairments to both the lexical–semantic route and the direct lexical route between orthography and phonology to explain why an individual such as M.R. is unable to read irregular words aloud. The absence of a reading (and spelling) route of this kind in the triangle model means that it can provide a more parsimonious account than the DRC–SLA of the developmental impairments that are needed to explain the irregular word reading (and spelling) deficits that M.R. experiences.

Finally, neither model can fully explain the nature of A.H. and G.M.'s spelling impairment. Because they appear to have preserved links from phonology to semantics and from semantics to orthography, the reason why they are unable to spell to dictation words with atypical sound–spelling correspondences remains obscure.

Acknowledgements

The authors would like to thank Brenda Rapp and an anonymous reviewer for their perceptive comments on earlier drafts. They also thank David Plaut for information about spelling and lexical decision in the triangle model and Chris Barry for supplying the words used in Experiment 3.

Disclosure statement

No potential conflict of interest was reported by the authors.

References

Angelelli, P., Marinelli, C. V., & Zoccolotti, P. (2010). Single or dual orthographic representations for reading and spelling? A study of Italian dyslexic–dysgraphic and normal children. *Cognitive Neuropsychology*, *27*, 305–333. doi:10.1080/02643294.2010.543539

Barry, C., & Seymour, P. H. K. (1988). Lexical priming and sound-to-spelling contingency effects in nonword spelling. *The Quarterly Journal of Experimental Psychology Section A*, *40*, 5–40. doi:10.1080/14640748808402280

Behrmann, M., & Bub, D. (1992). Surface dyslexia and dysgraphia: Dual routes, single lexicon. *Cognitive Neuropsychology*, *9*, 209–251. doi:10.1080/02643299208252059

Bergmann, J., & Wimmer, H. (2008). A dual-route perspective on poor reading in a regular orthography: Evidence from phonological and orthographic lexical decisions. *Cognitive Neuropsychology*, *25*(5), 653–676. doi:10.1080/02643290802221404

Blazely, A., Coltheart, M., & Casey, B. (2005). Semantic impairment with and without surface dyslexia: Implications for models of reading. *Cognitive Neuropsychology*, *22*, 695–717. doi:10.1080/02643290442000257

Castles, A., & Coltheart, M. (1996). Cognitive correlates of developmental surface dyslexia: A single case study. *Cognitive Neuropsychology*, *13*, 25–50. doi:10.1080/026432996382051

Coltheart, M., & Funnell, E. (1987). Reading and writing: One lexicon or two? In A. Allport, D. Mackay, W. Prinz, & E. Sheerer (Eds.), *Language perception and production*. London: Academic Press.

Coltheart, M., Rastle, K., Perry, C., Langdon, R., & Zeigler, J. (2001). DRC: A dual route cascaded model of visual word recognition and reading aloud. *Psychological Review*, *108*, 204–256. doi:10.1037/0033-295X.108.1.204

Crawford, J. R., & Garthwaite, P. H. (2005). Testing for suspected impairments and dissociations in single-case studies in neuropsychology: Evaluation of alternatives using Monte Carlo simulations and revised tests for dissociations. *Neuropsychology*, *19*, 318–331. doi:10.1037/0894-4105.19.3.318

Crawford, J. R., & Howell, D. C. (1998). Comparing an individual's test score against norms derived from small samples. *The Clinical Neuropsychologist (Neuropsychology, Development and Cognition: Section D)*, *12*(4), 482–486.

Douklias, S., Masterson, J., & Hanley, J. R. (2009). Surface and phonological developmental dyslexia in Greek. *Cognitive Neuropsychology*, *26*(8), 705–723. doi:10.1080/02643291003691106

Ellis, A. W., Lambon Ralph, M. A., Morris, J., & Hunter, A. (2000). Surface dyslexia, description, treatment, and interpretation. In E. Funnell (Ed.), *Case studies in the neuropsychology of reading* (pp. 85–123). Hove: Psychology Press.

Ellis, A. W., & Young, A. W. (1988). *Human cognitive neuropsychology*. Hove: Psychology Press.

Friedmann, N., & Lukov, L. (2008). Developmental surface dyslexias. *Cortex*, *44*, 1146–1160. doi:10.1016/j.cortex.2007.09.005

Goulandris, N. K., & Snowling, M. (1991). Visual memory deficits: A plausible cause of developmental dyslexia? Evidence from a single case study. *Cognitive Neuropsychology*, *8*, 127–154. doi:10.1080/02643299108253369

Gvion, A., & Friedmann, N. (2016). A principled relation between reading and naming in acquired and developmental anomia: Surface dyslexia following impairment in the phonological output lexicon. *Frontiers in Psychology: Language Sciences*, *7* (340), 1–16.

Hanley, J. R., & Gard, F. (1995). A dissociation between developmental surface and phonological dyslexia in two undergraduate students. *Neuropsychologia*, *33*, 909–914. doi:10.1016/0028-3932(95)00038-5

Hanley, J. R., Hastie, K., & Kay, J. (1992). Developmental surface dyslexia and dysgraphia: An orthographic processing impairment. *The Quarterly Journal of Experimental Psychology Section A*, *44*, 285–319. doi:10.1080/02724989243000046

Harm, M. W., & Seidenberg, M. S. (1999). Phonology, reading acquisition, and dyslexia: Insights from connectionist models. *Psychological Review*, *106*, 491–528. doi:10.1037/0033-295X.106.3.491

Holmes, V., & Carruthers, J. (1998). The relation between reading and spelling in skilled adult readers. *Journal of Memory and Language*, *39*, 264–289. doi:10.1006/jmla.1998.2583

Kay, J., Lesser, R., & Coltheart, M. (1992). *Psycholinguistic assessment of language processing in aphasia*. London: Lawrence Erlbaum Associates.

Loosemore, R. P. W., Brown, G. D. A., & Watson, F. L. (1991). A connectionist model of alphabetic spelling development and developmental and acquired dysgraphia. *Proceedings of the Thirteenth Annual Conference of the Cognitive Science Society, 13*, 61–66.

Niolaki, G., Terzopoulos, A., & Masterson, J. (2014). Varieties of developmental dyslexia in Greek children. *Writing Systems Research, 6*(2), 230–256. doi:10.1080/17586801.2014.893862

Patterson, K., & Lambon Ralph, M. A. (1999). Selective disorders of reading? *Current Opinion in Neurobiology, 9*, 235–239. doi:10.1016/S0959-4388(99)80033-6

Plaut, D. (1997). Structure and function in the lexical system: Insights from distributed models of word reading and lexical decision. *Language and Cognitive Processes, 12*, 765–806. doi:10.1080/016909697386682

Plaut, D. C., & Booth, J. R. (2006). More modeling but still no stages: Reply to Borowsky and Besner. *Psychological Review, 113*, 196–200. doi:10.1037/0033-295X.113.1.196

Plaut, D. C., McClelland, J. L., Seidenberg, M. S., & Patterson, K. (1996). Understanding normal and impaired word reading: Computational principles in quasi-regular domains. *Psychological Review, 103*, 56–115. doi:10.1037/0033-295X.103.1.56

Purcell, J. J., Shea, J., & Rapp, B. (2014). Beyond the visual word form area: The orthography–semantics interface in spelling and reading. *Cognitive Neuropsychology, 31*, 482–510. doi:10.1080/02643294.2014.909399

Rapp, B., & Lipka, K. (2011). The literate brain: The relationship between spelling and reading. *Journal of Cognitive Neuroscience, 23*, 1180–1197. doi:10.1162/jocn.2010.21507

Romani, C., Ward, J., & Olson, A. (1999). Developmental surface dysgraphia: What is the underlying cognitive impairment? *The Quarterly Journal of Experimental Psychology Section A, 52*(1), 97–128. doi:10.1080/713755804

Seidenberg, M. S, & McClelland, J. L. (1989). A distributed developmental model of word recognitionand naming. *Psychological Review, 96*, 523–568.

Snodgrass, J. G., & Vanderwart, M. (1980). A standardized set of 260 pictures: Norms for name agreement, image agreement, familiarity, and visual complexity. *Journal of Experimental Psychology: Human Learning and Memory, 6*(2), 174–215. doi:10.1037/0278-7393.6.2.174

Sotiropoulos, A. (2015). Surface and phonological developmental dyslexia among Greek University students in both Greek and English. *A thesis submitted for the degree of Doctor of Philosophy.* University of Essex, UK.

Sotiropoulos, A., & Hanley, J. R. (2017). Developmental surface and phonological dyslexia in both Greek and English. *Cognition, 168*, 205–216. doi:10.1016/j.cognition.2017.06.024

Temple, C. M. (1985). Developmental surface dysgraphia: A case report. *Applied Psycholinguistics, 6*, 391–406. doi:10.1017/S0142716400006329

Watt, S., Jokel, R., & Behrmann, M. (1997). Surface dyslexia in nonfluent aphasia. *Cognitive Neuropsychology, 56*, 211–233.

Wechsler, D. (1999). *Wechsler abbreviated scale of intelligence*. San Antonio, TX: Psychological Corporation.

Woollams, A. (2014). Connectionist neuropsychology: Uncovering ultimate causes of acquired dyslexia. *Philosophical Transactions of the Royal Society B, 369*, 1634.

Woollams, A. M., Lambon Ralph, M. A., Madrid, G., & Patterson, K. E. (2016). Do you read how I read? Systematic individual differences in semantic reliance amongst normal readers. *Frontiers in Psychology, 7*, 1052. doi:10.3389/fpsyg.2016.01757

Appendices

Appendix A

Words and pseudohomophones used in the English orthographic lexical decision task in Experiment 1.

Words	Pseudohomophones
speed	spead
learn	lern
need	nead
dream	dreem
yacht	yot
answer	anser
debt	det
year	yeer
cough	coff
muscle	mussle
girl	gerl
group	groop
green	grean
ceiling	cealing
mortgage	morgage
feed	fead
soup	soop
nurse	nerse
scream	skream
leaf	leef
cream	creem
keep	keap
mean	meen
fear	feer

Appendix B

Words and pseudohomophones used in the Greek orthographic lexical decision task in Experiment 1.

Words	Pseudohomophones
αυτοκίνητο	αφτοκίνητο
αυτοθαυμάζομαι	αφτοθαυμάζομαι
τρέχω	τραίχω
ξιφασκία	ξυφασκία
στρατόπεδο	στρατόπαιδο
ουτοπιστής	ουτωπιστής
εξαιρώ	εξερώ
ωφέλιμος	οφέλιμος
τσουρέκι	τσουραίκι
άφραγκος	αφραγγος
αγγλομαθής	αγκλομαθής
αγκάθι	αγγάθι
μέλισσα	μέλισα
αγιογραφώ	αγιογραφφώ
αυτοσεβασμός	αφτοσευασμός
αβασίλευτος	αυασίλεφτος
εύσωμος	έφσομος
καύσωνας	κάφσονας
κεραυνός	καιραβνός
περισσεύω	περισέβω
αυτεπάγγελτος	αφτεπάγκελτος
αυτοσυγκράτηση	αφτοσυγγράτηση
ήσυχος	ύσηχος
στρογγυλός	στρογκιλός
ήττα	ίτα
μοιραίος	μυρραίος
οπωροκηπευτικά	οπορωκηπευτικά
τυποποίηση	τιποποίυση
παγκόσμιος	παγγόσμειος
πρίγκιπας	πρύγγιπας

(Continued)

Continued.

Words	Pseudohomophones
αλληλεγγύη	αληλεγκύη
μαραγκός	μαρραγγός
θάλασσα	θάλλασα
εκκλησία	εκλλησία

Appendix C

Pairs of homophones used in the English semantic decision task in Experiment 2.

Triad (target meaning: pair of homophones)
be informed: no / **know**
fruit: **pear** / pair
destroy: brake / **break**
death: **bury** / berry
room: sweet / **suite**
family: **son** / sun
God: praise / **prays**
construct: **build** / billed
part of: sum / **some**
meat: **steak** / stake
large: grate / **great**
animal: **bear** / bare
nothing: nun / **none**
lost: **waste** / waist
all: hole / **whole**
bus: **route** / root
food: eight / **ate**
number: too / **two**

Note: *Correct item in bold.

Appendix D

The Greek picture names from Experiment 4.

τσεκούρι *(axe)*	**άλογο** *(horse)*	**καράβι** *(yacht/sailboat)*
μπάλα *(ball)*	**φεγγάρι** *(moon)*	**πατούσα** *(foot)*
φιόγκος *(bow)*	**πάπια** *(duck)*	**λεμονί** *(lemon)*
μπολ *(bowl)*	**βιβλίο** *(book)*	**κρεμμύδι** *(onion)*
ψωμί *(bread)*	**ήλιος** *(sun)*	**βουνό** *(mountain)*
παλτό *(coat)*	**ροδάκινο** *(peach)*	**βίδα** *(screw)*
χτένα *(comb)*	**γουρούνι** *(pig)*	**αγελάδα** *(cow)*
πόρτα *(door)*	**σκαμνί** *(stool)*	**βέλος** *(arrow)*
μάτι *(eye)*	**πιρούνι** *(fork)*	**καρέκλα** *(chair)*
φλογέρα *(flute)*	**πόδι** *(leg)*	**ποτήρι** *(glass)*
μύγα *(fly)*	**ρόδα** *(wheel)*	**ελέφαντας** *(elephant)*
γάντι *(glove)*	**ρολόι (τοίχου)** *(clock)*	**πουλί** *(bird)*
κατσικά *(goat)*	**τούρτα** *(cake)*	**σκάλα** *(ladder)*
κλειδί *(key)*	**στέμμα** *(crown)*	**κουνέλι** *(rabbit)*
μαχαίρι *(knife)*	**τύμπανο** *(drum)*	**αστέρι** *(star)*

πουκάμισο (*shirt*)	**πρόβατο** (*sheep*)	**βούρτσα** (*brush*)
παπούτσι (*shoe*)	**στυλό** (*pen*)	**φρυγανιέρα** (*toaster*)
φούστα (*skirt*)	**σύννεφο** (*cloud*)	**φώκια** (*seal*)
κύκνος (*swan*)	**μύτη** (*nose*)	**σκύλος** (*dog*)
αντίχειρας (*thumb*)	**αρκούδα** (*bear*)	**κούνια** (*swing*)
γραβάτα (*tie*)	**άγκυρα** (*anchor*)	**ψάρι** (*fish*)
ρολόι (*watch*)	**σίδερο** (*iron*)	**ζώνη** (*belt*)
μυρμήγκι (*ant*)	**καρδιά** (*heart*)	**ψαλίδι** (*scissors*)
μέλισσα (*bee*)	**μαϊμού** (*monkey*)	

Appendix E

Words used in the auditory comprehension test in Experiment 4

bird, calendar, number, bell, lunch, police, vacation, pet, balloon, transform, alligator, cart, blame, dance, purpose, entertain, famous, reveal, decade, tradition, rejoice, enthusiastic, improvise, impulse, haste, trend, intermittent, devout, impertinent, niche, presumptuous, formidable, ruminate, panacea.

πούλι, ημερολόγιο, νούμερο, κουδούνι, γεύμα, αστύνομια, διακοπές, κατοικίδιο, μπαλόνι, μεταμορφώνω, αλιγάτορας, καρότσι, κατηγορία, χορός, σκοπός, διασκεδάζω, διάσημος, αποκαλύπτω, δεκαέτια, παράδοση, ευφραίνομαι, ενθουσιώδης, αυτοσχεδιάζω, παρόρμηση, βιασύνη, τάση, διαλείπων, ένθερμος, άξεστος, εσοχή, ξιπασμένος, ανυπέρβλητος, αναμασώ, πανάκεια

Lexical processing and distributional knowledge in sound–spelling mapping in a consistent orthography: A longitudinal study of reading and spelling in dyslexic and typically developing children

Chiara Valeria Marinelli, Pamela Cellini, Pierluigi Zoccolotti and Paola Angelelli

ABSTRACT

This study examined the ability to master lexical processing and use knowledge of the relative frequency of sound–spelling mappings in both reading and spelling. Twenty-four dyslexic and dysgraphic children and 86 typically developing readers were followed longitudinally in 3rd and 5th grades. Effects of word regularity, word frequency, and probability of sound–spelling mappings were examined in two experimental tasks: (a) spelling to dictation; and (b) orthographic judgment. Dyslexic children showed larger regularity and frequency effects than controls in both tasks. Sensitivity to distributional information of sound–spelling mappings was already detected by third grade, indicating early acquisition even in children with dyslexia. Although with notable differences, knowledge of the relative frequencies of sound–spelling mapping influenced both reading and spelling. Results are discussed in terms of their theoretical and empirical implications.

Introduction

Language acquisition in part reflects learning the regularities of the language that a child is exposed to and occurs without an explicit intention to learn and without clear awareness of the regularities (Perruchet & Pacton, 2006). In fact, both oral and written language have a rich statistical structure that is being identified thanks to the analysis of large linguistic corpora (e.g., Arciuli & Simpson, 2012). Also, learning to read and spell reflects not only the acquisition of phoneme-to-grapheme correspondences (and vice versa), as it occurs through explicit instruction, but also the ability to detect the distributional properties of written language.

In languages with inconsistent orthographies, such as English and French, these regularities may be at different levels particularly with regard to their phonology, orthography, and sound–letter mappings. An example at the phonological level is phonotactic probability, which is a frequency measure for how often phones and biphones occur in words in a given language (for English see Luce & Large, 2001; Storkel, 2001). Stimuli with high phonotactic probability are more accurately spelled and recognized as correct than those with low phonotactic probabilities (e.g., Apel, Wolter, & Masterson, 2006). At the orthographic level, there are various types of regularities, such as single-letter positional frequency, which assist perception in letter search and word-recognition tasks (e.g., Mason, 1975) or graphotactic regularities, such as patterns involving the order and arrangement of letters in written words (e.g., Pacton, Fayol, & Perruchet, 2002; Treiman & Cassar, 1997). Studies of English- and French-speaking children show that they find it easier to read (e.g., Pacton, Perruchet, Fayol, & Cleeremans, 2001) and spell (e.g., Treiman, 1993) words with the most frequent orthographic patterns. Knowledge of orthographic regularities was also found to influence the recall of newly learned orthographic representations in French-speaking children and adults (e.g., Pacton, Sobaco, Fayol, & Treiman, 2013).

Furthermore, the sound–spelling (and vice versa) mappings found in inconsistent orthographies can be framed in probabilistic terms. For example, during their formal instruction in reading children are often explicitly taught to associate the letter "c" with the phoneme /k/ (e.g., as in the word "cat"). However, the letter "c" can also be associated with the phoneme /s/ (as in "circus"). Over time, even if children are not explicitly taught they discover that most words beginning with the letter "c" followed by the letter "i" start with the initial phoneme /s/, and become sensitive to the co-occurrence of letters (i.e., contextual cues; Arciuli & Simpson, 2012). Then, children implicitly acquire the distributional properties that characterize sound–spelling mappings (of a single letter or a sequence of letters/sounds) when processing stimuli sublexically.

Clearly, an alternative way of processing words in reading and spelling bypasses sublexical mapping through the acquisition of orthographic representations of each word in the input and output lexicons. To a large extent lexical processing is also sensitive to distributional properties: It is well known that the frequency with which a word is encountered in texts is also one of the best predictors of reading and spelling accuracy in children (for reading see, for example, Zoccolotti, De Luca, Di Filippo, Judica, & Martelli, 2009; for spelling see, for example, Lété, Peereman, & Fayol, 2008).

Contrary to widespread opinion, also in languages characterized by consistent orthographies (e.g., German, Spanish, Italian) is sound–spelling mapping not always highly predictable. In Italian (the focus of the present paper), in reading there is a unique case of unpredictability concerning stress assignment (see description below), while in spelling there are more instances of inconsistent sound–spelling mappings. For instance, the phonemic group [kw] can be transcribed with the orthographic sequences QU or CU. Since reliance on the sublexical procedure does not allow choosing among the two possible spelling options, a child with poor lexical knowledge may write *CUOTA instead of QUOTA ("rate") or *SQUOLA instead of SCUOLA ("school"). Similarly, the syllables [tʃe], [ʃe], [dʒe] may or may not require the I (e.g., [ʃena] is written SCENA and not *SCIENA ["scene"], but [ʃentsa] is written SCIENZA and not *SCENZA ["science"]). In these instances, phonological-to-orthographic conversion rules are insufficient to generate the correct spelling of words, and errors may indicate defective lexical processing. Thus, these cases were successfully used to test the efficiency of the lexical spelling route (e.g., Angelelli, Judica, Spinelli, Zoccolotti, & Luzzatti, 2004; Angelelli, Notarnicola, Judica, Zoccolotti, & Luzzatti, 2010).

However, these types of words may also be spelled with some degree of accuracy by relying on the distributional properties of sound–spelling mappings. In fact, there are clear asymmetries in the occurrence of each orthographic option. For example, the phonemic groups [tʃe], [ʃe], [kw] are more frequently mapped as CE, SCE, QU (they appear in 77.2 to 82.8% of cases according to the databases of Marconi, Ott, Pesenti, Ratti, & Tavella, 1993, and De Mauro, 1989, respectively) as compared to CIE, SCIE, CU, which appear less commonly (from 22.8% to 17.2% of cases according the two previously mentioned databases). Note that these various orthographic options cannot be predicted by the context in which they occur, as in other languages (e.g., see Pacton et al., 2002, for French orthography). In the present study, knowledge of the distributional properties of orthography was examined by evaluating children's sensitivity to the relative frequencies of sound–spelling mappings. In all cases lacking one-to-one mapping of sounds to letters, the choice of the most frequent sound–spelling mappings can be considered an index of reliance on knowledge of distributional properties at the sublexical level.

In consistent orthographies, such as Italian (Marinelli et al., 2016; Marinelli, Romani, Burani, & Zoccolotti, 2015; Notarnicola, Angelelli, Judica, & Zoccolotti, 2012), children learn the sublexical phoneme-to-grapheme (and grapheme-to-phoneme) mappings early and easily and mainly rely on this procedure, which allows correct reading and spelling of almost all Italian words (see Burani, Thornton, & Zoccolotti, 2017). Thus, the orthographic lexicon may be less critical than in inconsistent orthographies, at least in the early stages of reading and spelling acquisition (Marinelli et al., 2015, 2016). Therefore, the less reliance on the lexical procedure and the more reliance on sound–spelling mappings in consistent orthographies compared to inconsistent ones makes it impossible to generalize findings from inconsistent orthographies.

To our knowledge, in consistent orthographies only one study has examined how lexical information and knowledge of distributional properties of sound–spelling mappings interact in the spelling skills of first-, second-, and fourth-grade typically developing Italian children (Angelelli, Marinelli, Putzolu, et al.,

2017). Sensitivity to the relative frequencies of sound–spelling mappings was acquired quite early—that is, before the children optimized the acquisition of lexical orthographic representations. Already in first grade the children wrote words and pseudowords containing inconsistently spelled segments by choosing highly probable sound–spelling options more often than options with low probability. Therefore, sensitivity to distributional properties of sound–spelling mappings was already mastered by first graders, and increasing exposure to written language through school experience did not seem to increase this ability. However, accuracy on words with low-probability sound–spelling mappings emerged progressively in higher grades when orthographic representations were acquired and lexical processing became more efficient.

Also in reading, Italian adults (Sulpizio, Arduino, Paizi, & Burani, 2013) and children (Burani, Paizi, & Sulpizio, 2014) provided evidence of the use of distributional knowledge to improve accuracy. In the written-to-oral direction Italian is characterized by an almost perfect grapheme-to-phoneme correspondence. However, there is some unpredictability at the supra-segmental level. In fact, stress assignment in Italian polysyllabic words, is neither marked[1] nor predicted by rules. Most three- and four-syllable words are stressed on the penultimate syllable, which is regarded as the dominant (or "regular") stress. A smaller proportion of polysyllabic words are stressed on the antepenultimate syllable (non-dominant or "irregular" stress). On the basis of this disproportionate distribution, it was originally suggested that stress assignment in Italian might require item-specific learning (see Colombo, 1992). It was later discovered that adults, as well as fourth-grade typically developing children, assign stress by relying also on distributional information, such as stress neighbourhood (Burani & Arduino, 2004)—that is, the number of words that share their final sequence with the target (e.g., TAv*ola* "table") and have the same stress pattern (e.g., PENt*ola*, BAMb*ola*, "pot, doll"). Thus, readers know that some words have the same ending and the same stress pattern and use this information as a probabilistic cue for assigning stress in reading both words and pseudowords. Notably, younger Italian readers (second graders) had not acquired complete knowledge of stress neighbourhood and opted for the dominant stress (Sulpizio & Colombo, 2013). In agreement with Arciuli, Monaghan, and Seva (2010), these data suggest that the bias to assign the most common stress in the language decreases with age, and its role becomes progressively less influential than that of stress neighbourhood (for consistent results in Greek see Protopapas & Gerakaki, 2009).

Overall, knowledge of distributional properties of sound–spelling mappings is acquired quite early and supports reading and spelling also in consistent orthographies such as Italian. Furthermore, relative reliance on lexical and sublexical information changes as a function of age and reading/spelling experience.

The present study had three main aims: (a) to examine reliance on the lexical procedure in children with dyslexia; (b) to evaluate whether dyslexic children are sensitive to relative frequency of sound–spelling sublexical mappings in reading and spelling; and (c) to investigate the possible interaction between lexical and sublexical processes in reading and spelling in children with dyslexia.

As to the first aim, we wished to explore the lexical processing of children with dyslexia and control readers in reading and spelling as a function of reading experience. In Italian, children with dyslexia show a sequential mode of processing, which indicates the prevalent use of the sublexical procedure (Spinelli et al., 2005; Zoccolotti et al., 1999) and limited efficiency in lexical processing (Marinelli, Angelelli, Notarnicola, & Luzzatti, 2009). In spelling, failure to write words with inconsistent spellings correctly as well as a prevalence of phonologically plausible misspellings have been reported (Angelelli et al., 2004). Indeed, Italian children with dyslexia may suffer from a lexical orthographic deficit in both reading and spelling (Angelelli, Marinelli, & Zoccolotti, 2010), although rare cases with a prevalence of segmental errors in spelling have also been described (Angelelli, Putzolu, et al., 2016). Lexical deficit in spelling are particularly clear at the end of primary school, but second–third-grade dyslexic children present a concomitant fragility of the sublexical procedure (Angelelli, Notarnicola, et al., 2010). Overall, limited efficiency in lexical processing has been demonstrated in both reading and spelling (Angelelli, Marinelli, et al., 2010; Marinelli et al., 2009) although its expression may change during development (Angelelli, Notarnicola, et al., 2010).

Although lexical representations are not always accessed or available, we expect that Italian children with dyslexia will benefit to some extent from the presence of lexical activation in both reading and spelling. In fact, much evidence supports this in both reading and spelling. Thus, dyslexic children are facilitated in reading words with a large neighbourhood size (Marinelli, Traficante, Zoccolotti, & Burani, 2013) and show a spared word superiority effect (Marinelli, Traficante, & Zoccolotti, 2014). In reading, greater frequency effects in dyslexic children than in controls have been reported in Italian (Barca, Burani, Di Filippo, & Zoccolotti, 2006; Marinelli et al., 2013) as well as in other consistent languages such as German (e.g., Ziegler, Perry, Ma-Wyatt, Ladner, & Schulte-Körne, 2003). This larger frequency effect can be viewed as a deficit in lexical expansion—that is, a smaller number of orthographic representations in the lexicon than that in typically developing children. The lack of orthographic representations for low-frequency words, which makes the processing of these words particularly difficult compared to high-frequency words, may lead to the greater facilitation of high-frequency words in dyslexic children than in controls. Furthermore, in an orthographic judgment task (Marinelli et al., 2009), although dyslexic children were impaired in detecting pseudo-homophones, indicating their reliance on sublexical processing, they used the lexical procedure with over-learned words, with an advantage for high- over low-frequency words similar to that of control children.

In the present study, the lexical processing of dyslexic children was examined longitudinally in reading and spelling. In particular, we studied the factors that modulate the magnitude of the lexical deficit by varying the regularity and frequency of words in a dictation task and in an orthographic judgment task. A regularity effect was expected, with the dyslexic children having greater difficulty processing inconsistent words than processing regular words due to their lexical deficit. A larger frequency effect in both reading and spelling was also expected in the dyslexic children due to their smaller number of orthographic representations in the lexicon (compared to typically developing children). On the contrary, we expected that the control children would process not only high-frequency words lexically but also a proportion of low-frequency words. Note that better performance with high- than low-frequency words indicates the contribution of lexical processing in spelling and reading not only in localist but also in connectionist models. According to the dual-route model (Coltheart, Rastle, Perry, Ziegler, & Langdon, 2001), the rate at which activation occurs through the lexical route is proportional to word frequency—that is, the more common a word is, the sooner it will be processed. According to connectionist models, the extended experience accumulated with high-frequency words determines variations in the strengths of the network' connections and in the activation thresholds (e.g., Seidenberg & McClelland, 1989).

Apart from a main difficulty in processing lexical information, it is unclear whether dyslexic children are able to use knowledge of the relative frequency of sound–spelling mappings and to what extent this knowledge supports their performance when lexical processing fails. A study by Paizi, Zoccolotti, and Burani (2011) revealed that dyslexic children are able to successfully use the distributional properties of language for stress assignment in reading (similarly to control children, Sulpizio & Colombo, 2013). Regarding spelling, no evidence is as yet available. According to Barry and Seymour (1988), sublexical processing rests upon a set of probabilistic phoneme-to-grapheme mappings, weighted according to their frequencies of occurrence. In the present study, we examined whether or not dyslexic children, similarly to control children, were able to acquire and use knowledge of the relative frequency of sound–spelling mappings for phonemes with inconsistent spelling.

The third aim of the study was to examine whether or not in dyslexic children knowledge of the distributional properties of sound–spelling mappings are more clearly evident in the context of lexical orthographic deficits. There is much evidence (from control children as well as from developmental and acquired dyslexic/dysgraphic children) that lexical and sublexical processing interact in reading and in spelling (Burden, 1989; Campbell, 1983; Folk, Rapp, & Goldrick, 2002; Hillis, Rapp, & Caramazza, 1999; Seymour & Dargie, 1990; Tainturier, Bosse, Roberts, Valdois, & Rapp, 2013). Also, in consistent orthographies, such as Italian, lexical and sublexical interactions have been reported with different experimental paradigms, such as lexical priming (Angelelli, Marinelli, Putzolu, et al., 2017; Barry & De Bastiani, 1997) and single word reading (e.g., Barca et al., 2006) and in studies examining morphological (Angelelli, Marinelli, & Burani, 2014; Angelelli, Marinelli, De Salvatore, & Burani, 2017; Traficante, Marcolini,

Luci, Zoccolotti, & Burani, 2011) and neighbourhood size (Angelelli, Notarnicola, Marcolini, & Burani, 2014) effects.

Also, theoretical models support the view that lexical and sublexical procedures interact in spelling and reading (e.g., Houghton & Zorzi, 2003). According to Barry and Seymour (1988), the selection of a specific mapping (from a weighted list based on their probability of occurrence) may be influenced by lexical activation. Folk and Rapp (2004) suggested that in spelling the lexical system may exert an influence on sublexical processing at the level of graphemic representations. According to the "simultaneous activation" hypothesis (Rapp, Epstein, & Tainturier, 2002; see also Rapp, Folk, & Tainturier, 2000, for reading) both lexical and sublexical procedures simultaneously activate candidate graphemes: The most strongly activated candidates are selected for output. Note that both procedures send activations to candidate graphemic elements in the graphemic buffer; there, activation is combined but in an undamaged system that from the lexical system normally dominates the process. Subsequently, the activated graphemes send activation back to words through feedback from graphemes to lexeme nodes of the orthographic output lexicon (McCloskey, Macaruso, & Rapp, 2006). The output is finally selected as a consequence of this dynamic interaction of lexical and sublexical processing (through iterative feedforward/feedback processes). In this vein, if lexical activation is defective compared to sublexical activation (as in many dyslexic children), then the output might be predominantly determined by the sublexical procedure (as in the case of low-frequency words). Also in reading, according to the dual-route cascade model (Coltheart et al., 2001), a letter string activates both lexical and sublexical processes, and the various units underlying each procedure influence one another. In this view, even pseudoword reading will be influenced by the output from the lexical route (even though it may not be able to accomplish the task). The rate at which activation occurs through the lexical route is proportional to word frequency—that is, the more common a word is, the sooner it will be processed. Then, in reading low-frequency words, the lexical procedure is not sufficiently fast, and the output is mainly influenced by sublexical activation.

In the present study, the interaction between knowledge of the relative frequency of sound–spelling mappings and lexical processing was examined in both reading and spelling. Note that this interaction could manifest itself in one of two ways. One possibility is that dyslexic children fail to acquire lexical representations but are able to learn the most frequent sound–spelling mappings for phonemes with inconsistent spellings as well as control children do (Angelelli, Marinelli, Putzolu, et al., 2017). In this case, it should be expected that their sensitivity to distributional properties of sublexical mappings would allow them to partially compensate for their lexical difficulty, making it possible for them to correctly spell most lexical items with typical mappings but incorrectly spell those with atypical mappings. Alternatively, it could be that the presence of atypical sound–spelling mappings at the sublexical level makes the orthographic representations of certain words more distinctive, and this in turn facilitates their acquisition. In fact, some authors suggest that sublexical information strengthens targeted lexical representations (Folk et al., 2002; Houghton & Zorzi, 2003; Rapp et al., 2002). In the case of word recognition in reading, Grainger and Ziegler (2011) argued that letter combinations that are encountered less often are more diagnostic of the identity of a word, at least when readers are processing words along what they call the coarse-grained route to pre-lexical orthographic codes. Also in this case, a larger difference between performance with words with low-probability and that with words with high-probability sound–spelling mappings is expected in children with dyslexia than in control children. In fact, in control children who have good lexical processing and an orthographic lexicon containing almost all orthographic representations of words, the modulating role of sublexical sound–spelling distributional knowledge would be less detectable.

Overall, the present study aimed to shed some light on the efficiency of the lexical procedure in children with dyslexia learning a consistent orthography on their sublexical sound–spelling distributional knowledge and on the possible interaction between lexical and sublexical processes in both reading and spelling in children with dyslexia. We know from previous research (Angelelli, Notarnicola, et al., 2010) that the profile characterized by frequent phonologically plausible errors emerges progressively during the last years of primary school due to the reduction of implausible spellings with the children progressively mastering phoneme-to-grapheme mappings. Thus, we longitudinally followed a group of children with a reading disturbance and a group of control children and tested them when they were in third and fifth grade.

Method

Participants

Eighty-six control readers and 24 dyslexic children were first tested in third grade and then two years later in fifth grade. All participants scored above the 10th percentile on Raven's Coloured Progressive Matrices (CPM, according to data from Pruneti et al., 1996). Some demographic and clinical variables of the sample are presented in Table 1, as well as raw data and mean *z* score performance compared to normative samples.

The children with dyslexia (14 female and 10 male) were selected based on a marked reading delay (at least 1.65 *SD*s below normative data) in accuracy and/or speed on a standard reading test (MT reading test, Cornoldi & Colpo, 1998; for a description see Appendix A) while they were in third grade. Note that they also suffered from dysgraphia (based on Diagnosis of Orthographic Developmental Disturbances–2, DDO–2, spelling test, Angelelli, Marinelli, et al., 2016; for a description see Appendix A). This is consistent with previous studies of Italian dyslexic children showing a strictly parallelism between reading and spelling deficits (e.g., Angelelli, Marinelli, et al., 2010).

The performance of the children with dyslexia was compared with that of a control group of 86 typically developing readers (39 female, 47 male) selected from the same classes as those for the children with dyslexia. Criteria for inclusion in the control group included normal reading speed and accuracy on the MT reading test (Cornoldi & Colpo, 1998) in third grade. Control participants were comparable to children with dyslexia for sex ($\chi^2 = 1.27$, *ns*), and, as shown in Table 1, also for age; the performance of the two groups on Raven's CPM was similar at the fifth-grade evaluation, whereas the third-grade children with dyslexia scored worse than the control children.

As reported in Table 1, on the MT reading test (Cornoldi & Colpo, 1998) mean *z* scores of control participants were near zero for all parameters, while the children with dyslexia performed worse than the control children in reading accuracy and speed at both evaluation times—that is, in both third and fifth grade. Also in spelling, dyslexic children performed worse than control children in both third and fifth grade.

The parents were informed of the screening activities and authorized their child's participation by signing the appropriate informed consent. The study was conducted according to the principles of the Helsinki Declaration and was approved by the school authorities.

Materials and procedure

The same stimuli were used in the spelling-to-dictation and the orthographic judgment tasks.

Seventy-two words with inconsistent spellings due to the presence of a phonemic segment with two homophonic transcriptions (only one of which is orthographically correct) were selected from a corpus of 1,000,000 stimuli taken from a word

Table 1. Some demographic and clinical variables of the sample.

	Third grade						Fifth grade					
	Dyslexic children		Control children				Dyslexic children		Control children			
	M	*SD*	*M*	*SD*	*t*(109)	*p*	*M*	*SD*	*M*	*SD*	*t*(109)	*p*
Age (years)	8.59	0.30	8.55	0.33	0.62	.54	10.57	0.31	10.48	0.33	1.26	.21
Raven CPM error data	9.21	3.97	6.74	3.75	2.81	.006	4.42	2.57	3.64	2.78	1.23	.22
z scores	0.05	0.65	0.45	0.62			0.32	0.60	0.50	0.65		
MT test (seconds per syllable × 100)	60.42	15.11	32.43	8.72	11.62	.000	38.94	9.46	25.15	4.99	9.59	.000
z scores	−0.53	0.53	0.38	0.31			−0.85	0.52	0.28	0.61		
MT test: Error data	16.17	2.44	4.31	2.41	21.16	.000	12.06	6.19	3.95	2.72	9.34	.000
z scores	−2.28	0.50	0.08	0.50			−1.00	1.00	0.31	0.45		
Spelling test error data	26.54	16.75	14.24	9.13	4.76	.000	18.83	13.37	11.11	6.93	3.83	.000
z scores	−1.05	1.76	0.25	0.96			−1.26	1.91	−0.16	0.99		

Note: Mean raw data and *z* scores (with respect to normative data) are presented. For *z* scores, negative values indicate in all cases performance below the norm. CPM = Coloured Progressive Matrices.

frequency dictionary for children (Marconi et al., 1993). Words could contain the following inconsistently spelled segments: (a) the phonemic group [kw] that is sometimes transcoded as CU and other times as QU—for example, CUOCO ['kwɔko], cook, versus QUOTA ['kwɔta], quote; (b) the syllables [tʃe], [ʃe], [dʒe], which are written as CIE, SCIE, and GIE in some words and CE, SCE, and GE in others—for example, CIECO ['tʃɛko], blind, versus CECO ['tʃɛko], Czech; SCIENZA ['ʃɛntsa], science, versus ADOLESCENZA [adoleʃ'ʃɛntsa], adolescence; (c) words containing segments [nj]–[ɲ], which are homophonous in most Italian regional variants to the extent that [opinjone/ opiɲone] opinion may be spelled OPINIONE and not OPIGNONE, while [oɲuno/onjuno], everyone, may be spelled OGNUNO and not ONIUNO. Only these three types of inconsistently spelled segments were selected because they show a clear asymmetry in the frequency of occurrence of each of the two orthographic options according to Marconi et al.'s (1993) and De Mauro's (1989) dictionaries. Accordingly, the orthographic options CE, GE, SCE, QU, and GN were considered as high-probability mappings as they appear in 89.3% (according to Marconi et al.'s, 1993, dictionary) or 88.3% (according to De Mauro's, 1989, dictionary) of words including the phonemes considered in the present study. On the other hand, CIE, SCIE, GIE, CU, and NI were considered as low-probability mappings as they appear in 10.7% and 11.7% of cases in the two quoted databases, respectively. For the sake of brevity subsequently we refer to high- and low-probability sound–spelling mappings as *typical* and *atypical mappings*, respectively.

In particular, we selected 36 inconsistently spelled words with typical mappings and 36 inconsistently spelled words with atypical mappings. Half of each experimental set was made of high-frequency words ($M = 242.6$, $SD = 385$) and half of low-frequency words ($M = 5.6$, $SD = 5$) according to Marconi et al.'s (1993) database. As a control, 36 regular words (i.e., not containing any inconsistently spelled phonemic segment) were included; half were high-frequency words ($M = 233.2$, $SD = 263$), and half were low-frequency words ($M = 6.4$, $SD = 6$).

Overall, the six sets of experimental words (high- and low-frequency regular words, high- and low-frequency inconsistently spelled words with typical mappings, and high- and low-frequency inconsistently spelled words with atypical mappings) were matched for length (mean number of letters = 7.3, $SD = 1.6$), bigram frequency (according to Marconi et al.'s, 1993, database), presence of consonant clusters and geminate consonants, presence of contextual rules,[2] percentage of non-dominant stress, and number of nouns, adjectives, and verbs (all $Fs < 1$). Moreover, word frequency was matched across sets with similar word frequency ($Fs < 1$). In the case of inconsistently spelled words, the type of phonemic segment was also matched across sets (with six stimuli for each source of ambiguity).

For the orthographic judgment task, a pseudoword was created for each stimulus. Pseudowords derived from inconsistently spelled words were pseudo-homophones (i.e., they resulted in a string that could be read as homophonous to the target; e.g., *SQUOLA[3] derived from SCUOLA, school). Thus, they can be detected only by relying on the lexical procedure. There were two types of pseudo-homophones: They were either those obtained by transforming typical mappings into atypical ones (e.g., QUOTA, ['kwɔta], quote, written as *CUOTA) or vice versa (e.g., CUOIO, [kwɔio], leather, written as *QUOIO). Pseudowords derived from regular words resulted in strings that were non-homophonic because of the substitution or permutation of graphemes (e.g., DENORO derived from DENARO, money). They can be detected through either the lexical or the sublexical procedure. The same type of errors (insertions, deletions, and substitutions) were introduced in regular and inconsistently spelled words. There were no violations of Italian orthography—that is, all pseudowords were composed of legal letter sequences.

The whole list of words and pseudowords is reported in Appendix B.

In the spelling to dictation task, words were dictated by the experimenter, and the child had to spell them on a sheet of paper. No time limit was given. In the orthographic judgment task, stimuli were typewritten (font Palatino 24, triple spacing) at the centre of the page. Children saw one stimulus at a time; a white sheet of paper was laid over the other stimuli. There was a brief practice with six stimuli. Then, stimuli were presented in two blocks with a pause between blocks. Words and derived pseudowords were not included in the same block. Children were instructed to read silently and judge whether the word was orthographically correct or not. No time limit was given.

As the stimuli used in the two experimental tasks were the same, a week was allowed between test sessions, and the order of tasks was counterbalanced across participants.

Participants were tested individually. The experiment was carried out in a quiet room. No feedback was provided on any task. Only error (and not time) data were collected; in particular, the number of stimuli erroneously spelled/judged in each experimental condition was computed.

Data analysis

For the spelling to dictation task, two analyses of variance (ANOVAs) were performed on percentages of spelling errors with group (dyslexic children, control readers) as a between-subjects factor. In the first ANOVA, *grade* (3rd grade, 5th grade), *regularity* (regular words, inconsistently spelled words[4]), and *word frequency* (high-frequency words, low-frequency words) were entered as repeated measures. In the second one, *grade* (3rd grade, 5th grade), *mapping probability* (words with typical and atypical mappings), and *word frequency* (high-frequency words, low-frequency words) were entered as repeated measures. In this case, regular words were excluded from the analysis. Post hoc comparisons were carried out with the Tukey test.

We also examined the type of spelling errors made by the dyslexic and control children in inconsistently spelled words. In particular, the percentage of lexical (i.e., phonologically plausible errors due to the lack of lexical processing), segmental errors (i.e., errors of substitution, insertion, omission, or transpositions of letters causing a change in the phonemic make up of a word), and mixed errors (i.e., cases in which both a lexical and a phonological error were present) were computed. The percentage of the three types of errors in dyslexic and control children was compared as a function of age by means of an ANOVA with *grade* and *group* as between-subjects factors and *error type* (lexical, phonological, and mixed errors) as a repeated measure. Post hoc comparisons were carried out with the Tukey test.

Regarding the orthographic judgment task, the same analyses were carried out as those for the spelling task. In this case, the effect of *lexical status* (word, pseudoword) was also entered as repeated measure, in addition to the previously described factors. Note that in these analyses, the effect of frequency is different in the case of words (when it actually marks the frequency of the target) and in the case of pseudowords, where it marks the frequency of the base word from which the pseudoword was derived. Post hoc comparisons were carried out with the Tukey test. Note that for the orthographic judgment task, it was unfeasible to examine error type.

Results

Performance on the orthographic judgment and the spelling to dictation tasks was correlated in both third and fifth grade. For third-grade children, the median correlation was $r = .49$, with r values ranging from .40 to .68 in the various experimental conditions. For fifth-grade children, the median correlation was $r = .56$, with r values ranging from .21 to .63 across experimental conditions, with lower correlations for high-frequency regular words (probably because children were generally accurate in this condition, and variability was scarce).

Table 2 reports the significant main effects and interactions for the ANOVAs. Following is a description of the main findings in each task, with particular attention to interactions with the group factor.

Spelling: Spelling to dictation task

Regularity effect

As reported in Table 2, Section A, the ANOVA showed the significance of all main effects, indicating a higher rate of spelling errors for dyslexic than for skilled readers (20.9% vs. 11.0%, respectively), for children in third grade than for those in fifth grade (19.5% vs. 12.5%), for inconsistently spelled words than for regular words (25.4% vs. 6.5%), and for low-frequency than for high-frequency words (20.4% vs. 11.6%).

Regularity interacted with *word frequency*, with a larger frequency effect for inconsistently spelled words (difference between high- and low-frequency words = 15%, $p < .0001$) than for regular words (difference = 2.7%, $p < .001$). Inconsistently spelled words were always spelled less accurately than regular words (at least $p < .0001$), but this difference was larger for low- (difference = 25.0%) than for high-frequency words (12.8%).

The *group* by *regularity* interaction (see Figure 1) highlighted that both control and dyslexic children

Table 2. ANOVAs on data from the spelling to dictation task and the orthographic judgment tasks.

Effect	$F(1, 108)$	p
A. Spelling: Regularity effect		
Group	50.03	<.0001
Grade	166.34	<.0001
Regularity	588.19	<.0001
Word frequency	282.76	<.0001
Group × Regularity	15.19	<.0001
Group × Grade	23.32	<.0001
Frequency × Regularity	213.93	<.0001
Regularity × Grade	19.30	<.0001
Group × Word Frequency × Grade	6.33	<.05
B. Spelling: Word frequency and mapping probability in inconsistently spelled words		
Group	43.63	<.0001
Grade	125.40	<.0001
Mapping probability	74.90	<.0001
Word frequency	401.89	<.0001
Word frequency by mapping probability	307.07	<.0001
Mapping probability by grade	6.39	<.05
Group × Grade	5.80	<.05
Group × Grade × Word Frequency	3.29	.07
C. Orthographic judgment task: Regularity effect		
Group	64.17	<.0001
Grade	40.51	<.0001
Lexical status	378.33	<.0001
Word frequency	353.90	<.0001
Regularity	575.82	<.0001
Grade × Lexical Status × Word Frequency × Regularity	5.38	<.05
Group × Lexical Status × Word Frequency	8.97	<.01
Group × Lexical Status × Regularity	14.85	<.0001
Group × Grade × Word Frequency × Regularity	8.30	<.01
D. Orthographic judgment task: Word frequency and mapping probability in inconsistently spelled words		
Group	39.75	<.0001
Grade	55.35	<.0001
Lexical status	378.14	<.0001
Word frequency	400.17	<.0001
Mapping Probability × Grade	6.66	<.05
Grade × Lexical Status × Word Frequency	6.83	<.01
Group × Lexical Status × Mapping Probability × Word Frequency	7.88	<.01

Note: (A) Spelling: regularity effect; (B) spelling: word frequency and mapping probability in inconsistently spelled words; (C) orthographic judgment task: regularity effect; (D) orthographic judgment task: word frequency and mapping probability in inconsistently spelled words. For the sake of brevity only main effects and interactions that proved significant with at least $p < .10$ are reported. ANOVA = analysis of variance.

made more errors on inconsistently spelled words than on regular ones (at least $p < .0001$) while regularity influenced the spelling of children with dyslexia (regularity effect = 21.9%) more than that of control readers (15.9%). In fact, larger group differences were evident in spelling inconsistently spelled words (difference = 12.9%, $p < .0001$) than in spelling regular words (6.8%, $p < .01$) due to the high percentage of errors made by dyslexic children in spelling this type of word (31.9% errors, while controls made 19.0% errors).

The *group* by *grade* and the *group* by *grade* by *word frequency* interactions highlighted that age affected the performance of dyslexic children more than that of control children and that this difference was especially true for high-frequency words. While dyslexic children reduced their percentages of errors in spelling high-frequency words by 10.5% passing from third to fifth grade, controls were already accurate in spelling these stimuli by third grade. Thus, the reduction in the number of errors with age was smaller (3.2%). With low-frequency words the influence of age was more similar in the two groups (difference between 5th and 3rd grades = 9.0% and 5.7% for dyslexic and control children, respectively).

Word frequency and mapping probability in inconsistently spelled words

As reported in Table 2, Section B, the ANOVA showed the significance of all main effects, indicating a higher rate of spelling errors in dyslexic than in control readers (31.9% vs. 18.9%, respectively), for children in third than for those in fifth grade (30.0% vs.

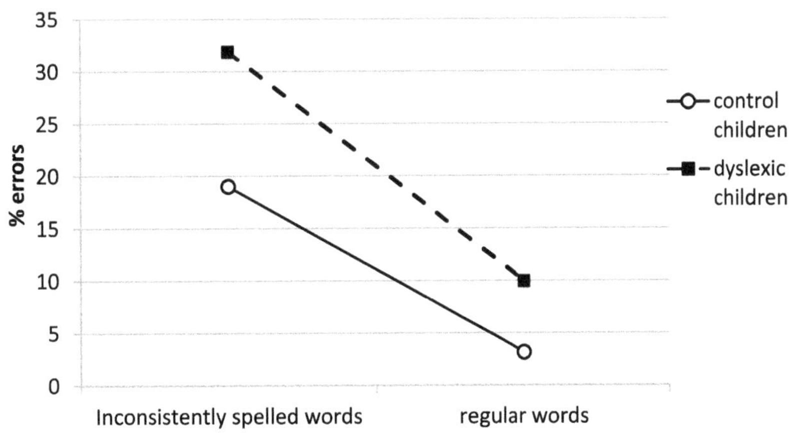

Figure 1. Group by regularity interaction in the spelling task. Percentage of errors (as a function of word regularity) in word spelling for dyslexic and control children.

20.7%), for words with atypical mappings than for words with typical mappings (31.1% vs. 19.6%), and for low-frequency than for high-frequency words (32.8% vs. 17.9%).

Word frequency interacted with *mapping probability*: In the case of low-frequency inconsistently spelled words there was a higher rate of error for those with atypical mappings (44.3%) than for those with typical ones (21.3%, $p < .0001$) but not in the case of high-frequency words (17.9% of errors for both typical and atypical mappings).

Mapping probability also interacted with *grade*, indicating larger mapping probability effects (i.e., larger difference between the spelling of typical and atypical mapping words) when children were in third than in fifth grade (difference = 14.0% and 8.9%, respectively, at least $p < .0001$). Furthermore, the interaction indicated a larger age effect in spelling words with atypical mappings (difference between 3rd- and 5th-grade performance = 11.9%, $p < .0001$) than in spelling words with typical ones (difference = 6.8%, $p < .0001$).

Note that *mapping probability* did not interact with *group* or with *word frequency* and *group*, indicating that the performance of dyslexic and control children was affected similarly by mapping probability (with a reduction of errors for words with typical mappings compared to atypical ones of 12.4% for controls and of 10.5% for dyslexic children) and that both groups were influenced by mapping probability in the case of low-frequency words (mapping probability effect = 23.4% and 22.6% for control and dyslexic children, respectively) but not in the case of high-frequency words. This pattern is shown in Figure 2.

Group interacted with *grade*, while the *group* by *grade* by *word frequency* interaction approached significance. Age had a greater effect on dyslexic performance (difference between 5th and 3rd grade = 11.3%, $p < .0001$) than on control performance (difference = 7.3%, $p < .0001$); larger group differences were detectable in spelling low-frequency words especially when children were in third grade (difference between dyslexic and control children = 16.7% in 3rd grade, $p < .001$, and 13.4% in 5th grade, $p < .05$; for high-frequency words the difference was about 11% and was not significant).

Error type analysis

Appendix C reports the mean percentages of lexical, segmental, and mixed errors in the spelling of dyslexic and control readers separately for each experimental category as a function of word regularity, sound–spelling mapping, and word frequency.

Significant main effects (see Table 3) highlighted a higher percentage of errors in dyslexic children than in controls (10.6% and 6.3%, respectively), in younger than in older children (10.0% and 6.9%, respectively) as well as a higher proportion of lexical errors (21.8%) than segmental (2.3%) and mixed errors (1.3%). The *group* by *error type* interaction showed that groups differed only in the percentage of lexical errors (26.8% in dyslexic children and 16.7% in control children, $p < .0001$) but not in segmental (3% for dyslexics and 1.5% for controls) and mixed errors (2.1% for dyslexics and 0.7% for controls). This pattern did not interact with *grade*, showing a higher incidence of lexical errors among dyslexics than among controls at both ages

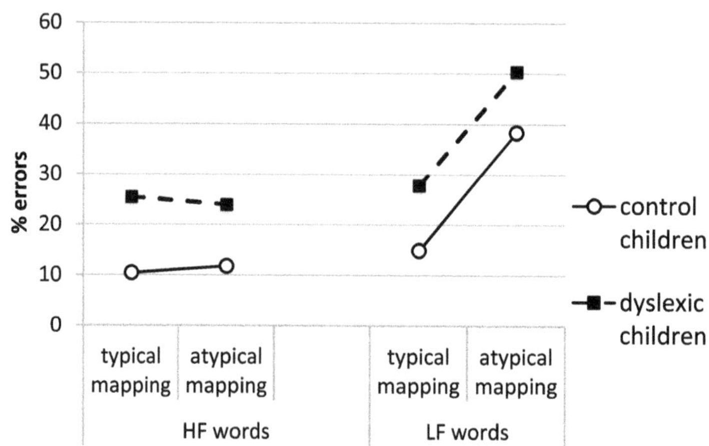

Figure 2. Group by word frequency by mapping probability interaction in the spelling task. Percentage of errors (as a function of word frequency and mapping probability) of dyslexic and control children in the spelling task. HF = high-frequency; LF = low-frequency.

Table 3. ANOVAs on error type data.

EFFECT	Spelling: Error type analysis $F(1, 108)$	p
A: Words with inconsistent spelling		
Group	42.73	<.0001
Grade	125.84	<.0001
Error type	632.93	<.0001
Group × Grade	5.52	<.05
Group × Error Type	29.76	<.0001
Grade × Error Type	49.01	<.0001
B: Regular words		
Group	38.56	<.0001
Grade	49.75	<.0001
Word frequency	20.97	<.0001
Group × Grade	23.69	<.0001

Note: (A) Inconsistently spelled words; (B) regular words. For the sake of brevity only main effects and interactions that proved significant (at least $p < .05$) are presented. ANOVA = analysis of variance.

examined. However, *grade* interacted with *group*, indicating a larger reduction of errors as a function of age in dyslexic children (3.8% passing from 3rd to 5th grade, $p < .0001$) than in control children (reduction of 2.5% passing from 3rd to 5th grade, $p < .001$) as well as larger group differences in younger children (difference between dyslexics and controls = 5.0% and 3.7% in 3rd and 5th grade, respectively, at least $p < .0001$). *Grade* also interacted with *error type:* With age the reduction of lexical errors (passing from 22.2% to 15.6%, $p < .0001$) was significant, although lexical errors remained prevalent, while segmental (from 2.3% to 1.4% of errors) and mixed errors (from 1.3% to 0.7%), already few in third grade, did not further decrease.

Reading: Orthographic judgment task

Regularity effect

As reported in Table 2, Section C, the ANOVA showed the significance of all main effects, indicating a higher rate of errors for dyslexic children than for control readers (22.9% vs. 14.0%, respectively), for children in third than for those in fifth grade (20.2% vs. 16.7%), for pseudowords than for words (27.8% vs. 9.1%), for low- than for high-frequency words (22.2% vs. 14.8%), and for inconsistently spelled words than for regular words (28.2% vs. 8.7%).

The *group* by *lexical status* by *regularity* interaction is presented in Figure 3. In the case of pseudowords, errors were 7.1% for control readers and 17.0% for dyslexic children in the case of non-homophonic foils. The difficulty in recognizing pseudowords increased dramatically in the case of pseudo-homophones (33.7% and 53.4% for control and dyslexic children, respectively). In the case of correct versions, errors were generally low, no group difference emerged, and inconsistently spelled words were judged less accurately than regular ones by both dyslexic (difference between regular and inconsistently spelled words: 6.5%, $p < .05$) and control (difference = 8.6%, $p < .001$) children. Note that control children outperformed dyslexic children more with pseudo-homophones (group effect = 19.7%, $p < .001$) than with non-homophonic foils (group effect = 9.9%, $p < .0001$) and that the regularity effect was larger among dyslexic (36.3%, $p < .0001$) than control (26.6%, $p < .0001$) children.

The *group* by *lexical status* by *word frequency* interaction highlighted that with correct words frequency affected in a similar way the performance of dyslexic (frequency effect = 8.4%, $p < .0001$) and control children (7.1%, $p < .0001$), while with pseudowords the frequency effect was larger in control (9.1%, $p < .0001$) than in dyslexic children (5.0%, $p < .001$). Groups did not differ in terms of performance with

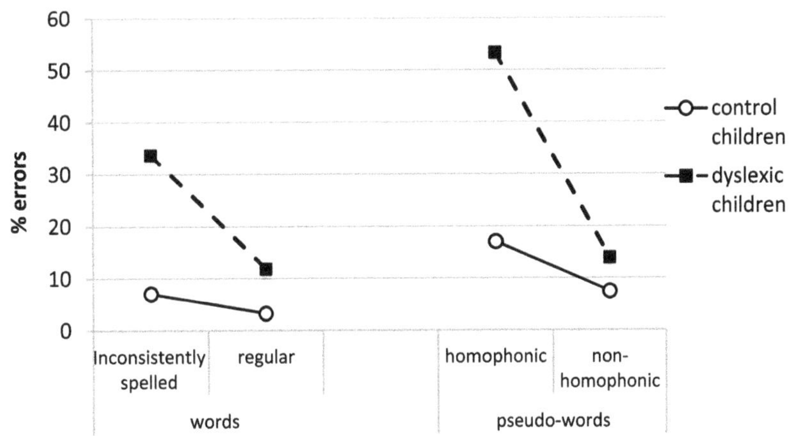

Figure 3. Group by lexical status by regularity interaction in the orthographic judgment task. Percentage of errors (as a function of word regularity) in judging correct words and pseudowords for dyslexic and control children.

the correct versions, but only with low-frequency derived pseudowords (difference between groups = 12.8%, $p < .0001$) and especially with high-frequency derived pseudowords (16.9%, $p < .0001$). In fact, in the latter condition controls partially compensated for their difficulty with pseudowords (15.8% of errors) whereas dyslexic children did not (32.7% of errors).

The *group* by *grade* by *word frequency* by *regularity* interaction indicates that word frequency of regular stimuli affected in a similar way the performance of dyslexic and control children in fifth grade (frequency effect = 1.9% and 1.6%, respectively), whereas in third grade word frequency affected the performance of dyslexic children more than that of control children (frequency effect = 7.5% and 3.4%, respectively). Regarding stimuli with inconsistent spellings, word frequency affected the performance of dyslexic and control children similarly when they were in fifth grade (frequency effect = 9.0% and 12.2%, respectively); however, in third grade the control children judged high-frequency stimuli quite well and showed a larger frequency effect (15.2%) than the dyslexic children (8.5%); thus, a larger group difference was evident for high- than for low-frequency stimuli (group difference = 13.6% and 6.9%, respectively).

Word frequency and mapping probability in inconsistently spelled words

As reported in Table 2, Section D, the ANOVA showed the significance of all main effects except *mapping probability*, indicating a higher rate of errors for dyslexic than for control readers (33.7% vs. 22.8%, respectively), for children in third than in fifth grade (31.1% vs. 25.3%), for pseudowords than for correct stimuli (43.5% vs. 12.9%), and for low- than for high-frequency words (33.8% vs. 22.6%).

The *group* by *lexical status* by *mapping probability* by *word frequency* interaction is illustrated in

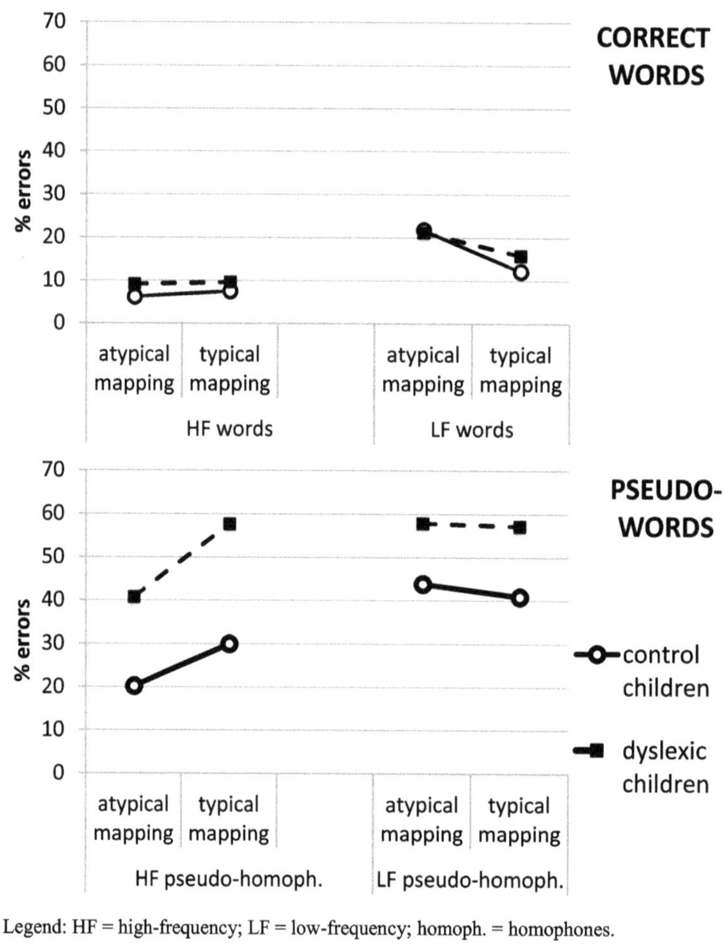

Figure 4. Group by lexical status by word frequency by mapping probability interaction in the orthographic judgment task. Percentage of errors (as a function of word frequency and mapping probability) of dyslexic and control children in the orthographic judgment task in third and fifth grade.

Figure 4. In the case of high-frequency correct words, both groups were very accurate, showing similar performance not affected by mapping probability. By contrast, with low-frequency correct words accuracy was lower for words with atypical than for those with typical mappings in both groups even if the effect tended to be larger for control readers (difference between atypical and typical mappings = 9.5%, $p < .0001$) than for children with dyslexia (difference = 5.3%, $p = .07$). Note that for correct low-frequency words with atypical mappings dyslexic and control children performed almost identically, while in the case of typical mappings errors decreased, especially in control children. For correct versions the word frequency effect was very large in the case of words with atypical mappings for both control and dyslexic children (15.6% and 12.0%, respectively, at least $p < .0001$) and smaller for typical ones (4.7% and 6.3% for control and dyslexic children, at least $p < .01$). Regarding pseudowords, the level of accuracy was generally lower than that for correct words, for each type of stimuli and for both groups. As shown in Figure 4, with low-frequency pseudowords, neither control nor dyslexic children were affected by mapping probability, and the error rate was very high (about 42% and 57% for the two groups, respectively). With high-frequency derived pseudowords, the dyslexics' errors were much lower when the pseudoword was made by substituting an atypical mapping with a typical one (40.7%, $p < .0001$) than the opposite (57.6%). Control children showed a smaller percentage of errors with high-frequency derived pseudowords (compared to low-frequency ones) in both cases (at least $p < .001$): Errors were 20.2% when pseudowords were made by substituting an atypical mapping with a typical one and 29.9% in the opposite case. Moreover, a frequency effect was evident for both controls (23.6%, $p < .0001$) and dyslexic children (17.1%, $p < .0001$) when the error was introduced in atypical mappings. When typical mappings were substituted with atypical mappings, a frequency effect was evident only in control readers (10.9%, $p < .0001$); the dyslexic children were unable to detect the errors even in the high-frequency stimuli.

Discussion

The first aim of the present study was to examine the use of the lexical procedure in children with dyslexia and dysgraphia and in control readers. Data show larger regularity and frequency effects in dyslexic children than in controls in both the spelling to dictation and orthographic judgment tasks. Italian dyslexic children have greater difficulty in writing words with inconsistent spelling (see Figure 1) and rejecting pseudo-homophones (see Figure 3) than do control children. This is due to over-reliance on the sublexical procedure rather than the lexical one. In fact, the regularity effect is an index of difficulty in lexical processing. Although both the lexical and the sublexical procedures allow for correct reading and spelling in the case of regular words, only the lexical procedure supports correct rejection of pseudo-homophones and accuracy in writing words with inconsistent spelling. The use of the sublexical procedure in spelling leads to difficulty with inconsistently spelled words (those with atypical mappings) and a high number of phonologically plausible errors. In the same vein, in the orthographic judgment task difficulty in recognizing pseudo-homophones highlights non-skilful use of orthographic lexical processing and a predominant use of the sublexical procedure. In fact, in processing pseudo-homophones, the lexical and sublexical procedures produce conflicting information: The lexical procedure allows for the detection of errors whereas the sublexical procedure may induce erroneous acceptance of pseudo-homophones because of their phonological plausibility. Therefore, a deficit in judging these stimuli may be ascribed to over-reliance on sublexical processing. Note that in both tasks regularity and frequency effects interact: Regularity affects performance especially on low-frequency words. High-frequency stimuli are processed lexically and then relatively quickly—that is, before the sublexical procedure generates conflicting output. This produces weak or absent regularity effects (see, e.g., Rapp et al., 2000; Seidenberg, Waters, Barnes, & Tanenhaus, 1984). For low-frequency words, orthographic representations in the lexicon may not be available, and then larger regularity effects are reported. The overreliance on the sublexical procedure and the poor lexical skills in reading and spelling of dyslexic children support previous findings in Italian (Angelelli et al., 2004; Angelelli, Marinelli, et al., 2010; Marinelli et al., 2009) and similar findings in other consistent orthographies (e.g., Bergmann & Wimmer, 2008).

However, a frequency effect was present, and indeed greater, in dyslexic children than in control children. This pattern is in keeping with previous studies in Italian dyslexic children (Barca et al., 2006; Marinelli et al., 2009, 2013). The smaller number of orthographic representations of words in the lexicon of dyslexic children (compared to controls) might be responsible for the greater frequency effect in this population: Dyslexic children performed very poorly with low-frequency words, indicating a possible lack or unavailability of orthographic representations for low-frequency words. With high-frequency words the presence of at least some representations in the lexicon allowed for reference to the lexical procedure and produced a frequency effect greater than that for control readers (for which both high- and at least some low-frequency words were processed lexically). Thus, the pattern of results for frequency points to a deficit in the expansion of the orthographic lexicon in children with dyslexia (Angelelli, Marinelli, et al., 2010; Bergmann & Wimmer, 2008; Hanley, Hastie, & Kay, 1992).

The second aim of the present study was to examine whether dyslexic children are sensitive to the relative frequency of sound–spelling mappings and use this knowledge to support reading and spelling when lexical processing is unavailable. Furthermore, we were interested in studying the interaction between lexical and sublexical processes in reading and spelling in children with dyslexia. This interaction may be of two different types. One possibility is that knowledge of the distributional properties of sublexical mappings also interacts with lexical processing in dyslexic children, allowing them to partially compensate for their lexical difficulties. An alternative view is that low-probability mappings may increase the distinctiveness of the orthographic representations of certain words, facilitating lexical processing. According to Grainger and Ziegler (2011) letter combinations that are rarely encountered may be more diagnostic of the identity of the word being processed. In the extreme, a combination of letters that only occurs in a single word in the language would be highly informative compared to word identity.

The present results indicate that knowledge of the relative frequency of sound–spelling mappings was acquired also by dyslexic children and influenced their performance. However, a different degree of reliance on this knowledge was detected in reading and spelling.

In both dyslexic children and controls, spelling was affected by mapping probability but only in the case of low-frequency words (see Figure 2). Thus, children were more accurate in spelling low-frequency words with typical mappings (such as QUOTA) than in spelling low-frequency words with atypical mappings (such as CUOIO). For high-frequency words, the presence of a typical or atypical mappings did not affect performance. Thus, it seems that these stimuli were processed lexically and that the probability of sound–letter mappings at the sublexical level was not relevant. Note that according to the dual-route cascaded model (Coltheart et al., 2001) the two procedures are always active together. Specifically for spelling, the "simultaneous activation" hypothesis (Rapp et al., 2002; Rapp et al., 2000) proposes that lexical and sublexical procedures are simultaneously engaged: A cooperative interaction takes place when both routines agree on a given spelling. When they do not agree, a competition takes place between candidate graphemes, and the most strongly activated candidates are selected for output. Then, the lexical procedure is faster (Coltheart et al., 2001) and produces a stronger activation (Rapp et al., 2002) than the sublexical one. For this reason, the output is determined by the lexical procedure for words with orthographic representations available in the lexicon (such as high-frequency words). This result was detected not only in control children but also in children with dyslexia. Note that for both groups low-frequency words with atypical mappings were most often misspelled: When orthographic representations were not acquired or accessible as for low-frequency words, reliance on the sublexical procedure, which encodes spelling options proportionate to their frequency, may lead to error. When the probability of sound–letter mappings is high, reliance on probabilistic cues allows for good accuracy even in the absence of lexical processing. Then, in spelling Italian, dyslexic children, as well as control children, showed that they had acquired the sound–spelling regularities and used this probabilistic knowledge, compensating for their difficulty when lexical processing was not available, ensuring at least the correct spelling of low-frequency words with typical mappings.

In this vein, data on typically developing children were consistent with those of a cross-sectional study that examined the effect of word frequency and mapping probability on the spelling of first-, second-, and fourth-grade control readers (Angelelli, Marinelli, Putzolu, et al., 2017). This study highlighted a mapping probability effect that was larger for low- than for high-frequency words and was present only for low-frequency words in the case of children in fourth grade, a literacy level similar to that of the children examined in the present study. Moreover, consistent with the present study, Angelelli, Marinelli, Putzolu, et al. (2017) found that typically developing readers were able to obtain higher levels of accuracy in spelling stimuli with atypical mappings in second but not in first grade, probably when lexical representations start to be established. This indicates that the sensitivity to distributional properties of sublexical mapping is acquired quite early, before children optimize the acquisition of lexical orthographic representations. The present study examined children from third to fifth grade longitudinally and found larger mapping probability effects when children were in third grade, indicating greater reliance on the distributional properties in sound–spelling mappings when children were younger (presumably because of their smaller reliance on the lexical procedure by this age). With increasing experience, performance improved in the spelling of words with atypical mappings. This effect was similar for control and dyslexic children, even though with age, relatively speaking, the performance of dyslexic children improved more than that of control readers.

In the orthographic judgment task, for words with atypical mappings dyslexic children acquire or have access only to orthographic representations of high-frequency words. They perform better when atypical mappings are substituted by typical ones while they have more difficulty in detecting pseudo-homophones obtained by substituting a typical mapping with a less common one (see Figure 4). For controls, in the case of high-frequency words, a similar pattern to that exhibited by dyslexic children was evident, even if they were less affected by sound–spelling mapping probability than the dyslexic children (and were generally more accurate). In fact, they seem to have acquired the orthographic representations of high-frequency words with both typical and atypical mappings. Therefore, both groups were able to acquire the orthographic representations of high-frequency words with distinctive characteristics such as the presence of an atypical mapping. In this vein, knowledge of the relative frequency of sound–spelling mappings at the sublexical level is a source of information for lexical learning. Note that for both groups this knowledge does not influence the performance of low-frequency words, which was generally more impaired than that of high-frequency words. Moreover, dyslexic children were unable to detect pseudo-homophones obtained with the introduction of a phonologically plausible error in a typical segment, irrespective of word frequency. In fact, they have difficulty in judging these stimuli, not only for low-frequency words, but even in the case of high-frequency stimuli (with identical performance on high- and low-frequency words). By contrast, control children also showed a frequency effect in detecting errors introduced in typical segments, with better performance on high-frequency words.

It seems that for words with atypical mappings, dyslexic children acquire or have access only to orthographic representations of high-frequency words with atypical mappings, and for these words are able to detect whether atypical mappings are substituted by typical ones; by contrast, they are unable to detect pseudo-homophones obtained by substituting an atypical mapping with a more common one or a phonological plausible error introduced in low-frequency words. The present data on dyslexic children are consistent with the findings of Treiman and Kessler (2006). They suggest that children store the most common spellings and individually memorize the lexical representations of words with less common mappings. Then, in the orthographic judgment task, dyslexic children do not simply apply probabilistic reasoning (that would prompt them to erroneously choose all the most frequent orthographic solutions), but use distributional knowledge, specifically the presence of atypical mappings, to store single instances as (available) orthographic representations in their lexicon. In fact, they are able to acquire the orthographic representations of words with distinctive characteristics, such as the presence of an atypical mapping, with sufficient exposure (as for high-frequency words). In this vein, knowledge of the relative frequency of sound–spelling mappings at the sublexical level is a source of information for lexical learning and, then, for lexical processing. This finding is consistent with Rapp et al. (2002) and Houghton and Zorzi's (2003) hypothesis that sublexical information strengthens targeted lexical representations (see also Folk et al., 2002), but also with the hypothesis of a coarse-grained representation that codes for the presence of informative letter combinations (Grainger & Ziegler, 2011).

Overall, knowledge of distributional properties of sound–spelling mappings plays a different role in the spelling to dictation task (i.e., output orthographic lexicon) and in the orthographic judgment task (i.e., input orthographic lexicon). In spelling, when the probability of sound–letter mappings is high, reliance on probabilistic cues allows for good accuracy supplying for the lack of lexical knowledge. In contrast, in reading (the orthographic judgment task) probabilistic cues and specifically low-probability sound–spelling mappings contribute to lexical processing, favouring the acquisition of lexical representations (together with lexical exposure, as ensured by high-frequency stimuli).

There may be multiple reasons for this difference. A first possibility is that there are two separate orthographic input and output lexicons, one used in reading and one in spelling, which—although both affected in dyslexic/dysgraphic children—have different developmental failures, which account for differences in error patterns in spelling and reading. Some researchers described developmental deficits on the basis of independent cognitive systems for reading and writing (e.g., Campbell, 1987; Temple, 1986), although this hypothesis may not be very parsimonious. Another possibility is related to the hypothesis of a unique orthographic lexicon but spelling and reading (the last investigated through the orthographic judgment task) make different demands on this single lexical orthographic system.

The spelling to dictation task is a retrieval task in which children have to recover the exact orthographic representations of words from their output lexicon in order to spell them correctly. In the orthographic judgment task, children have to recognize the orthographic representations of correct words from their input lexicon and to detect pseudo-homophones (despite the contrasting information coming from lexical and sublexical processing). Alternatively, the task may be carried out by checking the lexicon for the absence of the stimuli they see. Notably, a YES bias was present only in the case of the orthographic judgment task: For correct words both lexical and sublexical procedures induce responding that the stimulus is correct (i.e., a YES response). For pseudo-homophones sublexical processing induces erroneous responding that the stimulus is correct (YES response) while only the lexical one allows recognizing the misspelling (NO response). Thus, clear differences in task demands (retrieval vs. recognition) are present. Rather, it seems possible that task differences induced differential strategies with an overestimation of the distinctive characteristics in the orthographic judgement task compared to the spelling to dictation task. The performance of dyslexic children in recognizing correct words was similar to their spelling performance: With low-frequency words they were less accurate with words containing atypical mappings than with those containing typical ones. With pseudo-homophones, their performance was impaired with low-frequency stimuli, irrespective of mapping probability. With high-frequency stimuli it proved easy to recognize an error in the presence of an atypical mapping. Therefore, the different pattern is probably due to task differences. Even if pseudo-words recognition refers to a situation that has some similarity with real life (as children often correct their spelling mistakes when revising their own texts), the orthographic judgement task is substantially different from reading (in which children have to retrieve the corresponding phonological and/or semantic information, a process more similar to the retrieval of orthographic information for spelling). However, this task seems to represent a unique way of testing the input lexicon in consistent languages such as Italian (Marinelli et al., 2009). Note that in Angelelli, Marinelli, et al. (2010) a strict parallelism in the orthographic representations used in spelling and orthographic judgment tasks was found in fourth-grade dyslexic children as well as in control children with poor lexical processing due to their young age (2nd grade). Also in the present study, a high correlation between performance on the orthographic judgment and the spelling to dictation tasks was found, consistent with Angelelli, Marinelli, et al. (2010). In any case, a note of caution in generalizing the present findings to reading is in order. Alternatively, it is possible to imagine that task discrepancy is due to the developmental stage of the children examined in the present study. Stage models (e.g., Frith, 1980) hypothesize that reading and spelling processes are not necessarily parallel and that a child can master a strategy only in one of these tasks. Thus, one possibility is that the dyslexic children in the present study mastered the strategy based on the acquisition of distinctive characteristics in reading, but not yet in spelling (for which they still used only distributional information); a study extending into later grades would be necessary to test this hypothesis. In the same vein, a longitudinal evaluation over a larger temporal range might shed light on whether the dyslexics' delay might eventually diminish and disappear with reading experience and lexical exposure. Furthermore, the examination of younger typically developing children might highlight whether, before their lexical expansion, they have learning mechanisms similar to those shown by dyslexic children.

In both reading and spelling, the effects of word regularity and word frequency as well as mapping probability were observed both in third and fifth grade. Age affected performance more in dyslexic than in skilled readers, probably because the higher accuracy of the latter children made the developmental improvement less detectable. Note that group differences were generally larger when children were in third than when they were in fifth grade, showing an improvement in performance with age in dyslexic children, even though they still underperformed compared to typically developing children.

The present study provides useful information to plan intervention programmes as well as didactic strategies. First, it suggests that in a language with very few sources of ambiguity such as Italian, it may prove useful to foster knowledge of distributional sound–spelling mappings through explicit training to allow dyslexic children to compensate for their lexical deficit and improve their accuracy in spelling and reading. Rendering explicit to children that one of two possible spellings is more common should increase the probability to use common sound–spelling mappings (as opposed to having a chance behaviour) and be more accurate in processing items containing high-probability mappings. On the other hand, enhancing the salience of the more rare instances (containing low-probability mappings) and increasing expositions to words with atypical mappings, through repeated learning opportunities, may favour the acquisition of orthographic representations of words with infrequent mappings. In this vein, reinforcing the use of distributional knowledge, together with learning the few inconsistent words with atypical mappings, might also guarantee reading and spelling success in dyslexic children with a lexical deficit. In fact, children might refer by default to common mappings in spelling inconsistent segments and retrieve by memory only the inconsistent words with an uncommon segment. In this way, metacognitive didactics may reduce the lexical demand.

Finally, a note of caution seems in order. The present findings are based on a language with a consistent orthography and may not generalize to other, more inconsistent, orthographies. In fact, the high consistency of grapheme-to-phoneme (and vice versa) mappings in Italian may facilitate the acquisition of distributional properties of sound–spelling mapping more than in inconsistent orthographies. On the other hand, the very high number of sound–spelling correspondence rules in inconsistent orthographies, such as English (more than 1,000 rules according to the dual-route cascaded (DRC) model; Coltheart et al., 2001) might induce greater reliance on the emerging statistical regularities to compensate this difficulty. Furthermore, the small number of words with inconsistent spelling in Italian orthography might lead children to learn them by memorizing their distinctive characteristics, such as the presence of atypical mappings, also by a relatively limited set of declarative and metacognitive strategies. This strategy is probably not feasible in more inconsistent orthographies, due to the high number of inconsistent words. Thus, caution in generalizing the present findings to orthographies with different levels of regularity is clearly in order.

In conclusion, consistent with previous evidence (e.g., Angelelli, Marinelli, et al., 2010), this study shows reduced lexical processing ability in Italian dyslexic children compared to control readers in both spelling and reading tasks. However, these children also proved that they take into account the distributional properties of Italian sound–spelling mappings. This effect was present in both reading and spelling, although with notable differences as a function of word frequency and group, differences that may, at least in part, reflect the different requirements in the tasks used. Notably, sensitivity to the distributional properties of sound–spelling mappings was detected by third grade, indicating early acquisition of this skill even in children with dyslexia and dysgraphia.

Notes

1. Stress is only marked in the infrequent case in which it occurs on the last letter of a word (for example Società "Society").

2. In Italian, the orthographic transcription of sequences involving [k], [g], [tʃ], [dn] is determined by context-sensitive rules and depends on the letters that follow—for example, [k] in [kaza], (home) is spelled CASA, but in [kiesa], (church) is spelled CHIESA.
3. *The asterisk marks nonlexical spelling errors.
4. The error scores for inconsistently spelled words were the mean error scores of words with atypical and typical mappings.

Acknowledgement

The authors thank Dr. Claire Montagna for the style editing.

Disclosure statement

No potential conflict of interest was reported by the authors.

Funding

This work was supported by the Fondo di Sviluppo e Coesione 2007-2013–APQ Ricerca Regione Puglia Programma regionale a sostegno della specializzazione intelligente e della sostenibilità sociale ed ambientale–FutureInResearch.

ORCID

Chiara Valeria Marinelli http://orcid.org/0000-0002-8806-5655
Pierluigi Zoccolotti http://orcid.org/0000-0002-6351-2455
Paola Angelelli http://orcid.org/0000-0001-9870-6009

References

Angelelli, P., Judica, A., Spinelli, D., Zoccolotti, P., & Luzzatti, C. (2004). Characteristics of writing disorders in Italian dyslexic children. *Cognitive and Behavioral Neurology*, *17*, 18–31. doi:10.1097/00146965-200403000-00003

Angelelli, P., Marinelli, C., & Burani, C. (2014). The effect of morphology on spelling and reading accuracy: A study on Italian children. *Frontiers in Psychology*, *5*, 1–10. doi:10.3389/fpsyg.2014.01373

Angelelli, P., Marinelli, C. V., De Salvatore, M., & Burani, C. (2017). Morpheme-based reading and spelling in Italian children with developmental dyslexia and dysgraphia. *Dyslexia: An International Journal of Research and Practice*. doi:10.1002/dys.1554

Angelelli, P., Marinelli, C. V., Iaia, M., Notarnicola, A., Costabile, D., Judica, A., … Luzzatti, C. (2016). *DDO-2 Diagnosi dei disturbi ortografici in età evolutiva* [Diagnosis of Orthographic Deficits in Childhood]. Trento: Erickson.

Angelelli, P., Marinelli, C. V., Putzolu, A., Notarnicola, A., Iaia, M., & Burani, C. (2017). Learning to spell in a language with transparent orthography: Distributional properties of orthography and whole-word lexical processing. *The Quarterly Journal of Experimental Psychology*, *7*, 1–14. doi:10.1080/17470218.2016.1275715

Angelelli, P., Marinelli, C. V, & Zoccolotti, P. (2010). Single or dual orthographic representations for reading and spelling? A study on Italian dyslexic and dysgraphic children. *Cognitive Neuropsychology*, *27*, 305–333. doi:10.1080/02643294.2010.543539

Angelelli, P., Notarnicola, A., Judica, A., Zoccolotti, P., & Luzzatti C. (2010). Spelling impairments in Italian dyslexic children: Phenomenological changes in primary school *Cortex*, *46*, 1299–1311. doi:10.1016/j.cortex.2010.06.015

Angelelli, P., Notarnicola, A., Marcolini, S., & Burani, C. (2014). Interaction between the lexical and sublexical spelling procedures: A study on Italian primary school children. *Rivista Italiana di Psicolinguistica Applicata/Journal of Applied Psycholinguistics*, *14*, 23–43.

Angelelli, P., Putzolu, A., Iaia, M., Marinelli, C. V., Gasperini, F., Chilosi, A. M., & Brizzolara, D. (2016). Spelling impairments in Italian dyslexic children with and without a history of early language delay. *Are There any Differences? Frontiers in Psychology - Educational Psychology*, *7*, 1–13. doi:10.3389/fpsyg.2016.00527

Apel, K., Wolter, J. A., & Masterson J. J. (2006). Effects of phonotactic and orthotactic probabilities during fast mapping on 5-year-olds' learning to spell. *Developmental Neuropsychology*, *29*, 21–42. doi:10.1207/s15326942dn2901_3

Arciuli, J., Monaghan, P., & Seva, N. (2010). Learning to assign lexical stress during reading aloud: Corpus, behavioral, and computational, investigation. *Journal of Memory and Language*, *63*, 180–196. doi:10.1016/j.jml.2010.03.005

Arciuli, J., & Simpson, I. C. (2012). Statistical learning is related to reading ability in children and adults. *Cognitive Science*, *36*, 286–304. doi:10.1111/j.1551-6709.2011.01200.x

Barca, L., Burani, C., Di Filippo, G., & Zoccolotti, P. (2006). Italian developmental dyslexic and proficient readers: Where are the differences? *Brain and Language*, *98*, 347–351. doi:10.1016/j.bandl.2006.05.001

Barry, C., & De Bastiani, P. (1997). Lexical priming of nonword spelling in the regular orthography of Italian. *Reading and Writing*, *9*, 499–517. doi:10.1023/A:1007907431371

Barry, C., & Seymour, P. H. K. (1988). Lexical priming and sound-to-spelling contingency effects in nonword spelling. *The Quarterly Journal of Experimental Psychology Section A*, *40*, 5–40. doi:10.1080/14640748808402280

Bergmann, J., & Wimmer, H. (2008). A dual-route perspective on poor reading in a regular orthography: Evidence from phonological and orthographic lexical decisions. *Cognitive Neuropsychology*, *25*, 653–676. doi:10.1080/02643290802221404

Burani, C., & Arduino, L. S. (2004). Stress regularity or consistency? Reading aloud Italian polysyllables with different stress patterns. *Brain and Language*, *90*, 318–325. doi:10.1016/S0093-934X(03)00444-9

Burani, C., Paizi, D., & Sulpizio, S. (2014). Stress assignment in Italian: Friendship outweighs dominance. *Memory & Cognition*, *42*, 662–675. doi:10.3758/s13421-013-0379-5

Burani, C., Thornton, A. M., & Zoccolotti, P. (2017). Literacy acquisition in Italian. In L. Verhoeven & C. Perfetti (Eds.), *Reading acquisition across languages and writing systems: An international handbook* (pp. 181–210). Cambridge: Cambridge University Press.

Burden, V. (1989). A comparison of priming effects on the nonword spelling performance of good and poor spellers. *Cognitive Neuropsychology, 6*, 43–65. doi:10.1080/02643298908253284

Campbell, R. (1983). Writing nonwords to dictation. *Brain and Language, 19*, 153–178. doi:10.1016/0093-934X(83)90061-5

Campbell, R. (1987). One or two lexicons for reading and writing words: Can misspellings shed any light? *Cognitive Neuropsychology, 4*(4), 487–499. doi:10.1080/02643298708252049

Colombo, L. (1992). Lexical stress effect and its interaction with frequency in word pronunciation. *Journal of Experimental Psychology: Human Perception and Performance, 18*, 987–1003. doi:10.1037/0096-1523.18.4.987

Coltheart, M., Rastle, K., Perry, C., Ziegler, J., & Langdon, R. (2001). DRC: A dual route cascaded model of visual word recognition and reading aloud. *Psychological Review, 108*, 204–256. doi:10.1037/0033-295X.108.1.204

Cornoldi, C., & Colpo, G. (1998). *Prove* di Lettura *MT. Guida all'uso* [The MT Reading Test: User Manual]. Firenze, IT: Organizzazioni Speciali.

De Mauro, T. (1989). *VELI. Vocabolario elettronico della lingua Italiana* [VELI. Electronic dictionary of Italian language]. Milano: IBM Italia.

Folk, J. R., Rapp, B., & Goldrick, M. (2002). The interaction of lexical and sublexical information in spelling: What's the point? *Cognitive Neuropsychology, 19*, 653–671. doi:10.1080/02643290244000184

Folk, J. R., & Rapp, B. (2004). Interaction of lexical and sublexical information in spelling: Evidence from nonword spelling. *Applied Psycholinguistics, 25*, 565–585. doi:10.1017/S0142716404001274

Frith U. (1980). *Cognitive processes in spelling*. London: Academic Press.

Grainger, J., & Ziegler, J. C. (2011). A dual-route approach to orthographic processing. *Frontiers in Psychology, 2*, 1–13. doi:10.3389/fpsyg.2011.00054

Hanley, J. R., Hastie, K., & Kay, J. (1992). Developmental surface dyslexia and dysgraphia: An orthographic processing impairment. *The Quarterly Journal of Experimental Psychology Section A, 44*, 285–319. doi:10.1080/02724989243000046

Hillis, A. E., Rapp, B. C., & Caramazza, A. (1999). When a rose is a rose in speech but a tulip in writing. *Cortex, 35*, 337–356. doi:10.1016/S0010-9452(08)70804-9

Houghton, G., & Zorzi, M. (2003). Normal and impaired spelling in a connectionist dual-route architecture. *Cognitive Neuropsychology, 20*, 115–162. doi:10.1080/02643290242000871

Lété, B., Peereman, R., & Fayol, M. (2008). Consistency and word-frequency effects on spelling among !rst- to !fth-grade French children: A regression-based study. *Journal of Memory and Language, 58*, 952–977. doi:10.1016/j.jml.2008.01.001

Luce, P. A., & Large, N. R. (2001). Phonotactics, density, and entropy in spoken word recognition. *Language and Cognitive Processes, 16*, 565–581. doi:10.1080/01690960143000137

Marconi, L., Ott, M., Pesenti, E., Ratti, D., & Tavella, M. (1993). *Lessico elementare: Dati statistici sull'italiano scritto e letto dai bambini delle elementari* [Elementary lexicon: Statistical data for Italian written and read by elementary school children]. Bologna: Zanichelli.

Marinelli, C. V., Angelelli, P., Notarnicola, A., & Luzzatti, C. (2009). Do Italian dyslexic children use the lexical reading route efficiently? An orthographic judgment task. *Reading and Writing: An Interdisciplinary Journal, 22*, 333–351. doi:10.1007/s11145-008-9118-x

Marinelli, C. V., Romani, C., Burani, C., McGowan, V. A., Zoccolotti, P., & Perea, M. (2016). Costs and benefits of orthographic inconsistency in reading: Evidence from a cross-linguistic comparison. *PlosOne, 11*(6), e0157457. doi:10.1371/journal.pone.0157457

Marinelli, C. V., Romani, C., Burani, C., & Zoccolotti, P. (2015). Spelling acquisition in English and Italian: A cross-linguistic study. *Frontiers in Psychology - Educational Psychology, 6*, 1–13. doi:10.3389/fpsyg.2015.01843

Marinelli, C. V., Traficante, D., Zoccolotti, P., & Burani, C. (2013). Orthographic neighbourhood-size effects on the reading aloud of Italian children with and without dyslexia. *Scientific Studies of Reading, 17*, 333–349. doi:10.1080/10888438.2012.723080

Marinelli, C. V., Traficante, D., & Zoccolotti, P. (2014). Does pronounceability modulate the letter string deficit of children with dyslexia? Evidence from lexical decision task. *Frontiers in Psychology, 5*, 1–16. doi:10.3389/fpsyg.2014.01353

Mason, M. (1975). Reading ability and letter search time: Effects of orthographic structure defined by single-letter positional frequency. *Journal of Experimental Psychology: General, 104*, 146–166. doi:10.1037/0096-3445.104.2.146

McCloskey, M., Macaruso, P., & Rapp, B. (2006). Grapheme-to-lexeme feedback in the spelling system: Evidence from dysgraphia. *Cognitive Neuropsychology, 23*, 278–307. doi:10.1080/02643290442000518

Notarnicola, A., Angelelli, P., Judica, A., & Zoccolotti, P. (2012). Development of spelling skills in a shallow orthography: The case of Italian language. *Reading and Writing, 25*, 1171–1194. doi:10.1007/s11145-011-9312-0

Pacton, S., Fayol, M., & Perruchet, P. (2002). The acquisition of untaught orthographic regularities in French. In L. Verhoeven, C. Elbro, & P. Reitsma (Eds.), *Precursors of functional literacy* (pp. 121–136). Dordrecht: Kluwer.

Pacton, S., Perruchet, P., Fayol, M., & Cleeremans, A. (2001). Implicit learning out of the lab: The case of orthographic regularities. *Journal of Experimental Psychology: General, 130*, 401–426. doi:10.1037/0096-3445.130.3.401

Pacton, S., Sobaco, A., Fayol, M., & Treiman, R. (2013). How does graphotactic knowledge influence children's learning of new spellings? *Frontiers in Psychology, 4*, 1–10. doi:10.3389/fpsyg.2013.00701

Paizi, D., Zoccolotti, P., & Burani, C. (2011). Lexical stress assignment in Italian developmental dyslexia. *Reading and Writing, 24*, 443–461. doi:10.1007/s11145-010-9236-0

Perruchet, P., & Pacton, S. (2006). Implicit learning and statistical learning: One phenomenon, two approaches. *Trends in Cognitive Sciences, 10*, 233–238. doi:10.1016/j.tics.2006.03.006

Protopapas, A., & Gerakaki, S. (2009). Development of processing stress diacritics in reading Greek. *Scientific Studies of Reading, 13*, 453–483. doi:10.1080/10888430903034788

Pruneti, C. A., Fenu, A., Freschi, G., Rota, S., Cocci, D., Marchionni, M., … Baracchini Murratorio, G. (1996). Aggiornamento alla standardizzazione italiana del test delle Matrici Progressive Colorate di Raven (CPM). *Bollettino di Psicologia Applicata, 217*, 51–57.

Rapp, B., Epstein, C., & Tainturier, M. J. (2002). The integration of information across lexical and sublexical processes in spelling. *Cognitive Neuropsychology, 19*, 1–29. doi:10.1080/0264329014300060

Rapp, B., Folk, J., & Tainturier, M. J. (2000). Word reading. In B. Rapp (Ed.), *What deficits reveal about the human mind: A handbook of cognitive neuropsychology* (pp. 233–262). Philadelphia,PA: Psychology Press.

Seidenberg, M. S., & McClelland, J. L. (1989). A distributed, developmental model of word recognition and naming. *Psychological Review, 96*, 523–568. doi:10.1037/0033-295X.96.4.523

Seidenberg, M. S., Waters, G. S., Barnes, M. A., & Tanenhaus, M. K. (1984). When does irregular spelling or pronunciation influence word recognition?. *Journal of Verbal Learning and Verbal Behavior, 23*, 383–404. doi:10.1016/S0022-5371(84)90270-6

Seymour, P. H. K., & Dargie, A. (1990). Associative priming and orthographic choice in nonword spelling. *European Journal of Cognitive Psychology, 2*, 395–410. doi:10.1080/09541449008406215

Spinelli, D., De Luca, M., Di Filippo, G., Mancini, M., Martelli, M., & Zoccolotti, P. (2005). Length effect in word naming in reading: Role of reading experience and reading deficit in Italian readers. *Developmental Neuropsychology, 27*, 217–235. doi:10.1207/s15326942dn2702_2

Storkel, H. L. (2001). Learning new words: Phonotactic probability in language development. *Journal of Speech, Language, and Hearing Research, 44*, 1321–1337. doi:10.1044/1092-4388(2001/103

Sulpizio, S., Arduino, L. S., Paizi, D., & Burani, C. (2013). Stress assignment in reading Italian polysyllabic pseudowords. *Journal of Experimental Psychology: Learning, Memory, and Cognition, 39*, 51–68. doi:10.1037/a0028472

Sulpizio, S., & Colombo, L. (2013). Lexical stress, frequency and stress neighborhood effects in the early stages of Italian reading development. *The Quarterly Journal of Experimental Psychology, 66*, 2073–2084. doi:10.1080/17470218.2013.785577

Tainturier, M. J., Bosse, M. L., Roberts, D. J., Valdois, S., & Rapp, B. (2013). Lexical neighborhood effects in pseudoword spelling. *Frontiers in Psychology, 4*, 1–8. doi:10.3389/fpsyg.2013.00862

Temple, M. C. (1986). Developmental dysgraphias. *The Quarterly Journal of Experimental Psychology Section A, 38*, 77–110. doi:10.1080/14640748608401586

Traficante, D., Marcolini, S., Luci, A., Zoccolotti, P., & Burani, C. (2011). How do roots and suffixes influence reading of pseudowords: A study of young Italian readers with and without dyslexia. *Language and Cognitive Processes, 26*, 777–793. doi:10.1080/01690965.2010.496553

Treiman, R., & Cassar, A. G. (1997). Spelling acquisition in English. In C. Perfetti, L. Rieben, & M. Fayol (Eds.), *Learning to spell: Research, theory, and practice across languages* (pp. 61–80). Mahwah, NJ: Lawrence Erlbaum.

Treiman, R., & Kessler, B. (2006). Spelling as statistical learning: Using consonantal context to spell vowels. *Journal of Educational Psychology, 98*, 642–652. doi:10.1037/0022-0663.98.3.642

Treiman, R. (1993). *Beginning to spell: A study of first-grade children*. New York: Oxford University Press.

Ziegler, J. C., Perry, C., Ma-Wyatt, A., Ladner, A., & Schulte-Körne, G. (2003). Developmental dyslexia in different languages: Language-specific or universal? *Journal of Experimental Child Psychology, 86*, 169–193. doi:10.1016/S0022-0965(03)00139-5

Zoccolotti, P., De Luca, M., Di Filippo, G., Judica, A., & Martelli, M. (2009). Reading development in an orthographically regular language: Effects of length, frequency, lexicality and global processing ability. *Reading and Writing, 22*, 1053–1079. doi:10.1007/s11145-008-9144-8

Zoccolotti, P., De Luca, M., Di Pace, E., Judica, A., Orlandi, M., & Spinelli, D. (1999). Markers of developmental surface dyslexia in a language (Italian) with high grapheme-phoneme correspondence. *Applied Psycholinguistics, 20*, 191–216. doi:10.1017/S0142716499002027

Appendix A

MT reading test (Cornoldi & Colpo, 1998)

The child has to read a meaningful text passage aloud (within a 4-min time limit). Speed (time in seconds per syllable) and accuracy (number of errors adjusted for the amount of text read) were considered. Stimulus materials and related reference norms vary depending on school grade. Raw scores are converted to *z* scores according to standard reference data (Cornoldi & Colpo, 1998).

Diagnosis of Orthographic Developmental Disturbances–2 (DDO–2; Angelelli, Marinelli, et al., 2016)

The test consists of four sections:

- Section A ($N = 70$): regular words with complete one-sound-to-one-letter correspondence;
- Section B ($N = 10$): regular words requiring application of context-sensitive sound-to-spelling rules ($N = 10$). In Italian, context-sensitive rules are required when spelling of a consonant depends on the following sound. For instance, the phoneme [k] is spelled C when followed by a consonant (e.g., CLIMA [klima], climate) or by A, O, U (e.g., CASA [kaza], home), and CH when followed by E or I (e.g., BARCHE [barke], boats).
- Section C ($N = 55$): words with unpredictable transcription along the phonological-to-orthographic conversion route (e.g., [kw] in [ˈkwɔta], i.e., quota is transcribed as QUOTA and not *CUOTA);
- Section D ($N = 25$): non-words with one-sound-to-one-letter correspondence.

Words and non-words are presented in separate lists and in randomized order. The examiner reads each item aloud in a neutral tone—that is, without emphasizing the presence of clusters, double consonants, or orthographic ambiguities. Before writing each item, the children are asked to repeat it to make sure they have understood it. The number of words spelled correctly in each category is computed. Raw scores are converted to *z* scores according to standard reference data (Angelelli, Marinelli, et al., 2016).

Appendix B. Words and pseudowords used in the spelling and orthographic judgment task.

Word	Pseudoword	Mapping consistency	Word frequency	Probability of sound–spelling mapping	Length (n° letters)	Word frequency	Bigram frequency	Consonants cluster	Consonants geminate	Contextual rules	Stress
superficie	superfice	irreg	high	atypical	10	69	8.86	1	0	1	p
società	socetà	irreg	high	atypical	7	71	7.62	0	0	1	l
specie	spece	irreg	high	atypical	6	149	9.06	1	0	1	p
cielo	celo	irreg	high	atypical	5	493	1.00	0	0	1	p
cuoco	quoco	irreg	high	atypical	5	34	9.32	0	0	2	p
scuotere	squotere	irreg	high	atypical	8	36	9.98	1	0	1	ap
cuocere	quocere	irreg	high	atypical	7	40	9.98	0	0	2	ap
cuore	quore	irreg	high	atypical	5	310	10.05	0	0	1	p
acqua	aqua	irreg	high	atypical	5	1089	8.79	1	0	2	p
scuola	squola	irreg	high	atypical	6	1823	9.29	1	0	1	p
comunione	comugnione	irreg	high	atypical	9	32	9.68	0	0	1	p
ciminiera	cimigniera	irreg	high	atypical	9	24	9.80	0	0	1	p
matrimonio	matrimognio	irreg	high	atypical	10	31	9.74	1	0	0	p
niente	gniente	irreg	high	atypical	6	32	9.58	0	0	0	p
miniera	migniera	irreg	high	atypical	7	41	9.99	0	0	0	p
maniera	magniera	irreg	high	atypical	7	52	10.10	0	0	0	p
scienziato	scenziato	irreg	high	atypical	10	62	9.29	2	0	1	p
scienza	scenza	irreg	high	atypical	7	87	8.96	2	0	1	p
M					**7.17**	**248.61**	**8.95**	**0.56**	**0.00**	**0.94**	
SD				**1.79**	**472.25**	**2.08**	**0.70**	**0.00**	**0.64**		
aquila	acuila	irreg	high	typical	6	44	8.28	0	0	1	ap
quaderno	cuaderno	irreg	high	typical	8	115	9.97	0	0	1	p
quercia	cuercia	irreg	high	typical	7	40	9.90	1	0	2	p
pasqua	pascua	irreg	high	typical	6	56	8.57	1	0	1	p
squadra	scuadra	irreg	high	typical	7	215	8.40	2	0	1	p
inquinamento	incuinamento	irreg	high	typical	12	256	9.46	2	0	1	p
impegno	impegnio	irreg	high	typical	7	38	9.31	2	0	1	p
segnale	segniale	irreg	high	typical	7	42	9.48	1	0	1	p
ognuno	ogniuno	irreg	high	typical	6	113	9.08	1	0	1	p
montagna	montagnia	irreg	high	typical	8	369	9.44	2	0	1	p
compagno	compagnio	irreg	high	typical	8	748	9.52	2	0	1	p
signore	signiore	irreg	high	typical	7	878	10.03	1	0	1	p
conoscenza	conoscienza	irreg	high	typical	10	56	9.60	2	0	1	p
pesce	pescie	irreg	high	typical	5	432	9.93	1	0	1	p
discesa	disciesa	irreg	high	typical	7	39	9.69	1	0	1	p
scena	sciena	irreg	high	typical	5	51	9.50	1	0	1	p

(*Continued*)

Appendix B. Continued.

Word	Pseudoword	Mapping consistency	Word frequency	Probability of sound–spelling mapping	Length (*n*° letters)	Word frequency	Bigram frequency	Consonants cluster	Consonants geminate	Contextual rules	Stress
gente	giente	irreg	high	typical	5	524	9.54	0	0	1	p
ruscello	rusciello	irreg	high	typical	8	54	9.21	1	1	1	p
M					**7.17**	**226.11**	**9.38**	**1.17**	**0.06**	**1.06**	
SD				**1.76**	**261.81**	**0.52**	**0.71**	**0.24**	**0.24**		
cuoio	quoio	irreg	low	atypical	5	15	9.47	0	0	1	p
acquolina	aquolina	irreg	low	atypical	9	8	9.28	1		2	p
proficuo	profiquo	irreg	low	atypical	8	0	8.74	1	0	1	p
acquisto	aquisto	irreg	low	atypical	8	8	9.05	2	0	2	p
vacuo	vaquo	irreg	low	atypical	5	0	8.80	0	0	1	p
innocuo	innoquo	irreg	low	atypical	7	13	9.39	0	1	1	p
sbornia	sborgnia	irreg	low	atypical	7	0	8.53	2	0	0	p
ernia	ergnia	irreg	low	atypical	5	0	9.84	1	0	0	p
unione	ugnione	irreg	low	atypical	6	9	10.15	0	0	0	p
paniere	pagniere	irreg	low	atypical	7	10	10.34	0	0	0	p
dominio	domignio	irreg	low	atypical	7	11	9.82	0	0	0	p
opinione	opignione	irreg	low	atypical	8	12	9.79	0	0	0	p
efficienza	efficenza	irreg	low	atypical	10	0	8.39	1	1	1	p
socievole	socevole	irreg	low	atypical	9	8	9.04	0	0	1	ap
deficiente	deficente	irreg	low	atypical	10	0	9.22	0	1	1	p
crociera	crocera	irreg	low	atypical	8	0	9.52	2	0	2	p
igiene	igene	irreg	low	atypical	6	0	9.34	0	0	1	p
coscienza	coscenza	irreg	low	atypical	9	9	9.24	1	0	1	p
M					**7.44**	**5.72**	**9.33**	**0.61**	**0.18**	**0.83**	
SD				**1.62**	**5.55**	**0.53**	**0.78**	**0.39**	**0.71**		
sostegno	sostegnio	irreg	low	typical	8	10	9.54	2	0	1	p
menzogna	menzognia	irreg	low	typical	8	0	8.74	2	0	1	p
pugnale	pugniale	irreg	low	typical	7	7	8.63	1	0	1	p
lasagna	lasagnia	irreg	low	typical	7	8	9.07	1	0	1	p
usignolo	usigniolo	irreg	low	typical	8	8	9.57	1	0	1	p
insegna	insegnia	irreg	low	typical	7	9	9.18	2	0	1	p
inquilino	incuilino	irreg	low	typical	9	0	9.55	1	0	1	p
squama	scuama	irreg	low	typical	6	0	8.71	1	0	1	p
equo	ecuo	irreg	low	typical	4	0	7.59	0	0	1	p
delinquente	delincuente	irreg	low	typical	11	5	9.61	2	0	1	p
quota	cuota	irreg	low	typical	5	12	9.52	0	0	1	p
liquore	licuore	irreg	low	typical	7	7	9.11	0	0	1	p
diligenza	diligienza	irreg	low	typical	9	10	9.12	1	0	1	p
ancella	anciella	irreg	low	typical	7	8	9.72	0	1	1	p
strage	stragie	irreg	low	typical	6	8	9.30	2	0	1	p
carcere	carciere	irreg	low	typical	7	9	10.54	1	0	1	ap
scemo	sciemo	irreg	low	typical	5	5	9.19	1	0	1	ap
discepolo	disciepolo	irreg	low	typical	9	5	9.42	1	0	1	
M					**7.22**	**6.17**	**9.23**	**1.06**	**0.06**	**1.00**	
SD				**1.70**	**3.84**	**0.60**	**0.73**	**0.24**	**0.00**		
cristallo	cistallo	reg	high	–	9	40	9.61	2	1	1	p
elefante	elefane	reg	high	–	8	103	9.43	1	0	0	p
pericolo	percolo	reg	high	–	8	133	10.43	0	0	1	ap
bianco	binco	reg	high	–	6	681	9.79	1	0	1	P
carota	cariota	reg	high	–	6	38	10.01	0	0	1	p
serpente	serpenete	reg	high	–	8	89	9.86	2	0	0	p
caramella	craramella	reg	high	–	9	103	9.99	0	1	1	p
carnevale	carinevale	reg	high	–	9	310	9.38	1	0	1	p
fanciullo	faneciullo	reg	high	–	9	77	9.60	1	1	1	p
ciascuno	ciastuno	reg	high	–	8	94	9.75	1	0	3	
giardino	giarino	reg	high	–	8	386	10.15	1	0	1	p
inverno	inerno	reg	high	–	7	315	9.93	2	0	0	p
vasca	viasca	reg	high	–	5	42	9.28	1	0	2	p
denaro	denoro	reg	high	–	6	86	10.23	0	0	0	p
fango	fengo	reg	high	–	5	37	8.99	1	0	1	p
ragazzo	ragezzo	reg	high	–	7	1031	8.44	0	1	1	p
antico	ansico	reg	high	–	6	255	9.89	1	0	1	P
cambiare	crambiare	reg	high	–	8	378	9.97	1	0	1	P
M					**7.33**	**233.22**	**9.71**	**0.89**	**0.22**	**0.94**	
SD				**1.37**	**262.91**	**0.48**	**0.68**	**0.43**	**0.73**		

(*Continued*)

Appendix B. Continued.

Word	Pseudoword	Mapping consistency	Word frequency	Probability of sound–spelling mapping	Length ($n°$ letters)	Word frequency	Bigram frequency	Consonants cluster	Consonants geminate	Contextual rules	Stress
carciofo	carcofo	reg	low	–	8	0	9.16	1	0	2	p
catrame	catame	reg	low	–	7	0	9.69	1	0	1	p
clero	glero	reg	low	–	5	0	9.46	1	0	1	p
pugile	pugie	reg	low	–	6	0	8.76	0	0	1	ap
egiziano	egizitano	reg	low	–	8	6	9.25	0	0	1	p
cofano	cosfano	reg	low	–	6	0	9.60	0	0	1	ap
imbuto	imabuto	reg	low	–	6	0	8.82	1	0	0	p
vendetta	venadetta	reg	low	–	8	15	10.03	1	1	0	p
ambulante	ambilante	reg	low	–	9	6	9.16	2	0	0	p
bugiardo	brugiardo	reg	low	–	8	7	9.00	1	0	0	p
fregare	fegare	reg	low	–	7	5	10.01	1	0	0	p
categoria	crategoria	reg	low	–	9	13	9.39	0	0	2	p
scorpione	scorpone	reg	low	–	9	13	9.62	2	0	2	p
dogana	dosana	reg	low	–	6	0	9.19	0	0	1	p
burrasca	burrisca	reg	low	–	8	8	8.97	1	1	2	p
canguro	cangaro	reg	low	–	7	14	9.06	1	0	2	p
principio	prencipio	reg	low	–	9	14	9.44	2	0	1	p
confetto	cofetto	reg	low	–	8	15	9.29	1	1	1	p
M					**7.44**	**6.44**	**9.33**	**0.89**	**0.17**	**1.00**	
SD				**1.25**	**6.15**	**0.36**	**0.68**	**0.38**	**0.77**		

Note: Reg. = regular (consistent) sound–spelling mapping; irreg = irregular (inconsistent) sound–spelling mapping; *SD* = standard deviation. Stress: p = penultimate; ap = antepenultimate; l = last.

Appendix C. Percentage of lexical, phonological, and mixed errors of dyslexic and control children for each age and word type.

			Dyslexic children						Control children					
			Lexical errors		Phonological errors		Mixed errors		Lexical errors		Phonological errors		Mixed errors	
Word regularity	Sound–spelling mapping	Word frequency	*M*	*SE*	*M*	*SE*	*M*	*SE*	*M*	*SE*	*M*	*SE*	*M*	*SE*
					3rd Grade									
Inconsistent spelling	Atypical	Low	49.07	3.2	3.24	0.8	4.4	0.8	41.34	1.7	1.55	0.4	2.07	0.4
Inconsistent spelling	Atypical	High	26.39	2.2	1.39	0.5	3.24	0.5	13.5	1.2	1.29	0.3	0.84	0.3
Inconsistent spelling	Typical	Low	24.07	2.6	6.94	1	1.16	0.6	13.5	1.4	2.91	0.5	0.9	0.3
Inconsistent spelling	Typical	High	24.54	2.4	4.4	0.8	1.39	0.3	10.85	1.3	1.61	0.4	0.13	0.2
Regular	—	Low	—	—	15.28	1.8	—	—	—	—	5.23	1	—	
Regular	—	High	—	—	12.73	1.4	—	—	—	—	2.39	0.7	—	
					5th Grade									
Inconsistent spelling	Atypical	Low	39.35	2.7	1.16	0.6	3.47	0.7	29.52	1.4	1.49	0.3	0.9	0.4
Inconsistent spelling	Atypical	High	14.35	1.9	1.39	0.4	1.16	0.3	7.56	1	0.26	0.2	0	0.1
Inconsistent spelling	Typical	Low	17.59	2.2	4.4	0.8	1.39	0.5	9.75	1.2	2.39	0.4	0.45	0.2
Inconsistent spelling	Typical	High	18.98	1.9	0.93	0.4	0.69	0.3	7.62	1	0.71	0.2	0.19	0.1
Regular	—	Low	—	—	8.1	1.2	—	—	—	—	2.84	0.6	—	
Regular	—	High	—	—	3.7	0.8	—	—	—	—	1.81	0.4	—	

Note: Percentages with respect to the total number of words in each experimental set. Data are presented as a function of word regularity, sound–spelling mapping probability, and word frequency.

Motor control of handwriting in the developing brain: A review

Sarah Palmis, Jeremy Danna, Jean-Luc Velay and Marieke Longcamp

ABSTRACT
This review focuses on the acquisition of writing motor aspects in adults, and in 5-to 12-year-old children without learning disabilities. We first describe the behavioural aspects of adult writing and dominant models based on the notion of motor programs. We show that handwriting acquisition is characterized by the transition from reactive movements programmed stroke-by-stroke in younger children, to an automatic control of the whole trajectory when the motor programs are memorized at about 10 years old. Then, we describe the neural correlates of adult writing, and the changes that could occur with learning during childhood. The acquisition of a new skill is characterized by the involvement of a network more restricted in space and where neural specificity is increased in key regions. The cerebellum and the left dorsal premotor cortex are of fundamental importance in motor learning, and could be at the core of the acquisition of handwriting.

Introduction

Efficient handwriting is a prerequisite for successful academic achievement. Handwriting *quality* is also thought to predict the performance in related cognitive domains such as text composition (Connelly, Dockrell, Walter, & Critten, 2012; Graham, Berninger, Abbott, Abbot, & Whitaker, 1997; Jones & Christensen, 1999; Puranik & Al Otaiba, 2012), spelling and orthographic skills (Graham et al., 1997; Pontart et al., 2013), and reading (Guan, Perfetti, & Meng, 2015; Shatil, Share, & Levin, 2000). This review article focuses on the acquisition of the motor aspects of writing in children without learning disabilities. Learning how to write is a long and demanding process that starts as early as age 2 years, when the first graphic movements are produced, and ends in late adolescence. However, the most massive changes in the features of writing occur between ages 5 and 10 years.

In the first part of the article, we review the dominant models of skilled handwriting that are based on the notion of motor programs encoded in memory. We describe the behavioural characteristics of handwriting in skilled adults, and we outline the main behavioural changes occurring with learning. In the second part, we focus on the neural correlates of writing. We describe the handwriting brain network in adults. In order to better understand how this network is constructed, it is useful to consider general developmental brain changes in middle childhood, and their possible relationships with handwriting acquisition. It is also relevant to highlight the similarity between the trajectory followed by children to become expert writers and data from the field of motor learning. The neural changes that have been described in relation to motor learning and the acquisition of a motor expertise can inform us on how the brain correlates of handwriting evolve in children. In the final part, we review the existing neuroimaging studies on handwriting and related skills in children.

Models of handwriting and behavioural data

Models of expert handwriting

Models of writing originate either from cognitive neuropsychology with the analysis of errors of normal subjects and brain-damaged patients (Ellis, 1988; Margolin & Binder, 1984), or from the field of motor control (van Galen, 1991). They agree upon the hierarchical modular organization of writing, and upon the dissociation between "high-level" syntactic, semantic, and orthographic processes that converge in an orthographic working memory, and "low-level" motor processes. This general architecture has remained relatively unchanged over the last 30 years. Prior to the onset of motor processes, letter identities are still represented in an abstract way (Rothlein & Rapp, 2014). Those abstract letter representations can be externalized in several possible output modalities (oral spelling, typing, etc. . . . Ellis, 1988; Margolin & Binder, 1984). In terms of motor processes specific to handwriting, the model of van Galen (1991) is the most widely used because it relies on a large body of research on motor production in handwriting. At the core of this model lies the idea that letter-forms—that is, the possible instances of each letter (allographs) that have been learned, are stored in long-term memory in the form of "motor programs". At the so-called allographic level of processing, the motor programs would therefore be selected from a long-term motor memory store. Note that the early notion of motor programs (Keele, 1968; Schmidt, 1975) has more recently been redefined as internal models (Wolpert, Ghahramani, & Jordan, 1995). However, for sake of clarity, the term of motor programs is used in the present review. In handwriting, motor programs are codes that specify the number of basic motor units (strokes, see below for an operational definition of a stroke) and their spatiotemporal relations in an abstract, effector-independent way. Neuropsychological models developed a similar notion of "graphic motor pattern" or "motor engram". It originates from the observation of patients with apraxic agraphia, a condition in which writing is impaired despite intact spelling ability and normal sensorimotor skills (Ellis, 1982; Margolin & Binder, 1984). Apraxic agraphia is interpreted as a deficit affecting the graphic motor patterns caused by the brain lesion. In neuropsychological models, the selection of allographs is considered distinct from the selection of the motor programs itself. Finally, the idea that motor programs are specified at the level of a letter has been debated. It is supported by the results of experiments showing, for instance, that adding a letter to a sequence of letters increases the preparation time, whereas the number of strokes per letter does not affect this variable (Hulstijn & van Galen, 1983).

After the motor programs is retrieved, at the lower level, information about movement parametrization and muscular adjustments would be encoded and stored in a motor working memory to produce the trajectories, with the desired size and slant. Several models of handwriting have described this last level. They seek to explain how the central motor representations are actually implemented in the neuromuscular system, in a real-time biophysical context (Hollerbach, 1981; Plamondon, 1995a, 1995b; Viviani & Flash, 1995). At this late stage of execution (Plamondon, 1995a, 1995b; van Galen, 1991), the stroke is usually considered the basic motor unit of handwriting. A stroke is typically defined as the portion of the trajectory between two absolute velocity minima (Meulenbroek & van Galen, 1988), or between two points of zero "vertical" (in the *y*-axis) velocity (Hollerbach, 1981). Among those models, the kinematic model of Plamondon (1995a, 1995b) is currently the most accurate for skilled handwriting production. In this model, each stroke would result from a coordinated activity of the muscular system and would be defined by a velocity vector. Interestingly, only the orientation and amplitude of each velocity vector would be coded in the central nervous system.

The levels of representation in handwriting are summarized in Figure 1.

Main characteristics of skilled handwriting in adults

Handwriting production is usually characterized through the handwriting product—that is, the spatial accuracy of the written trace (shaping, size, legibility, etc.) and through the handwriting process—that is, the movement that generates this trace (Rosenblum, Weiss, & Parush, 2003; Tucha, Tucha, & Lange, 2008). Such coupled analysis of handwriting product and process is possible when writing is recorded on graphic tablets from which several kinematic variables can be computed, such as the mean velocity, the number of lifts and stops (Paz-Villagrán, Danna, & Velay, 2014), or the movement fluency (e.g., Danna, Paz-Villagrán, & Velay, 2013). Note that when a graphic tablet is not available, the writing speed (which has been also called frequency of production) can be roughly approximated by counting the number of letters produced per minute (Graham, Berninger, Weintraub, & Schafer, 1998). A fluent movement is characterized by a smooth velocity profile, and broad velocity fluctuations (see the velocity profile of adult writing in Figure 2). Conversely, the more numerous the velocity peaks, the greater the number of abnormal accelerations and decelerations and, therefore, the less fluent the movement. Finally, a possibly interesting index of the stability of the motor

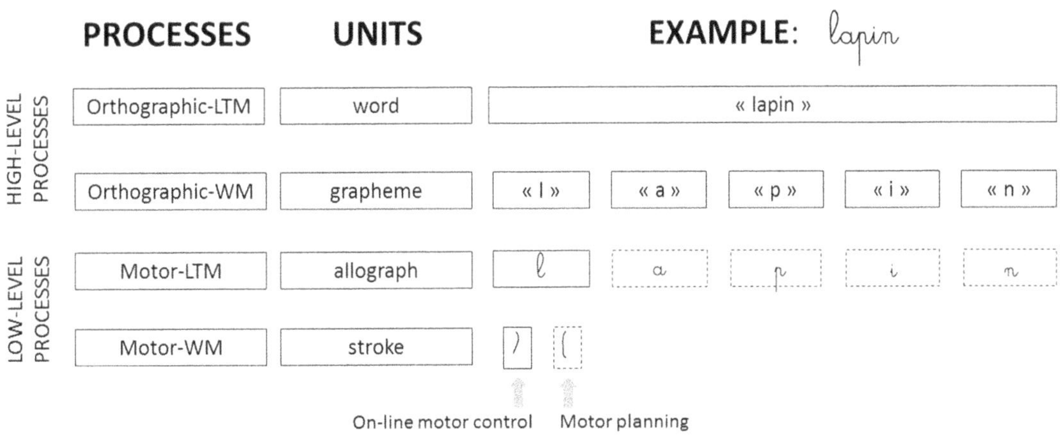

Figure 1. Schematic illustration of the different key processes and units activated during the production of the first stroke of the French word "lapin" (rabbit) in cursive handwriting. LTM = long-term memory; WM = working memory. At the high level, the orthographic-LTM is responsible for the long-term storage and retrieval of learned word spelling. The orthographic-WM is responsible for the online temporary storage and serial selection of graphemes for production. At the low level, the motor-LTM is responsible for the long-term storage and retrieval of the motor programs corresponding to the selected allographic representation of each letter that constitutes the word. Note that neuropsychological models postulate an extra step for selecting the allograph before the motor programs. Finally, the motor-WM is responsible for the online control of the current stroke production and for motor planning of the following stroke that constitutes the allograph.

programs is the intra-individual variability of the performance. However, indexes of variability are investigated more rarely (Mojet, 1991; Rueckriegel et al., 2008; Zesiger, 1992).

Skilled handwriting is characterized by an optimal control of spatial and temporal constraints in order to produce a legible trace as quickly as possible. Handwriting is considered a fast motor activity. Surprisingly, handwriting speed does not result from the pen velocity, which generally reaches about 10 cm/s (a velocity 100 times lower than that of a tennis racket), but from the very rapid succession of short movements with many fast changes in direction. Handwriting is a rhythmic activity that can reach a frequency of about 5 Hz when accounting for the successive ascending and descending strokes produced by the pen (see Figure 2, adult handwriting). Note that in studies comparing different styles of handwriting (e.g., cursive versus printing), the authors reported that cursive handwriting was slower than printing despite the numerous pen lifts in the latter case (Bara & Morin, 2013). Independently of the writing style, the high frequency limits the possibility of online control based on sensory information and imposes a mode of control so-called proactive, based on the execution of motor programs. The movement of a skilled writer can thus be considered as fully automated. Automation refers to the fact that writing is produced with minimal conscious "effort"—that is, with minimal attentional involvement (Hasher & Zacks, 1979; Tucha et al., 2008). Automation is crucial in handwriting as it allows the allocation of cognitive resources to other processes (Berninger & Swanson, 1994; Jones & Christensen, 1999). An illustrated example of the effect of disruption of the automatic movement control in adults can be found in Marquardt, Gentz, and Mai (1996). The participants were instructed to write while allocating attention to visually tracking the position of the tip of the pen. The timing and kinematics of the movement were dramatically deteriorated by this attentional instruction: The writing of the same word took a much longer time, and the velocity profile indicated a disruption of the fluency, with several accelerations and decelerations within the same stroke. For some authors, fluency is the most accurate index of automation. An automated movement can be characterized by a minimal number of changes in velocity during execution (Tucha et al., 2008).

In spite of its high degree of automation, skilled handwriting requires visual and proprioceptive (tactile and kinaesthetic) feedback. These two sensory systems play different and complementary roles in the integration and the processing of common features of handwriting, as, for instance, the trajectory orientation (Lajoie et al., 1992), or the curvature of the trace and velocity of the movement (see Danna et al., 2015 for review; Viviani & Stucchi,

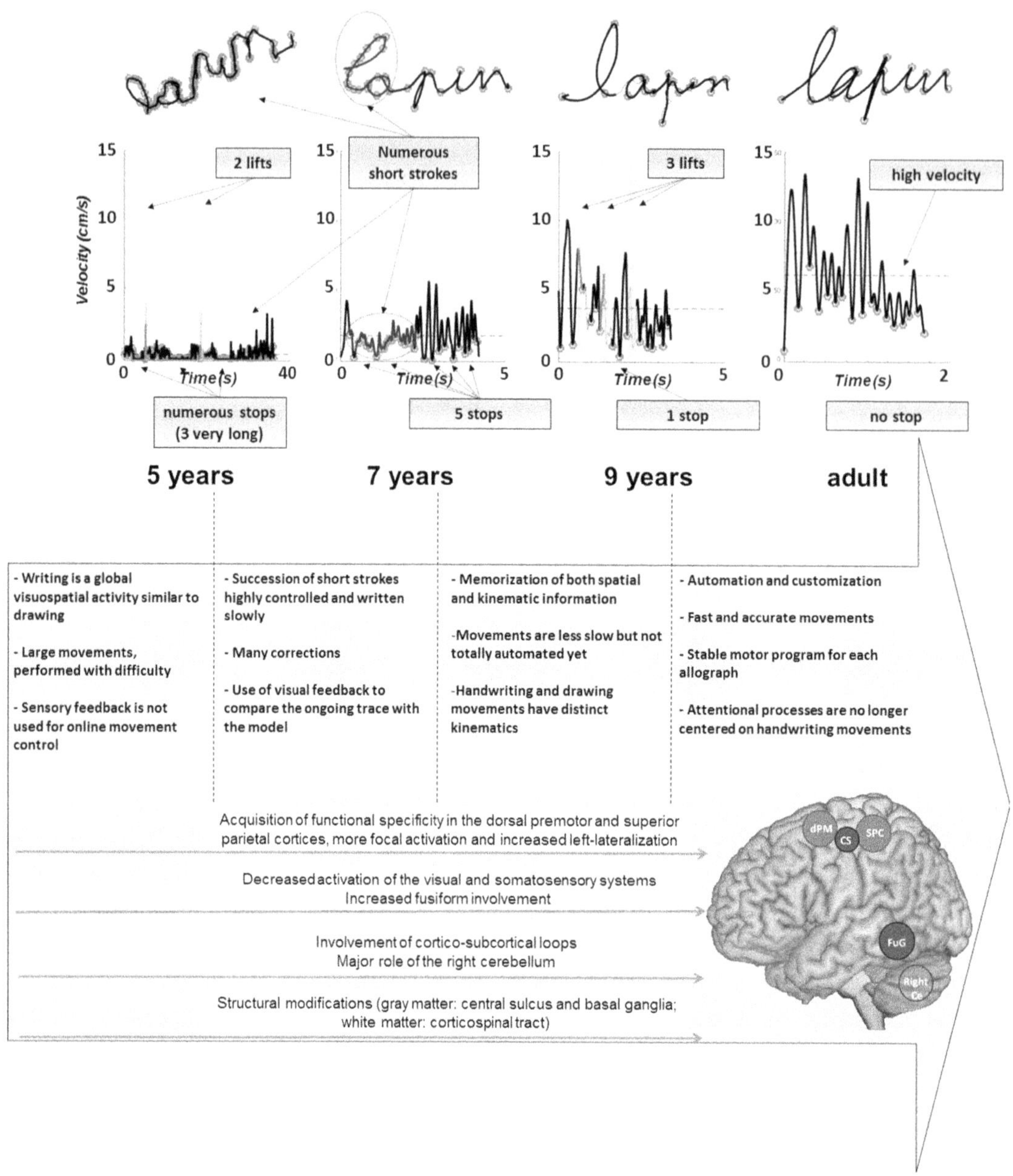

Figure 2. Time-frame showing the evolution of handwriting with learning and development. Top: typical exemplars of handwriting at age 5, 7, and 9, and from an adult, and corresponding velocity profiles. The red dots indicate the absolute velocity minima and their position in the trace. The time scale is different for the youngest child (40 s) and for the adult (2 s). Pen lifts and stops are indicated, and the dramatic evolution of movement fluency, mean velocity, total duration, and number of stops is clearly visible. Bottom: description of the main behavioural and brain changes, and view of the left hemisphere showing the position of the main regions involved in handwriting and discussed in the text. The core of the handwriting network (dPM = dorsal premotor cortex; SPC = superior parietal cortex; right Ce = right cerebellum, viewed in transparency) is in blue, and the associated regions (CS = central sulcus, position of the hand motor cortex; FuG = fusiform gyrus) are in purple. [To view this figure in colour, please see the online version of this Journal.]

1989). Smyth and Silvers (1987) evaluated adult handwriting in "blind" conditions, when vision was not allowed. They observed that the global spatial layout and the orientation of the words were impacted by the absence of visual feedback. However, the word shape and letter legibility were little deteriorated, except for letters with repetitive strokes ("n" and "m"; "u" and "w") where some strokes could be added or omitted. A possible explanation is that vision is used to update a motor buffer containing the strokes of each letter (see Figure 1). The role of proprioceptive feedback was evaluated by comparing the handwriting movements of deafferented subjects, who cannot perceive any tactile or kinaesthetic information about their movement or the position of their own body, to that of control adults (Hepp-Reymond,

Chakarov, Schulte-Mönting, Huethe, & Kristeva, 2009; Teasdale et al., 1993). Without proprioceptive feedback, the handwriting kinematics deteriorated because the subjects slow their pen down in order to control it visually. However, the word shape and letter legibility were not dramatically affected.

Visual and proprioceptive information can be used to adjust the parametrization phase (the last step in Figure 1, where strokes are the units of processing), but have a negligible effect on the shape of the letters. This spatial invariance that is maintained despite variations in the context of execution is a typical and remarkable feature of handwriting. It can be highlighted when observing the invariance in the written product when varying the size or speed (Kadmon Harpaz, Flash, & Dinstein, 2014; Viviani & Terzuolo, 1980), or the effector (left hand, toe, elbow, . . . Bernstein, 1947). This confirms that invariance results from the abstract nature of the information represented in the motor programs (Teulings & Schomaker, 1993).

Characteristics of writing evolution in childhood

Several years and thousands of hours of practice pass between the first time a child holds a pen to write their name and the time they write series of words fluently. The construction and consolidation of motor programs in long-term memory is therefore a long and extremely demanding process. Many studies (Meulenbroek & van Galen, 1988; Mojet, 1991; Zesiger, 1992) have tried to characterize the evolution of handwriting in childhood. Those studies display very variable methodologies both in the materials used (single letters, loops, bigrams, trigrams, words, sentences . . .) and in the variables considered (product and/or process). Figure 2 (top) presents the same word written by children aged 5, 7, or 9, and by an adult, as an illustration of the dramatic evolution of both the trace and the underlying process. The mean velocity increases (and therefore the duration of the whole word decreases). The number of absolute velocity minima (marked by red circles) decreases to reach an optimal value in the fluent adult handwriting. The trace becomes more legible. The low-skilled handwriting of 5-year-old children corresponds to a discrete succession of inaccurate strokes, produced with very variable velocity profiles, many stops, and pen lifts. The children have learned the writing primitives through the practice of graphomotor exercises (e.g., production of loops and zigzag) but they fail the transition from one stroke to the next in the context of writing. The early evolution, between ages 5 and 7, has been interpreted as a transition from a ballistic strategy characterized by an inability to use sensory feedback (about the age of 5) to a control based mainly on visual feedback (at about 7). The youngest children perform rapid short gestures followed by error evaluation, while older children are characterized by a progressive online integration of visual and proprioceptive information. Around 7–8 years, despite two years of practice, the writing is still not automated. The size decreases but the movement velocity is still low. Children still pay attention to the distal movements of their hand. The correct motor pattern is not yet memorized, and handwriting movement is mainly under the control of the online visual inspection of the trace. Finally, around 9–10 years, the children master and personalize their writing. Therefore, learning to write could be explained by a shift from a product-oriented (the written trace) to a process-oriented (the motor patterns generating the trace) control. Indeed, all authors agree upon the idea that children switch from a mainly retroactive mode of control at age 7, essentially based on visual feedback, to a proactive mode of control, based on stable motor representations, at age 10. The motor programs for producing letters are acquired gradually over long time-periods, and the performance becomes automatic, allowing the children to devote less attention to the task.

The monotonic versus non-monotonic nature of the evolution of motor control of handwriting with age has been a matter of debate. When the product is analysed, there is general agreement on data showing that the evolution of legibility is non-monotonic (Graham et al., 1998; Mojet, 1991). In a systematic cross-sectional study of both the product and the process of handwriting in a representative sample of children (respectively, 300 and 219) who were writing simple pseudowords, Mojet (1991) reported a marked increase of legibility at age 8–10 followed by a temporary decrease. This supports the idea of a phase of the acquisition where the children focus their handwriting on the respect of the calligraphic style, followed by a phase where they depart from standard letter shapes (de Ajuriaguerra, 1971). For kinematic indexes, the evolution is less clear. On the one hand, early studies have identified periods of temporary regression of performance. Between the ages of 7 and 9, Meulenbroek and van Galen (1988) reported a decrease of movement velocity and fluency in a letter production task. Rueckriegel et al. (2008) also observed a decrease in fluency in their group of 8–9-year-olds compared to the group of 6–7-year-olds in the same type of task. One interpretation of the non-monotonic variations of kinematic indexes with age is that the evolution of handwriting depends on the developmental course of the child, as has been shown for other motor skills. In reaching movements, for instance, Hay (1979) showed that 7–8-year-olds display velocity profiles that are more jerky than those of younger or older children. This loss of movement fluency is thought to occur because the maturation of the motor system in this age-group allows the use of sensory information during movement execution. On the other hand, some authors have reported a fully monotonic improvement in the performance for most of the indexes analysed (Mojet, 1991; Zesiger, 1992). Mojet (1991), for instance, reported no discontinuity in any of the kinematic variables derived from the graphic tablet. The most important changes were nonetheless observed within a limited age range (between 7 and 9 years old). After age 10, the performance did not greatly evolve (see also Rueckriegel et al., 2008; Zesiger, 1992). However, significant differences between 12-year-olds and adults indicate that handwriting continues to progress slightly during adolescence (Zesiger, 1992). A monotonic profile of evolution would be more compatible with the idea that writing performance is mainly determined by the increase of the size of the motor programs the child is able to implement, not by an abrupt change in sensorimotor strategies due to development. This idea is at the core of the AVITE-WRITE model (Grossberg & Paine, 2000; Paine, Grossberg, & Van Gemmert, 2004). This model accounts for the changes occurring during handwriting practice from the stroke to the letter production. It simulates an early, error-prone, learning stage consisting of visually guided short curves generated sequentially. The error between the actual and the desired position of the pen is visually estimated, and the motor command allowing error correction is computed. This process stops when the correct motor program is memorized and then used for automatic movement generation. In addition, the increasing ability of the child to anticipate the following strokes and letters could also be a determinant of the observed progressive improvements in the performance (Kandel & Perret, 2015).

This overview shows that, among the ages tested, a period of transition seems to occur between ages 7–8 and 10. Depending on the studies and variables, this age-range is characterized either by a temporary deterioration of the performance followed by an improvement, or by a massive improvement. Although the performance is not fully stabilized afterwards, kinematic indexes evolve slowly after age 10, and at this age writing starts to become automated. The motor programs for the allographs are likely to be acquired after this age, and writing can then be performed in an automatic way (Kandel & Perret, 2015).

Handwriting and the brain

Skilled handwriting brain network

How is motor control of handwriting implemented in the brain of skilled adults? The possible existence of a brain centre containing the "motor images" of writing has been debated since the nineteenth century (Roux, Draper, Köpke, & Démonet, 2010). Following the first observations by Exner (1881) of apraxic agraphia (Ellis, 1982; Margolin & Binder, 1984) after a brain lesion, it is assumed that a part of the left dorsal premotor cortex, located at the junction between the middle frontal gyrus and the precentral gyrus, codes for the implementation of graphic motor patterns (Anderson, Damasio, & Damasio, 1990). This region is referred to as Exner's area. Its specificity for writing is confirmed by neuroimaging studies showing that it is only minimally activated during linguistic tasks that do not involve writing movements (Planton, Jucla, Roux, & Démonet, 2013; Planton, Longcamp, Péran, Démonet, & Jucla, 2017; Purcell, Turkeltaub, et al.,; Rapcsak & Beeson, 2004; Sugihara, Kaminaga, & Sugishita, 2006). It also responds preferentially to writing than to matched control manual movements (e.g., loops, zigzags, circles; Planton et al., 2013; Purcell, Turkeltaub, et al., 2011) and even preferentially to writing letters than to digits (Longcamp et al., 2014). It is possible that this dorsal premotor region displays functional specificity to letters because the corresponding motor programs are practised more often and are therefore coded in a more stable fashion. In addition, Roux et al. (2009) have suggested that this region, which they termed the graphemic motor frontal area, serves as an interface between linguistic processes and motor programs specific to handwriting. In neuroimaging studies, however, the position of Exner's area along the precentral gyrus appears more dorsal than initially defined based on neurological observations. Neuroimaging studies indicate that Exner's area is located at the junction between the precentral gyrus and the superior frontal sulcus (Roux et al., 2009; Sugihara et al., 2006). The left dorsal premotor cortex is not the only part of the brain wherein lesions can cause motor deficits predominantly affecting writing. The left superior parietal cortex is also thought to play a key role in motor control of writing, as attested to by the number of cases of apraxic agraphia following a lesion in this region (Alexander, Fischer, & Friedman, 1992; Auerbach & Alexander, 1981; Basso, Taborelli, & Vignolo, 1978; Beeson, Rising, & Volk, 2003; Kinsbourne & Rosenfield, 1974; Magrassi, Bongetta, Bianchini, Berardesca, & Arienta, 2010; Roeltgen & Heilman, 1983; Sakurai et al., 2007; Takayama,Sugishita, Akiguchi, Kimura, 1994) and by neuroimaging studies focused on motor control of writing trajectory (Kadmon Harpaz et al., 2014; Menon & Desmond, 2001; Seitz et al., 1997). The left superior parietal involvement is consistent, irrespective of the type of linguistic task performed (Brownsett & Wise, 2010). Some authors have hypothesized that the motor programs for writing are actually stored in the dominant superior parietal lobe (Beeson et al., 2003). Indeed, in an experiment where participants had to write letters at different sizes, the left parietal cortex was found to code for scale-invariant representations, meaning that the pattern of activation varied as a function of the letter written, but remained similar for a given letter despite changes in size and therefore of muscular motor commands (Kadmon Harpaz et al., 2014). Interestingly, subcortical lesions (Ohno, Bando, Nagura, Ishii, & Yamanouchi, 2000; Vandenborre, van Dun, Engelborghs, & Mariën, 2015) and lesions of the right cerebellum (Mariën, De Smet, Paquier, & Verhoeven, 2010) have also been reported to cause apraxic agraphia. Writing impairments possibly occur through a reorganization of subcortico-cortical or cortico-cerebellar loops exerting a remote effect on premotor and parietal regions after the appearance of the lesion (Mariën et al., 2010; Ohno et al., 2000). Neuroimaging studies also demonstrated a very consistent involvement of the right posterior cerebellar hemisphere in studies where the control tasks are otherwise well matched in terms of their motor complexity (Planton et al., 2013). This portion of the cerebellum, ipsilateral to the writing hand, is therefore considered a writing-specific motor region. Haggard, Jenner, and Wing (1994) proposed that in cases of cerebellar lesions, impaired proactive control might induce important deficits in the timing, smoothness, and accuracy of writing movements due to over-dependence on cortical feedback loops for correcting errors. Although the exact function of the cerebellum in motor control remains debated, researchers agree upon its predominant involvement in motor learning and in the retention of motor skills. Consistent right cerebellar involvement in writing could stem from an initial implication in early stages of acquisition (Doyon & Benali, 2005), followed by a role in the retention of the acquired graphomotor skills. Among the theories of cerebellar function, some non-exclusive views attribute to the cerebellum the implementation of inverse models allowing error correction in the course of acquisition and storage of internal models allowing an automatic proactive movement (Manto et al., 2012).

The left parietal, dorsal premotor cortices and the right cerebellum may therefore constitute a network that codes for the effector-independent writing motor programs. Consistent with this idea, two studies demonstrated that when right-handed participants have to write with their dominant hand or with another effector (non-dominant hand or even toe), those three regions are consistently activated, among otherwise distinctly distributed sensorimotor activations (Rijntjes et al., 1999; Sugihara et al., 2006). The authors suggested that the motor representations of writing tend to cluster in brain regions initially devoted to controlling the movements of the dominant hand. The activation of the dorsal premotor and parietal cortices during writing is indeed right-lateralized in left-handers (Longcamp, Anton, Roth, & Velay, 2005; Siebner et al., 2002). In a single-case study, a left-handed agraphic patient with callosal disconnection produced well-formed letters but meaningless writing with the left hand and apraxic agraphia with the right hand (Varley, Cowell, Gibson, & Romanowski, 2005). The authors also concluded that the motor programs were stored in the right hemisphere in left-handers. In converted left-handers, who were forced to switch their writing hand in early childhood, the activation is more bilateral (Klöppel et al., 2007; Siebner et al., 2002). This confirms that the distribution of the writing network is determined both by the initial organization of the motor system and by training with a certain effector.

Finally, although the left fusiform cortex is not considered a part of the motor network, its role in writing processes should be acknowledged. First, the left fusiform gyrus is very consistently activated in spelling tasks (Planton et al., 2013; Purcell, Turkeltaub, Eden, & Rapp, 2011) as well as in reading tasks (Cohen et al., 2002; Flowers et al., 2004). Some researchers have proposed that it plays a key role in orthographic long-term memory because it is consistently found to be damaged in patients who produce more spelling errors on orthographically difficult (low-frequency or irregular) words (Rapp, Purcell, Hillis, Capasso, & Miceli, 2016). In this fusiform region, the identity of the letters is represented in an abstract form: The similarity of the patterns of activation is not determined by the physical, phonological, or motor similarity of the letters, but by their actual identity (for instance, visually presented "E" and "e" produce very similar patterns of activation in this region despite a different shape, whereas "b" and "p" do not despite similar physical and phonological features; Rothlein & Rapp, 2014).

How does this organization emerge to reach this expert state? Despite the scarcity of studies of handwriting in children with brain imaging tools, some elements can be found in the field of brain development, and of motor learning and expertise.

Brain changes in development and in motor learning, and relationships with handwriting acquisition

Learning how to write probably relies on very similar organizing principles to those for learning other types of motor tasks. The main feature of handwriting is that the acquisition of a highly complex new motor skill spans over several years, while the brain is developing (Dick, Leech, Moses, & Saccuman, 2006). In that sense, learning handwriting is similar to learning how to play a musical instrument.

General brain changes during middle childhood

By the time most of the writing skill has been acquired, between ages 6 and 10, children are in a phase of neuronal development characterized by significant changes in grey and white matter densities (up to 6–10 years), and then by an increase of total grey matter during middle childhood and a decrease during adolescence (Gogtay et al., 2004; Wilke, Krägeloh-Mann, & Holland, 2007). The cortico-spinal white matter system grows denser continuously (Barnea-Goraly et al., 2005; Giedd et al., 1999, 2009; Mills et al., 2016; Paus, 1999; Wilke et al., 2007). This neuronal maturation co-occurs with the development of motor abilities, with a decrease of latency, and with an increase in accuracy (Adi-Japha, Badir, Dorfberger, & Karni, 2014; Gogtay et al., 2004; Savion-Lemieux, Bailey, & Penhune, 2009). The basic sensorimotor brain network is already well segregated in young children when they start formal writing instruction, and its topography, extent, and connectivity vary little between ages 6 and 10 (Grayson & Fair, 2017; Zielinski, Gennatas, Zhou, & Seeley, 2010). Functionally, children between ages 6 and 12 display a relatively similar distribution of cortical activation during a visuomotor tracing task. However, older children display more accurate performance and less cortical motor activation than young children. This suggests a more efficient mobilization of the neural resources with age (Pangelinan, Hatfield, & Clark, 2013). In addition, as stated above, handwriting production is thought to rely on brain regions that display functional specificity for letters compared to other graphic shapes. Studies of the development, between ages 7 and 11, of the functional specificity to certain stimulus categories in the cortex, such as faces, show that the position of category-selective regions is determined early in childhood. However, the extent of category-specific tissue and the amplitude of the difference in activation between preferred and non-preferred categories increase with age (Golarai, Liberman, & Grill-Spector, 2015). This co-occurs with improved performance (better discrimination of faces; (Natu et al., 2016). In summary, the development of a given skill relies on both the focalization and increase of activity in regions crucial for the task and on the decrease in regions uncorrelated with the task (Durston et al., 2006). It is accompanied by changes from local and diffuse connectivity to longer range functional connectivity (Grayson & Fair, 2017; Kelly et al., 2009): Brain regions relevant to the task become more specialized, and better organized in long-range networks, in the course of development (Johnson, 2011).

Neural correlates of motor learning

Because learning how to write co-occurs with brain development, it is likely that motor learning in children is not fully comparable to motor learning in adults. For example, in children, stabilization in motor memory occurs faster and is less susceptible to interference than in adults (Adi-Japha et al., 2014; Ashtamker & Karni, 2013). However, despite those differences, existing studies suggest that generally, the evolution of the performance of children during learning, and the underlying processes, are similar to those of adults (Adi-Japha et al., 2014; Julius & Adi-Japha, 2015). At the brain level, motor learning may also rely on similar mechanisms. For instance, cortico-cerebellar networks, which crucially participate in motor learning in adults, also display dynamic changes of activation between the early phase of training and the retention of a new motor skill, in children aged 8–12 (Zwicker, Missiuna, Harris, & Boyd, 2011). Motor learning research could therefore constitute an interesting framework leading to better understand the brain correlates of learning how to write.

Short- and long-term motor learning

In adults, motor learning occurs in two stages: an early stage with fast improvements and a late stage with slower improvements. Both stages depend on two neural circuits: the cortico-cerebellar loop that is composed of cortical motor areas (mainly the primary motor, somatosensory, dorsal premotor, and parietal cortices), the thalamus, and the cerebellum, while the cortico-striatal loop is composed of the same motor cortical areas, the thalamus and basal ganglia (Doyon, Penhune, & Ungerleider, 2003; Hardwick, Rottschy, Miall, & Eickhoff, 2013). Prefrontal regions and the hippocampus interact with both circuits (Doyon & Benali, 2005; Floyer-Lea & Matthews, 2005; Schendan, Searl, Melrose, & Stern, 2003). The early motor stage is primarily driven by the cortico-cerebellar loop. It is characterized by slow and inaccurate movements, relying strongly on feedback, but the extent and rapidity of improvement are substantial. It has been shown that in the course of short-term training to new graphomotor sequences in adults, the pattern of activations is similar to that observed in other motor learning tasks (Swett, Contreras-Vidal, Birn, & Braun, 2010). Interestingly, when the activation in the very first trials of learning was contrasted to activation in the later trials, the authors observed an initially stronger activation of the visual system indicating visual coding of the sequences, followed by a shift towards a stronger subcortical (cerebellum and basal ganglia) activation indicating motor recoding. Long-term learning was not assessed in this study (Swett et al., 2010).

The late stage of motor learning corresponds to a slow phase during which the motor skill has been consolidated. Improvements still can be observed until the performance reaches an asymptotic level, and motor execution becomes fully automatic (Doyon, Owen, Petrides, Sziklas, & Evans, 1996; Grafton, Woods, & Tyszka, 1994). Movements become faster, more accurate, less dependent on feedback (Halsband & Lange, 2006), and less variable (Krakauer & Mazzoni, 2011). This indicates a long-term memorization of the motor skill, which can be elicited efficiently even after a long delay without practice. The kinematic changes are accompanied by a shift from anterior to more posterior brain areas (Floyer-Lea & Matthews, 2005), highlighting the decrease of executive control, working memory, and attention towards a more automatic performance (Kelly & Garavan, 2005). Important plastic changes have also been shown to occur in the primary motor cortex during slow learning, with a higher activation when performing the task and a decrease of excitability thresholds at the late stage, reflecting a more efficient recruitment of motor units with learning (Galea, Vazquez, Pasricha, de Xivry, & Celnik, 2011; Hardwick et al., 2013; Pascual-Leone et al., 1995). This suggests a role in the retention of learned movements through their repeated performance (Galea et al., 2011). Interestingly, although the left primary motor cortex is not considered part of the core network for representing handwriting movements, meta-analyses show that it is often more activated in handwriting tasks than in control tasks (Planton et al., 2013; Purcell, Turkeltaub, et al., 2011). It could therefore also play a role in the retention of handwriting movements (Kadmon Harpaz et al., 2014).

Left dorsal premotor cortex and motor learning

In a meta-analysis including a large number of functional magnetic resonance imaging (fMRI) studies of manual motor learning, Hardwick et al. (2013) found that motor learning was strongly and systematically associated with left dorsal premotor activation at a location close to the position of Exner's area, regardless of the type of task and of the time-scale. According to Hardwick et al. (2013), the left dorsal premotor cortex constitutes "the core of motor learning". This central role could stem from a pivotal function in the visuomotor control of movement, through the selection and updating of motor responses according to visual cues. The left dorsal premotor cortex holds multiple connections with primary motor, parietal, and prefrontal cortices and is a potential node of convergence between sensorimotor information, decision making, and other cognitive functions (Hardwick et al., 2015). It is therefore possible that the motor representations in Exner's area cluster at a subpart or in the close vicinity of the premotor region supporting motor learning. This fits well with the early idea that Exner's area is "especially trained from childhood through the formation of engrams to function as a writing center" (Nielsen, 1946).

Expertise

Importantly, the relative duration of fast and slow learning is highly task specific. Learning how to write is comparable to learning how to play a musical instrument, with the fast and slow stages and associated behavioural improvements extending over the course of months or even years (Dayan & Cohen, 2011). By the end of learning, expertise is achieved. Functionally, expert performance is associated with less strong and more focused overall brain activation whereas novice performance is associated with more widespread activation (Lotze, Scheler, Tan, Braun, & Birbaumer, 2003; Milton, Solodkin, Hluštík, & Small, 2007). In addition, the regions primarily activated by task performance in motor experts are located in the cortical motor networks and in the cerebellum, and are more strongly activated than in novices (Lotze et al., 2003; Milton et al., 2007). This pattern of activation is associated with better behavioural performance (Lotze et al., 2003). It indicates that with expertise, the memory trace is coded in regions that directly participate in the task performance. In the field of writing, the effects of expertise on functional brain activations have never been investigated. However, some insights can be found in the comparison of writing overlearned letter patterns to drawing pictures or unknown symbols. Drawing requires the implementation of similar graphomotor strokes, but non-automated and not coded as a single motor program in memory. At about 5–6, reliably distinct action sequences can be observed for writing and drawing (Brenneman, Massey, Machado, & Gelman, 1996), and around age 7 the movement kinematics (velocity, fluency, pause-time . . .) for writing letters and drawing geometric symbols otherwise similar in their shape diverge (Adi-Japha & Freeman, 2001). This indicates that the brain networks underpinning the two activities are different in experts. At the brain level, neuroimaging data on adults show that in fact, writing and drawing rely on overlapping frontoparietal regions. Strikingly, however, drawing recruits a much more extended amount of neural tissue (Harrington, Farias, Davis, & Buonocore, 2007; Planton et al., 2017; Yuan & Brown, 2015). In a recent study where they compared writing and drawing in a design controlled for minimizing possible kinematic differences between tasks, Planton et al. (2017) found that compared to writing, drawing overactivates the previously defined "handwriting network", including the left fusiform gyrus. Interestingly, however, the lateralization of the premotor activation was strikingly different for the two tasks: It was completely bilateral for drawing whereas it was strongly left-lateralized for writing (participants were right-handers). And indeed, as stated above, the lateralization of the premotor and parietal activations in handwriting seems to be determined by handedness (Klöppel et al., 2007; Longcamp, Anton, et al., 2005; Siebner et al., 2002). It is therefore possible that, in the brain, the specificity of writing stems from learning and developmental processes leading to expertise and allowing both its spatial focalization and its lateralization at the cortical level.

Expertise also induces structural reorganizations at the level of the grey matter, as shown in experts such as musicians (Gaser & Schlaug, 2003; Han et al., 2009) and athletes (Park et al., 2009), or after long-term training to juggling (Draganski et al., 2004). For instance, musicians present higher grey matter volumes in sensorimotor and premotor cortices and in the cerebellum than non-experts (Gaser & Schlaug, 2003; Hutchinson, Lee, Gaab, & Schlaug, 2003). Could the same type of modification occur in relation to the acquisition of writing? Interestingly, in converted left-handers, an early forced switch in the hand used to write leads to structural modifications in the asymmetry of the central sulcus and in the volume of the middle part of the putamen, a part of the striatum dealing with executive and associative functions (Kloppel, Mangin, Vongerichten, Frackowiak, & Siebner, 2010). In addition, structural modifications in the parietal cortex have been reported in expert typists (Cannonieri, Bonilha, Fernandes, Cendes, & Li, 2007). It is a good indication that, similar to experience with a musical instrument, writing experience shapes brain structure. Microstructural properties of the white matter, for instance in the corticospinal tract, are also modified after motor learning (Bengtsson et al., 2005; McKenzie et al., 2014; Schmithorst & Wilke, 2002). Although no direct evidence of such modifications exist in the field of handwriting, it is can be hypothesized that writing acquisition also modifies white matter tracts.

Neural correlates of writing acquisition in children

Few elements directly shed light on the neural mechanisms by which the key network for handwriting develops in children. Up to now, only two neuroimaging studies have directly assessed handwriting production in children (Richards et al., 2011, 2015). The lack of neuroimaging data in children is probably related to the sensitivity of the method to head movements induced by the mobilization of the hand and forearm, and by the difficulty to write in a supine position when the skill is not fully mastered. No study has yet compared children to adults.

The writing network described in adults seems to be active in children

In an fMRI study involving participants aged between 10 and 12, Richards et al. (2015) compared the brain activation resulting from the writing of an unfamiliar letter shape (pseudoletter), to that from a highly practised letter of comparable shape. It should be noted that, in this age-range, the children are likely to have automated their writing, as outlined in the first, behavioural, section. However, the degree of automation could be variable among children. Within this study, good writers were defined by an above-average rating on a legibility measure of handwriting. They were likely to display a fully automatized writing as they were more efficient in writing highly practised letters than the poor writers. On the contrary, the poor writers were less likely to have reached automation of the movements. Similar to that observed in studies comparing writing to drawing in adults (see above), the premotor and parietal cortices, the right cerebellum, and the fusiform gyrus were engaged more strongly when the children were writing a new letter (pseudoletter). However, this was only true in the case of the good writers, because the activation of those regions did not differ between newly taught and highly practised letters in the poor writers. Another important result was that efficient writing was linked to the involvement of a more restricted and focused brain network. The good writers engaged fewer neural regions to write a newly taught letter than did the poor writers. The poor writers displayed over-activation of the visual system, and extra parietal and cerebellar regions. Consistent with this finding, Richards et al. (2015) reported that efficient handwriting is associated with less functional connectivity than poor handwriting. In summary, the development of a more focal activation of the premotor and cerebellar regions while learning new letter shapes is associated with good writing skills whereas more widespread activation, and greater involvement of the visual system, of the left parietal cortex and of extra cerebellar regions is associated with poor writing skills. A possible interpretation of those findings is that, at least in children, good writers are better able to mobilize the brain systems for motor learning when learning a new symbol whereas poor writers display patterns of activation that resemble those of novice subjects in early learning phases.

Finally, the good and poor writers differed significantly in activation in left fusiform cortex when writing highly practised letters compared to writing a newly taught pseudo-letter (Richards et al., 2011). Good writers showed significantly stronger activation in this region than poor writers. This individual fusiform activation correlated with behavioural measures of writing legibility. This suggests that there are critical interactions between the visual and motor systems in the acquisition of writing, since the efficiency depends both on the pattern of activation on motor-related brain regions when practising new shapes and on the activation of the fusiform gyrus when writing highly practised shapes. In addition, the fusiform involvement significantly predicted other language skills. The results of this study should nonetheless be replicated in a larger sample of children, if possible also including younger children who have not yet automatized their writing.

Handwriting acquisition leads to modulations in other functions

It is likely that because of the thousands of hours of practice and of the corresponding functional and probably structural modifications, writing acquisition can impact other functions. For instance, writing acquisition can also affect the functioning of the visual system when processing written language. James and her collaborators studied the consequences of writing practice on functional brain activations during visual recognition of newly learned letters in preschoolers. The study of James (2010) revealed that writing training, but not visual-only training, induces increased activation in bilateral anterior fusiform gyri, the portion of the fusiform gyrus sensitive to the visual configuration of single letters (Flowers et al., 2004), when pre-training and post-training fMRI measures of letter recognition were compared. The stability of the visual representations of letters is therefore strengthened when letters are trained by writing them repeatedly. A subsequent study with the same age-group confirmed this finding by observing a greater effect of freely producing letters by hand than of tracing or typing them on the fusiform activation during letter perception (James & Engelhardt, 2012). When examining the whole-brain consequences of the training mode, James and Engelhardt (2012) found that compared to the control conditions, active handwriting training led to subsequent greater activation of the bilateral precentral gyri, at the level of the primary motor cortex. This interesting finding shows that the motor representations built in the course of learning can be reactivated by the mere visual processing of letters. This is in agreement with previous observations in the course of single letter perception in adults (James & Atwood, 2009; Longcamp, Anton, Roth, & Velay, 2003; Longcamp, Boucard, et al., 2008; Longcamp, Zerbato-Poudou, & Velay, 2005). However, contrary to what has been found to occur in adults, the motor activation was more caudal (corresponding to the primary motor cortex and not the premotor cortex) and was bilateral. This bilateral activation has been interpreted as relating to the immaturity of the motor system in preschoolers. In another study, Richards et al. (2009) have measured brain activity in groups of good and poor writers (again classified as being above or below the average level on a standardized measure of legibility of their writing) aged 10 to 12, who were engaged in a motor task involving a memorized finger sequence. They showed that the poor writers underactivated a broad frontoparietal network including the dorsal premotor cortex, the inferior occipito-temporal regions, and the cerebellum. Their conclusion was that efficient handwriting is related to optimal activation of the neural circuits supporting the planning of sequential movements.

Conclusion

Handwriting acquisition is characterized by massive changes in a series of kinematic parameters between ages 7 and 10. This is thought to correspond to the progressive integration in long-term motor memory of the various motor programs that are required to produce words fluently. This allows the motor system to be freed from attention and cognitive control. Handwriting can be produced in an automatic way. At the brain level, this is likely to induce a massive reorganization, both at the functional and at the structural levels. This reorganization is of the same type as that previously demonstrated in other kinds of motor expertise. It leads to the focalization of activations in a restricted network mainly composed of the left dorsal premotor cortex at the junction between the superior frontal sulcus and the precentral gyrus, of the left superior parietal lobule, and of the right cerebellum. The primary motor cortex is also a site of plasticity. The laterality of this network is probably inverted in left-handers.

The understanding of how motor control of writing emerges and stabilizes in the course of typical brain development will set the ground for the study of the neural bases of developmental dysgraphia. It will also contribute to the evaluation of potential interactions between cognitive and motor stages of processing in the acquisition of literacy.

Disclosure statement

No potential conflict of interest was reported by the authors.

Funding

This work was supported by a grant from the Agence Nationale de la Recherche (French National Research Agency), programme education et apprentissages [grant number ANR-14-CE30-0013 ECRIRE, ANR-16-CONV-0002 (ILCB), ANR-11- LABX-0036 (BLRI) and ANR-11-IDEX-0001-02 (A*MIDEX)].

References

Adi-Japha, E., Badir, R., Dorfberger, S., & Karni, A. (2014). A matter of time: Rapid motor memory stabilization in childhood. *Developmental Science*, *17*(3), 424–433. https://doi.org/10.1111/desc.12132

Adi-Japha, E., & Freeman, N. H. (2001). Development of differentiation between writing and drawing systems. *Developmental Psychology*, *37*(1), 101–114. http://doi.wiley.com/10.1111/desc.12132

Alexander, M. P., Fischer, R. S., & Friedman, R. (1992). Lesion localization in apractic agraphia. *Archives of Neurology*, *49* (3), 246–251. http://doi.org/10.1001/archneur.1992.0053027 0060019

Anderson, S. W., Damasio, A. R., & Damasio, H. (1990). Troubled letters but not numbers: Domain specific cognitive impairments following focal damage in frontal cortex. *Brain*, *113*, 749–766. https://doi.org/10.1093/brain/113.3.749

Ashtamker, L., & Karni, A. (2013). Motor memory in childhood: Early expression of consolidation phase gains. *Neurobiology of Learning and Memory*, *106*, 26–30. https://doi.org/10.1016/j.nlm.2013.07.003

Auerbach, S. H., & Alexander, M. P. (1981). Pure agraphia and unilateral optic ataxia associated with a left superior parietal lobule lesion. *Journal of Neurology, Neurosurgery, and Psychiatry*, *44*(5), 430–432. https://doi.org/10.1136/jnnp.44.5.430

Bara, F., & Morin, M. F. (2013). Does the handwriting style learned in first grade determine the style used in the fourth and fifth grades and influence handwriting speed and quality? A comparison between French and Quebec children. *Psychology in the Schools*, *50*(6), 601–617. http://doi.org/10.1002/pits.21691

Barnea-Goraly, N., Menon, V., Eckert, M., Tamm, L., Bammer, R., Karchemskiy, A., … Reiss, A. L. (2005). White matter development during childhood and adolescence: A cross-sectional diffusion tensor imaging study. *Cerebral Cortex (New York, N.Y.: 1991)*, *15*(12), 1848–1854. https://doi.org/10.1093/cercor/bhi062

Basso, A., Taborelli, A., & Vignolo, L. A. (1978). Dissociated disorders of speaking and writing in aphasia. *Journal of Neurology, Neurosurgery, and Psychiatry*, *41*(6), 556–563. https://doi.org/10.1136/jnnp.41.6.556

Beeson, P. M., Rising, K., & Volk, J. (2003). Writing treatment for severe aphasia: Who benefits? *Journal of Speech, Language, and Hearing Research: JSLHR*, *46*(5), 1038–1060. http://doi.org/10.1044/1092-4388

Bengtsson, S. L., Nagy, Z., Skare, S., Forsman, L., Forssberg, H., & Ullén, F. (2005). Extensive piano practicing has regionally specific effects on white matter development. *Nature Neuroscience*, *8*(9), 1148–1150. https://doi.org/10.1038/nn1516

Berninger, V., & Swanson, H. L. (1994). Children's writing: Toward a process theory of the development of skilled writing. In E. C. Butterfield, & J. Carlson (Eds.), *Modifying Hayes and flower's model of skilled writing to explain beginning and developing writing* (pp. 57–81). London: JAI Press.

Bernstein, N. A. (1947). *On the construction of movements*. Moscow: Medgiz (in Russian).

Brenneman, K., Massey, C., Machado, S. F., & Gelman, R. (1996). Young children's plans differ for writing and drawing. *Cognitive Development*, *11*(3), 397–419. https://doi.org/10.1016/S0885-2014(96)90011-8

Brownsett, S. L. E., & Wise, R. J. S. (2010). The contribution of the parietal lobes to speaking and writing. *Cerebral Cortex (New York, N.Y.: 1991)*, *20*(3), 517–523. https://doi.org/10.1093/cercor/bhp120

Cannonieri, G. C., Bonilha, L., Fernandes, P. T., Cendes, F., & Li, L. M. (2007). Practice and perfect: Length of training and structural brain changes in experienced typists. *Neuroreport*, *18* (10), 1063–1066. https://doi.org/10.1097/WNR.0b013e328 1a030e5

Cohen, L., Lehericy, S., Chochon, F., Lemer, C., Rivaud, S., & Dehaene, S. (2002). Language-specific tuning of visual cortex? Functional properties of the visual word form area. *Brain*, *125*(5), 1054–1069. https://doi.org/10.1093/brain/awf094

Connelly, V., Dockrell, J. E., Walter, K., & Critten, S. (2012). Predicting the quality of composition and written language bursts from oral language, spelling, and handwriting skills in children with and without specific language impairment. *Written Communication*, *29*(3), 278–302. https://doi.org/10.1177/0741088312451109

Danna, J., & Velay, J.-L. (2015). Basic and supplementary sensory feedback in handwriting. *Frontiers in Psychology*, *6*. https://doi.org/10.3389/fpsyg.2015.00169

Dayan, E., & Cohen, L. G. (2011). Neuroplasticity subserving motor skill learning. *Neuron*, *72*(3), 443–454. https://doi.org/10.1016/j.neuron.2011.10.008

de Ajuriaguerra, J. (1971). *L' écriture de L'enfant: L' évolution de L' écriture et ses Difficultés*. Neuchâtel: Delachaux et Niestlé. (Vol. 1).

Dick, F., Leech, R., Moses, P., & Saccuman, M. C. (2006). The interplay of learning and development in shaping neural organization. *Developmental Science*, *9*(1), 14–17. https://doi.org/10.1111/j.1467-7687.2005.00457.x

Doyon, J., & Benali, H. (2005). Reorganization and plasticity in the adult brain during learning of motor skills. *Current Opinion in Neurobiology*, *15*(2), 161–167. https://doi.org/10.1016/j.conb.2005.03.004

Doyon, J., Owen, A. M., Petrides, M., Sziklas, V., & Evans, A. C. (1996). Functional anatomy of visuomotor skill learning in human subjects examined with positron emission tomography. *The European Journal of Neuroscience*, *8*(4), 637–648. http://doi.org/10.1111/j.1460-9568.1996.tb01249.x

Doyon, J., Penhune, V., & Ungerleider, L. G. (2003). Distinct contribution of the cortico-striatal and cortico-cerebellar systems to motor skill learning. *Neuropsychologia*, *41*, 252–262. https://doi.org/10.1016/S0028-3932(02)00158-6

Draganski, B., Gaser, C., Busch, V., Schuierer, G., Bogdahn, U., & May, A. (2004). Neuroplasticity: Changes in grey matter induced by training. *Nature*, *427*(6972), 311–312. https://doi.org/10.1038/427311a

Durston, S., Davidson, M. C., Tottenham, N., Galvan, A., Spicer, J., Fossella, J. A., & Casey, B. J. (2006). A shift from diffuse to focal cortical activity with development. *Developmental Science, 9* (1), 1–8. https://doi.org/10.1111/j.1467-7687.2005.00454.x

Ellis, A. W. (1982). Spelling and writing (and reading and speaking). In A. W. Ellis (Ed.), *Normality and pathology in cognitive functions* (pp. 113–146). London: Academic Press.

Ellis, A. W. (1988). Normal writing processes and peripheral acquired dysgraphias. *Language and Cognitive Processes, 3* (2), 99–127. https://doi.org/10.1080/01690968808402084

Exner, S. (1881). *Untersuchungen über die Localisation der Functionen in der Grosshirnrinde des Menschen.* Wien: Wilhelm Braumüller.

Flowers, D., Jones, K., Noble, K., VanMeter, J., Zeffiro, T., Wood, F., & Eden, G. (2004). Attention to single letters activates left extrastriate cortex. *NeuroImage, 21*(3), 829–839. https://doi.org/10.1016/j.neuroimage.2003.10.002

Floyer-Lea, A., & Matthews, P. M. (2005). Distinguishable brain activation networks for short- and long-term motor skill learning. *Journal of Neurophysiology, 94*(1), 512–518. https://doi.org/10.1152/jn.00717.2004

Galea, J. M., Vazquez, A., Pasricha, N., de Xivry, J.-J. O., & Celnik, P. (2011). Dissociating the roles of the cerebellum and motor cortex during adaptive learning: The motor cortex retains what the cerebellum learns. *Cerebral Cortex (New York, N.Y.: 1991), 21*(8), 1761–1770. https://doi.org/10.1093/cercor/bhq246

Gaser, C., & Schlaug, G. (2003). Brain structures differ between musicians and non-musicians. *The Journal of Neuroscience: The Official Journal of the Society for Neuroscience, 23*(27), 9240–9245.

Giedd, J. N., Blumenthal, J., Jeffries, N. O., Castellanos, F. X., Liu, H. L., Zijdenbos, A. … Rapoport, J. I. (1999). Brain development during childhood and adolescence: A longitudinal MRI study. *Nature Neuroscience, 2*(10), 861–863. http://doi.org/10.1038/13158

Giedd, J. N., Lalonde, F. M., Celano, M. J., White, S. L., Wallace, G. L., Lee, N. R., & Lenroot, R. K. (2009). Anatomical brain magnetic resonance imaging of typically developing children and adolescents. *Journal of the American Academy of Child and Adolescent Psychiatry, 48*(5), 465–470. https://doi.org/10.1097/CHI.0b013e31819f2715

Gogtay, N., Giedd, J. N., Lusk, L., Hayashi, K. M., Greenstein, D., Vaituzis, A. C., … Thompson, P. M. (2004). Dynamic mapping of human cortical development during childhood through early adulthood. *Proceedings of the National Academy of Sciences, 101*(21), 8174–8179. https://doi.org/10.1073/pnas.0402680101

Golarai, G., Liberman, A., & Grill-Spector, K. (2015). Experience shapes the development of neural substrates of face processing in human ventral temporal Cortex. *Cerebral Cortex*, bhv314. https://doi.org/10.1093/cercor/bhv314

Grafton, S. T., Woods, R. P., & Tyszka, M. (1994). Functional imaging of procedural motor learning: Relating cerebral blood flow with individual subject performance. *Human Brain Mapping, 1*(3), 221–234. https://doi.org/10.1002/hbm.460010307

Graham, S., Berninger, V. W., Abbott, R. D., Abbot, S., & Whitaker, D. (1997). Role of mechanics in composing of elementary school students: A New methodological approach. *Journal of Educational Psychology, 89*(1), 170–182. https://doi.org/10.1037/0022-0663.89.1.170

Graham, S., Berninger, V., Weintraub, N., & Schafer, W. (1998). Development of handwriting speed and legibility in grades 1–9. *The Journal of Educational Research, 92*(1), 42–52. https://doi.org/10.1080/00220679809597574

Grayson, D. S., & Fair, D. A. (2017). Development of large-scale functional networks from birth to adulthood: A guide to the neuroimaging literature. *NeuroImage*. https://doi.org/10.1016/j.neuroimage.2017.01.079

Grossberg, S., & Paine, R. W. (2000). A neural model of cortico-cerebellar interactions during attentive imitation and predictive learning of sequential handwriting movements. *Neural Networks, 13*(8–9), 999–1046. https://doi.org/10.1016/S0893-6080(00)00065-4

Guan, C. Q., Perfetti, C. A., & Meng, W. (2015). Writing quality predicts Chinese learning. *Reading and Writing, 28*(6), 763–795. https://doi.org/10.1007/s11145-015-9549-0

Haggard, P., Jenner, J., & Wing, A. (1994). Coordination of aimed movements in a case of unilateral cerebellar damage. *Neuropsychologia, 32*(7), 827–846. https://doi.org/10.1016/0028-3932(94)90021-3

Halsband, U., & Lange, R. K. (2006). Motor learning in man: A review of functional and clinical studies. *Journal of Physiology-Paris, 99*(4–6), 414–424. https://doi.org/10.1016/j.jphysparis.2006.03.007

Han, Y., Yang, H., Lv, Y.-T., Zhu, C.-Z., He, Y., Tang, H.-H., … Dong, Q. (2009). Gray matter density and white matter integrity in pianists' brain: A combined structural and diffusion tensor MRI study. *Neuroscience Letters, 459*(1), 3–6. https://doi.org/10.1016/j.neulet.2008.07.056

Hardwick, R. M., Lesage, E., Eickhoff, C. R., Clos, M., Fox, P., & Eickhoff, S. B. (2015). Multimodal connectivity of motor learning-related dorsal premotor cortex. *NeuroImage, 123*, 114–128. https://doi.org/10.1016/j.neuroimage.2015.08.024

Hardwick, R. M., Rottschy, C., Miall, R. C., & Eickhoff, S. B. (2013). A quantitative meta-analysis and review of motor learning in the human brain. *NeuroImage, 67*, 283–297. https://doi.org/10.1016/j.neuroimage.2012.11.020

Harrington, G. S., Farias, D., Davis, C. H., & Buonocore, M. H. (2007). Comparison of the neural basis for imagined writing and drawing. *Human Brain Mapping, 28*(5), 450–459. https://doi.org/10.1002/hbm.20286

Hasher, L., & Zacks, R. T. (1979). Automatic and effortful processes in memory. *Journal of Experimental Psychology: General, 108*(3), 356–388. https://doi.org/10.1037/0096-3445.108.3.356

Hay, L. (1979). Spatial-temporal analysis of movements in children: Motor programs versus feedback in the development of reaching. *Journal of Motor Behavior, 11*(3), 189–200. https://doi.org/10.1080/00222895.1979.10735187

Hepp-Reymond, M.-C., Chakarov, V., Schulte-Mönting, J., Huethe, F., & Kristeva, R. (2009). Role of proprioception and vision in handwriting. *Brain Research Bulletin*, *79*(6), 365–370. https://doi.org/10.1016/j.brainresbull.2009.05.013

Hollerbach, J. M. (1981). An oscillation theory of handwriting. *Biological Cybernetics*, *39*, 139–156. https://doi.org/10.1007%2FBF00336740

Hulstijn, W., & van Galen, G. P. (1983). Programming in handwriting: Reaction time and movement time as a function of sequence length. *Acta Psychologica*, *54*(1–3), 23–49. https://doi.org/10.1016/0001-6918(83)90021-5

Hutchinson, S., Lee, L. H.-L., Gaab, N., & Schlaug, G. (2003). Cerebellar volume of musicians. *Cerebral Cortex (New York, N.Y.: 1991)*, *13*(9), 943–949. https://doi.org/10.1093/cercor/13.9.943

James, K. H., & Atwood, T. P. (2009). The role of sensorimotor learning in the perception of letter-like forms: Tracking the causes of neural specialization for letters. *Cognitive Neuropsychology*, *26*(1), 91–110. https://doi.org/10.1080/02643290802425914

James, K. H., & Engelhardt, L. (2012). The effects of handwriting experience on functional brain development in pre-literate children. *Trends in Neuroscience and Education*, *1*(1), 32–42. https://doi.org/10.1016/j.tine.2012.08.001

James, K. H. (2010). Sensori-motor experience leads to changes in visual processing in the developing brain. *Developmental Science*, *13*(2), 279–288. https://doi.org/10.1111/j.1467-7687.2009.00883.x

Johnson, M. H. (2011). Interactive specialization: A domain-general framework for human functional brain development? *Developmental Cognitive Neuroscience*, *1*(1), 7–21. https://doi.org/10.1016/j.dcn.2010.07.003

Jones, D., & Christensen, C. A. (1999). Relationship between automaticity in handwriting and students' ability to generate written text. *Journal of Educational Psychology*, *91*(1), 44–49. https://doi.org/10.1037/0022-0663.91.1.44

Julius, M. S., & Adi-Japha, E. (2015). Learning of a simple graphomotor task by young children and adults: Similar acquisition but age-dependent retention. *Frontiers in Psychology*, *6*, 215. https://doi.org/10.3389/fpsyg.2015.00225

Kadmon Harpaz, N., Flash, T., & Dinstein, I. (2014). Scale-invariant movement encoding in the human motor system. *Neuron*, *81*(2), 452–462. https://doi.org/10.1016/j.neuron.2013.10.058

Kandel, S., & Perret, C. (2015). How does the interaction between spelling and motor processes build up during writing acquisition? *Cognition*, *136*, 325–336. https://doi.org/10.1016/j.cognition.2014.11.014

Keele, S. W. (1968). Movement control in skilled motor performance. *Psychological Bulletin*, *70*(6), 387–403. https://doi.org/10.1037/h0026739

Kelly, A. M. C., Di Martino, A., Uddin, L. Q., Shehzad, Z., Gee, D. G., Reiss, P. T., … Milham, M. P. (2009). Development of anterior cingulate functional connectivity from late childhood to early adulthood. *Cerebral Cortex (New York, N.Y.: 1991)*, *19*(3), 640–657. https://doi.org/10.1093/cercor/bhn117

Kelly, A. M. C., & Garavan, H. (2005). Human functional neuroimaging of brain changes associated with practice. *Cerebral Cortex (New York, N.Y.: 1991)*, *15*(8), 1089–1102. https://doi.org/10.1093/cercor/bhi005

Kinsbourne, M., & Rosenfield, D. B. (1974). Agraphia selective for written spelling. *Brain and Language*, *1*(3), 215–225. https://doi.org/10.1016/0093-934X(74)90037-6

Kloppel, S., Mangin, J.-F., Vongerichten, A., Frackowiak, R. S. J., & Siebner, H. R. (2010). Nurture versus nature: Long-term impact of forced right-handedness on structure of pericentral Cortex and basal ganglia. *Journal of Neuroscience*, *30*(9), 3271–3275. https://doi.org/10.1523/JNEUROSCI.4394-09.2010

Klöppel, S., van Eimeren, T., Glauche, V., Vongerichten, A., Münchau, A., Frackowiak, R. S. J., … Siebner, H. R. (2007). The effect of handedness on cortical motor activation during simple bilateral movements. *NeuroImage*, *34*(1), 274–280. https://doi.org/10.1016/j.neuroimage.2006.08.038

Krakauer, J. W., & Mazzoni, P. (2011). Human sensorimotor learning: Adaptation, skill, and beyond. *Current Opinion in Neurobiology*, *21*(4), 636–644. https://doi.org/10.1016/j.conb.2011.06.012

Lajoie, Y., Paillard, J., Teasdale, N., Bard, C., Fleury, M., Forget, R., & Lamarre, Y. (1992). Mirror drawing in a deafferented patient and normal subjects: Visuoproprioceptive conflict. *Neurology*, *42*(0028-3878), 1104–1106. https://doi.org/10.1212/WNL.42.5.1104

Longcamp, M., Anton, J. L., Roth, M., & Velay, J. L. (2003). Visual presentation of single letters activates a premotor area involved in writing. *NeuroImage*, *19*(4), 1492–1500. https://doi.org/10.1016/S1053-8119(03)00088-0

Longcamp, M., Anton, J.-L., Roth, M., & Velay, J.-L. (2005). Premotor activations in response to visually presented single letters depend on the hand used to write: A study on left-handers. *Neuropsychologia*, *43*(12), 1801–1809. https://doi.org/10.1016/j.neuropsychologia.2005.01.020

Longcamp, M., Boucard, C., Gilhodes, J. C., Anton, J. L., Roth, M., Nazarian, B., & Velay, J. L. (2008). Learning through hand- or typewriting influences visual recognition of new graphic shapes: Behavioral and functional imaging evidence. *Journal of Cognitive Neuroscience*, *20*(0898–929X (Print)), 802–815. https://doi.org/10.1162/jocn.2008.20504

Longcamp, M., Lagarrigue, A., Nazarian, B., Roth, M., Anton, J.-L., Alario, F.-X., & Velay, J.-L. (2014). Functional specificity in the motor system: Evidence from coupled fMRI and kinematic recordings during letter and digit writing. *Human Brain Mapping*, *35*(12), 6077–6087. https://doi.org/10.1002/hbm.22606

Longcamp, M., Zerbato-Poudou, M.-T., & Velay, J.-L. (2005). The influence of writing practice on letter recognition in preschool children: A comparison between handwriting and typing. *Acta Psychologica*, *119*(1), 67–79. https://doi.org/10.1016/j.actpsy.2004.10.019

Lotze, M., Scheler, G., Tan, H.-R. M., Braun, C., & Birbaumer, N. (2003). The musician's brain: Functional imaging of amateurs and professionals during performance and imagery. *NeuroImage*, *20*(3), 1817–1829. https://doi.org/10.1016/j.neuroimage.2003.07.018

Magrassi, L., Bongetta, D., Bianchini, S., Berardesca, M., & Arienta, C. (2010). Central and peripheral components of writing critically depend on a defined area of the dominant superior parietal gyrus. *Brain Research, 1346*, 145–154. https://doi.org/10.1016/j.brainres.2010.05.046

Manto, M., Bower, J. M., Conforto, A. B., Delgado-García, J. M., da Guarda, S. N. F., Gerwig, M., ... Timmann, D. (2012). Consensus paper: Roles of the cerebellum in motor control —The diversity of ideas on cerebellar involvement in movement. *Cerebellum (London, England), 11*(2), 457–487. https://doi.org/10.1007/s12311-011-0331-9

Margolin, D. I., & Binder, L. (1984). Multiple component agraphia in a patient with atypical cerebral dominance: An error analysis. *Brain and Language, 22*, 26–40. https://doi.org/10.1016/0093-934X(84)90077-4

Mariën, P., De Smet, H. J., Paquier, P. F., & Verhoeven, J. (2010). Cerebellocerebral diaschisis and postsurgical posterior fossa syndrome in pediatric patients. *AJNR. American Journal of Neuroradiology*, 31(9), E82;author reply E83. https://doi.org/10.3174/ajnr.A2198

Marquardt, C., Gentz, W., & Mai, N. (1996). On the role of vision in skilled handwriting. In M. L. Simner, C. G. Leedham, & A. J. W. M. Thomassen (Eds.), *Handwriting and drawing research: Basic and applied issues* (pp. 87–97). Amsterdam: IOS Press.

McKenzie, I. A., Ohayon, D., Li, H., Paes de Faria, J., Emery, B., Tohyama, K., & Richardson, W. D. (2014). Motor skill learning requires active central myelination. *Science, 346*(6207), 318–322. https://doi.org/10.1126/science.1254960

Menon, V., & Desmond, J. E. (2001). Left superior parietal cortex involvement in writing: Integrating fMRI with lesion evidence. *Cognitive Brain Research, 12*, 337–340. https://doi.org/10.1016/S0926-6410(01)00063-5

Meulenbroek, R. G. J., & van Galen, G. P. (1988). The acquisition of skilled handwriting: Discontinuous trends in kinematic variables. In *Advances in psychology* (Vol. 55, pp. 273–281). Elsevier. Retrieved from http://linkinghub.elsevier.com/retrieve/pii/S0166411508606275

Mills, K. L., Goddings, A.-L., Herting, M. M., Meuwese, R., Blakemore, S.-J., Crone, E. A., ... Tamnes, C. K. (2016). Structural brain development between childhood and adulthood: Convergence across four longitudinal samples. *NeuroImage, 141*, 273–281. https://doi.org/10.1016/j.neuroimage.2016.07.044.

Milton, J., Solodkin, A., Hluštík, P., & Small, S. L. (2007). The mind of expert motor performance is cool and focused. *NeuroImage, 35*(2), 804–813. https://doi.org/10.1016/j.neuroimage.2007.01.003

Mojet, J. (1991). Development of graphic skills. In J. Wann, A. M. Wing, & N. Sovik (Eds.), *Characteristics of the developing handwriting skill in elementary education* (pp. 53–75). London: Academic Press.

Natu, V. S., Barnett, M. A., Hartley, J., Gomez, J., Stigliani, A., & Grill-Spector, K. (2016). Development of neural sensitivity to face identity correlates with perceptual discriminability. *The Journal of Neuroscience, 36*(42), 10893–10907. https://doi.org/10.1523/JNEUROSCI.1886-16.2016

Nielsen, J. M. (1946). *Agnosia, apraxia, aphasia: Their value in cerebral localization* (2nd ed). New York, NY: Paul B. Hoeber https://doi.org/10.1192/bjp.94.395.469-a

Ohno, T., Bando, M., Nagura, H., Ishii, K., & Yamanouchi, H. (2000). Apraxic agraphia due to thalamic infarction. *Neurology, 54*, 2336–2339. https://doi.org/10.1212/WNL.54.12.2336

Paine, R. W., Grossberg, S., & Van Gemmert, A. W. A. (2004). A quantitative evaluation of the avitewrite model of handwriting learning. *Human Movement Science, 23*(6), 837–860. https://doi.org/10.1016/j.humov.2004.08.024

Pangelinan, M. M., Hatfield, B. D., & Clark, J. E. (2013). Differences in movement-related cortical activation patterns underlying motor performance in children with and without developmental coordination disorder. *Journal of Neurophysiology, 109*(12), 3041–3050. https://doi.org/10.1152/jn.00532.2012

Park, I. S., Lee, K. J., Han, J. W., Lee, N. J., Lee, W. T., Park, K. A., & Rhyu, I. J. (2009). Experience-dependent plasticity of cerebellar vermis in basketball players. *Cerebellum (London, England), 8*(3), 334–339. https://doi.org/10.1007/s12311-009-0100-1

Pascual-Leone, A., Dang, N., Cohen, L. G., Brasilneto, J. P., Cammarota, A., & Hallett, M. (1995). Modulation of muscle responses evoked by transcranial magnetic stimulation daring the acquisition of new fine motor skills. *Journal of Neurophysiology, 74*, 1037–1045.

Paus, T., Zijdenbos, A. , Worsley, K., Collins, D. L., Blumenhal, J., Giedd, J. N., Rapoport, J. N. Evans, A. C.. (1999). Structural maturation of neural pathways in children and adolescents: in vivo study.. *Science, 283*(2), 1908–1911.

Paz-Villagrán, V., Danna, J., & Velay, J.-L. (2014). Lifts and stops in proficient and dysgraphic handwriting. *Human Movement Science, 33*, 381–394. https://doi.org/10.1016/j.humov.2013.11.005

Plamondon, R. (1995a). A kinematic theory of rapid human movements. Part I. Movement representation and generation. *Biological Cybernetics, 72*(4), 295–307. https://doi.org/10.1007/BF00202785

Plamondon, R. (1995b). A kinematic theory of rapid human movements. Part II. Movement time and control. *Biological Cybernetics, 72*(4), 309–320. https://doi.org/10.1007/BF00202786

Planton, S., Jucla, M., Roux, F.-E., & Démonet, J.-F. (2013). The "handwriting brain": a meta-analysis of neuroimaging studies of motor versus orthographic processes. *Cortex; a Journal Devoted to the Study of the Nervous System and Behavior, 49*(10), 2772–2787. https://doi.org/10.1016/j.cortex.2013.05.011

Planton, S., Longcamp, M., Péran, P., Démonet, J.-F., & Jucla, M. (2017). How specialized are writing-specific brain regions? An fMRI study of writing, drawing and oral spelling. *Cortex, 88*, 66–80. https://doi.org/10.1016/j.cortex.2016.11.018

Pontart, V., Bidet-Ildei, C., Lambert, E., Morisset, P., Flouret, L., & Alamargot, D. (2013). Influence of handwriting skills during spelling in primary and lower secondary grades. *Frontiers in Psychology, 4*. https://doi.org/10.3389/fpsyg.2013.00818

Puranik, C. S., & Al Otaiba, S. (2012). Examining the contribution of handwriting and spelling to written expression in kindergarten children. *Reading and Writing*, *25*(7), 1523–1546. https://doi.org/10.1007/s11145-011-9331-x

Purcell, J. J., Turkeltaub, P. E., Eden, G. F., & Rapp, B. (2011). Examining the central and peripheral processes of written word production through meta-analysis. *Frontiers in Psychology*, *2*, 239. https://doi.org/10.3389/fpsyg.2011.00239

Rapcsak, S. Z., & Beeson, P. M. (2004). The role of left posterior inferior temporal cortex in spelling. *Neurology*, *62*(12), 2221–2229. https://doi.org/10.1212/01.WNL.0000130169.60752.C5

Rapp, B., Purcell, J., Hillis, A. E., Capasso, R., & Miceli, G. (2016). Neural bases of orthographic long-term memory and working memory in dysgraphia. *Brain: A Journal of Neurology*, *139*(Pt 2), 588–604. https://doi.org/10.1093/brain/awv348

Richards, T. L., Berninger, V. W., Stock, P., Altemeier, L., Trivedi, P., & Maravilla, K. (2009). Functional magnetic resonance imaging sequential-finger movement activation differentiating good and poor writers. *Journal of Clinical and Experimental Neuropsychology*, *31*(8), 967–983. doi:10.1080/13803390902780201

Richards, T. L., Berninger, V. W., Stock, P., Altemeier, L., Trivedi, P., & Maravilla, K. R. (2011). Differences between good and poor child writers on fMRI contrasts for writing newly taught and highly practiced letter forms. *Reading and Writing*, *24*(5), 493–516. https://doi.org/10.1007/s11145-009-9217-3

Richards, T. L., Grabowski, T. J., Boord, P., Yagle, K., Askren, M., Mestre, Z., … Berninger, V. (2015). Contrasting brain patterns of writing-related DTI parameters, fMRI connectivity, and DTI–fMRI connectivity correlations in children with and without dysgraphia or dyslexia. *NeuroImage: Clinical*, *8*, 408–421. https://doi.org/10.1016/j.nicl.2015.03.018

Rijntjes, M., Dettmers, C., Büchel, C., Kiebel, S., Frackowiak, R. S. J., & Weiller, C. (1999). A blueprint for movement: Functional and anatomical representations in the human motor system. *The Journal of Neuroscience*, *19*(18), 8043–8048.

Roeltgen, D., & Heilman, K. M. (1983). Apractic agraphia in a patient with normal praxis. *Brain and Language*, *18*, 35–46. https://doi.org/10.1016/0093-934X(83)90004-4

Rosenblum, S., Weiss, P. L., & Parush, S. (2003). Product and process evaluation of handwriting difficulties. *Educational Psychology Review*, *15*(1), 41–81. https://doi.org/10.1023/A:1021371425220

Rothlein, D., & Rapp, B. (2014). The similarity structure of distributed neural responses reveals the multiple representations of letters. *NeuroImage*, *89*, 331–344. https://doi.org/10.1016/j.neuroimage.2013.11.054

Roux, F.-E., Draper, L., Köpke, B., & Démonet, J.-F. (2010). Who actually read exner? Returning to the source of the frontal "writing centre" hypothesis. *Cortex*, *46*(9), 1204–1210. https://doi.org/10.1016/j.cortex.2010.03.001

Roux, F.-E., Dufor, O., Giussani, C., Wamain, Y., Draper, L., Longcamp, M., & Démonet, J.-F. (2009). The graphemic/motor frontal area exner's area revisited. *Annals of Neurology*, *66*(4), 537–545. https://doi.org/10.1002/ana.21804

Rueckriegel, S. M., Blankenburg, F., Burghardt, R., Ehrlich, S., Henze, G., Mergl, R., & Hernáiz Driever, P. (2008). Influence of age and movement complexity on kinematic hand movement parameters in childhood and adolescence. *International Journal of Developmental Neuroscience*, *26*(7), 655–663. https://doi.org/10.1016/j.ijdevneu.2008.07.015

Sakurai, Y., Onuma, Y., Nakazawa, G., Ugawa, Y., Momose, T., Tsuji, S., & Mannen, T. (2007). Parietal dysgraphia: Characterization of abnormal writing stroke sequences, character formation and character recall. *Behavioural Neurology*, *18*(2), 99–114. https://doi.org/10.1155/2007/906417

Savion-Lemieux, T., Bailey, J. A., & Penhune, V. B. (2009). Developmental contributions to motor sequence learning. *Experimental Brain Research*, *195*(2), 293–306. https://doi.org/10.1007/s00221-009-1786-5

Schendan, H. E., Searl, M. M., Melrose, R. J., & Stern, C. E. (2003). An FMRI study of the role of the medial temporal lobe in implicit and explicit sequence learning. *Neuron*, *37*(6), 1013–1025. https://doi.org/10.1016/S0896-6273(03)00123-5

Schmidt, R. A. (1975). A schema theory of discrete motor skill learning. *Psychological Review*, *82*(4), 225–260. https://doi.org/10.1037/h0076770

Schmithorst, V. J., & Wilke, M. (2002). Differences in white matter architecture between musicians and non-musicians: A diffusion tensor imaging study. *Neuroscience Letters*, *321*(1–2), 57–60. https://doi.org/10.1016/S0304-3940(02)00054-X

Seitz, R. J., Canavan, A. G. M., Yágüez, L., Herzog, H., Tellmann, L., Knorr, U. … Hömberg, V. (1997). Representations of graphomotor trajectories in the human parietal cortex: Evidence for controlled processing and automatic performance. *European Journal of Neurosciences*, *9*, 378–389. http://doi.org/10.1111/j.1460-9568.1997.tb01407.x

Shatil, E., Share, D. L., & Levin, I. (2000). On the contribution of kindergarten writing to Grade 1 literacy: A longitudinal study in Hebrew. pp. 1–21.

Siebner, H. R., Limmer, C., Peinemann, A., Drzezga, A., Bloem, B. R., Schwaiger, M., & Conrad, B. (2002). Long-term consequences of switching handedness: A positron emission tomography study. *Journal of Neuroscience*, *22*(7), 2816–2825.

Smyth, M. M., & Silvers, G. (1987). Functions of vision in the control of handwriting. *Acta Psychologica*, *65*(1), 47–64. https://doi.org/10.1016/0001-6918(87)90046-1

Sugihara, G., Kaminaga, T., & Sugishita, M. (2006). Interindividual uniformity and variety of the "writing center": a functional MRI study. *NeuroImage*, *32*(4), 1837–1849. https://doi.org/10.1016/j.neuroimage.2006.05.035

Swett, B. A., Contreras-Vidal, J. L., Birn, R., & Braun, A. (2010). Neural substrates of graphomotor sequence learning: A combined fMRI and kinematic study. *Journal of Neurophysiology*, *103*(6), 3366–3377. https://doi.org/10.1152/jn.00449.2009

Takayama, Y., Sugishita, M., Akiguchi, I., & Kimura, J. (1994). Isolated Acalculia due to Left Parietal Lesion. *Archives of Neurology*, *51*, 286–291. http://doi.org/10.1001/archneur.1994.00540150084021

Teasdale, N., Forget, R., Bard, C., Paillard, J., Fleury, M., & Lamarre, Y. (1993). The role of proprioceptive information for the production of isometric forces and for handwriting tasks. *Acta Psychologica*, *82*(0001-6918), 179–191. https://doi.org/10.1016/0001-6918(93)90011-F

Teulings, H. L., & Schomaker, L. R. B. (1993). Invariant properties between stroke features in handwriting. *Acta Psychologica*, *82*(1–3), 69–88. https://doi.org/10.1016/0001-6918(93)90005-C

Tucha, O., Tucha, L., & Lange, K. W. (2008). Graphonomics, automaticity and handwriting assessment: Graphonomics, automaticity and handwriting assessment. *Literacy*, *42*(3), 145–155. https://doi.org/10.1111/j.1741-4369.2008.00494.x

Vandenborre, D., van Dun, K., Engelborghs, S., & Mariën, P. (2015). Apraxic agraphia following thalamic damage: Three new cases. *Brain and Language*, *150*, 153–165. https://doi.org/10.1016/j.bandl.2015.05.011

van Galen, G. P. (1991). Handwriting: Issues for a psychomotor theory. *Human Movement Science*, *10*(2–3), 165–191. https://doi.org/10.1016/0167-9457(91)90003-G

Varley, R., Cowell, P., Gibson, A., & Romanowski, C. (2005). Disconnection agraphia in a case of multiple sclerosis: The isolation of letter movement plans from language. *Neuropsychologia*, *43*(10), 1503–1513. https://doi.org/10.1016/j.neuropsychologia.2004.12.011

Viviani, P., & Flash, T. (1995). Minimum-jerk, two-thirds power law, and isochrony: Converging approaches to movement planning. *Journal of Experimental Psychology: Human Perception and Performance*, *21*(1), 32–53. https://doi.org/10.1037/0096-1523.21.1.32

Viviani, P., & Stucchi, N. (1989). The effect of movement velocity on form perception: Geometric illusions in dynamic displays. *Perception and Psychophysics*, *46*(3), 266–274. https://doi.org/10.3758/BF03208089

Viviani, P., & Terzuolo, C. (1980). Space-time invariance in learned motor skills. In G. Stelmach, & J. Requin (Eds.), *Tutorials in motor behavior* (pp. 525–533). Amsterdam: North Holland https://doi.org/10.1016/S0166-4115(08)61967-6

Wilke, M., Krägeloh-Mann, I., & Holland, S. K. (2007). Global and local development of gray and white matter volume in normal children and adolescents. *Experimental Brain Research*, *178*(3), 296–307. https://doi.org/10.1007/s00221-006-0732-z.

Wolpert, D. M., Ghahramani, Z., & Jordan, M. I. (1995). An internal model for sensorimotor integration. *Science*, *269*, 1880–1882. http://www.jstor.org/stable/2889276

Yuan, Y., & Brown, S. (2015). Drawing and writing: An ALE meta-analysis of sensorimotor activations. *Brain and Cognition*, *98*, 15–26. https://doi.org/10.1016/j.bandc.2015.05.004

Zesiger, P. (1992). *L' écriture chez l'enfant de 8 à 12 ans et chez l'adulte. Aspects perceptivo-moteurs et effets linguistiques.*

Zielinski, B. A., Gennatas, E. D., Zhou, J., & Seeley, W. W. (2010). Network-level structural covariance in the developing brain. *Proceedings of the National Academy of Sciences*, *107*(42), 18191–18196. https://doi.org/10.1073/pnas.1003109107

Zwicker, J. G., Missiuna, C., Harris, S. R., & Boyd, L. A. (2011). Brain activation associated with motor skill practice in children with developmental coordination disorder: An fMRI study. *International Journal of Developmental Neuroscience*, *29*(2), 145–152. https://doi.org/10.1016/j.ijdevneu.2010.12.002

OPEN ACCESS

Understanding handwriting difficulties: A comparison of children with and without motor impairment

Mellissa Prunty and Anna L. Barnett

ABSTRACT

The nature of handwriting difficulties have been explored in children with specific developmental disorders. The aim of this study was to investigate the nature of handwriting difficulties in children with dysgraphia, a less studied group who have significant handwriting difficulties in the absence of motor control or cognitive difficulties. The performance of a dysgraphia group aged 8-14 years was compared to a group with Developmental Coordination Disorder and to typically developing (TD) controls. Participants completed two handwriting tasks on a digitizing writing tablet. The amount and accuracy of the handwriting product was measured, plus various temporal and spatial features of the writing process. There were no significant differences in performance between the two groups with handwriting difficulties but both performed more poorly than the TD group. Individual differences in the type and severity of handwriting impairments suggest the need for a range of classroom assessments to tailor intervention appropriately.

Introduction

The skill of handwriting is an important gateway to academic success (Graham, Berninger, Weintraub, & Schafer, 1998) as it supports participation in the classroom and provides a valuable source of self-esteem in children (Engel-Yeger, Nagauker-Yanuv, & Rosenblum, 2009). It is a complex skill, often referred to as "language by hand" (Berninger, Abbott, Abbott, Graham, & Richards, 2002), which reflects the complex integration of cognitive and motor processes that underpin the task (Van Galen, 1991). As such, handwriting skill takes time to develop (Barnett, Henderson, Scheib, & Schulz, 2007; Graham et al., 1998). Initially, correct letter formation (including size and shape) are taught in the classroom (5–6 years; Department for Education, DfE, 2013) followed by an emphasis on speed and fluency later on (8–9 years of age; DfE, 2013). The development of handwriting speed in particular plays an important role in the overall task of writing, as the number of words produced per minute has been found to predict compositional quality in both typically (Graham, Berninger, Abbott, Abbott, & Whitaker, 1997; Puranik & Al Otaiba, 2012) and atypically developing children (Connelly, Dockrell, Walter, & Critten, 2012; Prunty, Barnett, Wilmut, & Plumb, 2016; Sumner, Connelly, & Barnett, 2014). Therefore, if a child has difficulties with aspects of handwriting performance such as speed and/or legibility, it can significantly hamper progress in the classroom and lead to academic underachievement (Graham, Harris, & Fink, 2000).

According to Van Hartingsveldt, De Groot, Aarts, and Nijhuis-Van Der Sanden (2011) up to 27% of school-aged children experience difficulties with handwriting. Handwriting difficulties are varied in their presentation and may be explained by a range of factors. Van Galen's (1991) psychomotor model of handwriting can provide a useful lens for considering handwriting difficulties in children, as it describes the range of cognitive and motor processes involved in the skill. At the top level, Van Galen (1991) refers to higher level cognitive processes including attention (activation of the intention to write) and language (semantic retrieval and syntactical construction). These processes have been linked to poor handwriting in children with various developmental disorders including attention deficit hyperactivity disorder (ADHD; Adi-Japha et al., 2007; Rosenblum, Epsztein,

& Josman, 2008) and specific language impairment (SLI; Connelly & Dockrell, 2015; Connelly et al., 2012). In children with SLI, for example, language ability was found to constrain handwriting speed and fluency (Connelly & Dockrell, 2015; Connelly et al., 2012) as they produced fewer words per minute and paused for longer during writing than typically developing peers.

Below the levels of language, Van Galen (1991) describes the process of spelling. This can be programmed in two ways: through the mapping of phoneme-to-grapheme (sound to letter) rules or through knowledge of spelling a familiar word (orthographic representations; Miceli & Capasso, 2006; Rapp, Purcell, Hillis, Capasso, & Miceli, 2016). Indeed spelling difficulties, found in children with dyslexia, have been linked to poor handwriting performance. Sumner, Connelly, and Barnett (2013) found that children with dyslexia produced fewer words per minute than typically developing peers. By analysing the location of writing pauses, Sumner et al. (2013) revealed that the dyslexic group had a tendency to pause within misspelled words, which impacted on their handwriting speed. However, the notion of spelling as a constraint on handwriting also applies to typically developing individuals where word-structure has been found to mediate the kinematics of handwriting (Kandel, Soler, Valdois, & Gros, 2006). For example, the process of phoneme to grapheme mapping can constrain handwriting speed (Kandel et al., 2006), as can the number of syllables in a word (Lambert, Kandel, Fayol, & Esperet, 2008). It is therefore apparent that language and spelling are important components to consider when examining handwriting difficulties in children, as these factors alone can constrain performance.

According to Van Galen's (1991) model, there are three motor processes involved in handwriting production. The first is the selection of the *allograph*,[1] which according to Van Galen's model refers to the activation of the motor programme (retrieval of an action pattern from long-term motor memory) and the selection of the type of script (joined, un-joined, capital letters, small letters). Following this, the parameterization process occurs under *size control* where the size, speed, and spacing of allographs are programmed (Van Galen, 1991). This is followed by *recruitment of muscle synergies*, which results in the real-time movement of the pen (Van Galen, 1991). These three motor processes (selection of allograph, size/speed control, muscular adjustment) are complex in nature, and any one may be associated with handwriting difficulties. One population known for their difficulties with motor skill are children with developmental coordination disorder (DCD; American Psychiatric Association, APA, 2013). DCD is the term used to describe children who have motor coordination difficulties that are unexplained by a general medical condition, intellectual disability, or neurological impairment (APA, 2013). They commonly present with slow and poorly formed handwriting (Prunty, Barnett, Wilmut, & Plumb, 2014; 2016; Rosenblum & Livneh-Zirinski, 2008) and have a tendency to pause for a greater percentage of writing tasks than typically developing peers (indicating a lack of automatization; Prunty et al., 2014). They also produce a higher percentage of errors during the process of letter formation including incorrect starting position and inaccuracy in the number, direction, and sequence of letter strokes (Prunty and Barnett, 2017). These difficulties appear to straddle the three motor processes in Van Galen's model.

Van Galen's model is useful in outlining the processes involved in the skill of handwriting and, as outlined above, how these are impacted by cognitive or motor impairments associated with developmental disorders. However, teachers also commonly report handwriting difficulties in children in the absence of motor or cognitive impairment, and these have been referred to by some as "dysgraphia" (Di Brina, Niels, Overvelde, Levi, & Hulstijn, 2008; Dohla & Heim, 2015; Rosenblum, Parush, & Weiss, 2003; Smits-Engelsman & Schoemaker, 2017). This term is not formally described in either of the international classification systems, *Diagnostic and Statistical Manual of Mental Disorders–Fifth Edition* (DSM–5) or *International Classification of Diseases–10th Revision* (ICD–10) but the literal translation of the Greek term is "bad writing", which includes handwriting, spelling, and written expression. While "dysgraphia" has been used by some to describe children with spelling difficulties (e.g., Miceli & Capasso, 2006), many have used the term to denote children with handwriting difficulties (e.g., Di Brina et al., 2008; Dohla & Heim, 2015; Rosenblum et al., 2003; Smits-Engelsman & Schoemaker, 2017), and that is the focus of the current paper. Studies that have focused on handwriting performance in children with dysgraphia reported difficulties such as slow and illegible handwriting with a tendency to pause during writing (Rosenblum et al., 2003). Although this seems very similar to features of handwriting in DCD, no study has directly compared handwriting performance across these groups. Smits-Engelsman and Schoemaker (2017) found no differences between a DCD and "dysgraphia" group on a drawing task, in which children copied a series of patterns from a computer screen as quickly and accurately as possible. Although both groups had slower movement velocity, had a smaller trajectory length, and were less accurate than typically developing controls, the DCD and "dysgraphia" groups did not differ from each other. However, the results may be quite different for a handwriting task involving the production of language by hand. In previous research, distinctions between the handwriting difficulties of children with different developmental disorders suggest different approaches to intervention for these groups. In the same vein, further investigation of those with dysgraphia is needed to inform tailored interventions for these children.

While previous studies tend to focus on group findings, the heterogeneity of groups is acknowledged, and it is recognized that individual differences may be masked (Sugden & Chambers, 2007). Moreover, handwriting difficulties can take various forms, as mentioned above, and children may have different profiles of proficiency across various temporal and spatial measures of handwriting performance (e.g., letter accuracy, legibility, pausing, and overall speed). Therefore, the main aim of this study was to examine handwriting performance in children with dysgraphia (handwriting difficulties), compared to children with DCD (general motor difficulties) and a typically developing control group using tools commonly used by teachers and health professionals in an attempt to tap into the motor processes outlined in Van Galen's (1991) model. Measures of the handwriting product (speed and legibility) were supplemented with more detailed temporal aspects (process measures) of performance across two handwriting tasks. Group analyses were supplemented with an examination of individual performance profiles within and across the three groups.

Method

Two groups of children with handwriting difficulties were included, a dysgraphia and a DCD group. Handwriting difficulties were determined by scores either below the 15th percentile on the Detailed Assessment of Speed of Handwriting (DASH; Barnett et al., 2007), indicating slow handwriting, or below average on the Handwriting Legibility Scale (HLS; Barnett, Prunty, & Rosenblum, 2013).

Participants

Twenty-eight children with handwriting difficulties were recruited to the study, ranging from 8 to 14 years of age. For 14 of these children their handwriting difficulties were accompanied by a diagnosis of DCD (14 boys); the remaining 14 had handwriting difficulties with no significant motor impairment (dysgraphia group). There was a third group of 14 typically developing children (TD group) with neither handwriting difficulties nor movement difficulties. All three groups were age and gender matched in the study. The recruitment procedure for each group is outlined below.

Dysgraphia group

This group was recruited through local primary and secondary schools. Teachers were asked to use their professional judgement to identify children with handwriting difficulties without motor, reading/spelling difficulties and without intellectual impairment. The children were also individually tested on the Movement Assessment Battery for Children 2nd edition Test (MABC–2 Test; Henderson, Sugden, & Barnett, 2007), British Picture Vocabulary Scale 2nd edition (BPVS–2; Dunn, Dunn, Whetton, & Burley, 1997), and the reading and spelling components of the British Ability Scales 2nd Edition (BAS–II; Elliot, 1996). Children in this group had a MABC–2 score above the 15th percentile and standard scores above 85 on the BPVS and reading/spelling measures, indicating performance within the expected range. None had a diagnosis of dyslexia.

DCD group

The children with DCD were recruited from a database of children previously assessed and who met the formal diagnostic criteria from the DSM–5 (APA, 2013). The children had significant motor difficulties, with performance below the 10th percentile (13 were below the 5th, 1 below the 10th) on the MABC–2 (Henderson et al., 2007). These difficulties had a significant impact on their activities of daily living, as reported by their parents and evident on the MABC–2 Checklist (Henderson et al., 2007). A developmental, educational, and medical history was taken from the parents, which confirmed that there was no history of neurological or intellectual impairment and no medical condition that might explain the motor deficit. The BPVS–2 (Dunn et al., 1997) was used to give a measure of receptive vocabulary, which correlates highly with verbal IQ (Glenn & Cunningham, 2005). This was in at least the average range (above a standard score of 85) for all children. The Strengths and Difficulties Questionnaire (SDQ; Goodman, 1997) was also used to note any other behavioural difficulties reported by the parent, which commonly occur with DCD, such as ADHD (Miller, Missiuna, Macnab, Malloy-Miller, & Polatajko, 2001). The parent interviews revealed that no children had been given a diagnosis of ADHD from a health professional. The children were also assessed on the reading and spelling components of the BAS–II. None had a diagnosis of dyslexia.

Typically developing (TD) control group

Teachers in local primary and secondary schools were asked to use their professional judgement to identify children without any handwriting, motor, or reading/spelling difficulties and without intellectual impairment. To ensure that the children identified were free of these difficulties, they were individually tested on the MABC–2 Test, the BPVS–2, and the reading and spelling components of the BAS–II. Children were included in the control group if they scored at least at the typical level expected for their age on all measures.

Exclusion criteria

Children from all groups with a diagnosis of dyslexia and/or those who had English as a second language were excluded from the study. Children who had a reported physical, sensory, or neurological impairment or who were born before 35 weeks gestational age were also excluded. This was to ensure that handwriting difficulties could not be attributed to other disorders. See Table 1 for performance profiles of all groups.

Assessments

The detailed assessment of speed of handwriting (DASH; Barnett et al., 2007)

The DASH is a standardized handwriting speed test with UK norms for 9- to 16-year-olds. It is commonly used among teachers and health care professionals to identify children with handwriting difficulties (Blank, Smits-Engelsman, Polatajko, & Wilson, 2012). In this study two tasks from the DASH were implemented: alphabet writing and free writing. The demands of both tasks were deemed acceptable for use with children aged 8 years as they align with practice in the classroom and have been successfully used in our previous work (Prunty, Barnett, Wilmut, & Plumb, 2013, 2014); they are outlined below.

Alphabet writing. The participants wrote the alphabet repeatedly from memory as fast as possible for one minute. They were instructed to write it in the correct order using lower-case letters, making sure that every letter was readable.

Free writing. The participants wrote on the topic of "my life". A spider diagram, offering different writing suggestions, was presented prior to writing, in order to elicit ideas from the child. The content of their writing was not assessed, but they were instructed to try and write continuously over a 10-minute period using their everyday handwriting. They were

Table 1. Mean age and scores for dysgraphia, DCD, and TD groups on selection measures.

Selection measures	D ($n = 14$)	DCD ($n = 14$)	TD ($n = 14$)	p	
Age in years	10.55 (1.77)	10.61 (1.82)	10.47 (2.00)	.981	
MABC–2 Test percentiles					
Total test score	32.00 (21.15)	6.41 (8.12)	48.28 (26.32)	<.001*	DCD < D < TD
Manual Dexterity component	36.21 (24.60)	7.42 (9.14)	55.85 (30.92)	<.001*	DCD < D < TD
BPVS–2 standard score	105.43 (11.3)	111.21 (17.44)	106.77 (12.79)	.532	
BAS–II spelling standard score	104.00 (12.78)	100.36 (10.58)	112.21 (10.11)	.023*	DCD = D; D = TD; DCD < TD
BAS–II reading standard score	113.80 (9.48)	113.71 (11.04)	121.86 (11.60)	.101	

Note: Standard deviations in parentheses. MABC–2 = Movement Assessment Battery for Children test component; BPVS–2 = British Picture Vocabulary Scale; BAS–II = British Ability Scale; D = dysgraphia; DCD = developmental coordination disorder; TD = typically developing group.
*$p \leq .050$.

first given one minute to think of some ideas before writing. No instructions were given regarding writing style, and children used their usual way of writing. In the UK there is no single, prescribed writing style; some schools teach fully joined ("cursive") from the start, but a semi-joined script is most common, and this was reflected in our sample.

Performance on these two tasks was scored and analysed in various ways, as described in the "Data Analysis" section below.

The Handwriting Legibility Scale (HLS; Barnett et al., 2013)

The HLS examines five different components of handwriting legibility including global legibility (overall readability of the text on first reading), effort to read the script, layout on the page, letter formation, and alterations to writing (attempts made to rectify written work). The HLS is applied retrospectively to the DASH free-writing task. Each component is scored on a scale of 1 to 5 with 1 representing good performance and 5 representing poor performance. Each component is summed to give a total score for legibility with total scores ranging from 5 to 25, with higher scores reflecting poorer legibility. Inter-rater reliability and internal consistency have been reported to be high ($\alpha = .92$ in each case), with all components loading on just one factor. The total HLS score for each group is recorded. The analysis involving the HLS is described below.

Apparatus

When completing the two DASH tasks the participants wrote with an inking pen on paper placed on a Wacom Intuos 4 digitizing writing tablet (325.1 mm × 203.2 mm) to record the movement of the pen during handwriting. The writing tablet transmits information about the spatial and temporal data of the pen as it moves across the surface. The data were sampled at 100 Hz via a laptop computer. Eye & Pen Version 2 (EP2) software (Alamargot, Chesnet, Dansac, & Ros, 2006) was used to analyse the tablet data.

Measures

From the above assessments, a range of measures were obtained, aligned as closely as possible with the motor processes from Van Galen's (1991) model. Although these do not provide a pure measure of each process, they indicate how commonly used clinical tools can be used to begin to examine different components of the model.

Motor Process 1: Selection of the allograph

Quality of letter formation

According to Van Galen (1991), the first stage in the motor aspect of handwriting is the selection of the allograph. Using Van Galen's definition of an allograph we examined this process across the three groups. To do so, we examined the quality of letter form production, as this might reflect incomplete (or erroneous) knowledge about the proper form of the allograph. The participants completed the alphabet task from the DASH (Barnett et al., 2007; described above). The alphabet was chosen as it would naturally facilitate an examination of each of the individual letter forms required for handwriting. Using EP2's video function, which allows for the replay of handwriting production in real time on a laptop, the alphabet task was initially played and replayed in slow motion. The video was paused if needed to allow for accurate coding of the process. In the UK children may be taught different handwriting styles, which include variations of joined or un-joined letterforms, so the coding in this study only focused on incorrect letterforms and directions that the children would not be taught in the school system regardless of style.

The quality of letter formation was examined using the following codes.

1. Letter stroke in wrong direction: This occurred in letters that "looked" appropriate on paper but when replayed revealed incorrect letter stroke directions. An example of this was a clockwise rather than anticlockwise direction when forming the letter "a" or "o".
2. Incorrect start place: This occurred if a letter started in a position that would not be taught. An example of this includes the letters "r", "n", or "i" starting at the baseline rather than at the top of the letter.
3. Letters with missing strokes: This occurred if a letter was missing a required stoke. An example of this includes the letters "t" and "f" without the cross stroke or "r", "n", "u" completed with one stroke rather than two.
4. Letters with added strokes: This occurred through over-writing on a letter. An example of this is repeating strokes already formed.

5. Letter reversals: This occurred if a letter was formed in the opposite direction. An example of this is the letter "b" appearing as "d".

The percentage of letters in the alphabet task with formation errors was calculated and reported for each group. The inter-rater reliability for this measure is .89 as reported previously in Prunty and Barnett (2017).

Motor Process 2: Size/speed control

The second motor process outlined in Van Galen's (1991) model is size control, which refers to the parameterization of the allograph. This is where the size, speed, and spacing of allographs are programmed.

Size and spacing

To examine letter size and spacing we used two measures of legibility on the free-writing task including the HLS total score (as described above) and the percentage of illegible words identified using the instructions from the DASH manual. The HLS score takes into account an overview of both letter size and spacing while the percentage of illegible words provides an additional word-level analysis. While issues with legibility may be attributed to difficulties in other areas (i.e., the level of the allograph—quality of letter forms), we made the assumption based on Di Brina et al.'s (2008) findings that parameterization including poor spacing and size could also contribute to legibility issues. In their study they reported that difficulties with letter spacing were independent of the difficulties observed in letter form production (Di Brina et al, 2010).

Handwriting speed

To examine the speed of handwriting the scoring instructions from the DASH manual were applied to the 10-min free-writing task. The number of words per minute were averaged over the 10-min period. Indeed the number of words per minute is a frequently used measure of handwriting speed in the literature on writing (Connelly et al., 2012; Sumner et al., 2013).

Motor Process 3: Muscular adjustment and real-time trajectory of pen

The final stage described in Van Galen's model is thought to represent the recruitment of muscle synergies and the real-time movement of the pen. We examined this process through the temporal aspects of performance measured using the digitizing writing tablet (as described above) and the EP2 software (Alamargot et al., 2006). In particular, we examined execution speed to explore muscular adjustment and writing pauses to explore any interference with the real-time trajectory.

The following variables obtained from EP2 were ascertained for the alphabet and free-writing tasks:

1. Execution speed (cm s^{-1}): The speed of the pen when it is in contact and moving on the page. This does not include when the pen is pausing on the page.
2. Pause duration (% of writing time): The percentage of time during the task where the pen was either off the page (in-air pause), or halted on the page (on-paper pause). A pause was defined as three successive digital samples without movement (a halt >30 ms) (Alamargot et al., 2006). This threshold has been used by other researchers in the case of handwriting in dyslexia, in speech and language impairments, and in typically developing populations (Alamargot et al., 2006; Connelly et al., 2012; Sumner et al., 2013). It is the minimum threshold available with the EP2 software and is thought to capture all writing events.

Individual performance profiles

In order to ascertain whether the children in the dysgraphia and DCD groups were performing more poorly than TD peers on handwriting measures, the mean and standard deviation from the TD group were used to denote typical or average performance. The number of standard deviations from the TD mean was calculated to demonstrate the severity of difficulties in the dysgraphia and DCD groups in comparison to TD peers. This was calculated for the following measures:

1. Speed: Number of words per minute on the free-writing task.
2. Legibility: Total score of the HLS.
3. Percentage of pausing on the free-writing task.
4. Percentage of errors in letter formation on the alphabet task.

Initially the numbers and percentages of participants who were poor on each measure (at least below 1 *SD* of the TD mean) were calculated. A common cut-off to determine poor performance on a measure is more than one standard deviation from the mean (Cascio, Alexander, & Barrett, 1988). This was then extended across the measures to ascertain the number and percentage of participants who were poor on two and three measures.

Procedure

The study was approved by the University Research Ethics Committees at Oxford Brookes University and Brunel University London. Parents were required to sign a consent form, and children were asked to either assent (below 11 years) or countersign the parent consent form (over 11 years).

The handwriting component of this study took place over one 60-min session. Each child met with the first author and completed the reading, spelling, and handwriting tasks. The sessions were completed either at the child's home or school or at Oxford Brookes University or Brunel University London. During the handwriting tasks the children were seated at a height-adjustable table and chair, with knees positioned at approximately 90°. The participants were invited to manoeuvre the tablet to a position that was comfortable for them when writing.

Data analysis

Group differences

To examine group differences on a range of handwriting measures, one-way analyses of variance (ANOVAs; or non-parametric equivalent) were used. Significant group effects were broken down using pairwise comparisons. An analysis of covariance (ANCOVA) was used with age as a co-variate on handwriting speed and pausing measures due to the relationship between these variables and age and the wide age-range of participants. Two-way mixed ANCOVAs were used to examine group differences across handwriting execution speed. Significant main effects and interactions were broken down using post hoc tests and simple main effects, respectively. For all analyses, significance levels were set at .05, with Bonferroni corrections used to control for multiple comparisons.

Correlations

Partial bivariate correlations (controlling for age) were also conducted to examine the relationship between reading/spelling/vocabulary/motor skills and the handwriting measures (quality of letter formation, handwriting speed, legibility, and pausing). The correlations were calculated for each group separately and for all participants together.

Results

Motor Process 1: Selection of the allograph

The quality of letter formation

Kruskal–Wallis *H* tests showed that there was a significant effect of group in the percentage of errors in letter production produced, $\chi^2(2) = 7.37$, $p = .025$ (mean rank 21.39 for dysgraphia, 27.82 for DCD, 15.29 for TD). Mann–Whitney *U* tests (with Bonferroni corrections) revealed that the dysgraphia group ($U =$ 42.25. $Z = -2.56$, $p = .010$) performed significantly below the TD group but did not differ from the DCD group ($U = 65.0$. $Z = -1.52$, $p = .129$; see Table 2).

Motor Process 2: Size/speed control

Size and spacing

Handwriting Legibility Scale. There was a significant effect of group for performance on the HLS, $\chi^2(2) =$ 22.96, $p < .001$ (mean rank 27.61 for dysgraphia, 28.18 for DCD, 8.71 for TD). The TD group demonstrated significantly better performance on the HLS than the dysgraphia ($U = 14.0$, $Z = -3.87$, $p < .001$) and DCD ($U = 3.00$. $Z = -4.38$, $p < .001$) groups, which did not differ from each other ($U = 96.5$. $Z = -0.69$, $p = .945$).

Percentage of illegible words. Kruskal–Wallis *H* tests showed that there was a significant effect of group in the percentage of illegible words produced in the DASH free-writing task, $\chi^2(2) = 22.72$, $p < .001$ (mean rank 27.21 for DCD, 28.18 for dysgraphia, 9.11 for TD). Mann–Whitney *U* tests (with Bonferroni corrections) revealed that the TD group performed significantly better than both the dysgraphia ($U = 7.50$, $Z = -4.44$, $p < .001$) and DCD ($U = 15.0$, $Z = -4.14$, $p < .001$) groups, which did not differ from each other ($U = 95.0$, $Z = -1.38$, $p = .890$; see Table 2).

Table 2. A comparison of the handwriting performance measures for the dysgraphia, DCD, and TD groups.

Measures	Dysgraphia ($n = 14$) *M (SD)*	DCD ($n = 14$) *M (SD)*	TD ($n = 14$) *M (SD)*	
Handwriting product				
Alphabet (lpm)	41.07 (23.28)	42.93 (16.17)	52.57 (15.66)	
Free writing (wpm)*	12.43 (3.83)	12.34 (4.22)	15.38 (4.48)	TD > (D = DCD)
HLS (total score)*	16.57 (3.61)	17.64 (4.10)	9.57 (2.06)	TD < (D = DCD)
% Illegible words*	4.98 (4.53)	6.55 (8.22)	0.001 (0.005)	TD < (D = DCD)
Handwriting process				
Execution speed (cm/s)				
Alphabet	2.63 (1.02)	2.46 (0.82)	2.74 (0.73)	
Free writing	2.85 (0.61)	2.67 (0.63)	2.64 (0.61)	
Percentage of pausing				
Alphabet	60.74 (9.08)	56.94 (9.44)	58.28 (9.08)	
Free writing*	61.20 (7.15)	62.19 (8.66)	53.52 (8.70)	TD < (D = DCD)
Percentage of errors in letter production				
Alphabet*	13.79 (8.94)	24.38 (18.30)	9.63 (5.37)	TD < (D = DCD)

Note: Means (standard deviations in parentheses) or median. D = dysgraphia; DCD = developmental coordination disorder; TD = typically developing group; wpm = words per minute; lpm = letters per minute.
*$p \leq .050$.

Handwriting speed

One-way ANCOVAs (Group × Writing Task with age as covariate) revealed no significant effect of group for the alphabet task, as the three groups produced a similar number of letters during the one-minute task, $F(2, 38) = 1.92$, $p = .160$, $\eta^2 = .092$. The covariate, age, was significantly related to the number of letters produced in the alphabet task, $F(1, 38) = 7.55$, $p < .009$, $\eta^2 = .166$.

On the free-writing task there was a significant effect of group for the number of words written, $F(2, 38) = 3.50$, $p = .040$, $\eta^2 = .156$. Pairwise comparisons indicated that the TD group produced a higher number of words per minute than the dysgraphia ($p = .032$) and DCD groups ($p = .024$) who did not differ from each other ($p = .910$). The covariate, age, was significantly related to the number of words produced, $F(2, 38) = 14.48$, $p < .001$, $\eta^2 = .276$. See Table 2 for group means.

Motor process 3: Muscular adjustment and real-time trajectory of pen

Execution speed

The execution speed (the speed of the pen when it is in contact and moving on the page) for both groups averaged between 2 and 3 cm s^{-1} in both tasks. A two-way mixed ANCOVA (Group × Writing Task) was used to examine group differences across the two tasks. The co-variate age was significantly related to execution speed, $F(1, 38) = 14.61$, $p < .001$, $\eta^2 = .278$. There was no effect of group, $F(2, 38) = 0.389$, $p = .681$, $\eta^2 = .020$, indicating that the three groups performed in a similar way. There was also no effect of task, $F(1, 38) = 2.38$, $p = .131$, $\eta^2 = .59$ (degrees of freedom corrected for violation of sphericity with a Greenhouse–Geisser correction).

Pausing percentage

There was no group effect for the percentage of pausing on the alphabet task, $F(2, 38) = 0.599$, $p = .554$, $\eta^2 = .031$. However, there was a significant group effect for the free-writing task, $F(2, 38) = 4.93$, $p = .012$, $\eta^2 = .206$. Pairwise comparisons indicated that the dysgraphia ($p = .016$) and DCD ($p = .007$) groups spent a significantly longer percentage of time pausing than their TD peers but did not differ from each other ($p = .735$; see Table 2).

Performance profiles across the handwriting measures

Tables 3 and 4 show the individual performance profiles of children in the dysgraphia and DCD groups, respectively. It can be seen that, within each group, children differ both in the severity of impairment and in the pattern of performance across the measures. Comparing the frequency of difficulties on the handwriting measures between the DCD and dysgraphia groups using chi-square tests of independence revealed no significant group differences. Based on 1 standard deviation, 7/14 (50%) participants in the dysgraphia group had difficulties with handwriting speed, and 5/14 (36%) participants in the DCD group, $\chi^2(2) = 0.667$, $p = .717$. On the HLS 11/14 (79%) in the dysgraphia group were above (indicating

Table 3. Performance profiles of children with dysgraphia across four measures.

Participant	Errors in letter formation[a] (%) TD *M* (*SD*) = 9.63 (5.37)	Speed (wpm) TD *M* (*SD*) = 15.38 (4.48)	Legibility[a] (HLS) TD *M* (*SD*) = 9.07 (2.06)	Pausing[a] (%) TD *M* (*SD*) = 53.52 (8.70)
37	−1	−1	−2	0
08	+2	−1	+4	+2
10	+1	+1	+3	0
124	+3	−2	+3	+1
133	+1	0	+2	+1
144	−2	0	+2	0
45	+1	0	+2	+1
46	+1	−1	+2	+1
147	+1	+1	+1	−1
48	−1	−2	+1	0
49	+1	−2	+2	+2
51	0	0	+1	+1
156	−1	0	0	0
118	+3	−1	0	−1

Note: HLS = Handwriting Legibility Scale; TD = typically developing group; wpm = words per minute. 0 = within 1 *SD* of the TD mean.
[a]Positive *SD* indicates performance below that of TD group.

poor performance) 1 standard deviation, and 12/14 (86%) children in the DCD group, $\chi^2(2) = 0.377$, $p = .828$. For the percentage of pausing, 7/14 (50%) children in the dysgraphia group were below their TD peers (showing greater pausing) and 9/14 (64%) in children with DCD, $\chi^2(2) = 1.74$, $p = .420$. For the percentage of errors in letterform production an equal number of children in the DCD and dysgraphia groups 9/14 (64%) were at least 1 standard deviation below their TD peers on this measure, $\chi^2(2) = 1.66$, $p = .435$ (see Table 5).

Table 4. Performance profiles of children in the DCD group across four measures.

Participant	Errors in letter formation[a] (%) TD *M* (*SD*) = 9.63 (5.37)	Speed (wpm) TD *M* (*SD*) = 15.38 (4.48)	Legibility[a] (HLS) TD *M* (*SD*) = 9.07 (2.06)	Pausing[a] (%) TD *M* (*SD*) = 53.52 (8.70)
02	+6	−1	+3	+2
05	+8	+1	+3	−1
15	+7	−1	+7	+1
18	0	0	+1	+1
19	+1	0	+1	+1
20	+1	0	+2	0
28	+1	−1	+1	+1
24	+1	0	+1	+1
30	−1	+2	0	−1
39	+9	−2	+2	+1
33	0	0	+2	+2
41	0	−1	+2	0
42	−1	0	−1	−1
53	+3	0	+1	+1

Note: DCD = developmental coordination disorder; HLS = Handwriting Legibility Scale; TD = typically developing group; wpm = words per minute. 0 = within 1 *SD* of the TD mean.
[a]Positive *SD* indicates performance below that of TD group.
**p* ≤ .050.

In relation to the severity of difficulties, chi-square tests of independence revealed no significant group differences. For example, for the quality of letter formation, while 5/14 (35%) children in the DCD group appeared to score between 3 and 9 standard deviations below the TD group mean compared to 2/14 (14%), this was not significant, $\chi^2(3) = 3.21$, $p = .360$.

Results across measures

Out of the 14 children with DCD, 12/14 (86%) were poor on at least two measures with four of them (29%) scoring below 1 standard deviation on all four measures followed by three (21%) across three measures. Only two (14%) children with DCD scored within the TD range on all measures. Similar profiles emerged in the dysgraphia group with 11/14 (79%) poor on at least two measures, 4/14 (29%) on four, and 2/14 (14%) on three. Tables 3 and 4 indicate the performance profiles of the DCD and dysgraphia groups on the four measures.

Correlations with vocabulary, reading, spelling, and motor measures

Partial correlations (controlling for age) conducted on each group separately revealed no significant relationships between any of the literacy measures (vocabulary, reading, spelling, manual dexterity) and the handwriting measures (quality of letter formation, handwriting speed, legibility, execution speed, and pausing). When conducted with all participants together there were significant relationships between spelling, vocabulary, and manual dexterity with some of the handwriting measures. For example, poorer letter formation and overall legibility were associated with both poorer spelling and poorer manual dexterity. Faster writing was associated with

Table 5. Percentage of children in the dysgraphia and DCD groups with scores below 1 standard deviation of TD group mean.

Measure	TD *M* (*SD*)	Dysgraphia (%)	DCD (%)
Speed (wpm)	15.38 (4.48)	50	36
Legibility (HLS)	9.07 (2.06)	79	86
% Pausing	53.52 (8.70)	50	64
% Errors in letter formation	9.63 (5.37)	64	64

Note: Standard deviations in parentheses. DCD = developmental coordination disorder; HLS = Handwriting Legibility Scale; TD = typically developing group; wpm = words per minute.

Table 6. Correlations between reading, spelling, vocabulary, and manual dexterity with the handwriting measures.

	Reading		Spelling		Vocabulary		Manual dexterity	
Measure	*r*	*p*	*r*	*p*	*r*	*p*	*r*	*p*
Quality of letter formation (% incorrect letter forms)	−.309	.067	−.383	.021*	−.033	.846	−.351	.036*
Free writing (wpm)	.079	.648	.322	.056	−.409	.013*	.262	.123
HLS total score (1–25)[a]	−.276	.103	−.397	.017*	.261	.125	−.658	<.001*
Execution speed (cms^{-1})	.123	.477	.155	.367	−.093	.590	−.112	.515
% Pausing on free writing	−.099	.565	−.361	.031*	.367	.028*	−.399	.016*

Note: $N = 42$. HLS = Handwriting Legibility Scale; wpm = words per minute.
[a]Higher scores on HLS reflect poorer legibility.
*$p \leq .050$.

poorer vocabulary, and more pausing in the writing was associated with poorer manual dexterity, vocabulary, and spelling. There were no significant correlations with reading ability (see Table 6).

Discussion

Previous research on handwriting has focused on identifying performance deficits in groups of children with different developmental disorders (Adi-Japha et al., 2007; Connelly et al., 2012; Prunty et al., 2013; Rosenblum et al., 2008; Sumner et al., 2014). However, there are many children who have significant handwriting difficulties in the absence of specific developmental disorders (Di Brina et al., 2008; Dohla & Heim, 2015; Rosenblum et al., 2003; Smits-Engelsman & Schoemaker, 2017). Often referred to as dysgraphia, this particular group causes concern to teachers and can severely impact on progress for the children. While work has been done on understanding handwriting difficulties in atypically developing children, this particular group has not received as much attention in the literature. As a consequence, it is unclear how they differ from other groups of children and how best to support them in school.

Using a range of measures accessible to health and educational professionals to help understand different aspects of performance, we examined handwriting in children with dysgraphia compared to children with and without DCD. In doing so we took into consideration additional factors that might impact on handwriting performance such as motor coordination, language, reading, and spelling skill. Our findings generally reflect those of Smits-Engelsman and Schoemaker (2017) who compared the performance of children with dysgraphia and DCD on a drawing task and found no group differences. This pattern held for the comprehensive range of measures used in our study, examining aspects of both the product and process of handwriting, considering both temporal features and the quality/accuracy of letter formation. This was an interesting finding as none of the children in the dysgraphia group had a significant motor difficulty, all with scores above the 16th percentile on the MABC-2 (and scores on the Manual Dexterity component in the average range for their age). It seems that despite the extensive range of measures used in this study we were unable to clearly distinguish between the dysgraphia and DCD groups. Both the DCD and dysgraphia groups displayed difficulties across the range of measures in comparison to the TD controls, including handwriting speed, legibility, and the handwriting process measures (pausing and letter formation).

The three motor processes outlined in Van Galen's (1991) model serve as a useful lens for discussion as we used the model as a framework for investigation. However, as there are no clinical tools specifically designed to assess each of these, we attempted to align our clinical assessments to this model. We recognize that there are limitations to this as while the measures align to some degree with the motor processes outlined by Van Galen (1991), the alignment is not perfect, and each measure probably reflects processing at several levels. Nonetheless the first process examined was the selection of the allograph, which we evaluated through studying the quality of letter formation in real time. We considered that poor letter formation might reflect poor knowledge about the proper form of the allograph. Previous studies such as Di Brina et al. (2010) reported inaccuracy of letter formation using single letters in children with dysgraphia. However, in the current study we were interested in identifying letters across the alphabet that were formed in a way that would not be taught in schools. Interestingly the DCD and dysgraphia groups had an equal percentage of children with difficulties in this area (64%). As such, it would appear that both groups align with previous descriptions of poor writers where a higher percentage of inaccurate letter forms were reported compared to TD peers (Di Brina et al, 2010; Smits-Engelsman & Van Galen, 1997). However, it is difficult to speculate on the underlying mechanisms for this issue in both groups as while deficits in motor sequence learning and procedural learning may be an issue in the DCD group (Bo et al, 2014; Wilson, Ruddock, Smits-Engelsman, Polatajko, & Blank, 2013), this has yet to be examined in children with dysgraphia. Indeed the considerable variation in performance on this measure adds another layer of complexity as while some children appeared to be more severely affected than others (3–9 *SD*s below TD group mean), there were five children in both groups who did not appear to have any difficulties on this measure. However, the allograph is only one level of analyses. According to Di Brina et al (2010) the inaccuracy of letterforms reported in their dysgraphia group was independent of difficulties with size control (in their case trajectory length and velocity). As such, the process of size control (parameterization), which was the second area of consideration in this study, may provide more insight.

To examine the motor process of size/speed control we used measures of handwriting speed and legibility. Size control here refers to the parameterization of the motor programme where the size, speed, and spacing of allographs are programmed (Van Galen, 1991). Looking at the individual data it seems that both the dysgraphia and DCD groups demonstrated significant difficulties with parameterization evident through a high percentage of children in each group with difficulties on the HLS. The HLS examines aspects of legibility including the size and spacing within and between words. Pending the correct sequencing of strokes at the allograph level, paramaterization would be a key factor, which could impact on global legibility as measured by the HLS. Interestingly, both groups had difficulties with handwriting speed as measured through the number of words produced per minute. However, many factors could contribute to this finding including higher level cognitive processes such as planning (Berninger & Swanson, 1994), and as such it may not be exclusively an issue with motor processing. Looking at the individual data on handwriting speed, 50% of the dysgraphia group had difficulties, compared to 36% in the DCD group. However, this difference was not significant. The issue of heterogeneity within the groups was again apparent, and it remains unclear why some children within either group had difficulties writing quickly while others did not.

The final motor process in Van Galen's (1991) model is the recruitment of muscle synergies, which results in the real-time movement of the pen. While physiological examinations of muscle activation and recruitment (i.e., electromyography/biofeedback) were beyond the scope of this study, we examined the execution speed of the pen and the percentage of pausing during writing to identify slowness and dysfluency in the real-time movement of the pen. Interestingly both the dysgraphia and DCD groups did not differ from the TD group on execution speed, indicating that they were able to move the pen as quickly as their peers. However, both the DCD and dysgraphia groups paused for a greater percentage of the task, indicating some dysfluency in the movement of the pen. According to Smits-Engelsman and Van Galen (1997), this motor process includes muscular initiation, which can be impacted by neuromotor noise in children with handwriting difficulties. While we did not consider the control of movement beyond measures of manual dexterity and execution speed of the pen, an examination at this level could help differentiate between children with dysgraphia and DCD. Indeed Smits-Engelsman and Van Galen (1997) suggested that poor writers are unable to adapt their fine distal musculature movements to the demands of an accurate handwriting task. Furthermore, it has been hypothesized that children with handwriting difficulties are unable to apply effective biomechanical strategies such as "stiffness" to reduce neuromotor noise (Van Galen & De Jong, 1995; Van Galen, Portier, Smits-Engelsman, & Schomaker, 1993). According to Smits-Engelsman and Wilson (2013), neuromotor noise involves unpredictable fluctuations and disturbances during movement, which can have a neural, neuromuscular, or environmental origin. The inability to apply movement strategies to counteract noise in the system may result in crude movements, which according to Van Galen et al. (1993) have an impact on the quality of handwriting. These crude movements described by Van Galen et al (1993) align with the idea that poor writers resort to using the wrist or the elbow as pivots of action. This may result in larger movements, which are not conducive to accurate performance on a task such as handwriting (Smits-Engelsman & Van Galen, 1997). However, while there are some hypotheses in the literature surrounding neuromotor noise and the biomechanical influences, these were outside the scope of this study. Further research is needed to investigate the process of muscular adjustment in more detail to examine possible differences between handwriting difficulties in dysgraphia and DCD.

A limitation of this study was the relatively small sample size, which may have impacted on power and overall null group differences. If supported in larger studies, these findings suggest that it may be helpful to include other groups of children such as those with dyslexia and specific language impairment, to begin to understand the nature of handwriting difficulties in these different groups. Full diagnostic assessment is important to differentiate the groups and should include a range of literacy and motor measures that may impact on handwriting production. Although our samples were too small to identify any significant relationships between measures within each of the groups, some significant correlations were found when we considered all groups together. For example, better manual dexterity scores and better spelling scores were each associated with better letter formation/legibility and less pausing during writing. This seems to reflect the importance of manual dexterity and spelling ability to aspects of handwriting production. Some other correlations are more difficult to interpret and need further investigation. A further limitation of our work is that, while we applied Van Galen's (1991) model as a framework for investigation, our clinical measures were not specifically designed to tap into these processes. Nonetheless, the extensive range of measures used allowed us to gain greater insight into the heterogeneity and presentation of handwriting difficulties in children with dysgraphia. The within-group variability found across the measures showed that no one assessment was able to capture every child with a handwriting difficulty. This suggests that in both research and clinical practice a range of measures needs to be included to more fully understand handwriting profiles. In addition, one area that was not considered in this study was the influence of external factors such as the way in which handwriting is taught in the schools of the participants and the amount of handwriting practice they engaged in (Molyneaux, Barnett, Glenny, & Davies, 2013; Smits-Engelsman & Van Galen, 1997). These are societal-based factors, which were outside the scope of this study but do warrant further investigation.

In summary, our examination of handwriting performance in children with dysgraphia spanned across the three motor processes of Van Galen's (1991) model and found that children in this group had difficulties in all three areas. Further work needs to be done to understand these processes in more detail as despite poor performance at a group level on all of our clinical measures, the individual variability within and across the measures illustrates the complex nature of handwriting difficulties. The results advance our knowledge of handwriting difficulties in children with dysgraphia but more research is needed in order to understand the underlying mechanisms of their difficulties. Further research needs to unpick the motor processes in more detail to aid in the provision of evidence for planning future interventions in this group.

Note

1. In the literature the term "allograph" is used in different ways including to describe the visual (non-motor) representation of a letter (Teulings, 1996). The present study uses Van Galen's (1991) definition.

Acknowledgements

We would like to thank all of the participants, their families, and the schools who took part in this study.

Disclosure statement

No potential conflict of interest was reported by the authors.

ORCID

Mellissa Prunty http://orcid.org/0000-0001-5149-9153

References

Adi-Japha, E., Landau, Y., Frenkel, L., Teicher, M., Gross-Tsur, V., & Shalev, R. (2007). ADHD and dysgraphia: Underlying mechanisms. *Cortex*, *43*(6), 700–709.

Alamargot, D., Chesnet, D., Dansac, C., & Ros, C. (2006). Eye and Pen: A new device for studying reading during writing. *Behavior Research Methods*, *38*(2), 287–299.

American Psychiatric Association (APA). (2013). *DSM-5. Diagnostic and statistical manual of mental disorders* (5th ed.). Washington: American Psychiatric Association.

Barnett, A., Henderson, S., Scheib, B., & Schulz, J. (2007). *The detailed assessment of speed of handwriting*. London: Harcourt Assessment.

Barnett, A., Prunty, M., & Rosenblum, S. (2013, June). *Development of the handwriting legibility scale (HLS): An examination of reliability and validity*. Paper presented at the International Graphonomics Society Conference, Nara, Japan.

Berninger, V., Abbott, R., Abbott, S., Graham, S., & Richards, T. (2002). Writing and reading: Connections between language by hand and language by eye. *Journal of Learning Disabilities*, *35*, 39–56.

Berninger, V., & Swanson, L. (1994). Modifying Hayes & Flower's model of skilled writing to explain beginning and developing writing. In E. Butterfield (Ed.), *Children's writing: Toward a process theory of development of skilled writing* (pp. 57–81). Greenwich, CT: JAI Press.

Blank, R., Smits-Engelsman, B., Polatajko, H., & Wilson, P. (2012). European academy for childhood disability (EACD): Recommendations on the definition, diagnosis and intervention of developmental coordination disorder (long version). *Developmental Medicine and Child Neurology*, *54*(1), 54–93.

Bo, J., Colbert, A., Lee, C., Schaffert, J., Oswald, K., & Neill, R. (2014). Examining the relationship between motor assessments and handwriting consistency in children with and without probable developmental coordination disorder. *Research in Developmental Disabilities*, *35*(9), 2035–2043.

Cascio, W. F., Alexander, R. A., & Barrett, G. V. (1988). Setting cutoff scores: Legal, psychometric, and professional issues and guidelines. *Personnel Psychology*, *41*(1), 1–24.

Connelly, V., & Dockrell, J. (2015). The role of oral language in underpinning the text generation difficulties in children with specific language impairment. *Journal of Research in Reading*, *38*(1), 18–34.

Connelly, V., Dockrell, J., Walter, K., & Critten, S. (2012). Predicting the quality of composition and written language bursts from oral language, spelling and handwriting skills in children with and without specific language impairment. *Written Communication*, *29*, 278–302.

Department for Education (DfE). (2013). The national curriculum in England. Retrieved March 2017, from https://www.gov.uk/government/collections/national-curriculum

Di Brina, C., Niels, R., Overvelde, A., Levi, G., & Hulstijn, W. (2008). Dynamic time warping: A new method in the study of poor handwriting. *Human Movement Science*, *27*(2), 242–255.

Dohla, D., & Heim, S. (2015). Developmental dyslexia and dysgraphia: what can we learn from the one about the other? *Frontiers in Psychology*, *6*(2045). 10.3389/fpsyg.2015.02045

Dunn, L., Dunn, L., Whetton, C., & Burley, J. (1997). *The British picture vocabulary scale* (2nd ed.). London: NFER Nelson Publishing Company Ltd.

Elliot, C. (1996). *British ability scales (II): Administration and scoring manual*. London: NFER Nelson Publishing Company Ltd.

Engel-Yeger, B., Nagauker-Yanuv, L., & Rosenblum, S. (2009). Handwriting performance, self-reports, and perceived self-efficacy among children with dysgraphia. *American Journal of Occupational Therapy*, *63*, 182–192.

Glenn, S., & Cunningham, C. (2005). Performance of young people with Down syndrome on the Leiter-R and British picture vocabulary scales. *Journal of Intellectual Disability Research*, *49*, 239–244.

Goodman, R. (1997). The strengths and difficulties questionnaire: A research note. *Journal of Child Psychology and Psychiatry*, *38*, 581–586.

Graham, S., Berninger, V., Abbott, R., Abbott, S., & Whitaker, D. (1997). Role of mechanics in composing of elementary school students: A new methodological approach. *Journal of Educational Psychology*, *89*, 170–182.

Graham, S., Berninger, V., Weintraub, N., & Schafer, W. (1998). Development of handwriting speed and legibility in grades 1–9. *The Journal of Educational Research*, *92*(1), 42–52.

Graham, S., Harris, K., & Fink, B. (2000). Is handwriting causally related to learning to write? Treatment of handwriting problems in beginning writers. *Journal of Educational Psychology*, *92*, 620–633.

Henderson, S., Sugden, D., & Barnett, A. (2007). *Movement assessment battery for children* (2nd ed). (Movement ABC-2). Examiner's Manual. London: Pearson Assessment.

Kandel, S., Soler, O., Valdois, S., & Gros, C. (2006). Graphemes as motor units in the acquisition of writing skills. *Reading and Writing*, *19*, 313–337.

Lambert, E., Kandel, S., Fayol, M., & Esperet, E. (2008). The effect of the number of syllables on handwriting production. *Reading and Writing*, *21*, 859–883.

Miceli, G., & Capasso, R. (2006). Spelling and dysgraphia. *Cognitive Neuropsychology*, *23*(1), 110–134.

Miller, L., Missiuna, C., Macnab, J., Malloy-Miller, T., & Polatajko, H. (2001). Clinical description of children with developmental coordination disorder. *Canadian Journal of Occupational Therapy*, *68*, 5–15.

Molyneaux, A., Barnett, A., Glenny, G., & Davies, R. (2013, June). *The association between handwriting practice and lexical richness: An analysis of the handwritten output of children aged 9–10 years.* Paper presented at the International Graphonomics Society Conference, Nara, Japan.

Prunty, M., & Barnett, A. (2017). Accuracy and consistency of letter formation in children with developmental coordination disorder. *Journal of Learning Disabilities*, Manuscript submitted for publication.

Prunty, M., Barnett, A., Wilmut, K., & Plumb, M. (2013). Handwriting speed in children with developmental coordination disorder: Are they really slower? *Research in Developmental Disabilities*, *34*(9), 2927–2936.

Prunty, M., Barnett, A., Wilmut, K., & Plumb, M. (2014). An examination of writing pauses in the handwriting of children with developmental coordination disorder. *Research in Developmental Disabilities*, *35*(11), 2894–2905.

Prunty, M., Barnett, A., Wilmut, K., & Plumb, M. (2016). The impact of handwriting difficulties on compositional quality in children with developmental coordination disorder. *British Journal of Occupational Therapy*, *79*(10), 591–597.

Puranik, C. S., & Al Otaiba, S. (2012). Examining the contribution of handwriting and spelling to written expression in kindergarten children. *Reading and Writing, 25*, 1523–1546.

Rapp, B., Purcell, J., Hillis, A., Capasso, R., & Miceli, G. (2016). Neural bases of orthographic long-term memory and working memory in dysgraphia. *Brain, 139*(2), 588–604.

Rosenblum, S., Epsztein, L., & Josman, N. (2008). Handwriting performance of children with attention deficit hyperactive disorders: A pilot study. *Physical & Occupational Therapy in Pediatrics, 28*(3), 219–234.

Rosenblum, S., & Livneh-Zirinski, M. (2008). Handwriting process and product characteristics of children diagnosed with developmental coordination disorder. *Human Movement Science, 27*(2), 200–214.

Rosenblum, S., Parush, S., & Weiss, P. (2003). Computerized temporal handwriting characteristics of proficient and non-proficient handwriters. *American Journal of Occupational Therapy, 57*(2), 129–138.

Smits-Engelsman, B., & Schoemaker, M. (2017). Comparability of graphic performance in children with pure dysgraphia and children with dysgraphia as part of developmental coordination disorder (DCD). In A. L. Barnett, & D. A. Sugden (Eds.), *Moving, developing and learning. A Festschrift in celebration of the career of Sheila E. Henderson* (pp. 81–95). Oxford: Oxford Brookes University.

Smits-Engelsman, B., & Van Galen, G. (1997). Dysgraphia in children: Lasting psychomotor deficiency or transient developmental delay? *Journal of Experimental Child Psychology, 67* (2), 164–184.

Smits-Engelsman, B., & Wilson, P. (2013). Noise, variability, and motor performance in developmental coordination disorder. *Developmental Medicine & Child Neurology, 55*(4), 69–72.

Sugden, D., & Chambers, M. (2007). Stability and change in children with developmental coordination disorder. *Child: Care, Health and Development, 33*(5), 520–528.

Sumner, E., Connelly, V., & Barnett, A. (2013). Children with dyslexia are slow writers because they pause more often and not because they are slow at handwriting execution. *Reading and Writing, 26*(6), 991–1008.

Sumner, E., Connelly, V., & Barnett, A. (2014). The influence of spelling ability on handwriting production: Children with and without dyslexia. *Journal of Experimental Psychology: Learning, Memory, and Cognition, 40*(5), 1441–1447.

Teulings, H. L. (1996). Handwriting movement control. In S. W. Keele, & H. Heuer (Eds.), *Handbook of perception and action. Vol.2: Motor skills* (pp. 561–613). London: Academic Press. ISBN 0-12-516162-X (reformatted).

Van Galen, G., & De Jong, W. (1995). Fitts' law as the outcome of a dynamic noise filtering model of motor control. *Human Movement Science, 14*(4–5), 539–571.

Van Galen, G. (1991). Handwriting: Issues for a psychomotor theory. *Human Movement Science, 10*, 165–191.

Van Galen, G., Portier, S. J., Smits-Engelsman, B., & Schomaker, L. (1993). Neuromotor noise and poor handwriting in children. *Acta Psychologica, 82*, 161–178.

Van Hartingsveldt, M., De Groot, I., Aarts, P. B., & Nijhuis-Van Der Sanden, M. W. (2011). Standardized tests of hand-writing readiness: A systematic review of the literature. *Developmental Medicine & Child Neurology, 53*, 506–515.

Wilson, P., Ruddock, S., Smits-Engelsman, B., Polatajko, H., & Blank, R. (2013). Understanding performance deficits in developmental coordination disorder: A meta-analysis of recent research. *Developmental Medicine & Child Neurology, 55*(3), 217–228.

The impact of developmental dyslexia and dysgraphia on movement production during word writing

Sonia Kandel, Delphine Lassus-Sangosse, Géraldine Grosjacques and Cyril Perret

ABSTRACT
This study investigated how deficits in orthographic processing affect movement production during word writing. Children with dyslexia and dysgraphia wrote words and pseudo-words on a digitizer. The words were orthographically regular and irregular of varying frequency. The group analysis revealed that writing irregular words and pseudo-words increased movement duration and dysfluency. This indicates that the spelling processes were active while the children were writing the words. The impact of these spelling processes was stronger for the children with dyslexia and dysgraphia. The analysis of individual performance revealed that most dyslexic/dysgraphic children presented similar writing patterns. However, selective lexical processing deficits affected irregular word writing but not pseudo-word writing. Selective poor sublexical processing affected pseudo-word writing more than irregular word writing. This study suggests that the interaction between orthographic and motor processing constitutes an important cognitive load that may disrupt the graphic outcome of the children with dyslexia/dysgraphia.

Introduction

Most studies on written language processing focused on reading skills. They paid less attention to writing processes (cf. Afonso, Suárez-Coalla, & Cuetos, 2015). The asymmetry is not merely quantitative, but also qualitative. There are many unanswered questions and important theoretical gaps concerning writing processes. This is surprising because everything we read has to be written somewhere by someone. Getting a more complete understanding of writing skills is therefore as necessary as investigating reading skills. Research in developmental dyslexia is also unbalanced in this sense because it mainly focuses on the reading difficulties (Berninger, Nielsen, Abbott, Wijsman, & Raskind, 2008). However, some children with dyslexia have more problems with writing than reading (Berninger, 2006; Berninger, Abbott, Thomson, & Raskind, 2001; Mortimore & Crozier, 2006). Many studies on dyslexia examined spelling skills but with the aim of identifying the underpinnings of the reading deficits (e.g., phonological, visuo-attentional), not to answer questions on writing performance per se (see, for instance, Ramus, Marshall, Rosen, & van der Lely, 2013; Saksida et al., 2016; Valdois et al., 2011). The present research intends to shed some light into word-writing processes of children with dyslexia and dysgraphia. We focused on how their difficulties with spelling processes affect the motor aspects of word writing. This could explain why many children with dyslexia and dysgraphia produce very irregular and/or unreadable writing during word production despite the absence of motor disorders (Valdois et al., 2011).

Word writing involves the proficiency of two complex processes: spelling retrieval and motor production. Spelling retrieval refers to the central processes that activate information on the letter components of a word from long-term memory (Costa, Fischer-Baum, Capasso, Miceli, & Rapp, 2011). The motor aspects of letter production are modulated by peripheral processes that regulate movement execution (Van Galen, 1991). According to dual-route models of spelling processes we retrieve spelling information by means of lexical and sublexical procedures (Rapp, Epstein, & Tainturier, 2002). Spelling retrieval via the lexical route involves the activation of its orthographic representation in a long-term memory system known as the orthographic lexicon.

This is particularly useful for writing orthographically irregular or inconsistent words that have to be memorized as a whole unit. They cannot be written correctly by applying the most frequent sound–letter conversion rules. For example, if we apply these rules to write the French word *monsieur* (/møsjø/, sir) the result would be pseudo-words such as "mecieu" or "meussieux", but never a letter sequence with a *mon* beginning. In contrast, *montagne* (/mɔ̃taɲ/, mountain) is an orthographically regular or consistent word because the most frequent sound–letter mappings lead to the correct spelling: /m/ = *m*, /ɔ̃/ = *on*, /t/ = *t*, /a/ = *a*, /ɲ/ = *gn*, // = *e*. The other spelling procedure—known as the sublexical route—involves the application of phonology to orthography conversion rules. Sublexical processing is useful when having to write new words and pseudo-words. Lexical and sublexical routes are active during the spelling processes and interact. The outcome of these processes is integrated and is kept in orthographic working memory for written production (Costa et al., 2011). Many researchers called this kind of working memory the "graphemic buffer" but we refer to it as orthographic working memory because we believe it is a more appropriate term to describe it (see Costa et al., 2011). At this stage, the spelling processes are concluded. The information on the spelling of the word is an abstract letter sequence that will "unwrap" sequentially during the execution of motor processes. In this view, the timing of motor production should be identical when writing *mon* in the orthographically irregular word *monsieur* and the regular word *montagne*.

The peripheral processes that are devoted to movement production have been described by Van Galen's (1991) model of handwriting production. The model includes a one-route "spelling" module that processes the orthographic components of the words. This module generates an abstract letter sequence that is stored temporarily in the "orthographic buffer" (i.e., the orthographic working memory). It is a linear letter string containing information on letter identity and order (e.g., *monsieur* = $m_1o_2n_3s_4i_5e_6u_7r_8$). It is the input to the following processing level, namely the "selection of allographs" module. Allographs refer to the shapes the letters will have. They determine geometrical parameters and writing style (e.g., cursive lower case). Once we know which shape each letter in the word should have, we activate the corresponding motor programmes for movement production. Motor programmes provide information on letter shape, stroke order, and direction. For the word *monsieur*, it would be, for example, m_1 = *m*, o_2 = *o*, n_3 = *n*, s_4 = *s*, i_5 = *i*, e_6 = *e*, u_7 = *u*, r_8 = *r*. Then, the "size control" module will process a series of local parameters like size, force, speed, so we adapt to the local constraints of the writing task, and the letters can be produced efficiently. Once all this information is set, the "muscular adjustment" module prepares for movement production. The muscles of the arm–hand system contract and produce the writing movements (e.g., *monsieur*). As dual-route models, this conception of word writing implies that the spelling processes are over when we start processing the peripheral components of the writing movements. Again, writing *mon* in the orthographically irregular word *monsieur* and the regular word *montagne* should involve the same kind of processing. Recent experimental data indicate, however, that spelling processes are not finished when peripheral processes start (Afonso, Álvarez, & Kandel, 2015; Afonso, Suárez-Coalla, et al., 2015; Álvarez, Cottrell, & Afonso, 2009; Buchwald & Falconer, 2014; Delattre, Bonin, & Barry, 2006; Kandel, Peereman, & Ghimenton, 2013, 2014; Lambert, Alamargot, Larocque, & Caporossi, 2011; Lambert, Sausset, & Rigalleau, 2015; Roux, McKeeff, Grosjacques, Afonso, & Kandel, 2013; Sausset, Lambert, Olive, & Larocque, 2012). Spelling and motor processes are not independent and may interact.

To investigate the way spelling and motor processes communicate, researchers recorded the graphic movements while the participants wrote the words on a digitizer or digitizing tablet. This provides online information on the writing movement that leads to letter production. In Roux et al. (2013) French adult participants wrote orthographically irregular (e.g., *monsieur*) and regular words (e.g., *montagne*) as well as pseudo-words (e.g., *mondrote*) on a digitizer. The data revealed that the type of letter sequence modulated the kinematics of movement production. Movement duration for producing letters *mon* in the orthographically irregular word *monsieur* was longer than in the regular word *montagne* and, in turn, in the pseudo-word *mondrote*. These differences at the peripheral level could be accounted for in terms of non-matching outcomes of lexical and sublexical processing at the central level (Afonso, Suárez-

Coalla, et al., 2015; Rapp et al., 2002; Roux et al., 2013). When these outputs are integrated at the grapheme level a conflict arises. Solving this conflict results in a temporal delay that affects the timing of motor production. This means that the spelling information that is coded in orthographic working memory refers to aspects of lexical and sublexical processing other than merely letter identity and order. This idea is not new, and there is abundant neuropsychological (e.g., Caramazza & Miceli, 1990) and experimental (e.g., Kandel, Álvarez, & Vallée, 2006; Kandel, Peereman, Grosjacques, & Fayol, 2011; Kandel & Spinelli, 2010) data supporting it. However, the orthographic regularity and lexicality effects on the timing of motor production point to an impact of orthographic processes *while* producing the writing movements. This is at odds with dual-route models and Van Galen's approach of handwriting production. These results indicate that orthographic retrieval processes are not finished when the motor processes are initiated. Lexical and sublexical processes are still active. They can modulate peripheral processing. In other words, the abstract letter sequence that results from spelling processes and is kept in orthographic working memory is not just "unwrapped" for motor production mechanically, in a letter-by-letter fashion.

To gain understanding on the way orthographic and motor processes interact during word writing, we investigated a situation in which orthographic processing is impaired and motor processing is not. We examined word-writing processes in children with dyslexia. Children with dyslexia are in general poor spellers and present a variety of spelling deficits (e.g., Afonso, Suárez-Coalla, et al., 2015; Chilosi et al., 2009). They may also be considered as presenting *central* dysgraphia. These orthographic deficits seem to have an impact on motor processing. The writing of children with dyslexia is often very irregular and difficult to read (Valdois et al., 2011). Sometimes, children with dyslexia are diagnosed with *peripheral* dysgraphia—that is, a pathology that refers to a deficit involving the mechanics of writing—even when no praxic, motor, or spatial impairments are detected (Berninger, Richards, & Abbott, 2015). Some motor skills can be deficient in dyslexia, like the ones related to the control of timing (Nicolson, Fawcett, & Dean, 2001; Wolff, Cohen, & Drake, 1984). However, these processes are not necessarily related to the motor control required for graphomotor production and manual dexterity. Ramus (2003) examined this specific point and did not find a direct relation between these motor deficits and reading skills.

The impact of orthographic processing difficulties on writing

Difficulties with orthographic processing may affect the quality and quantity of word writing. Abbott and Berninger (1993; Abbott, Berninger, & Fayol, 2010) showed that orthographic abilities predicted handwriting skills all throughout primary school. Maggio, Lété, Chenu, Jisa, and Fayol (2012) presented data of older children (ages 10–15 years) indicating that spelling processes affected motor production during composition by regulating pause production and writing rate. More recently, Rodriguez and Villaroel (2016) collected writing samples produced by Spanish-speaking first and third graders who were assessed on spelling skills. The children had to perform a series of writing tasks, including writing to dictation of inconsistent words and pseudo-words. Then their productions had to be rated by external judges as "poor handwriters" or "good handwriters". The results revealed that the children with low scores in the spelling tasks were the ones that were rated as poor writers. The authors concluded that handwriting difficulties can be predicted through the assessment of spelling abilities.

Most studies investigating the impact of dyslexia on writing were concerned with text composition, not word writing per se (Berninger et al., 2001, for children; Connelly, Dockrell, & Barnett, 2005, for adults). Some studies examined writing quality and legibility. Martlew (1992) observed poor legibility when dyslexic children had to copy verbal material. Most of the studies report that children with dyslexia are generally very slow in a variety of writing tasks (see Sumner, Connelly, & Barnett, 2012, for a review). Søvik and Arntzen's (1986) study indicated that children with dyslexia take more time to copy sentences than typically developing children of the same age. More recent research found, however, that dyslexic children are not slower when they write. These studies used digitizing tablets so they could have a very precise quantification of movement time and trajectory. These measures are important because execution speed refers to the ratio between these two parameters. Paz-Villagran, Gilhodes, and Velay (2013) presented a group study in which children with dyslexia and peripheral dysgraphia had to write a word eight times on the digitizer. They failed to find speed differences between the children with dyslexia and the controls. They observed instead that the children with peripheral dysgraphia wrote slower than the age-matched controls. In another experiment conducted by Brun-Henin, Velay, Beecham, and Cariou (2013) dyslexic and age-matched peers had to write a sentence on the digitizer. They had to produce it five times in cursive lower-case letters or print upper-case letters. The results revealed significant duration differences between the two groups during pen lifts (either between letters or between words) but no speed differences during movement production.

Sumner et al. (2012) examined movement speed differences between English-speaking children with and without dyslexia. The children had to write the alphabet and compose a text on the digitizer. Execution speed was equivalent in the dyslexic group and the age-matched peers. However, there were significant differences in pause production. The children with dyslexia paused more often and during more time than the age-matched group during the composition task. The pause pattern of the dyslexic group resembled the one of the spelling-matched controls. Pausing during text composition was thus related to spelling difficulties and their impact on having to deal simultaneously with the strong cognitive loads resulting from text planning and argumentation. To avoid the compositional loads related to writing, Sumner, Connelly, and Barnett (2014) conducted another experiment in which the children had to copy sentences. The results confirmed the previous findings. The execution speed of the dyslexic group was equivalent to their age-matched peers. Children with dyslexia seem slower because they pause more, particularly within words. Sumner et al. (2012, 2014) concluded that the lack of proficiency or automation with spelling skills did not affect the speed of motor production but led the children with dyslexia to produce more pauses during handwriting production. The absence of differences in execution speed should, however, be taken with caution. It is likely that important cognitive loads due to text composition and syntax processing may have masked small speed differences in movement production. This "null" effect could also be due to insufficient statistical power (Type II error).

In the present study we intended to gain more understanding of how the spelling deficits of children with dyslexia and dysgraphia affect writing. We restricted our investigation to word writing, so we could focus on orthographic retrieval and avoid text and sentence processing loads that could mask lexical and/or sublexical effects. Many studies related spelling deficits in dyslexia to difficulties with phonological processing (e.g., Friend & Olson, 2008; Saksida et al., 2016). This should mainly affect the sublexical processes involved in word writing. Spelling deficits can also be due to difficulties with the elaboration of orthographic representations. This should have a direct impact on lexical processing in word writing. Orthographic representations may be non-existent, lack specification on specific letter components, and/or vary in stability (Angelelli, Judica, Spinelli, Zoccolotti, & Luzzati, 2004, 2010; Di Betta & Romani, 2006; Goulandris & Snowling, 1991; Hanley, Hastie, & Kay, 1992). To our knowledge, the only experiment examining the impact of dyslexia on word writing using digitizer measures was conducted by Afonso, Suárez-Coalla, et al. (2015). Spanish adults with dyslexia copied words or wrote them to dictation. The results revealed that the participants with dyslexia took longer to initiate their writing movements (i.e., latency) than controls. Latency refers to the time lapse between stimulus presentation and the moment the participant starts to write. They also exhibited longer movement durations on letter and inter-letter writing and produced more errors. The participants with dyslexia had particular difficulties with low-frequency words before starting to write but not during motor production. Phoneme-to-orthography consistency had an impact on latencies and inter-letter intervals, but the differences between the participants with dyslexia and the controls failed to reach significance. The authors also found that word length had a stronger impact on the participants with dyslexia. This points to an impairment of the processes that keep information on letter identity and order in orthographic working memory during the writing process. Taken together, these results provided evidence that the spelling difficulties that the participants with dyslexia had during word writing affected the kinematic aspects of movement production. The results pointed to an effect of lexical processing (word frequency) and the operations that take place in the orthographic working memory (word length). As the authors say, the impact of phonology-to-orthography consistency requires further investigation. The lack of significant differences could be due to the fact that Spanish has a very shallow orthography so the number of orthographic inconsistencies is quite limited (Seymour, Aro, & Erskine, 2003). In the present research we assessed the impact of orthographic inconsistency in French, which is a language with a deep orthography and the presence of many exception words (Seymour et al., 2003). In addition, the impact of dyslexia on word writing may evolve with age (Angelelli, Notarnicola, Judica, Zoccolotti, & Luzzati, 2010). It is therefore likely that phonology-to-orthography consistency may have a strong effect on the way French children with dyslexia write words.

Learning how to write words

Before examining the impact of dyslexia and dysgraphia on word writing, we must understand how typically developing children learn how to write words. At school, children learn spelling and graphomotor skills at the same time. Both kinds of skills are extremely demanding at the beginning of the acquisition period. Several theoretical accounts of spelling acquisition indicate that the children learn the letter components of words by generating orthographic representations that become progressively more and more specified (e.g., Frith, 1986; Nation, Angell, & Castles, 2007; Share, 1995, 1999). On the graphomotor side, letter production is particularly demanding (Berninger et al., 1992). At the beginning, between ages 5 to 8 years, the children produce their writing movements slowly and control their productions throughout the whole word. They focus on reproducing the teacher's letters correctly. While doing so, they elaborate sensory-motor maps for each letter. With practice, these maps become more detailed and stable (Halsband & Lange, 2006). They are the basis for the motor programmes that contain information on letter shape, stroke order, and direction (Meulenbroek & van Galen, 1989a, 1989b; Schmidt, 1975; Schmidt & Lee, 2005). Progressively, the children produce letters by activating the motor programme and relying less on visual and kinaesthetic feedback. Motor programmes are stable when they contain all the information to produce a given letter correctly with a fast and smooth movement (Meulenbroek & van Galen, 1989a, 1989b). Writing automation is achieved when spelling retrieval and graphomotor production are no longer strong cognitive loads (Hayes, 2012; Maeland & Karlsdottir, 1991). The attentional and mnemonic resources can be devoted to higher functions of writing such as syntax processing and text planning (Berninger & Winn, 2006; Graham, Berninger, Abbott, Abbott, & Whitaker, 1997; Graham, Berninger, Weintraub, & Schafer, 1998). Writing becomes an instrument for written communication. A recent developmental study revealed that spelling and motor processes start to interact when the motor aspects of letter production become automatic (Kandel & Perret, 2015a).

Kandel and Perret (2015a) did the same experiment as Roux et al. (2013) but with children. They chose to work with children of ages 8 through 10 years because this is the period when letter production starts to become automatic (Mojet, 1991). The children copied orthographically regular and irregular words of varying frequency on a digitizer. The kinematic data indicated that irregular words produced longer movement duration and more dysfluency than regular words. The impact of orthographic regularity was stronger for the 9- and 10 year-olds than for the 8-year-olds. Furthermore, low-frequency words exhibited longer movement durations than high-frequency words, irrespective of age. This pattern of results suggests that the spelling–motor interaction starts to build up around age 9 with the *automation of graphomotor skills*. Before age 9, the children were so concentrated in producing letter shapes correctly and articulating the writing gestures from one letter to another that they could not deal with spelling processes at the same time. In dyslexia and central dysgraphia the children have difficulties with the *automation of orthographic skills*. This should affect the way spelling and motor processes communicate during word writing.

Phonological deficits in dyslexia should produce lexical and/or sublexical route dysfunctions (Saksida et al., 2016). This should affect word writing in different ways. The consequence for lexical processing deficits is that the orthographic representations that should be activated for word writing are underspecified or absent (Share, 1995, 1999). This makes it particularly difficult to write orthographically irregular or inconsistent words like the French word *monsieur*. The consequence for sublexical processing—that is, deficits when having to apply phoneme-to-grapheme conversion rules—is that the child has serious difficulties in writing new words or pseudo-words. In the present study, we examined word production in a group of French children with dyslexia and dysgraphia. We hypothesized that the difficulties with spelling automation that these children usually have should affect word writing. The children with dyslexia/dysgraphia who participated in this research were at least 10 years old. At age 10, handwriting automation should be fully achieved (Kandel & Perret, 2015b; Medwell & Wray, 2007; Overvelde & Hulstijn, 2011), and the dyslexia/dysgraphia diagnosis should be more stable and precise than at earlier ages. The spelling processes during word writing were assessed by varying orthographic regularity (regular words vs. irregular words), word frequency (high-frequency words vs. low-frequency words), and lexical status (regular words vs. pseudo-words). We instructed the children with dyslexia/dysgraphia (*dyslexics* hereafter) and a group of matched typically developing children in reading and writing abilities (*controls* hereafter) to copy the words and pseudo-words on a digitizing tablet or digitizer. We analysed movement duration and fluency as kinematic parameters that inform on motor production. To get more insight into the nature of the pauses that the children produced while writing, we noted every time they looked back to the model to be written on the screen of the computer. These "gaze lifts" are done to get more information on the spelling of the word while producing it. This constitutes supplementary evidence that orthographic processing has not yet finished while the child writes. We also measured latency, which is the temporal interval between word presentation and the moment the child starts to write the word.

Figure 1 presents the processes involved in copying the words and pseudo-words. The copying task gives the children the possibility of writing the letter sequences correctly with a letter-by-letter strategy (Figures 1a and 1b top left). If a child has difficulties in writing the item, he or she will be able to do the task correctly without having to apply lexical and/or sublexical processes. In this case, we should not observe regularity, frequency, or lexicality effects.

Orthographic regularity effects, as the ones reported by Kandel and Perret (2015a) in typically developing children of age 10, may result from conflicting outputs of lexical and sublexical processing. For example, the irregular French word *monsieur*

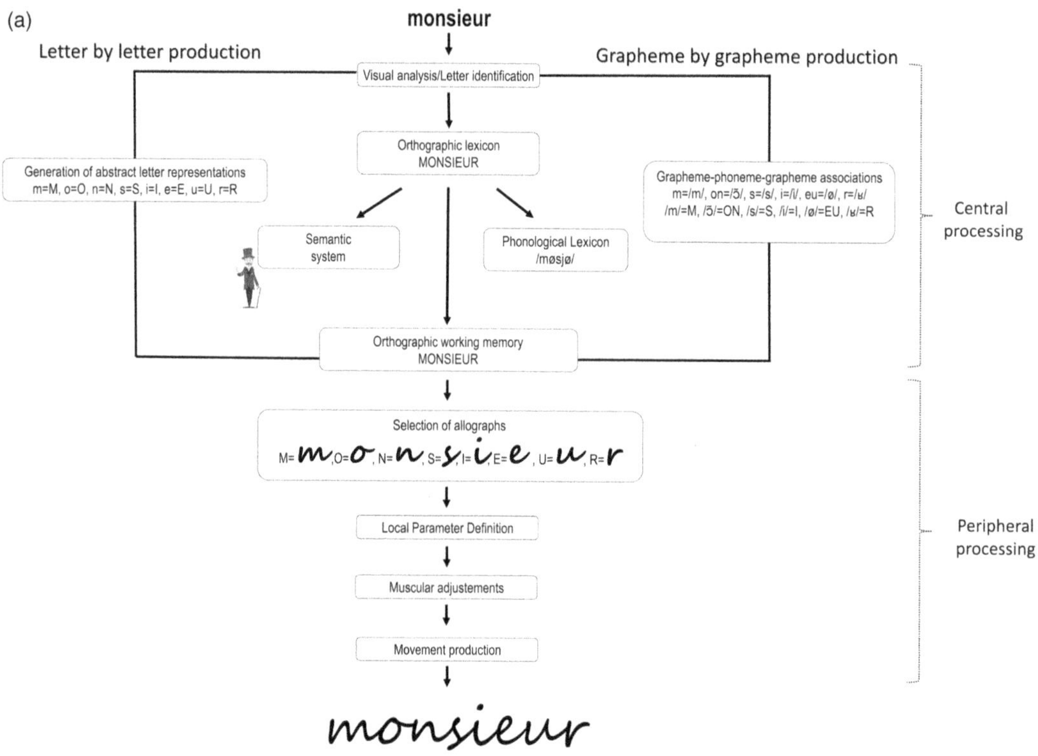

Figure 1. Lexical and sublexical processing in a copying task. Upper-case letters represent abstract letter representations. (1a) Writing the orthographically irregular word *monsieur*. Letter-by-letter production (left), lexical processing (centre), sublexical processing (right). (1b) Writing the pseudo-word *mondrote*. Letter-by-letter production (left), sublexical processing (right).

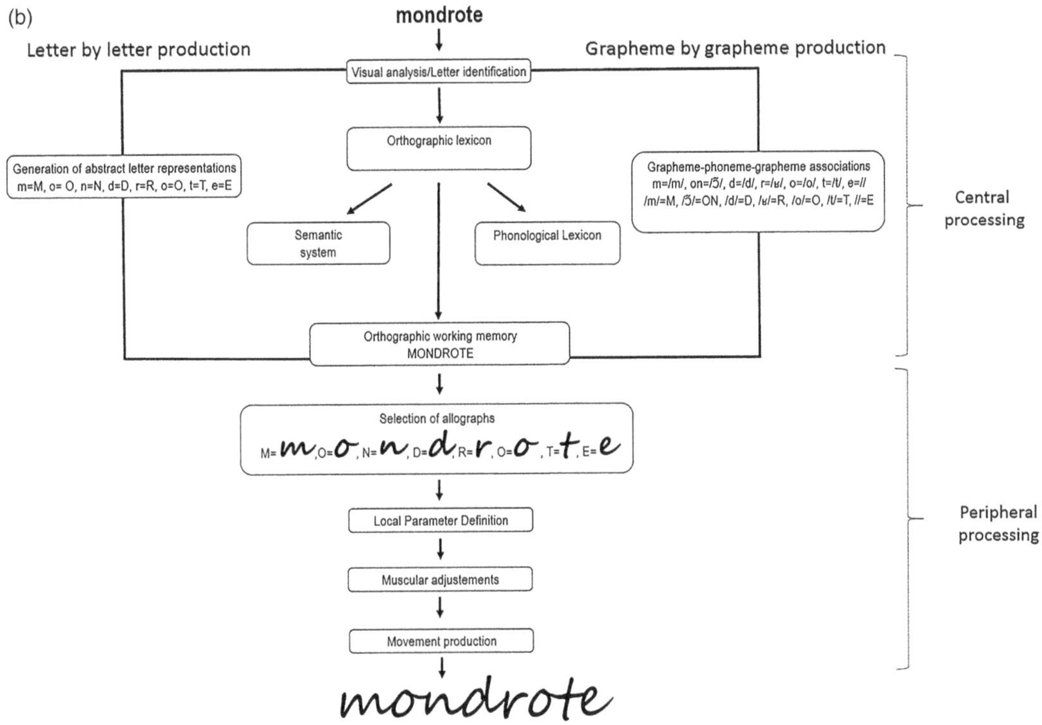

Figure 1. Continued.

should yield longer movement durations than the regular word *montagne*. Figure 1a outlines the processes involved in writing *monsieur*. Lexical processing concerns the middle upper part of the figure. The activation of the orthographic lexicon yields the correct letter sequence (i.e., MONSIEUR; upper-case letters in the figure represent abstract letter representations) and activates the phoneme sequence /møsjø/. Sublexical processing concerns the right upper part of the figure. The output is a different phoneme sequence /mɔ̃sjœʁ/. These output differences produce a conflict that does not arise with regular words. Another kind of conflict could arise between the outputs of the letter-by-letter processing strategy (Figure 1a left upper part) and sublexical processing (Figure 1a right upper part). Producing irregular words was more time consuming and produced more dysfluency than when producing regular words. So the processes that were activated before starting to write were not finished when movement production started.

Kandel and Perret (2015a) also reported word frequency effects on children's movement production. These effects can be accounted for in terms of lexical processing only (Figure 1a middle upper part). High-frequency words should be activated earlier than low-frequency words. Again, if these timing differences were limited to reading processes, they should be concluded before starting to write the words. The data revealed instead that word frequency modulated the kinematic parameters of movement production. Finally, Figure 1b outlines the sublexical processes involved in copying a pseudo-word like *mondrote* (/mɔ̃dʁɔt/). The serial nature of sublexical processing should be more time consuming than lexical processing. Roux et al.'s (2013) adult data indicated that sublexical processing was still active during the production of pseudo-words.

When lexical and sublexical processes are deficient, like in dyslexia and dysgraphia, the communication between spelling and motor processes should be altered. If the spelling–motor interaction is stronger or weaker in dyslexics than in controls, we should observe the same kind of pattern as in Kandel and Perret (2015a) and Roux et al. (2013), but with significant differences between the two groups. Yet another possibility is that the orthographic deficits of the children with dyslexia/dysgraphia are so hard to deal with that spelling and motor processes cannot interact at all. If so, the children with dyslexia/dysgraphia should write all the words in a letter-by-letter fashion (Figures 1a and 1b upper left part). We should not observe any effect of orthographic regularity, word frequency, or lexicality on any of the measures. We should also observe that selective deficits have specific impacts on writing. If a child with dyslexia/dysgraphia has selective deficits with lexical processing, this should affect word frequency and orthographic regularity effects on word writing. If the deficits only concern sublexical processing, we should observe lexicality and orthographic regularity effects on writing production. If the deficits with both procedures are too severe, the child can write the items with a letter-by-letter strategy to avoid having to deal with lexical and sublexical processing. In this case there should be no regularity, frequency, and lexicality effects.

Method

Participants

Seventeen dyslexic children participated in this experiment. They had a mean age of 11;5 years ($SD=11$ months; Appendix A). They were all native French-speakers. They received a formal diagnosis of developmental dyslexia and central dysgraphia at the "Centre Référent pour les Troubles du Langage et des Apprentissages Scolaires" (CRTLA), which is a specialized centre in language pathologies that belongs to the Paediatrics department at Grenoble Hospital. A neuropsychologist conducted a complete interview and neuropsychological screening. The children presented average intellectual performance. They exhibited a score higher than 85 in the WISC's verbal or performance batteries (Wechsler Intelligence Scale for Children IV; Wechsler, 2005) or higher than the 10th centile in the Raven Matrices (Raven, Court, & Raven, 1998). Previous to their arrival at the CRTLA, the children went through a complete clinical examination conducted by a paediatrician who excluded neurological, psychiatric, motor, and praxic disorders. Visual and auditory disorders were also excluded by a complete examination by an ophthalmologist and otolaryngologist prior to the arrival at the hospital. Co-morbidity for attentional disorders (e.g., attention-deficit/hyperactivity disorder, ADHD) were excluded. Eleven repeated or were repeating a grade. They attended school regularly. They attended different schools in the Grenoble urban area. All the dyslexic children were right-handed.

The diagnosis was established following the guidelines of the ICD-10 classification of mental and behavioural disorders (World Health Organization, 1992). The reading delay was of at least 18 months on the French standard reading text Alouette (Lefavrais, 1967; Appendix A). The children also presented deficits in reading regular and irregular words as well as pseudo-words (*z*-scores for reading scores and reading time <-1.65; Appendix B). Central dysgraphia was diagnosed on the basis of a deficient spelling performance on regular words, irregular words, and pseudo-words (*z*-scores for performance <-1.65; Appendix C). The patterns of performance determined impairment of lexical (deficits on irregular words in reading and spelling) and/or sublexical (deficits on pseudo-words in reading and spelling) processing from a neuropsychological perspective.

Each dyslexic child was matched to a child with average reading and writing skills (control group). We tried to match them as much as possible on age, gender, and language background at home. The 17 children in the control group had a mean age of 10;7 ($SD=10$). All the children except one were right-handed and native French-speakers. They attended different schools in the Grenoble urban area. They all had normal or corrected-to-normal vision and no hearing or auditory impairments, or brain lesions. All the children participated in the experiment under parental written consent. The study received approval by the Grenoble ethical committee for research in cognitive science (CERNI n° 2016-06-01-10).

Neuropsychological assessment of the dyslexic children

We did two sets of neuropsychological tests. The first set only concerned the children with dyslexia. The objective was to gather more information on the difficulties of the dyslexic children in relation to writing. They were administered tests that evaluated general performance, other skills related to writing, and language abilities. They were tested at the CRTLA. The tests lasted a whole day or a day and a half. The second set of tests concerned the dyslexic and control groups. It evaluated reading performance as well as meta-phonological abilities. The children of the control group were tested at their school in a quiet room.

General assessment

We conducted a series of tests to rule out deficits that could affect graphomotor performance during the writing task. Table 1 presents the results. Globally, all the children presented average performance for their age in all the tasks.

We used the Wechsler Intelligence Scale for Children–Fourth Edition (WISC–IV) (Wechsler, 2005) forward and backward digit span tasks to evaluate the children's working memory abilities. All the children exhibited a performance in the normal range (all *z*-score> −2σ). With the NEPSY Battery (Korkman, Kiri, & Kemp, 1998) we checked the children's auditory and visual attentional capacities. With the London Tower Test (Lussier, Guerin, Dufresne, & Lassonde, 1998) we evaluated executive functions and found efficient planning abilities. We also used other NEPSY tests to exclude disorders related to sensorimotor, visuospatial, and visuomotor abilities.

We did a letter identification task. We presented letters in the centre of the screen. They were immediately followed by a mask. The child had to name the letter as soon as possible. We varied letter presentation time: 33 ms, 50 ms, 67 ms, 84 ms, and 101 ms. There were 10 items for each presentation time. The score refers to the number of letters that were named correctly (max = 50). Dyslexic children performed in the normal range in all of these tasks. Finally, we evaluated the visuoattentional span with the global and partial report tasks that have been widely used for this kind of evaluation in France (e.g., Bosse & Valdois, 2009). There were six dyslexic children whose *z*-scores were lower than −2σ in the global report task and two dyslexic children in partial report task.

Table 1. General neuropsychological assessment of the dyslexic children.

	Dyslexic group *M* (*SD*)	Normative score standard (*SD*)	*Z*-score mean *M* (*SD*)
Working memory (WISC–IV)			
Forward digit span	4.4 (0.8)	5.5 (1.1)	−1.1 (0.7)[a]
Backward digit span	3.3 (0.5)	4 (1)	−0.7 (0.4)[a]
Attention (NEPSY)			
Auditory attention	10.7 (1.1)	10 (3)	0.3 (0.3)[a]
Visual attention	8.3 (2.3)	10 (3)	−0.3 (1.1)[a]
Executive functions (London Tower)			
Successful 1st trial (/12)	7.6 (0.9)	6.8 (1.5)	0.6 (0.5)[a]
Nb of trials (*N*)	19.6 (3.6)	22.4 (4.7)	0.7 (0.7)[a]
Mean planning time	3.6 (1.8)	5.2 (2.2)	−0.6 (0.8)[a]
Sensorimotor abilities (NEPSY)			
Finger distinction dominant hand (/18)	16.6 (0.9)		all percentile > 11°
Finger distinction non-dominant hand (/18)	15.8 (1.5)		all percentile >11°
Hand position imitation	11.1 (2.3)	10 (3)	0.4 (0.8)[a]
Tapping	8.5 (1.3)	10 (3)	−0.5 (0.4)[a]
Visuospatial abilities (NEPSY)			
Arrows	8.7 (2.3)	10 (3)	−0.4 (0.8)[a]
Orientation (/10)	7.6 (1.5)		all percentile > 26°
Visuomotor abilities (NEPSY)			
Visuomotor precision	10.6 (1.3)	10 (3)	0.2 (0.5)[a]
Cubes	11.3 (2.2)	10 (3)	0.8 (0.7)[a]
Figure copying	10.1 (1.2)	10 (3)	0 (0.4)[a]
Letter identification			
33 ms	7.6 (2.2)	6.41 (3.02)	0.39 (0.72)[a]
50 ms	9.3 (0.8)	8.23 (2.3	0.46 (0.34)[a]
67 ms	9.6 (0.7)	9.27 (1.59)	0.24 (0.44)[a]
84 ms	9.8 (0.4)	9.66 (0.99)	0.11 (0.44)[a]
101 ms	9.9 (0.3)	9.75 (0.93)	0.14 (0.36)[a]
Visuoattentional abilities			
Global report (/100)	78.24 (11.26)	85.11 (9.8)	−0.70 (1.15)[b]
Partial report (/50)	43.12 (3.76)	43.33 (0.73)	−0.29 (5.15)[c]

Note: WISC–IV = Wechsler Intelligence Scale for Children–Fourth Edition.
[a]all $z > -1.65\sigma$. [b]6 $z < -2\sigma$. [c]2 $z < -2\sigma$.

Language assessment

This series of tests aimed at evaluating the language abilities of the dyslexic children that may influence writing quantity or quality. Table 2 presents the results of this part of the assessment. The results of these tests globally revealed that the children in the dyslexic group presented important difficulties for their age with reading and spelling tasks.

Oral language

We conducted several tasks that evaluated the children's oral language capacities. We used a subset of the BALE battery (Batterie Analytique du Langage Écrit: Jacquier-Roux, Lequette, Pouget, Valdois, & Zorman, 2010) to assess phonemic discrimination and oral comprehension. We also evaluated verbal fluency. In the phonemic fluency task the child had to say as many words as possible within a minute that begin with phoneme /p/. In the semantic fluency task the child had to give as many animal names as possible within a minute. This assessment globally indicated that the children in the dyslexic group did not present any specific oral language deficit.

Written language

These tests aimed at getting more insight into the children's abilities in written language processing. The children read the "Monsieur Petit" text during one minute (BALE; Jacquier-Roux et al., 2010). This is a standard reading test used in France. All the dyslexic children presented a significant reading delay. The children's knowledge of grapheme-to-phoneme conversion rules (BALE; Jacquier-Roux et al., 2010) were within average. The written comprehension task

Table 2. Neuropsychological language assessment of the dyslexic children.

	Dyslexic group *M (SD)*		Control group 5th grade *M (SD)*	*Z*-score mean *M (SD)*
Oral language assessment				
Phonemic discrimination (/14)	13.9 (0.3)		13.81 (0.6)	0.2 (0.5)
Phonemic fluency	8.7 (3.5)		10.21 (3.37)	−0.4 (1)
Semantic fluency	15 (2.8)		14.78 (4.46)	0.1 (0.7)
Pseudo-word repetition(/92)	83.5 (6)		86.47 (2.69)	−1.1 (2.2)
Oral comprehension(/20)	16.2 (3.2)		17.54 (1.7)	−0.8 (1.9)
Written language assessment				
Text reading (Monsieur Petit)	106.9 (39.9) words (*n*)	4.8 errors (*n*)	264.2 (37.2)	−2.6 (0.7)[a]
Grapheme–phoneme conversion (/46)	39 (4.3)		43.33 (2.49)	−1.7 (1.7)[b]
Written comprehension (/10)	8.2 (1.5)		9.5 (0.9)	0.9 (1.2)[c]
Text copying	29.1 (10.2) words (*n*)		38.2 (8.7)	−1.2(0.8)[d]
Spelling abilities (Dictation)				
Regular words (/22)	15.8 (3.24)		19.58 (1.89)	−2 (1.19)
Inconsistent words (/22)	8.13 (3.91)		17.82 (3.31)	−2.93 (1.18)
Very inconsistent words (/22)	3.56 (2.8)		14.08 (4.49)	−2.34 (0.62)
Pseudo-words (/20)	14 (3.3)		18.31 (1.76)	−2.45 (1.87)

[a]all $z < -1.65$. [b]6 $z < -1.65$. [c]2 $z < -1.65$. [d]3 $z < -1.65$.

(BALE; Jacquier-Roux et al., 2010) was done correctly by most of the group. In the copying task, the child had to copy a text during three minutes (see Bosse, Kandel, Prado, & Valdois, 2014, for details on this task). Most children copied an average number of words for their age. This part of the assessment indicated that the reading deficit did not affect the ability to copy a text correctly.

Spelling abilities

We paid particular attention to the children's spelling abilities because the goal of the present study was to examine how difficulties with orthographic representation affected word writing. The individual performance of each child is presented in Appendix C. This section consisted of a series of spelling-to-dictation exercises. The first exercise was a dictation of 66 words (see Martinet & Valdois, 1999, for more details). The words were matched in length (4 to 9 letters long) and word frequency. There were 22 regular words in which phono-graphemic complexity was minimal (e.g., CONFITURE, /kɔ̃fityʁ/, jam). Ten children presented below-average spelling scores (i.e., $z < -1.65$). There were 22 inconsistent words that included one or more inconsistent graphemes (e.g., OCÉAN, /oseã/, ocean). Fourteen children presented below-average spelling scores. There were 22 very inconsistent words that included a particular orthographic feature and/or a very infrequent grapheme (e.g., TECHNIQUE, /teknik/, technical). Twelve children presented below-average spelling scores. We also asked the children to write 20 pseudo-words; 10 had two syllables (e.g., GONTRA, /gɔ̃tʁa/), and 10 had three syllables (e.g., PONTANEUR, /pɔ̃tanœʁ/). Eleven children presented below-average spelling scores. All the children presented a below-average score in at least one of the spelling tasks. Taken together, these results indicate that the spelling abilities were very impaired. We therefore consider that the children in the dyslexic group were also dysgraphic.

Neuropsychological assessment of the dyslexic and control groups

This part of the neuropsychological assessment concerned the dyslexic children and the controls. We evaluated their performance on a standard reading test, word and pseudo-word reading, and meta-phonological skills. The results of this assessment are presented in Table 3. It lasted about an hour and a half. The children could rest between tests if they were tired. The children with dyslexia did the tests at the CRTLA. These tests were done first, and, at least one week after, they did the writing experiment. The control children also did the tests and the writing experiment in two sessions. They were carried out in a quiet room at school.

To compare the two groups on all the tasks we used a Bayesian approach. In contrast with classical null-hypothesis significance testing (NHST), this method allows us to report the degree of confidence in both null (H_0) and experimental hypotheses (H_1; see Rouder, Speckman, Sun, Morey, & Iverson, 2009). If B_{10} is higher than 3, the groups present different patterns (evidence supports H_1); if B_{10} is lower than 0.33, the groups present equivalent patterns (evidence supports H_0). We applied the same approach to analysing the linguistic material (see section later, "Material for the writing experiment").

Reading performance

Text reading. We administered the French standard Alouette reading test (Lefavrais, 1967). It provides an estimation of the child's general text reading level. The children with dyslexia had at least an 18-month reading level delay, except one dyslexic child who had a 17-month delay (see Appendix A), whereas controls exhibited a reading level that corresponded to their age. The reading performance of the dyslexic children was significantly lower than that of the control group.

Word reading. The children read lists of isolated words and pseudo-words taken from the ODEDYS (Outil de Dépistage de la Dyslexie)–2 battery (Jacquier-Roux, Valdois, & Zorman, 2002). There were 20 high-frequency and 20 low-frequency regular words, 20 high-frequency and 20 low-frequency irregular words, and 40 pseudo-words that were matched to the regular words. The individual performance of each child in the dyslexic group is presented in Appendix B. The dyslexic children presented deficits on reading performance and were particularly below average on reading time. The reading performance of the dyslexic children was significantly lower than that of the control group for all the items.

Meta-phonological abilities

We used three subtests from the ODEDYS battery to evaluate the children's meta-phonological abilities (Jacquier-Roux et al., 2002). The individual performance of each child in the dyslexic group is presented in Appendix D.

Segmentation. In this task 15 words were presented auditorily. The child had to pronounce successively each phoneme in the word (e.g., FONTAINE, fountain, /f/-/ɔ̃/-/t/-/ɛ/-/n/). Only one dyslexic child was slower than controls; none of them had lower scores.

Deletion. In the phoneme deletion task, the children had to delete the initial phoneme of a word and produce the resulting pseudo-word (e.g., FONTAINE, /ɔ̃/-/t/-/ɛ/-/n/). There were 20 words. Some words began with a vocalic phoneme corresponding to a multiple letter grapheme (like OU in OUTIL, /uti/, tool) so that the omission of the first letter (instead of the first phoneme) yielded incorrect responses. Eight children with dyslexia had lower scores or were slower than controls.

Table 3. Mean reading performance and phonological skills of the children in the dyslexic and control groups.

	Dyslexics	Controls	B_{10}
Reading			
Text (Alouette)	97 (12.9)	140 (19.6)	4,426,117
HF regular words (/20)	19 (0.9)	20 (0.2)	11
Time (s)	24 (9.9)	17 (5.5)	9
LF regular words (/20)	16 (2.6)	19 (1.3)	92
Time (s)	34 (14.0)	19 (4.9)	309
HF irregular words (/20)	16 (3.0)	19 (0.8)	764
Time (s)	33 (16.1)	17 (5.0)	152
LF irregular words (/20)	10 (4.5)	17 (2.6)	21,320
Time (s)	46 (20.0)	21 (5.2)	1755
Pseudo-words matched to HF words (/20)	15 (3.5)	18 (1.4)	7
Time (s)	37 (13.9)	22 (5.8)	187
Pseudo-words matched to LF words (/20)	14 (2.4)	18 (1.0)	147,322
Time (s)	40 (17.5)	24 (5.7)	49
Phonological tasks			
Segmentation (/15)	10 (4.3)	12 (2.4)	4
Time (s)	111 (38.5)	91 (36.1)	6
Deletion (/20)	16 (3.5)	18 (1.6)	4
Time (s)	99 (27.3)	79 (21.9)	5
Acronyms (/10)	8 (1.1)	8 (1.6)	0.25
Time (s)	81 (32.5)	82 (33.9)	4

Note: Standard deviations in parentheses. If B_{10} is higher than 3, then the groups present different patterns (evidence supports H_1); if B_{10} is lower than 0.33, then the groups present different patterns (evidence supports H_0). HF = high-frequency; LF = low-frequency.

Acronyms. In this task, two words were presented successively in a one-second interval (e.g., FONTAINE then ASSIS, /asi/, seated). The words were presented auditorily. The child had to extract the first phoneme of each word and put them together to produce a syllable (/fa/). The onset of the first word was always a consonant and of the second word a vowel. There were 10 word pairs extracted from the BELEC (Batterie d'évaluation du langage écrit) battery (Mousty, Leybaert, Alegria, Content, & Morais, 1994). The two groups had equivalent scores but two dyslexics were slower than controls.

Taken together, the results of these meta-phonological tasks indicate that the children with dyslexia globally presented average performance. The reason for this is that the children with dyslexia would have been going through many years of therapy. In France, therapy focuses on meta-phonological training and a wide variety of exercises devoted to developing phonological awareness. This is considered as the most important underpinning for dyslexia (see the review presented by Saksida et al., 2016). However, despite all this training in phonological awareness tasks, phonological processing continues to be impaired in reading and spelling tasks (see Appendices B and C).

Material for the writing experiment

We constructed the linguistic material to manipulate three variables (Appendix E): orthographic regularity (irregular vs. regular words), word frequency (high-frequency words vs. low-frequency words), and lexicality (regular words vs. pseudo-words). There were 31 irregular words (e.g., *fusil*, /fysi/, rifle). A word was considered as irregular when it was an "exception word" (i.e., it is read incorrectly when applying graphophonological conversion rules) or had very low sound-to-spelling consistency (see Appendix F). We matched them to 31 orthographically regular words (e.g., *futur*, /fytyʁ/, future) with highly consistent sound-to-spelling correspondences. Since we had to compare letter duration between the regular and irregular words we tried to select words that shared at least the initial letter and up to the first three letters (e.g., *fusil* vs. *futur*). The irregular and regular words were also matched for word frequency. There were 28 high-frequency irregular and regular words and 34 low-frequency irregular and regular words. Appendix F presents all the factors for which the items were controlled. The values were extracted from Lexique 2 (New, Pallier, Brysbaert, & Ferrand, 2004): number of letters and phonemes, uniqueness point, grapheme, bigram and trigram frequencies. The developmental lexical frequency values (*U* values) were taken from Manulex (Lété, Sprenger-Charolles, & Colé, 2004) and phoneme–grapheme association from Manulex-Infra (Peereman, Lété, & Sprenger-Charolles, 2007). To compare the conditions we also used a Bayesian approach. If B_{10} is higher than 3, the differences are significant because H_1 is confirmed. If B_{10} is lower than 0.33, we have a null hypothesis (H_0). Finally, to avoid eventual supplementary processing loads due to morphological processing (Kandel, Spinelli, Tremblay, Guerassimovitch, & Álvarez, 2012), all the selected words were nouns [except for one verb in infinitive (*sortir*, to go out) and two adjectives in masculine (*meilleur*, better, and *gentil*, nice)]. Then, we matched the regular words to 31 pseudo-words (e.g., *furut*, /fyʁy/) on several aspects presented in Appendix F and syllable structure. We tried to produce pseudo-words that shared the initial letter and some of the following letters with the regular words (e.g., *furut* vs. *futur*). All the items were bi-syllabic to avoid eventual differences in the data due to syllable effects. They are frequently observed in French (Kandel & Valdois, 2006, for children; Kandel et al., 2006, for adults).

Procedure

The experiment consisted of a word and pseudo-word copying task. Although copying involves reading processes, and this might be misleading when working with children who have reading deficits, there were several reasons for using this kind of task. First, presenting the spelling of the model minimized the number of spelling errors. This was essential for measuring the movement production data. For example, to compare regular word *auteur* (/otœʁ/, author) and pseudo-word *autoir* (/otwaʁ/) for a lexicality effect, we needed the children to write *au* in the initial position in both items. Since in French /o/ = *au* and *o*, many children would have written *o* instead of *au* in a writing-to-dictation task. If a child wrote *auteur* for the word and *otoir* for the pseudo-word, we would not be able to compare *o* and *au* and would thus lose the kinematic data produced by this child. Second, presenting the letter sequence to be written on the screen and leaving it available throughout the whole trial was important because the children could write it with a letter-by-letter strategy (see Figure 1). They could write the letter sequence correctly by applying letter recognition processes. This would allow the children to write the correct spelling of the word even when they did not know it (Figure 1a left) and the correct letter sequence for pseudo-words (Figure 1b left). This gave the children the possibility of doing the task correctly irrespective of the severity of their reading and spelling deficits. If orthographic regularity, word frequency, and/or lexicality effects appear on movement production, despite the fact that the child can write the letter sequence letter by letter, lexical and sublexical processing are active during writing. This reinforces the strength of our data. Moreover, with the copying task we can observe the moments at which the children need more spelling information to finish writing the word or pseudo-word by noting when and where the child has to look up to the model to continue writing (see Bosse et al., 2014). It is also noteworthy that other tasks that have been used in spelling studies are problematic when having to work with a population of children with dyslexia. Writing to dictation involves auditory word recognition. It is well established that these processes are directly regulated by phonological processing. Since reading and spelling deficits in dyslexia/dysgraphia are related to difficulties with phonological processing (e.g., Friend & Olson, 2008; Saksida et al., 2016) we thought that a writing-to-dictation task would not be very adapted to the kind of study we intended to conduct. In addition, the study by Afonso, Suárez-Coalla, et al. (2015) with dyslexic participants indicated that writing-to-dictation and copying tasks only differ on latency measures. These authors did not observe any differences between the two tasks on the kinematic variables (writing duration and inter-letter intervals). Regarding picture naming, this kind of task is also problematic. Several studies have shown that children with dyslexia exhibit rapid automatized naming deficits. Moreover, rapid automatized naming skills may predict spelling abilities, at least in languages with deep orthographies (Savage, Pillay, & Melidona, 2008; Strattman & Hodson, 2005). There are other reasons that make the copying task the most suited to conducting this study. Sumner et al. (2014) presented a short review on the advantages of using a copying task in this kind of investigation.

The presentation of the words and pseudo-words was controlled by Ductus (Guinet & Kandel, 2010). Each trial began by a beep and a fixation point that appeared at the centre of the screen of a laptop during 100 ms. Then, the word or pseudo-word was presented in lower-case Times New Roman size 18. The child was instructed to copy the item on a lined paper (vertical limit = 0.8 cm, horizontal limit = 17 cm) stuck to the digitizer that recorded the writing movements (Wacom Intuos 2, sampling frequency 200 Hz, accuracy 0.02 mm). The paper was taken from the notebooks that the children usually use to write in when they are in school. They wrote with a special pen (Intuos Inking Pen) that is detected by the digitizer. The children had to copy the items "as they did in class". In France, most of the time reading is done in print style but writing in cursive handwriting. The children had to start writing "as soon as they could", but they could write at their "normal" speed. The words and pseudo-words remained on the screen so that the child could see the spelling of the item as many times as he or she wished during the trial. When the child finished writing the item, the experimenter clicked on a button to start the presentation of the following trial. The children became familiar with the pen and digitizer by writing their name. Then there were two practice items. The words were randomized across participants. The pseudo-words were presented in a separate block. We told the children that they would have to write "invented words". The experiment lasted between 20 to 30 minutes. The dyslexic children did the experiment at the CRTLA. The control group did the experiment in a quiet room provided by the school.

Data analysis

We analysed several measures provided by Ductus. Figure 2 presents an example of the word *flocon* (/flokɔ̃/, flake). *Latency* was the temporal interval between the presentation of the item and the moment the child started to write it on the digitizer. The beginning of the item was determined by pen pressure > 0 for the production of the first letter. The end of the word corresponded to pen pressure = 0 after the production of the last letter. We analysed movement duration and fluency. The former refers to the time it took to write the whole item whereas the latter concerns the movements' number of absolute velocity peaks produced during writing (Kandel & Perret, 2015a, 2015b; Meulenbroek & van Galen, 1989a, 1989b). Movement duration and fluency measures were taken when the pen touched the surface of the digitizer (pen pressure > 0). This excluded the moments in which the hand of the child was in air and pauses (pen pressure = 0). This detail is important because it excludes the within-word pausing time observed by Sumner et al. (2014). It means that the differences that we may observe concern the time of motor production.

The words and pseudo-words the children wrote were made up of different letters of varying stroke numbers. To compare the measures of all the items we divided total movement time and number of velocity peaks by the number of strokes in each item. The number of strokes for a given item was the sum of the strokes in each letter. The number of strokes in each letter was taken from the cursive letter segmentation presented by Meulenbroek and van Galen (1990). Therefore, for each item we obtained a mean stroke duration and mean stroke number of velocity peaks. We also counted the number of times the child looked back on the screen to see the item after the initial fixation. We named this measure *gaze lifts* (GL). The GL was also recorded by Ductus. It was marked by the experimenter by pressing the spacebar on the keyboard of the laptop. We only present gaze lifts for the dyslexic children because the controls hardly ever looked back to the model to get supplementary spelling information. This is in agreement with Kandel and Valdois (2006) who showed, with a word and pseudo-word copying task, that after Grade 3 (i.e., around age 9) typically developing children can extract enough spelling information before starting to write and do not produce gaze lifts while writing. Misspelled items were not analysed.

Statistical analysis

We excluded from the analyses the data that exceeded ±2.5 standard deviations from each participant mean across all stimuli for each condition. We then set the missing values (i.e., outliers and errors) following the procedure proposed by Slaoui and Nuel (2014). We conducted two series of analyses. First we tested for orthographic regularity, word frequency, and lexicality effects on the whole data set. The goal of this analysis was to examine (a) whether these effects were present in the whole population; and

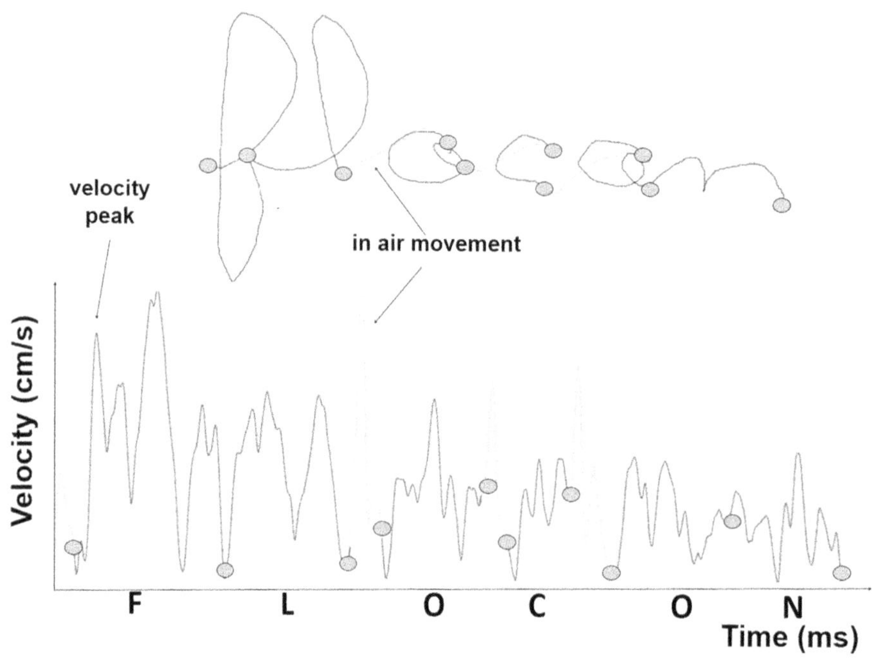

Figure 2. Example of the word "flocon" (flake, /flokɔ̃/) produced by one of the children in the control group: graphic production (above) and velocity profile (below). The black lines show the movements on the surface of the digitizer (pressure > 0); the grey lines show the movements in air (pressure = 0). The dots on the trajectory and the velocity profile indicate the beginning and end of each letter. The velocity profile shows how the word was segmented into letters. A dot corresponds to a velocity minimum and/or a point in which pressure = 0 or pressure > 0.

(b) whether these effects varied as a function of the presence or absence of dyslexia/dysgraphia. Then, we conducted supplementary analyses on the dyslexic group to get more insight into the impact of these effects on word and pseudo-word writing.

Group analyses

The statistical analyses were conducted on latencies, stroke duration, and fluency values. We ran analyses of variance (ANOVAs) using mixed-effect analyses (Pinheiro & Bates, 2000; Snijders & Bosker, 1999) with R-software (R Version 3.1.1; R Core Team, 2014). Items and participants were random-effect variables. We did two distinct analyses. The first one included orthographic regularity (regular words, irregular words), word frequency (high-frequency words, low-frequency words), and group (dyslexic, control) as fixed-effects variables. The second one concerned lexicality (regular words, pseudo-words) and group (dyslexic, control) as fixed-effects variables.

The most complex adequate adjustment model (Bar, Levy, Scheepers, & Tily, 2013)—that is, the adjustment on intercept and slopes—was included on all the models. All the mixed effects were tested using likelihood ratio tests (Pinheiro & Bates, 2000; lmerTest packages, Kuznetsova, Brockhoff, & Christensen, 2014). Goodness-of-fit for each model (Pitt & Myung, 2002) was evaluated using the Bayesian information criterion (BIC, Schwarz, 1978). The model with the most complex adjustment but with the smallest BIC was conserved. For all the fixed-effects tests, *p* values were obtained reporting *F* values on the Fisher distribution (Type III ANOVA) with error degree of freedom calculation based on Satterthwaite's approximation (Kuznetsova et al., 2014) for latency analyses. Gaze lift analysis was conducted using a generalized hierarchical mixed-effect model with a Poisson distribution. As suggested by Agresti (2013), log–linear count distribution allows accounting for multinomial data. The fixed effects were tested using likelihood ratio tests (Pinheiro & Bates, 2000; lmerTest packages, Kuznetsova et al., 2014) with BIC as criterion of goodness-of-fit (Pitt & Myung, 2002).

Individual analyses of the dyslexic group

For each child in the dyslexic group, we tested for orthographic regularity, word frequency, and lexicality effects on all the measures: 17 children × 3 effects × 3 measures = 153 *t* tests. The number of comparisons was extremely high, and the measures correlated between them, so we could not use the classical frequentialist analyses (i.e., *p*-value calculations). The risk of a dramatic increase of a Type I error was too high. We thus used the Bayesian approach (Dienes, 2016). We conducted the 153 *t* tests by calculating the Bayes factor (B_{10}). It refers to the ratio between the probability of observing an absence of effect (H_0) given the data and the probability of observing the presence of the effect (H_1) given the data (Rouder et al., 2009). Then we counted the number of times B_{10} supported H_1 (higher than 3), supported H_0 (smaller than 0.33), or was undetermined (between 3 and 0.33). We then reported a percentage of presence of each effect for the whole group. It is noteworthy that this approach tests not only the presence of an effect but also its direction.

Results

Group analyses

Orthographic regularity and word frequency

Movement duration. Fifty-eight errors (2.60%) and 45 outlier values (2.02%) were excluded from the analyses and imputed. None of the mixed-effect analyses (interaction between fixed-effect variables and random-effect variables) reached significance (χ^2s < 1). Figure 3 presents mean stroke duration values for irregular and regular words for low- and high-frequency words for each group. The orthographic regularity effect was significant: Mean stroke durations were longer for irregular than for regular words, $F(1, 58) = 11.03$, $p = .002$. Effects of lexical frequency and group did not reach significance (Fs < 1).

Orthographic regularity interacted with group, $F(1, 2136.08) = 4.93$, $p = .038$. For both groups, the durations were shorter for regular than for irregular words, but the impact of orthographic regularity was more pronounced for the dyslexic children, $t(60) = -2.73$, $p = .001$, for the dyslexic children, and $t(60) = -3.37$, $p = .001$, for the controls. None of the other interactions reached significance.

To summarize, the data revealed that writing irregular words produced longer movement durations than writing regular words. This was observed in both groups. The impact of orthographic irregularity

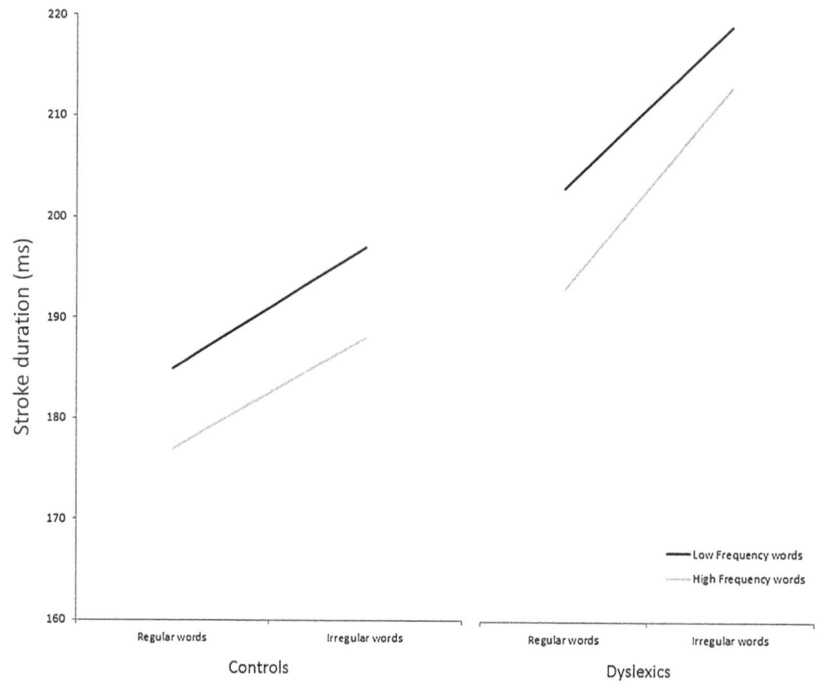

Figure 3. Mean stroke durations (ms) of the dyslexic children and controls for regular and irregular high- and low-frequency words.

was stronger for the dyslexic group than for controls. The children with dyslexia/dysgraphia had more difficulties with irregular words than did controls. The differences between the groups did not reach significance for regular words. Word frequency did not affect motor production.

Movement fluency. Fifty-eight errors (2.60%) and 26 outlier values (1.16%) were excluded from the analyses and imputed. None of the mixed-effect analyses (interaction between fixed-effect variables and random-effect variables) reached significance (χ^2s < 1). Figure 4 presents the mean number of velocity

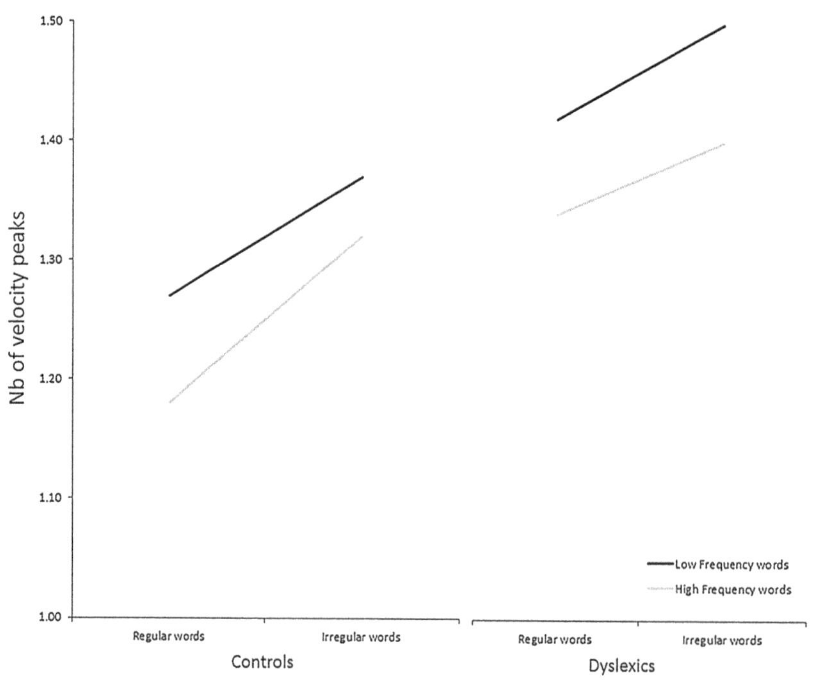

Figure 4. Mean stroke velocity peak numbers of the dyslexic children and controls for regular and irregular high- and low-frequency words. Nb = number.

peaks per stroke for irregular and regular words for low- and high-frequency words for each group. The orthographic regularity effect was significant: The writing movements were more fluent for regular than for irregular words, $F(1, 58) = 11.97$, $p = .001$. Lexical frequency and group did not reach significance ($Fs < 1$).

The interaction between orthographic regularity and group was significant, $F(1, 2132) = 4.14$, $p = .042$. For both groups, the writing movements were more fluent for regular than for irregular words, but the impact of orthographic regularity was more pronounced for the dyslexic children, $t(60) = -3.49$, $p < .001$, for the dyslexic children, and $t(60) = -2.61$, $p = .011$ for the controls. None of the other interactions reached significance.

In sum, the results indicated that writing irregular words rendered writing movements more dysfluent in the two groups. Orthographic irregularity had a stronger effect in the dyslexic group than in controls. As for movement duration, the children with dyslexia/dysgraphia exhibited more dysfluent movements when they had to write irregular words. The patterns of results for regular words were equivalent in both groups. Word frequency did not affect motor production.

Latency. Thirty-eight errors (1.70%) and 58 outlier values (2.60%) were excluded from the analyses and imputed. None of the mixed-effect analyses (interaction between fixed-effect variables and random-effect variables) reached significance (χ^2s < 1). Figure 5 presents the latency values for high- and low-frequency irregular and regular words for each group. The frequency effect was significant: Latencies were longer for low-frequency words than for high-frequency words, $F(1, 58) = 10.83$, $p = .002$. The group effect was significant: The children with dyslexia/dysgraphia presented longer latencies than the controls, $F(1, 34.01) = 7.12$, $p = .012$. Orthographic regularity did not influence latencies ($F < 1$).

The interaction between orthographic regularity and group was significant, $F(1, 2188.96) = 7.61$, $p = .006$. The simple-effect analyses indicated that orthographic regularity affected the dyslexic children, $t(60) = -2.34$, $p = .023$, but not controls ($t < 1$). None of the other interactions reached significance.

The analysis on latencies indicated that globally the dyslexic children took longer to start writing the words than the controls. Both groups had longer latencies for low-frequency than for high-frequency words. Orthographic regularity, however, only affected the dyslexic group. The dyslexic children had particular difficulties with the spelling of the irregular words. Orthographic regularity did not affect the children in the control group. This is consistent with previous studies with typically developing children of age 10 and adults, who did not exhibit

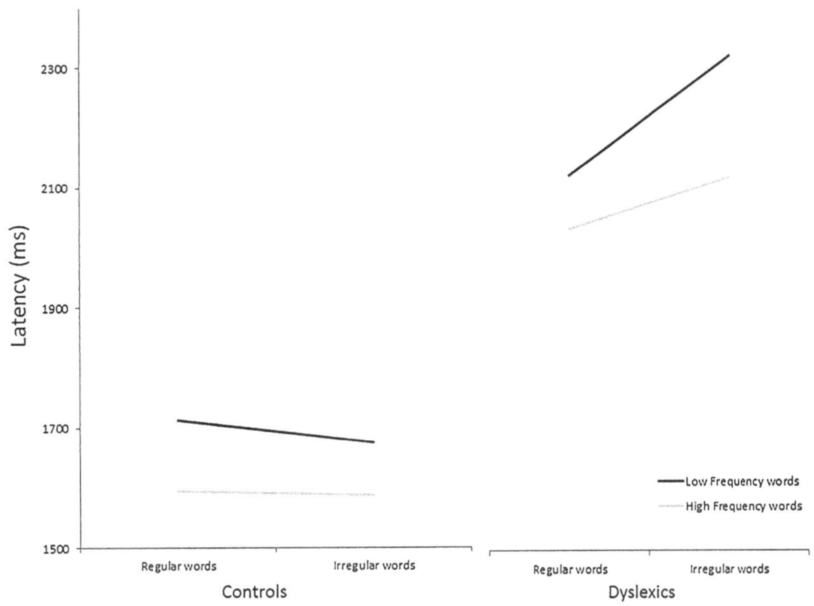

Figure 5. Latencies (ms) of the dyslexic children and controls for regular and irregular high- and low-frequency words.

Table 4. Mean number of gaze lifts of the dyslexic group for regular and irregular high- and low-frequency words, and pseudo-words.

	Words		
	High frequency	Low frequency	
Irregular words	149	221	
Regular words	98	143	241
Pseudo-words			360

latency differences when copying irregular and regular words (Kandel & Perret, 2015a; Roux et al., 2013, respectively).

Gaze lifts. The children in the control group hardly ever lifted their gaze (8%). This is in line with previous studies on word and pseudo-word copying, indicating that after ages 8–9 years, typically developing children can copy the items without looking at the model while writing (Kandel & Valdois, 2006). In contrast, the dyslexic children lifted their gaze for 20% of the words. We therefore restrict the analysis to the dyslexic group. There were 14 errors (1.25%) that were excluded from the analyses. None of the mixed-effect analyses (interaction between fixed-effect variables and random-effect variables) reached significance (χ^2s < 1). Table 4 presents the mean number of gaze lifts of the dyslexic group for regular and irregular high- (HF) and low-frequency (LF) words.

The orthographic regularity effect was significant: Irregular words produced more gaze lifts than regular words, $\chi^2(1) = 11.35$, $p < .001$. The frequency effect was significant: Low-frequency words produced more gaze lifts than high-frequency words, $\chi^2(1) = 5.67$, $p = .017$.

The gaze lift data also indicate that word frequency and orthographic regularity had an impact on the dyslexic children's performance.

Lexicality

Figure 6 presents the data produced by the children with dyslexia and controls for durations, fluency, and latency in regular words and pseudo-words.

Movement duration. Sixty errors (2.77%) and 57 outlier values (2.63%) were excluded from the analyses and imputed. None of the mixed-effect analyses (interaction between fixed-effect variables and random-effect variables) reached significance (χ^2s < 1). The interaction between lexicality and group was significant, $F(1, 1965.75) = 10.68$, $p = .001$. Stroke

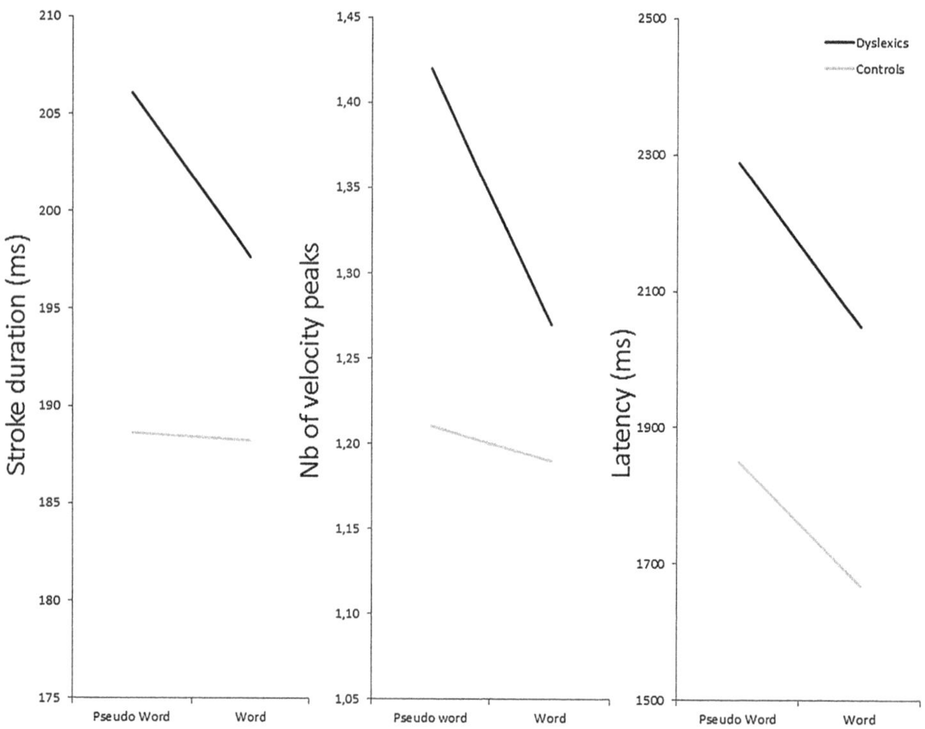

Figure 6. Mean stroke durations (ms, left), mean stroke velocity peak numbers (middle), and latencies (ms, right) of the dyslexic children and controls for regular words and pseudo-words.

durations were longer for pseudo-words than for words only for the dyslexic children, $t(60.36) = -2.91$, $p = .005$.

The data globally revealed that the children with dyslexia/dysgraphia took longer to write pseudo-words than the regular words. Lexicality did not affect motor production in the control group.

Movement fluency. Sixty errors (2.77%) and 43 outlier values (1.98%) were excluded from the analyses and imputed. None of the mixed-effect analyses (interaction between fixed-effect variables and random-effect variables) reached significance (χ^2s < 1). Figure 6 presents the mean number of velocity peaks per stroke in regular words and pseudo-words for each group. The lexicality effect was significant: Dysfluency was higher for pseudo-words than for words, $F(1, 61.10) = 10.46$, $p = .002$. The interaction between lexicality and group was significant, $F(1, 2076.02) = 229.34$, $p < .001$. We observed more dysfluency for pseudo-words than for words only for the dyslexic children, $t(59.92) = -7.68$, $p < .001$.

The results also indicated, as for duration, that the children with dyslexia/dysgraphia exhibited more dysfluency when writing pseudo-words than writing the regular words. Lexicality did not affect the control group.

Latency. Thirty-eight errors (1.75%) and 74 outlier values (3.40%) were excluded from the analyses and imputed. None of the mixed-effect analyses (interaction between fixed-effect variables and random-effect variables) reached significance (χ^2s < 1). Figure 6 presents the latency values for words and pseudo-words for each group. The group effect was significant: The latencies were higher for the dyslexic children than for the controls, $F(1, 33.01) = 4.31$, $p = .04$. The lexicality effect was significant: Latencies were higher for pseudo-words than for words, $F(1, 60.23) = 25.36$, $p < .001$. The interaction did not reach significance ($F < 1$).

The data indicated that both groups had longer latencies for pseudo-words than for words. The children with dyslexia/dysgraphia took longer than controls to start writing.

Gaze lifts. Twenty errors (1.25%) were excluded from the analyses. None of the mixed-effect analyses (interaction between fixed-effect variables and random-effect variables) reached significance (χ^2s < 1). Table 4 presents the dyslexic children's mean number of gaze lifts for regular words and pseudo-words. The lexicality effect was significant: Pseudo-words produced more gaze lifts than words, $\chi^2(1) = 14.779$, $p < .001$.

The results revealed that the children with dyslexia/dysgraphia had to look at the model more often when having to write pseudo-words than words.

Table 5. Mean stroke durations of the dyslexic children for orthographic regularity, word frequency, and lexicality.

Child	IRR	REG	1_B_{10}	HF	LF	2_B_{10}	PW	3_B_{10}
1	335	302	6.57 (H_1)	302	332	4.94 (H_1)	328	5.59 (H_1)
2	257	224	16.5 (H_1)	245	237	0.24 (H_0)	241	5.7 (H_1)
3	264	244	4.51 (H_1)	250	254	0.19 (H_0)	262	4.6 (H_1)
4	237	221	6.68 (H_1)	222	234	0.31 (H_0)	213	5.25 (H_1)
5	159	150	4.91 (H_1)	153	156	0.23 (H_0)	146	0.26 (H_0)
6	208	194	5.54 (H_1)	198	203	0.23 (H_0)	186	3.29 (H_1)
7	249	233	5.67 (H_1)	236	245	0.3 (H_0)	275	19.07 (H_1)
8	184	179	0.22 (H_0)	181	182	0.19 (H_0)	176	0.19 (H_0)
9	225	196	11.05 (H_1)	213	208	0.21 (H_0)	187	4.29 (H_1)
10	119	116	0.25 (H_0)	113	121	0.76 (Ind)	120	7.4 (H_1)
11	163	157	0.32 (H_0)	154	164	0.95 (Ind)	163	4.29 (H_1)
12	256	223	6.51 (H_1)	239	241	0.19 (H_0)	236	5.57 (H_1)
13	259	221	41.88 (H_1)	232	247	0.32 (H_0)	263	103.96 (H_1)
14	192	185	0.34 (Ind)	187	189	0.2 (H_0)	212	47.67 (H_1)
15	169	161	5.3 (H_1)	163	166	0.2 (H_0)	157	0.21 (H_0)
16	207	208	0.19 (H_0)	200	214	1.09 (Ind)	207	0.19 (H_0)
17	234	216	5.5 (H_1)	220	230	0.31 (H_0)	215	0.19 (H_0)
			70.59%			5.88%		70.59%

Note: Stroke durations in ms. Orthographic regularity: regular words (REG) versus irregular words (IRR). Word frequency: high-frequency words (HF) versus low-frequency words (LF). Lexicality: regular words (REG) versus pseudo-words (PW). 1_B_{10}: Individual comparisons between REG and IRR. 2_B_{10}: Individual comparisons between HF and LF. 3_B_{10}: individual comparisons between REG and PW. If B_{10} is higher than 3, the two data sets present different patterns (evidence supports H_1); if B_{10} is lower than 0.33, the two data sets present equivalent patterns (evidence supports H_0); if B_{10} = Ind, it is impossible to determine whether the evidence supports H_1 or H_0. The numbers below 1_B_{10}, 2_B_{10}, 3_B_{10} indicate the percentage of children in the group that presented a significant effect.

Table 6. Mean number of velocity peaks of the dyslexic children for orthographic regularity, word frequency, and lexicality.

Child	IRR	REG	1_B_{10}	HF	LF	2_B_{10}	PW	3_B_{10}
1	2.00	1.79	7.78 (H_1)	1.83	1.95	0.3 (H_0)	1.82	5.23 (H_1)
2	1.44	1.27	9.72 (H_1)	1.31	1.39	0.029 (H_0)	1.31	7.33 (H_1)
3	1.70	1.54	6.74 (H_1)	1.64	1.61	0.2 (H_0)	1.63	5.36 (H_1)
4	1.28	1.25	0.26 (H_0)	1.21	1.31	0.32 (H_0)	1.22	0.19 (H_0)
5	1.02	0.96	7.6 (H_1)	0.95	1.02	0.7 (Ind)	0.97	4.2 (H_1)
6	1.13	1.11	0.19 (H_0)	1.10	1.14	0.25 (H_0)	1.04	0.54 (Ind)
7	1.52	1.41	4.49 (H_1)	1.40	1.52	0.28 (H_0)	1.63	15.33 (H_1)
8	1.28	1.19	4.44 (H_1)	1.20	1.26	0.27 (H_0)	1.19	7.21 (H_1)
9	1.41	1.19	11.01 (H_1)	1.26	1.33	0.27 (H_0)	1.15	0.23 (H_0)
10	0.97	0.85	15.4 (H_1)	0.88	0.94	0.32 (H_0)	0.86	7.19 (H_1)
11	1.15	1.14	0.19 (H_0)	1.11	1.17	0.47 (Ind)	1.14	0.19 (H_0)
12	1.61	1.32	29.83 (H_1)	1.45	1.48	0.2 (H_0)	1.49	10.03 (H_1)
13	1.69	1.40	49.35 (H_1)	1.43	1.63	3.16 (H_1)	1.64	15.77 (H_1)
14	1.26	1.15	5.11 (H_1)	1.18	1.23	0.28 (H_0)	1.29	12.82 (H_1)
15	1.15	1.12	0.23 (H_0)	1.15	1.13	0.21 (H_0)	1.08	0.28 (H_0)
16	1.18	1.14	0.24 (H_0)	1.10	1.22	2.1 (Ind)	1.08	0.32 (H_0)
17	1.49	1.39	4.45 (H_1)	1.39	1.48	0.3 (H_0)	1.34	0.23 (H_0)
			70.59%			5.88%		58.82%

Note: Orthographic regularity: regular words (REG) versus irregular words (IRR); word frequency: high-frequency words (HF) versus low-frequency words; lexicality: regular words (REG) versus pseudo-words (PW). 1_B_{10}: Individual comparisons between REG and IRR. 2_B_{10}: Individual comparisons between HF and LF. 3_B_{10}: individual comparisons between REG and PW. If B_{10} is higher than 3, the two data sets present different patterns (evidence supports H_1); if B_{10} is lower than 0.33, the two data sets present equivalent patterns (evidence supports H_0); if B_{10} = Ind, it is impossible to determine whether the evidence supports H_1 or H_0. The numbers below 1_B_{10}, 2_B_{10}, 3_B_{10} indicate the percentage of children in the group that presented a significant effect.

Individual analyses of the dyslexic group

We investigated whether poor spelling abilities—that is, lexical and/or sublexical deficits—in dysgraphia have a specific impact on word writing. We did an individual analysis of the results to examine whether the children in the dyslexic group presented effects of orthographic regularity, word frequency, and lexicality on word and pseudo-word production. Table 5 presents the individual values for mean stroke duration. The analyses revealed that 70.59% of the children in the dyslexic group presented orthographic regularity and lexicality effects. Word frequency only affected Child 1 (5.88%).

Table 6 presents the individual values for mean number of velocity peaks. The analyses revealed that 70.59% of the children in the dyslexic group presented an orthographic regularity effect and 58.82% a lexicality effect. Word frequency only affected Child 13 (5.88%).

Table 7 presents the individual values for latencies. The analyses revealed that 76.47% of the children in the dyslexic group presented orthographic regularity, word frequency, and lexicality effects.

Table 7. Latencies of the dyslexic children for orthographic regularity, word frequency, and lexicality.

Child	IRR	REG	1_B_{10}	HF	LF	2_B_{10}	PW	3_B_{10}
1	3834	3556	6.26 (H_1)	3658	3726	6.19 (H_1)	3237	0.2 (H_0)
2	1381	1396	0.19 (H_0)	1342	1427	6.24 (H_1)	1602	9.83 (H_1)
3	2352	2228	8.24 (H_1)	2142	2412	6.54 (H_1)	2320	6.22 (H_1)
4	1733	1691	5.23 (H_1)	1703	1720	3.89 (H_1)	1723	0.36 (Ind)
5	1506	1535	0.2 (H_0)	1456	1574	8.46 (H_1)	1618	8.27 (H_1)
6	2833	2466	6.65 (H_1)	2434	2827	5.77 (H_1)	2734	5.77 (H_1)
7	3019	2769	4.35 (H_1)	2645	3099	13.41 (H_1)	2902	8.23 (H_1)
8	2425	2360	4.19 (H_1)	2508	2298	0.29 (H_0)	2546	11.83 (H_1)
9	2084	2179	0.26 (H_0)	2174	2096	0.24 (H_0)	2238	0.16 (H_0)
10	1928	1695	8.54 (H_1)	1773	1843	7.21 (H_1)	1902	9.25 (H_1)
11	1170	1036	8.59 (H_1)	1082	1120	8.21 (H_1)	954	0.24 (H_0)
12	2427	2458	0.2 (H_0)	2249	2603	6.53 (H_1)	3206	10.02 (H_1)
13	1031	907	7.62 (H_1)	988	953	0.21 (H_0)	1040	7.29 (H_1)
14	1510	1376	4.4 (H_1)	1441	1444	0.19 (H_0)	1420	8.25 (H_1)
15	2432	2273	7.26 (H_1)	2161	2510	9.99 (H_1)	2593	8.35 (H_1)
16	3594	3017	5.24 (H_1)	3216	3379	8.22 (H_1)	4141	1631 (H_1)
17	3029	2763	8.27 (H_1)	2706	3053	6.34 (H_1)	3263	9.34 (H_1)
			76.47%			76.47%		76.47%

Note: Latencies in ms. Orthographic regularity: regular words (REG) versus irregular words (IRR); word frequency: high-frequency words (HF) versus low-frequency words (LF); lexicality: regular words (REG) versus pseudo-words (PW). 1_B_{10}: Individual comparisons between REG and IRR. 2_B_{10}: Individual comparisons between HF and LF. 3_B_{10}: individual comparisons between REG and PW. If B_{10} is higher than 3, the two data sets present different patterns (evidence supports H_1); if B_{10} is lower than 0.33, the two data sets present equivalent patterns (evidence supports H_0); if B_{10} = Ind, it is impossible to determine whether the evidence supports H_1 or H_0. The numbers below 1_B_{10}, 2_B_{10}, 3_B_{10} indicate the percentage of children in the group that presented a significant effect.

We focused on the movement duration and fluency measures, because these are the indicators of modulations in motor production. We do not consider word frequency effects because they were not significant (H_0) or not concluding (Ind) for any of the children in the dyslexic group except for Child 1. This suggests, as for the control group, that word frequency does not affect movement production. The results on latencies indicate that this lexical variable affected the processes that were active before starting to write. However, it is difficult to conclude because these frequency effects can be linked to the lexical aspects involved in reading processes.

To get more insight into how lexical and sublexical deficits affected writing production, we constituted three subgroups on the basis of the spelling performance in the writing-to-dictation task (see Appendix C). Poor lexical processing was associated to deficits in writing inconsistent and/or very inconsistent words. Poor sublexical processing was associated to deficits in writing pseudo-words. Group L– concerned six children with poor lexical processing but average sublexical processing (Children 3, 7, 9, 10, 11, and 13). Group S– concerned three children with average lexical processing but poor sublexical processing (Children 5, 14, and 17). Group L–S– concerned seven children with poor lexical and sublexical processing (Children 1, 2, 4, 6, 8, 15, and 16). Child 12 was excluded from this analysis because the data on lexical spelling performance were not available.

The analyses of orthographic regularity effects revealed that in group L–, four children exhibited an orthographic regularity effect for duration and five for movement fluency. In group S–, all the children exhibited an orthographic regularity effect for movement duration and fluency. In group L–S–, five children exhibited an orthographic regularity effect for duration but only three for movement fluency. The latter could indicate that having both kinds of deficits generates more movement dysfluency. More focused studies should be conducted to confirm this pattern of results. Taken together, these results suggest that selective lexical and sublexical processing deficits affected the production of irregular words in similar ways. The children took longer and produced more dysfluent movements when producing letters that are embedded in irregular than in regular words. The analyses presented in the previous section indicated that these differences between irregular and regular words were bigger for the children in the dyslexic than in the control group. This could be due to a stronger conflict arising between the outcomes of the two routes (see Figure 1a). It seems as though the L– group activated orthographic representations of irregular words even if these representations were underspecified. This activation was sufficient to produce a mismatch with the letter string resulting from sublexical processing. The children in the S– group also did sublexical processing even when they knew it is not very efficient and the result may not be satisfactory. The outcome of this procedure did not correspond to the orthographic representation activated though lexical processing. So the L– and S– children start some kind of lexical and sublexical processing even if they know it is likely to be deficient. They do this even when they know they can write the words correctly with a letter-by-letter strategy (Figure 1a left). It seems as though the children with dyslexia/dysgraphia have more difficulties when dealing with a conflict than typically developing readers and spellers. This could explain why the children in the dyslexic group exhibited stronger orthographic regularity effects than the control group. This pattern of results could also be due to slower lexical processing for the children in the L– group and slower sublexical processing for the children in the S– group. Although we cannot exclude completely this possibility, it seems unlikely because the children should also be slower when writing regular words.

Regarding lexicality effects, all the children in group L– presented longer durations for pseudo-word than for word writing. The lexicality effect was not significant on movement fluency for two children. This result indicates that the children with deficient lexical processing did not privilege sublexical strategies during word processing. They activated orthographic representations, and this facilitated letter production with respect to pseudo-word writing. In group S–, one child exhibited a lexicality effect for movement duration and two children for fluency. In group L–S–, four children exhibited lexicality effects for duration and three for movement fluency. The results of the S– and L–S– groups are difficult to interpret because there is no clear pattern of behaviour. Some children exhibited lexicality effects. This is in line with the idea that sublexical deficits should produce strong lexicality effects (see Figure 1b right).

Our analyses do not tell us whether these lexicality effects were stronger than the ones observed in the L– group. The group analyses indicated that the differences between word and pseudo-word writing were much bigger for the children in the dyslexic than for the control group. In other cases, the children with sublexical deficits did not exhibit lexicality effects. This absence of effects could indicate that the children produced the words and pseudo-words letter by letter (see Figure 1b left).

It is also noteworthy that lexical and sublexical deficits may produce distinct patterns of writing behaviour. Child 10 presented lexical processing deficits (group L–) but average sublexical processing, in both reading and spelling tasks. This child did not exhibit orthographic regularity effects so the writing behaviour was similar for irregular and regular words. This could be due to a letter-by-letter writing strategy (Figure 1a left) for both kinds of words. However, this is unlikely because the child did exhibit lexicality effects. This means that the child wrote words faster than pseudowords. In other words, despite the lexical processing deficits, the child activated some kind of orthographic representation that facilitated word writing with respect to pseudo-word writing. The absence of regularity effects could be due to the fact that the child did not deal with the mismatch between the outcomes of the lexical and sublexical routes (Figure 1a centre and right) or did not even notice it. Further tests should be conducted to answer these questions. Child 17 presented the opposite pattern: average lexical processing but poor sublexical processing (group S–). This child exhibited orthographic regularity effects but no lexicality effects. This indicates that despite the selective sublexical impairment there is still a conflict between the outcomes of the lexical and sublexical routes (Figure 1a centre and right) that increases writing duration and produces more dysfluency. The fact that this child did not exhibit lexicality effects—that is, regular words and pseudo-words were produced the same way—suggests that this child could have adopted "lexical" strategies to process pseudo-words. In other words, the child might have associated the pseudo-words to words (e.g., processed pseudo-word *sirtar*, /siʁtaʁ/, as the word *sortir*, /sɔʁtiʁ/, to go out).

Finally, it is likely that Children 11 and 16 wrote most of the words and pseudo-words with a letter-by-letter strategy because they did not exhibit regularity and lexicality effects. This means that movement duration and dysfluency were not higher for the letters in irregular words and pseudo-words than in regular words. Moreover, these two children are the ones whose word frequency effect is impossible to determine in the Bayesian analyses, whereas it was clearly absent for the rest of the children and the control group.

Discussion

This study investigated how the difficulties that children with dyslexia and dysgraphia have with spelling processes affect movement production during word writing. We conducted an experiment in which children with diagnosed dyslexia and dysgraphia wrote words and pseudo-words on a digitizer. We compared their writing performance with a group of typically developing children without reading or spelling deficits. The results revealed that spelling processes modulated motor production in both groups of children. The spelling processes were still active while the children were writing the words. However, the impact of spelling processes was stronger for the children with dyslexia and dysgraphia. Their difficulties with orthographic processing increased movement duration and rendered writing execution more dysfluent.

The first series of group analyses indicated that irregular words increased movement duration and dysfluency for both groups of children, irrespective of word frequency. The interactions between orthographic regularity and group revealed that the children with dyslexia/dysgraphia took longer and exhibited more dysfluent movements when they wrote the irregular words. The impact of the orthographic regularity was thus stronger for the dyslexic children than controls. The gaze lift data also show that the children with dyslexia/dysgraphia had more difficulties with orthographic irregularities. They had to look up at the model more often when the spelling of the word was irregular than when it was regular. The analysis of movement duration and dysfluency also revealed that word frequency did not affect writing production. The latency and gaze lift data tell us, however, that the children with dyslexia/dysgraphia had more difficulties when they wrote low-frequency words than when they wrote high-frequency ones. We do not discuss the latency data because this measure includes reading processes. Since the children in the dyslexic group also exhibited reading deficits, it was problematic to disentangle the timing of reading and spelling processes. The latency differences could be due to reading processes, and they could be enhanced by the reading deficits. The gaze lift results show that the children with dyslexia and dysgraphia looked up at the model more when they had to write low-frequency words. This means that they did not have enough information on the spelling of the end of the word. This could be due to the activation of an orthographic representation that did not contain enough information or was unavailable. The children had to stop writing, get more spelling information, and then continue writing. So word frequency affected pausing but not movement production. This suggests that orthographic irregularities produced stronger processing loads on word writing than low-frequency words. The second series of analyses concerned lexicality. The children in the dyslexic group produced longer durations and were more dysfluent when writing pseudo-words than when writing words. Movement production for the controls was not affected by lexicality. The differences between the two groups resided on pseudo-word production. The differences on word production did not reach significance. We observed more numerous gaze lifts for pseudo-words than for words. Both groups exhibited longer latencies for pseudo-words than for words.

The analyses of individual performance in the dyslexic group revealed that most children had similar writing patterns, irrespective of their specific orthographic processing deficits. Most of them presented longer movement durations and more dysfluency when writing irregular than regular words. A majority exhibited an absence of word frequency effects. Also, an important proportion of the children with dyslexia/dysgraphia had more difficulties when writing pseudo-words. The results were very clear for movement duration and less for the fluency measure (although more than half of the children in the group exhibited a lexicality effect). In other words, most children in the dyslexic group have the same pattern of behaviour as the children in the control group. Some children of course had different writing behaviours. We observed that selective lexical processing deficits could affect irregular word writing but not pseudo-word writing. In addition, selective sublexical processing deficits affected pseudo-word writing more than irregular word writing. These selective impairments led some children to produce the words or pseudo-words with a letter-by-letter strategy. In these cases, the difficulties were so strong that the children copied the items without activating orthographic processes but rather by reproducing the letter shapes one after the other.

The results of our writing experiment revealed that spelling processes were active while the children were writing the words and pseudo-words. The difficulties with orthographic processing affected motor processing by increasing movement time and producing more dysfluency while writing. Orthographic regularity and lexicality affected the children's writing, but in diverging ways. The difficulties with irregular words were more pronounced for the children with dyslexia/dysgraphia than for controls. Writing pseudo-words generated difficulties only in the dyslexic group. Since word frequency failed to produce significant effects on word production, it is likely that what mostly affected word writing in the dyslexic group were sublexical processing deficits. However, the absence of mixed effects in the group analysis and the performance observed in individual analyses show that most of the children with dyslexia/dysgraphia presented similar writing patterns, irrespective of their specific lexical or sublexical deficits. Furthermore, the results indicate that none of the children had a complete absence of effects.

Taken together, this study provides further evidence for an interaction between central orthographic processes and peripheral motor production. It challenges both dual-route and Van Galen's (1991) accounts of word production. These conceptions cannot explain why specific spelling variables like orthographic regularity and lexicality regulate movement production. We need to get more understanding on how sublexical processing affects motor production. Moreover, the way orthographic working memory operates in this interaction is still unclear (Costa et al., 2011). This point is critical since it is widely admitted that the short-term memory system is often impaired in developmental dyslexia (Menghini, Finzi, Carlesiom, & Vicari, 2011; Ramus & Szenkovits, 2008). These questions should be addressed in future research.

The differences between the groups point to the strength of the interaction between orthographic and motor processes. The children with dyslexia and dysgraphia systematically exhibited longer and more dysfluency than controls. This means that the spelling activation spread into motor processes in a stronger manner. In other words, and this we believe is the main contribution of our study, the spelling–motor interaction was stronger for the dyslexic group than for controls. Former research with age 10 typically developing children revealed that the strength of the spelling–motor interaction differs with the nature of the spelling processes that are being activated (Kandel & Perret, 2015a). Orthographic regularity, which involves sublexical processing, affected more the children with dyslexia/dysgraphia than the controls. Adult data also indicate that the strength of the interaction depends on the position of the irregularity (Roux et al., 2013). The spelling processes remain active until the irregularity in the word is "solved". The interaction is therefore stronger when the irregularity is in final position than in word initial position because it affects the durations of all the letters that precede the irregularity (e.g., *parf* in the irregular word *parfum*, perfume vs. *m* in *monsieur*, sir; the irregularity is underlined). In the present study it seems as though the activation level of the spelling processes was high when the children with dyslexia and dysgraphia wrote the irregular words. This activation level produced interference in the peripheral processes and increased movement duration and dysfluency. Thus, deficits in sublexical processing generate more interaction. This idea is supported by the lexicality effects. Pseudo-word writing—which necessarily involves sublexical processes—produced longer movement duration and more dysfluency in the group with dyslexia/dysgraphia but not in the control group. Since a lexical variable such as word frequency did not modulate the motor component of the production process, it is likely that the strength of the spelling–motor interaction is linked to deficits with sublexical processing. The strength of the interaction could eventually explain why the writing movements of some dyslexic children often lack coordination, seem irregular, and produce low-quality handwriting. The interference of spelling processes on motor production can be so strong that certain dyslexic children are diagnosed with peripheral dysgraphia when in fact they do not have any motor or praxic disorders. So under age 10, when the automation of *motor processes* is not fully achieved, we do not observe spelling–motor interactions (Kandel & Perret, 2015a). In the case of dyslexia/dysgraphia, when the automation of *spelling processes* is not fully achieved, we observe a stronger spelling–motor interaction. It is also noteworthy that in our copying task the child had the spelling of the irregular words and pseudo-words available during the whole trial. They did not need to keep the spelling of the items active during motor production. Nonetheless, our results indicate that the children kept the spelling processes active while writing them. The children could have chosen to copy the items letter by letter. This strategy would have also led them to copy the items correctly. Our data do not support this possibility. A letter-by-letter strategy would yield equivalent movement durations and fluency values for all kinds of items: Regular word production should be equivalent to irregular word production as well as pseudo-word production. Our data do not support this hypothesis.

The stronger interaction between spelling and motor processes can be accounted for by the phonological component of word writing (Afonso & Álvarez, 2011; Qu, Damian, Zhang, & Zhu, 2011; Zhang & Damian, 2010). It is widely admitted that children with dyslexia have serious difficulties with phonological processes (e.g., Saksida et al., 2016) so it is not surprising that the children in the dyslexic group had trouble with irregular words. They are similar to the exception words or the words that present more inconsistent phoneme-to-grapheme correspondences used in the reading and spelling studies on dyslexia. Lexical status also affected the children throughout the writing process since they had difficulties in writing pseudo-words. This confirms previous research in dyslexia indicating that dealing with new letter strings represents an extremely heavy cognitive load (e.g., Brady & Shankweiler, 1991; Snowling, Goulandris, Bowbly, & Howell, 1986). The results on word frequency require further investigation because this variable did not yield significant differences on movement production. This is consistent with a developmental study by Afonso, Suárez-Coalla, González-Martín, and Cuetos (2017) in Spanish. They observed that word frequency affected writing durations in second-graders (age 7) but were equivalent for fourth- and sixth-graders (ages 9 and 11, respectively). The latter were the same age as the children in our study (ages 10–11). This is also in agreement with Afonso, Suárez-Coalla, et al.'s (2015) adult data. These authors did not observe a frequency effect on writing durations or inter-letter intervals. Moreover, Afonso et al.

(2017) reported that infrequent words yielded higher written latencies than frequent words, as in our study. They suggested that the effect of lexical processing loads on motor processing decreases as the children grow up and may even disappear with automation. It should finally be pointed out that we observed that low-frequency words produced more gaze lifts than high-frequency words. This is in line with previous research indicating that children with dyslexia have more difficulties in accessing the spelling of low- than high-frequency words (Rüsseler, Probst, Sönke, & Münte, 2003).

Our results could be interpreted as being in contradiction to those presented by Sumner et al. (2012, 2014). Their studies revealed that children with dyslexia seem slower writers but that in fact they are not. They seem slower because they pause more often and during longer periods. When the authors focused only on movement production and excluded pausing time, the execution speed of the children with dyslexia was equivalent to the one observed for the age-matched controls. We believe that Sumner et al.'s (2012, 2014) results are not contradictory but rather complementary to our results. Sumner et al. examined text composition in the 2012 study and sentence copying in 2014. Text composition and sentence processes involve orthographic processes but also many other kinds of processing that might have affected or interfered with movement time and masked eventual effects of spelling deficiencies. They could be due to text planning and sentence processing like subject–verb agreements or simply getting more information on the end of the sentence. In addition, since the compositions were extremely variable from one child to another, movement time is difficult to compare. We therefore restrict our discussion to the Sumner et al. (2014) sentence copying study. They observed that the children with dyslexia and the age-matched peers exhibited equivalent movement speed. As we mentioned in the Introduction, one might argue that this corresponds to a null effect or H_0, which is a Type II error. Another reason why Sumner et al. (2014) did not find speed differences between the two groups might be because they analysed the production of only one sentence containing a total of nine words. It is likely that we observed differences because our analysis concerned 62 words and 31 pseudo-words, making a total 93 items, which is much more writing material. Our study also manipulated the difficulty of the words to be written (irregular words and pseudo-words). We would like to point out that in our experiment, the differences between the groups were restricted to the interactions with orthographic regularity and lexicality. The main effects of group were only observed for latency—that is, for the processes that took place before starting to write. This means that globally speaking, the children with dyslexia/dysgraphia did not take longer than the controls or were more dysfluent. They needed more time and were more dysfluent when having to write letter sequences—irregular words and pseudo-words—that required more sublexical processing.

Regarding the pause analysis, our results are in line with the findings by Sumner et al. (2014). They showed that the children with dyslexia produced longer within-word pauses than the age-matched group. These pauses were probably due to their need for more information on the spelling of the words. Our data on gaze lifts are in agreement with these results since the gaze lifts were produced to extract information on the spelling of the end of the word or pseudo-word. Many of the between-word pauses that Sumner et al. observed during sentence writing could be related to the time the children took to activate spelling information before they started to write these words. These pauses were longer for the dyslexic group than for the age-matched peers. In our study, we measured latency to quantify the time lapse before movement initiation. We found longer latencies in the dyslexic group than in controls.

In conclusion, the present study provides evidence that spelling deficits render the spelling–motor interaction stronger. The impairments with sublexical processing spread onto motor execution processes. The difficulties with the phonological component of orthographic processing slow down the writing movements and make them more dysfluent. These modulations of motor *processes* affect the handwriting *product*, as Rosenblum and colleagues have observed with children with peripheral dysgraphia (Rosenblum, Weiss, & Parush, 2003). This may account for bad quality, irregular, and sometimes illegible writing that is often observed in children with dyslexia (Valdois et al., 2011). Finally, the strength of the interaction between the spelling and motor processes in word writing may explain why the graphomotor component of handwriting has such an important impact on text composition or note taking (Jones, 2004 for children; Connelly, Campbell, MacLean, & Barnes, 2006, for college students).

Acknowledgements

We acknowledge the financial support from the Institut Universitaire de France (attributed to Sonia Kandel); and the Agence Nationale de la Recherche [grant number ANR ECRIRE 14-C30-0013-01] (attributed to Sonia Kandel and Cyril Perret); as well as the technical support from the Poitiers MSHS (Maison des Sciences de l'Homme et de la Société) [grant number USR-CNRS 3565].

Disclosure statement

No potential conflict of interest was reported by the authors.

References

Abbott, R., Berninger, V., & Fayol, M. (2010). Longitudinal relationships of levels of language in writing and between writing and reading in grades 1 to 7. *Journal of Educational Psychology, 102*, 281–298.

Abbott, R. D., & Berninger, V. W. (1993). Structural equation modeling of relationships among developmental skills and writing skills in primary and intermediate grade writers. *Journal of Educational Psychology, 85*, 478–508.

Afonso, O., & Álvarez, C. J. (2011). Phonological effects in handwriting production: Evidence from the implicit priming paradigm. *Journal of Experimental Psychology: Learning, Memory, and Cognition, 37*, 1474–1483.

Afonso, O., Álvarez, C. J., & Kandel, S. (2015). Effects of grapheme-to-phoneme probability on writing durations. *Memory & Cognition, 43*, 579–592.

Afonso, O., Suárez-Coalla, P., & Cuetos, F. (2015). Spelling impairments in spanish dyslexic adults. *Frontiers in Psychology, 6*, 3. doi:10.3389/fpsyg.2015.00466

Afonso, O., Suárez-Coalla, P., González-Martín, N., & Cuetos, F. (2017). The impact of word frequency on peripheral processes during handwriting: A matter of age. *The Quarterly Journal of Experimental Psychology*, 13, 1–9.

Agresti, A. (2013). *Categorical data analysis* (3rd ed.). New York, NY: Wiley.

Álvarez, C. J., Cottrell, D., & Afonso, O. (2009). Writing dictated words and picture names: Syllabic boundaries affect execution in spanish. *Applied Psycholinguistics, 30*, 205–223.

Angelelli, P., Judica, A., Spinelli, D., Zoccolotti, P., & Luzzati, C. (2004). Characteristics of writing disorders in Italian dyslexic children. *Cognitive and Behavioral Neurology, 17*, 18–31.

Angelelli, P., Notarnicola, A., Judica, A., Zoccolotti, P., & Luzzati, C. (2010). Spelling impairments in Italian dyslexic children: Phenomenological changes in primary school. *Cortex, 46*, 1299–1311.

Bar, D. J., Levy, R., Scheepers, C., & Tily, H. J. (2013). Random effects structure for confirmatory hypothesis testing: Keep it maximal. *Journal of Memory and Language, 68*, 255–278.

Berninger, V. (2006). A developmental approach to learning disabilities. In I. Siegel, & A. Renninger (Eds.), *Handbook of child psychology, child psychology and practice. IV* (pp. 420–452). New York, NY: John Wiley & Sons.

Berninger, V., Abbott, R., Thomson, J., & Raskind, W. (2001). Language phenotype for reading and writing disability: A family approach. *Scientific Studies of Reading, 5*, 59–106.

Berninger, V., Nielsen, K., Abbott, R., Wijsman, E., & Raskind, W. (2008). Writing problems in developmental dyslexia: Under-recognized and under-treated. *Journal of School Psychology, 46*, 1–21.

Berninger, V., Richards, T., & Abbott, R. (2015). Differential diagnosis of dysgraphia, dyslexia, and OWL LD: Behavioral and neuroimaging evidence. *Reading and Writing. An Interdisciplinary Journal, 28*, 1119–1153.

Berninger, V., & Winn, W. (2006). Implications of advancements in brain research and technology for writing development, writing instruction, and educational evolution. In C. MacArthur, S. Graham, & J. Fitzgerald (Eds.), *Handbook of writing research* (pp. 96–114). New York, NY: Guilford.

Berninger, V., Yates, C., Cartwright, A., Rutberg, J., Remy, E., & Abbott, R. (1992). Lower level developmental skills in beginning writing. *Reading and Writing. An Interdisciplinary Journal, 4*, 257–280.

Bosse, M. L., Kandel, S., Prado, C., & Valdois, S. (2014). Does visual attention span relate to eye movements during reading and copying? *International Journal of Behavioral Development, 38*, 81–85.

Bosse, M. L., & Valdois, S. (2009). Influence of the visual attention span on child reading performance: A cross sectional study. *Journal of Research in Reading, 32*, 230–253.

Brady, S., & Shankweiler, D. (1991). *Phonological processes in literacy*. Hillsdale, NJ: Erlbaum.

Brun-Henin, F., Velay, J.-L., Beecham, Y., & Cariou, S. (2013). Troubles d'écriture et dyslexie: revue théorique, aspects cliniques et approche expérimentale. *Développements*, 4–27.

Buchwald, A., & Falconer, C. (2014). Cascading activation from lexical processing to letter-level processing in written word production. *Cognitive Neuropsychology, 31*, 606–621.

Caramazza, A., & Miceli, G. (1990). The structure of graphemic representations. *Cognition, 37*, 243–297.

Chilosi, A. M., Brizzolara, D., Lami, L., Pizzoli, C., Gasperini, F., Pecini, C., … Zoccolotti, P. (2009). Reading and spelling disabilities in children with and without a history of early language delay: A neuropsychological and linguistic study. *Child Neuropsychology, 15*(6), 582–604.

Connelly, V., Campbell, S., MacLean, M., & Barnes, J. (2006). Contribution of lower order skills to the written composition of college students with and without dyslexia. *Developmental Neuropsychology, 29*, 175–196.

Connelly, V., Dockrell, J. E., & Barnett, J. (2005). The slow handwriting of undergraduate students constrains overall performance in exam essays. *Educational Psychology, 25*, 99–107.

Costa, V., Fischer-Baum, S., Capasso, R., Miceli, G., & Rapp, B. (2011). Temporal stability and representational distinctiveness: Key functions of orthographic working memory. *Cognitive Neuropsychology, 28*, 338–62.

Delattre, M., Bonin, P., & Barry, C. (2006). Written spelling to dictation: Sound-to-spelling regularity affects both writing latencies and durations. *Journal of Experimental Psychology: Learning, Memory, and Cognition, 32*, 1330–1340.

Di Betta, A. M., & Romani, C. (2006). Lexical learning and dysgraphia in a group of adults with developmental dyslexia. *Cognitive Neuropsychology*, 23, 376–400.

Dienes, Z. (2016). How Bayes factors change scientific practice. *Journal of Mathematical Psychology, 72*, 78–89.

Friend, A., & Olson, R. K. (2008). Phonological spelling and reading deficits in children with spelling disabilities. *Scientific Studies of Reading, 12*(1), 90–105.

Frith, U. (1986). A developmental framework for developmental dyslexia. *Annals of Dyslexia, 36*, 67–81.

Goulandris, N. K., & Snowling, M. (1991). Visual memory deficits: A plausible cause of developmental dyslexia? Evidence from a single case study. *Cognitive Neuropsychology, 8*, 127–154.

Graham, S., Berninger, V., Abbott, R., Abbott, S., & Whitaker, D. (1997). The role of mechanics in composing of elementary school students: A new methodological approach. *Journal of Educational Psychology, 89*(1), 170–182.

Graham, S., Berninger, V., Weintraub, N., & Schafer, W. (1998). Development of handwriting speed and legibility in grades 1–9. *The Journal of Educational Research, 92*, 42–52.

Guinet, E., & Kandel, S. (2010). Ductus: A software package for the study of handwriting production. *Behavior Research Methods, 42*, 326–332.

Halsband, U., & Lange, R. K. (2006). Motor learning in man: A review of functional and clinical studies. *Journal of Physiology, 99*, 414–424.

Hanley, J. R., Hastie, K., & Kay, J. (1992). Developmental surface dysLexia and dysgraphia: An orthographic processing impairment. *Quarterly Journal of Experimental Psychology, 94*, 34–43.

Hayes, J. R. (2012). Modeling and remodeling writing. *Written Communication, 29*, 369–388.

Jacquier-Roux, M., Lequette, C., Pouget, G., Valdois, S., & Zorman, M. (2010). *Batterie Analytique du Langage Écrit*. Grenoble: Laboratoire cogni-sciences, Laboratoire de Psychologie et NeuroCognition.

Jacquier-Roux, M., Valdois, S., & Zorman, M. (2002). *Odedys: Outil de dépistage des dyslexies*. Grenoble: Laboratoire cogni-sciences, IUFM de Grenoble.

Jones, D. (2004). *Automaticity of the transcription process in the production of written text*. (Doctor of philosophy thesis). Graduate School of Education, University of Queensland, Australia.

Kandel, S., Álvarez, C. J., & Vallée, N. (2006). Syllables as processing units in handwriting production. *Journal of Experimental Psychology: Learning, Memory, and Cognition, 32*, 18–31.

Kandel, S., Peereman, R., & Ghimenton, A. (2013). Further evidence for the interaction between central and peripheral processes: The impact of double letters in writing English words. *Frontiers in Psychology (Research Topic "Writing Words : From Brain to Hand(s)" – Section Cognitive Science), 4*, 729.

Kandel, S., Peereman, R., & Ghimenton, A. (2014). How do we code the letters of a word when we have to write it? Investigating double letter representation in French. *Acta Psychologica, 148*, 56–62.

Kandel, S., Peereman, R., Grosjacques, G., & Fayol, M. (2011). For a psycholinguistic model of handwriting production: Testing the syllable-bigram controversy. *Journal of Experimental Psychology: Human Perception and Performance, 37*, 1310–1322.

Kandel, S., & Perret, C. (2015a). How does the interaction between spelling and motor processes build up during writing acquisition? *Cognition, 136*, 325–336.

Kandel, S., & Perret, C. (2015b). How do movements to produce letters become automation during writing acquisition? Investigating the development of motor anticipation. *International Journal of Behavioral Development, 39*, 113–120.

Kandel, S., & Spinelli, E. (2010). Processing complex graphemes in handwriting production. *Memory & Cognition, 38*(6), 762–770.

Kandel, S., Spinelli, E., Tremblay, A., Guerassimovitch, H., & Álvarez, C. J. (2012). Processing prefixes and suffixes in handwriting production. *Acta Psychologica, 140*, 187–195.

Kandel, S., & Valdois, S. (2006). Syllables as functional units in a copying task. *Language and Cognitive Processes, 21*, 432–452.

Korkman, M., Kiri, U., & Kemp, S. (1998). *Nepsy: A developmental neuropsychological assessment*. San Antonio, TX: The Psychological Corporation.

Kuznetsova, A., Brockhoff, P. B., & Christensen, R. H. B. (2014). *Lmertest: Tests for random and fixed effects for linear mixed effect models* (lmer objects of lme4 packages. Retrieved from URL http:// CRAN.R-project.org/package = lmerTest/

Lambert, E., Alamargot, D., Larocque, D., & Caporossi, G. (2011). Dynamics of the spelling process during a copy task: Effects of regularity and frequency. *Canadian Journal of Experimental Psychology/Revue Canadienne de Psychologie Expérimentale, 65*(3), 141–150.

Lambert, E., Sausset, S., & Rigalleau, F. (2015). The ortho-syllable as a processing unit in handwriting: The mute e effect. *Reading and Writing, 28*, 683–698.

Lefavrais, P. (1967). *Test de l'Alouette* [The Lark test] (2nd ed.). Paris: Editions du Centre de Psychologie Appliquée.

Lété, B., Sprenger-Charolles, L., & Colé, P. (2004). Manulex: A grade-level lexical database from French elementary school readers. *Behavior Research Methods, Instruments, & Computers, 36*, 156–166.

Lussier, F., Guerin, F., Dufresne A., & Lassonde, M. (1998). Etude normative developpementale des fonctions executives: la tour de Londres. *ANAE*, 47, 42–52.

Maeland, A. F., & Karlsdottir, R. (1991). Development of reading, spelling, and writing skills from third to sixth grade in normal and dysgraphic children. In J. Wann, A. M. Wing, & N. Søvik (Eds.), *Development of graphic skills* (pp. 179–189). London: Academic Press.

Maggio, S., Lété, B., Chenu, F., Jisa, H., & Fayol, M. (2012). Tracking the mind during writing: Immediacy, delayed, and anticipatory effects on pauses and writing rate. *Reading & Writing: An Interdisciplinary Journal, 25*, 2131–2151.

Martinet, C., & Valdois, S. (1999). L'apprentissage de l'orthographe d'usage et ses troubles dans la dyslexie developpementale de surface. / learning to spell words: Difficulties in developmental surface dyslexia. *L'Année Psychologique, 99*, 577–622.

Martlew, M. (1992). Handwriting and spelling: Dyslexic children's abilities compared with children of the same chronological age and younger children of the same spelling level. *British Journal of Educational Psychology*, 62, 375–390.

Medwell, J., & Wray, D. (2007). Handwriting: What do we know and what do we need to know? *Literacy, 41*, 10–15.

Menghini, D., Finzi, A., Carlesiom, G. A., & Vicari, S. (2011). Working memory impairment in children with developmental dyslexia: Is it just a phonological deficit? *Developmental Neuropsychology, 36*, 199–213.

Meulenbroek, R.G.J., & van Galen, G.P. (1989a). The acquisition of skilled handwriting: Discontinuous trends in kinematic variables. In A. M. Colley, J. R. Beech (Eds.) *Cognition and action in skilled behaviour* (pp. 93–101). North Holland: Elsevier Science Publishers BV.

Meulenbroek, R. G. J., & van Galen, G. P. (1989b). The production of connecting strokes in cursive writing: Developing co-articulation in 8 to 12 year-old children. In R Plamondon, CY Suen, & ML Simner (Eds.), *Computer recognition and human production of handwriting* (pp. 105–118). Singapore: World Scientific.

Meulenbroek, R. G. J., & van Galen, G. P. (1990). Perceptual-motor complexity of printed and cursive letters. *The Journal of Experimental Education, 58*, 95–110.

Mojet, W. (1991). Characteristics of developing handwriting skills in elementary education. In J Wann, A Wing, & N Sovik (Eds.), *Development of graphic skills* (pp. 53–75). London: Academic Press.

Mortimore, T., & Crozier, R. (2006). Dyslexia and difficulties with study skills in higher education. *Studies in Higher Education, 31*, 235–251.

Mousty, P., Leybaert, J., Alegria, J., Content, A., & Morais, J. (1994). Belec: Une batterie d'évaluation du langage écrit et de ses troubles. In J. Grégoire, & B. Piérart (Eds.), *Evaluer les troubles de la lecture : les nouveaux modèles théoriques et leurs implications diagnostiques* (pp. 127–145). Bruxelles: De Boeck.

Nation, K., Angell, P., & Castles, A. (2007). Orthographic learning via self-teaching in children learning to read English: Effects of exposure, durability, and context. *Journal of Experimental Child Psychology, 96*, 71–84.

New, B., Pallier, C., Brysbaert, M., & Ferrand, L. (2004). Lexique 2: A new French lexical database. *Behavior Research Methods, Instruments, & Computers, 36*, 516–524.

Nicolson, R. I., Fawcett, A. J., & Dean, P. (2001). Dyslexia, development and the cerebellum. *Trends in Neurosciences, 24*, 515–16.

Overvelde, A., & Hulstijn, W. (2011). Handwriting development in grade 2 and grade 3 primary school children with normal, at risk, or dysgraphic characteristics. *Research in Developmental Disabilities, 32*, 540–548.

Paz-Villagran, V., Gilhodes, J.-C., & Velay, J.-L. (2013). Les enfants dysgraphiques sont-ils réellement plus lents que les autres? *Développements*, 38–44.

Peereman, R., Lété, B., & Sprenger-Charolles, L. (2007). Manulex-infra: Distributional characteristics of grapheme-phoneme mappings, and infralexical and lexical units in child-directed written material. *Behavior Research Methods, 39*, 579–589.

Pinheiro, J. C., & Bates, D. M. (2000). *Mixed-effects models in S and S-PLUS*. New York, NY, USA: Springer.

Pitt, M. A., & Myung, I. J. (2002). When a good fit can be bad. *Trends in Cognitive Sciences, 6*, 421–425.

Qu, Q., Damian, M. F., Zhang, Q., & Zhu, X. (2011). Phonology contributes to writing: Evidence from written production in nonalphabetic language. *Psychological Science, 22*, 1107–1112.

Ramus, F. (2003). Developmental dyslexia: Specific phonological deficit or general sensorimotor dysfunction? *Current Opinion in Neurobiology, 13*, 212–218.

Ramus, F., Marshall, C. R., Rosen, S., & van der Lely, H. K. J. (2013). Phonological deficits in specific language impairment and developmental dyslexia: Towards a multidimensional model. *Brain: A Journal of Neurology, 136*, 630–645.

Ramus, F., & Szenkovits, G. (2008). What phonological deficit? *The Quarterly Journal of Experimental Psychology, 61*, 129–141.

Rapp, B., Epstein, C., & Tainturier, M.-J. (2002). The integration of information across lexical and sublexical processes in spelling. *Cognitive Neuropsychology, 19*, 1–29.

Raven, J. C., Court, J. H., & Raven, J. (1998). *Progressive matrices standard (PM38)*. Paris: EAP.

R Core Team. (2014). *R: A language and environment for statistical computing. R foundation for statistical computiong.* Vienna, Austria. Retrieved from URL http://www.R-project.org/

Rodriguez, C., & Villaroel, R. (2016). Predicting handwriting difficulties through spelling processes. *Journal of Learning Disabilities, 50*(5), 504–510.

Rosenblum, S., Weiss, P. L., & Parush, S. (2003). Product and process evaluation of handwriting difficulties: A review. *Educational Psychology Review, 15*, 41–81.

Rouder, J. N., Speckman, P. L., Sun, D., Morey, R. D., & Iverson, G. (2009). Bayesian t-tests for accepting and rejecting the null hypothesis. *Psychonomic Bulletin and Review, 16*, 225–237.

Roux, S., McKeeff, T. J., Grosjacques, G., Afonso, O., & Kandel, S. (2013). The interaction between central and peripheral processes in handwriting production. *Cognition, 127*, 235–241.

Rüsseler, J., Probst, S., Sönke, J., & Münte, T. (2003). Recognition memory for high- and Low-frequency words in adult normal and dyslexic readers: An event-related brain potential study. *Journal of Clinical and Experimental Neuropsychology (Neuropsychology, Development and Cognition: Section A), 25*, 815–829.

Saksida, A., Ianuzzi, S., Bogliotti, C., Chaix, Y., Démonet, J.-F., … Ramus, F. (2016). Phonological skills, visual attention span, and visual stress in developmental dyslexia. *Developmental Psychology, 52*, 1503–1516.

Sausset, S., Lambert, E., Olive, T., & Larocque, D. (2012). Processing of syllables during handwriting: Effects of graphomotor constraints. *The Quarterly Journal of Experimental Psychology, 65*, 1872–1879.

Savage, R., Pillay, V., & Melidona, S. (2008). Rapid serial naming is a unique predictor of spelling in children. *Journal of Learning Disabilities, 41*(3), 235–250.

Schmidt, R. A., & Lee, T. D. (2005). *Motor control and learning: A behavioral emphasis*. Champaign, IL: Human Kinetics.

Schmidt, R. a. R. (1975). A schema theory of discrete motor skill learning. *Psychological Review, 82*(4), 225–260.

Schwarz, G. (1978). Estimating the dimension of a model. *The Annals of Statistics, 6*, 461–464.

Seymour, P. H., Aro, M., & Erskine, J. M. (2003). Foundation literacy acquisition in European orthographies. *British Journal of Psychology, 94*(2), 143–174.

Share, D. L. (1995). Phonological recoding and self-teaching: Sine qua non of reading acquisition. *Cognition, 55*, 151–218.

Share, D. L. (1999). Phonological recoding and orthographic learning: A direct test of the self-teaching hypothesis . *Journal of Experimental Child Psychology, 72*, 95–129.

Slaoui, Y., & Nuel, G. (2014). Parameter estimation in a hierarchical random intercept model with censored response: An approach using a SEM algorithm and gibbs sampling. *Sankhy¯a : The Indian Journal of Statistics, 76*, 210–233.

Snijders, T. A. B., & Bosker, R. J. (1999). *Multilevel analysis: An Introduction to basic and advanced multilevel modeling*. London: Sage Publishers.

Snowling, M. J., Goulandris, N., Bowbly, M., & Howell, P. (1986). Segmentation and speech perception in relation to reading skill: A developmental analysis. *Journal of Experimental Child Psychology, 41*, 489–507.

Søvik, N., & Arntzen, O. (1986). A comparative study of the writing/spelling performances of "normal", dyslexic, and dysgraphic children. *European Journal of Special Needs Education, 1*, 85–101.

Strattman, K., & Hodson, B. W. (2005). Variables that influence decoding and spelling in beginning readers. *Child Language Teaching and Therapy, 21*, 165–190.

Sumner, E., Connelly, V., & Barnett, A. L. (2012). Children with dyslexia are slow writers because they pause more often and not because they are slow at handwriting execution. *Reading & Writing: An Interdisciplinary Journal, 40*, 1441–1447.

Sumner, E., Connelly, V., & Barnett, A. L. (2014). The influence of spelling ability on handwriting production: Children With and without dyslexia. *Journal of Experimental Psychology: Learning, Memory, and Cognition, 40*, 1441–1447.

Valdois, S., Bidet-Ildei, C., Lassus-Sangosse, D., Reilhac, C., N'Guyen, M. A., Guinet, E., & Orliaguet, J. P. (2011). A visual processing but no phonological disorder in a child with mixed dyslexia. *Cortex, 47*, 1197–1218.

Van Galen, G. P. (1991). Handwriting: Issues for a psychomotor theory. *Human Movement Science, 10*, 165–191.

Wechsler, D. (2005). *WISC-IV: Echelle d'Intelligence de Wechsler pour Enfants* [Wechsler Intelligence Scale for Children] (4th ed.). Paris: Editions du Centre de Psychologie Appliquée.

Wolff, P. H., Cohen, C., & Drake, C. (1984). Impaired motor timing control in specific reading retardation. *Neuropsychologia, 22*, 587–600.

World Health Organization. (1992). *The ICD-10 classification of mental and behavioural disorders: Clinical descriptions and diagnostic guidelines*. Geneva: Author.

Zhang, Q., & Damian, M. F. (2010). Impact of phonology on the generation of handwritten responses: Evidence from picture-word interference tasks. *Memory & Cognition, 38*, 519–528.

Appendix A

Chronological age and lexical age determined by performance on the French standard reading text "Alouette"

Child	Chronological age (months)	Lexical age (months)	Reading delay (months)
1	120	83	−18
2	136	86	−50
3	130	92	−38
4	122	87	−35
5	140	97	−43
6	154	99	−55
7	150	90	−60
8	124	91	−33
9	121	99	−22
10	146	122	−24
11	147	130	−17
12	141	88	−53
13	122	81	−41
14	149	104	−45
15	146	102	−44
16	141	95	−46
17	144	99	−45

Appendix B

Word and pseudo-word reading performance of the dyslexic children

Table B1. Regular words.

	High-frequency regular words									Low-frequency regular words								
	Individual performance		Age group							Individual performance		Age group						
			Score		Time		*z*-score					Score		Time		*z*-score	
Child	Score/ 20	Time s	*M*	*SD*	*M*	*SD*	Score	Time		Score/20	Time s	*M*	*SD*	*M*	*SD*	Score	Time
1	18	41	19.67	0.74	18.66	5.73	**−2.26**	**−3.90**		9	46	18.44	2.00	26.48	8.12	**−4.72**	**−2.40**
2	19	24	19.72	0.83	16.85	4.94	−0.87	−1.45		15	31	19.04	1.56	24.05	8.91	**−2.59**	−0.78
3	18	30	19.67	0.74	18.66	5.73	**−2.26**	**−1.98**		16	31	18.44	2.00	26.48	8.12	−1.22	−0.56
4	19	26	19.72	0.83	16.85	4.94	−0.87	**−1.85**		15	35	19.04	1.56	24.05	8.91	**−2.59**	−1.23
5	20	18	19.77	0.58	14.51	3.57	0.40	−0.98		19	34	19.09	1.01	20.40	7.49	−0.09	**−1.82**
6	20	17	19.77	0.58	14.51	3.57	0.40	−0.70		17	27	19.40	0.80	17.80	5.70	**−3.00**	−1.61
7	20	25	19.77	0.58	14.51	3.57	0.40	**−2.94**		18	42	19.40	0.80	17.80	5.70	**−1.75**	**−4.25**
8	19	26	19.67	0.74	18.66	5.73	−0.91	−1.28		15	40	18.44	2.00	26.48	8.12	**−1.72**	**−1.67**
9	19	19	19.67	0.74	18.66	5.73	−0.91	−0.06		17	30	18.44	2.00	26.48	8.12	−0.72	−0.43
10	19	18	19.77	0.58	14.51	3.57	−1.33	−0.98		19	23	19.09	1.01	20.40	7.49	−0.09	−0.35
11	20	12	19.77	0.58	14.51	3.57	0.40	0.70		18	19	19.40	0.80	17.80	5.70	**−1.75**	−0.21
12	20	26	19.72	0.83	16.85	4.94	0.34	**−1.85**		18	33	19.04	1.56	24.05	8.91	−0.67	−1.00
13	19	52	19.72	0.83	16.85	4.94	−0.87	**−7.12**		12	80	19.04	1.56	24.05	8.91	**−4.51**	**−6.28**
14	20	16	19.77	0.58	14.51	3.57	0.40	−0.42		17	22	19.09	1.01	20.40	7.49	**−2.07**	−0.21
15	20	17	19.77	0.58	14.51	3.57	0.40	−0.70		17	26	19.09	1.01	20.40	7.49	**−2.07**	−0.75
16	17	18	19.77	0.58	14.51	3.57	**−4.78**	−0.98		16	22	19.09	1.01	20.40	7.49	**−3.06**	−0.21
17	20	23	19.77	0.58	14.51	3.57	0.40	**−2.38**		18	37	19.09	1.01	20.40	7.49	−1.08	**−2.22**

Note: *z*-scores in bold indicate that the child presented a deficit in the skill.

Table B2. Irregular words.

	High-frequency irregular words								Low-frequency irregular words							
	Individual performance		Age group						Individual performance		Age group					
			Score		Time		*z*-score				Score		Time		*z*-score	
Child	Score /20	Time s	*M*	*SD*	*M*	SD	Score	Time	Score /20	Time s	*M*	*SD*	*M*	*SD*	Score	Time
1	10	49	18.25	1.54	20.31	6.54	**−5.36**	**−4.39**	0	64	13.22	3.88	30.22	10.38	**−3.41**	**−3.25**
2	16	32	19.03	1.49	18.24	6.83	**−2.03**	**−2.01**	4	46	15.90	3.66	26.61	10.62	**−3.25**	**−1.83**
3	13	31	18.25	1.54	20.31	6.54	**−3.41**	−1.63	6	55	13.22	3.88	30.22	10.38	**−1.86**	**−2.39**
4	14	34	19.03	1.49	18.24	6.83	**−3.38**	**−2.31**	9	46	15.90	3.66	26.61	10.62	**−1.89**	**−1.83**
5	14	34	19.58	0.57	14.34	3.72	**−9.79**	**−5.28**	10	49	17.68	2.07	21.11	6.72	**−3.71**	**−4.15**
6	14	30	19.58	0.57	14.34	3.72	**−9.79**	**−4.21**	7	30	17.10	2.60	19.70	6.80	**−3.88**	−1.51
7	20	31	19.58	0.57	14.34	3.72	0.74	**−4.48**	18	56	17.10	2.60	19.70	6.80	0.35	**−5.34**
8	13	32	18.25	1.54	20.31	6.54	**−3.41**	**−1.79**	10	50	13.22	3.88	30.22	10.38	−0.83	**−1.91**
9	13	30	18.25	1.54	20.31	6.54	**−3.41**	−1.48	10	33	13.22	3.88	30.22	10.38	−0.83	−0.27
10	16	26	19.58	0.57	14.34	3.72	**−6.28**	**−3.13**	7	26	17.68	2.07	21.11	6.72	**−5.16**	−0.73
11	19	14	19.58	0.57	14.34	3.72	−1.02	0.09	16	24	17.10	2.60	19.70	6.80	−0.42	−0.63
12	15	49	19.03	1.49	18.24	6.83	**−2.70**	**−4.50**	10	62	15.90	3.66	26.61	10.62	−1.61	**−3.33**
13	15	83	19.03	1.49	18.24	6.83	**−2.70**	**−9.48**	8	105	15.90	3.66	26.61	10.62	**−2.16**	**−7.38**
14	20	20	19.58	0.57	14.34	3.72	0.74	−1.52	15	32	17.68	2.07	21.11	6.72	−1.29	−1.62
15	16	26	19.58	0.57	14.34	3.72	**−6.28**	**−3.13**	12	37	17.68	2.07	21.11	6.72	**−2.74**	**−2.36**
16	19	14	19.58	0.57	14.34	3.72	−1.02	0.09	9	24	17.68	2.07	21.11	6.72	**−4.19**	−0.43
17	20	22	19.58	0.57	14.34	3.72	0.74	**−2.06**	15	40	17.68	2.07	21.11	6.72	−1.29	**−2.81**

Note: *Z*-scores in bold indicate that the child presented a deficit in the skill.

Table B3. Pseudo-words.

	Pseudo-words matched to high-frequency words								Pseudo-words matched to low-frequency words							
	Individual performance		Age group						Individual performance		Age group					
			Score		Time		*z*-score				Score		Time		*z*-score	
Child	Score /20	Time s	*M*	*SD*	*M*	*SD*	Score	Time	Score /20	Time s	*M*	*SD*	*M*	*SD*	Score	Time
1	8	44	16.59	2.40	27.44	8.91	**−3.58**	−1.14	5	44	17.27	2.14	33.18	9.46	**−5.73**	**−1.86**
2	11	40	17.36	1.98	25.98	8.31	**−3.21**	−0.59	14	39	17.77	1.99	32.94	11.92	**−5.73**	−1.57
3	14	36	16.59	2.40	27.44	8.91	−1.08	−0.30	18	35	17.27	2.14	33.18	9.46	0.34	−0.85
4	10	43	17.36	1.98	25.98	8.31	**−3.72**	−0.84	11	40	17.77	1.99	32.94	11.92	**−3.40**	**−1.69**
5	13	33	17.36	1.98	25.98	8.31	**−2.20**	−0.01	19	33	17.77	1.99	32.94	11.92	0.62	−0.84
6	16	25	17.80	1.90	25.98	8.31	−0.95	−0.07	19	27	17.77	1.99	24.50	7.50	0.62	−0.12
7	14	75	17.80	1.90	25.98	8.31	**−2.00**	**−6.73**	17	59	17.77	1.99	24.50	7.50	−0.39	**−3.97**
8	17	55	16.59	2.40	27.44	8.91	0.17	**−2.31**	13	40	17.27	2.14	33.18	9.46	**−2.00**	−1.41
9	13	29	16.59	2.40	27.44	8.91	−1.50	0.44	18	26	17.27	2.14	33.18	9.46	0.34	0.16
10	16	24	17.36	1.98	25.98	8.31	−0.69	0.75	18	22	17.77	1.99	32.94	11.92	0.12	0.48
11	17	15	17.80	1.90	25.98	8.31	−0.42	1.27	17	24	17.77	1.99	24.50	7.50	−0.39	0.24
12	15	48	17.36	1.98	25.98	8.31	−1.19	−1.26	15	44	17.77	1.99	32.94	11.92	−1.39	**−2.17**
13	13	81	17.36	1.98	25.98	8.31	**−2.20**	**−4.03**	17	74	17.77	1.99	32.94	11.92	−0.39	**−5.78**
14	14	30	17.36	1.98	25.98	8.31	**−1.70**	0.25	17	26	17.77	1.99	32.94	11.92	−0.39	0.00
15	15	36	17.36	1.98	25.98	8.31	−1.19	−0.26	15	29	17.77	1.99	32.94	11.92	−1.39	−0.36
16	13	24	17.36	1.98	25.98	8.31	**−2.20**	0.75	13	20	17.77	1.99	32.94	11.92	**−2.40**	0.72
17	14	41	17.36	1.98	25.98	8.31	**−1.70**	−0.68	15	40	17.77	1.99	32.94	11.92	−1.39	**−1.69**

Note: *Z*-scores in bold indicate that the child presented a deficit in the skill.

Appendix C

Word and pseudo-word spelling performance of the dyslexic children

	Regular words				Inconsistent words				Very inconsistent words				Pseudo-words			
	Score	Age group			Score	Age group			Score	Age group			Score	Age group		
Child	/22	*M*	*SD*	*z*-score	/22	*M*	*SD*	*z*-score	/22	*M*	*SD*	*z*-score	/20	*M*	*SD*	*z*-score
1	17	19.58	1.89	−1.37	7	17.82	3.31	**−3.27**	1	14.08	4.49	**−2.91**	14	18.31	1.76	**−2.45**
2	12	19.58	1.89	**−4.01**	7	17.82	3.31	**−3.27**	2	14.08	4.49	**−2.69**	13	18.31	1.76	**−3.02**
3	16	19.58	1.89	**−1.89**	6	17.82	3.31	**−3.57**	2	14.08	4.49	**−2.69**	17	18.31	1.76	−0.74
4	15	19.58	1.89	**−2.42**	7	17.82	3.31	**−3.27**	5	14.08	4.49	**−2.02**	9	18.31	1.76	**−5.29**
5	18	19.58	1.89	−0.84	13	17.82	3.31	−1.46	7	14.08	4.49	−1.58	15	18.31	1.76	**−1.88**
6	16	19.58	1.89	**−1.89**	6	17.82	3.31	**−3.57**	1	14.08	4.49	**−2.91**	10	18.31	1.76	**−4.72**
7	17	19.58	1.89	−1.37	10	17.82	3.31	**−2.36**	8	14.08	4.49	−1.35	17	18.31	1.76	−0.74
8	15	19.58	1.89	**−2.42**	4	17.82	3.31	**−4.18**	1	14.08	4.49	**−2.91**	11	18.31	1.76	**−4.15**
9	NA			NA	3	17.82	3.31	**−4.48**	1	14.08	4.49	**−2.91**	18	18.31	1.76	−0.18
10	16	19.58	1.89	**−1.89**	3	17.82	3.31	**−4.48**	1	14.08	4.49	**−2.91**	18	18.31	1.76	−0.18
11	15	19.58	1.89	**−2.42**	11	17.82	3.31	**−2.06**	2	14.08	4.49	**−2.69**	19	18.31	1.76	0.39
12	NA			NA	NA			NA	NA			NA	9	18.31	1.76	**−5.29**
13	15	19.58	1.89	**−2.42**	12	17.82	3.31	**−1.76**	4	14.08	4.49	**−2.24**	16	18.31	1.76	−1.31
14	18	19.58	1.89	−0.84	15	17.82	3.31	−0.85	7	14.08	4.49	−1.58	15	18.31	1.76	**−1.88**
15	11	19.58	1.89	**−4.54**	3	17.82	3.31	**−4.48**	2	14.08	4.49	**−2.69**	10	18.31	1.76	**−4.72**
16	16	19.58	1.89	**−1.89**	11	17.82	3.31	**−2.06**	4	14.08	4.49	**−2.24**	13	18.31	1.76	**−3.02**
17	20	19.58	1.89	0.22	12	17.82	3.31	**−1.76**	9	14.08	4.49	−1.13	14	18.31	1.76	**−2.45**

Note: Spelling performance in writing to dictation. The *z*-scores in bold indicate that the child presented a deficit in the skill. NA = not available.

Appendix D

Individual dyslexic performance in meta-phonological tasks

	Phoneme deletion task				Phoneme segmentation task				Acronyms			
	Individual performance		*z*-score		Individual performance		*z*-score		Individual performance		*z*-score	
Child	Score /20	Time s	Score	Time	Score /15	Time s	Score	Time	Score /10	Time s	Score	Time
1	10	70	**−1.66**	0.18	14	60	1.47	1.37	9	54	0.38	0.65
2	17	94	0.15	−0.97	12	76	0.98	0.92	9	76	0.38	−0.02
3	20	80	0.93	−0.30	15	72	1.72	1.03	10	55	0.81	0.62
4	15	129	−0.37	**−2.65**	13	87	1.22	0.62	8	66	−0.05	0.28
5	19	70	0.67	0.18	5	70	−0.77	1.09	9	78	0.38	−0.09
6	20	108	0.93	**−1.64**	13	64	1.22	1.26	9	85	0.38	−0.30
7	20	80	0.93	−0.30	12	81	0.98	0.78	10	56	0.81	0.59
8	18	96	0.41	−1.06	12	56	0.98	1.48	7	65	−0.48	0.31
9	15	102	−0.37	−1.35	5	44	−0.77	1.81	9	64	0.38	0.34
10	10	97	**−1.66**	−1.11	2	100	−1.52	0.25	8	71	−0.05	0.13
11	20	55	0.93	0.90	14	54	1.47	1.54	9	40	0.38	1.07
12	14	162	−0.63	**−4.23**	9	150	0.23	−1.14	9	75	0.38	0.01
13	11	124	−1.41	**−2.41**	4	125	−1.02	−0.44	7	95	−0.48	−0.60
14	15	130	−0.37	**−2.70**	4	119	−1.02	−0.27	6	120	−0.91	−1.37
15	19	74	0.67	−0.01	10	74	0.48	0.98	7	75	−0.48	0.01
16	18	98	0.41	−1.16	12	178	0.98	**−1.92**	8	146	−0.05	**−2.16**
17	19	118	0.67	**−2.12**	14	90	1.47	0.53	9	160	0.38	**−2.59**

Note: *Z*-scores in bold indicate that the child presented a deficit in the skill.

Appendix E

Words used in the writing experiment

Irregular words				Regular words				Pseudo-words	
High frequency		Low frequency		High frequency		Low frequency		High	Low
second	24.62	aplomb	3.35	sortir	181.82	agneau	35.77	sirtar	agnoin
aspect	24.77	album	11.68	auteur	100.80	aigle	34.01	autoir	angui
alcool	7.35	escroc	0.92	autrui	0.77	endive	0.72	autrit	embave
femme	230.16	asthme	0.02	forme	204.50	arceau	0.20	farne	arcein
respect	13.46	canyon	0.01	recours	1.74	castor	7.67	receurt	castal
moyen	76.64	fœtus	0.01	matin	474.82	fourmi	33.18	matol	foirta
monsieur	656.24	gadget	0.76	meilleur	31.60	gadoue	0.01	meissoin	gadord
parfum	37.85	camping	14.89	pardon	2.06	candeur	0.01	pirtin	coitair
gentil	92.26	oignon	8.66	goutte	35.61	orteil	8.50	geumme	ordeir
tabac	10.02	compteur	1.64	tissu	49.74	chaudron	10.59	tasso	choidran
instinct	3.73	dolmen	0.03	index	18.50	dicton	0.01	indom	dirtal
compte	66.28	accroc	0.29	chacun	299.01	aiglon	0.20	chipen	aigrin
fusil	63.38	chorale	2.64	futur	101.50	chameau	37.15	furut	chamoin
wagon	18.89	faisan	11.18	vigne	11.74	flocon	6.33	vagli	flesan
		millier	1.89			moisson	3.91		moichan
		galop	23.74			gazon	16.44		gobin
		Sirop	38.10			Satin	6.96		soron

Appendix F

Linguistic variables for which the words were controlled

	Irregular words	Regular words	B_{10} regularity	Pseudo-words	B_{10} lexicality	LF words	HF words	B_{10} frequency
Nb letters	6.06	5.97	0.28	6.00	0.26	6.12	5.89	0.29
Nb phonemes	4.45	4.42	0.26	4.26	0.32	4.53	4.32	0.32
Uniqueness point	5.55	5.45	0.27	4.87	0.29	5.41	5.61	0.32
Grapheme frequency	37,515.77	38,921.62	0.29	38,115.87	0.27	34,867.66	42,287.81	10.13
Bigram frequency	3,803.62	4,262.83	0.29	3,011.31	2.60	3,377.53	4,829.43	3.57
Trigram frequency	710.23	782.17	0.27	266.37	30.72	517.88	1,023.44	3.71
Lexical frequency	43.70	55.38	0.28	—	—	9.48	98.19	48.73
P–G association	62.59	82.79	250,440	71.81	12.04	72.33	73.13	0.26

Note: Nb = number; P–G = phoneme–grapheme; LF = low-frequency; HF = high-frequency. If B_{10} is higher than 3, the two data sets present different patterns (evidence supports H_1); if B_{10} is lower than 0.33, the two data sets present equivalent patterns (evidence supports H_0).

Index

For Product Safety Concerns and Information please contact our EU
representative GPSR@taylorandfrancis.com
Taylor & Francis Verlag GmbH, Kaufingerstraße 24, 80331 München, Germany

www.ingramcontent.com/pod-product-compliance
Ingram Content Group UK Ltd.
Pitfield, Milton Keynes, MK11 3LW, UK
UKHW050757180926
475701UK00007B/1106
* 9 7 8 0 3 6 7 5 3 5 7 4 2 *